THE LAST GREAT COLONIAL LAWYER

THE LAST GREAT COLONIAL LAWYER

The Life and Legacy of Jeremiah Gridley

Charles R. McKirdy

UNIVERSITY OF MASSACHUSETTS PRESS
Amherst & Boston

Copyright © 2018 by University of Massachusetts Press
All rights reserved
Printed in the United States of America
ISBN 978-1-62534-350-5 (paper); 349-9 (hardcover)

Designed by Sally Nichols
Set in Monotype Dante
Printed and bound by Maple Press, Inc.
Cover design by Sally Nichols
Cover art: *Antique book bound with decorative texture, from nineteenth century*, Shutterstock.com

Library of Congress Cataloging-in-Publication Data

Names: McKirdy, Charles Robert, 1943– author.
Title: The last great colonial lawyer : the life and legacy of Jeremiah Gridley / Charles R. McKirdy.
Description: Amherst : University of Massachusetts Press, [2018] | Includes bibliographical references and index. |
Identifiers: LCCN 2017050257 (print) | LCCN 2017055350 (ebook) | ISBN 9781613765906 (e-book) | ISBN 9781613765913 (e-book) | ISBN 9781625343499 (hardcover) | ISBN 9781625343505 (pbk.)
Subjects: LCSH: Gridley, Jeremiah, 1701–1767. | Lawyers—Massachusetts—Biography. | Lawyers—United States—History. | United States—History—Colonial period, ca. 1600–1775.
Classification: LCC KF363.G75 (ebook) | LCC KF363.G75 M33 2018 (print) | DDC 340.092 [B]—dc23
LC record available at https://lccn.loc.gov/2017050257

British Library Cataloguing-in-Publication Data
A catalog record for this book is available from the British Library.

For Kathie

CONTENTS

Preface
ix

Acknowledgments
xi

Introduction
1

Chapter One
Student, Teacher, Editor (1702–1733)
4

Chapter Two
Gridley's Law Practice
The First Ten Years (1732–1742)
19

Chapter Three
The Land Bank Crisis (1740–1742)
34

Chapter Four
The American Magazine (1743–1746)
43

Chapter Five
Iron and Land
53

Chapter Six
Fletcher v. Vassall (1752)
65

Chapter Seven
The House of Representatives
War, Influence, and Opportunity Lost (1755–1757)
80

Chapter Eight
Gridley's Law Practice in the 1750s and 1760s
105

Chapter Nine
The Writs of Assistance (1760–1761)
126

Chapter Ten
Sugar and Stamps (1762–1766)
155

Chapter Eleven
Death and Legacy
180

Notes
201
Index
269

PREFACE

I have known Jeremiah Gridley (1702–1767) for a long, long time. We first met when I was a history graduate student at Northwestern University. At the time, he did not leave a lasting impression. I was writing a dissertation on Massachusetts lawyers in the revolutionary and early Federalist periods, and although Gridley played a role in the early disputes with Britain, he died before things really heated up. For the next twenty years or so, our relationship remained somewhat distant. I was concerned with colonial lawyers as a social group—their politics, their education, and their degree of professionalization. Although Gridley found some mention in my studies, except for the part that he played in the legal education of John Adams, Gridley's role was a minor one.

My interest in Gridley began to change when my life changed. I went to law school and, after graduating, became a practicing lawyer, a litigator. I still pursued my study of colonial lawyers, but my focus shifted from an interest in lawyers as an element of society to a concern with them as legal practitioners. Once this shift occurred, it did not take long for me to discover that, in the twenty-five years before the colony became torn by internecine strife, the most revered lawyer in Massachusetts was Jeremiah Gridley. I also learned—much to my surprise—that despite his acknowledged stature, little has been written about Gridley or, in particular, about his legal practice.

My preliminary research led me to conclude that Gridley deserved far more attention than he had received. Gridley was the greatest lawyer of his generation. Mentor to future great lawyers, he tried some very important cases, including one now seen as a harbinger of the American Revolution. But Gridley was more than a lawyer. He edited a newspaper and a magazine, served in a wartime legislature, and was very much a colonial type, a man of his time—a time that was running out. Although Massachusetts was rapidly approaching the threshold of violent change, Gridley, the son of a tradesman, was one of many who still saw royal patronage as the key to high office and the higher social status that he craved.

Researching and writing this book was challenging, enjoyable, and satisfying. The challenge stemmed from the paucity of traditional primary sources, which required me to explore avenues of research somewhat off the beaten path. My enjoyment was the enjoyment that we all experience when we learn things that we did not know. The somewhat unusual sources that I used cast new light not only on Jeremiah Gridley but on the texture of his times as well. Finally, I must admit to some degree of satisfaction from rescuing this fascinating, influential, and all but forgotten man from an undeserved obscurity.

ACKNOWLEDGMENTS

As noted, this book can trace its origins to my studies at Northwestern University, which means that in order to acknowledge those who most assisted and encouraged me in its pursuit, I must go back about fifty years to the late Clarence Ver Steeg, who was professor of American colonial history there. Clarence had an uncanny ability to transmit his love of the study of history to his grad students, and I was one of them, lucky enough to have him as my thesis adviser. Enthusiastically promoting scholarship, over the years Clarence always reviewed my work, including the beginnings of this one, with a critical but helpful and kindly eye.

John D. Cushing was another early positive influence. John, now also gone, was the librarian of the Massachusetts Historical Society when I arrived there many years ago on a snowy January morning with no idea whatsoever how to go about doing what I wanted to do. He quickly recognized the situation and promptly set about rectifying it. Along with his wonderful staff, John gave me invaluable training in the trenches about the means and methods of historical research.

In more recent years, I have had the good fortune to enjoy the friendship, guidance, and unflagging support of Daniel R. Coquillette, the dean of American legal historians. As busy as he is (and Dan is always busy), he invariably has found the time to cheerfully look over a draft, provide unique and valuable insights, and lift my spirits when my spirits were in need of lifting.

At this point it is not too early to thank my editors. Most authors thank their editors somewhere near the end of their acknowledgments, but Matt Becker, a scholar in his own right, and Rachael DeShano at the University of Massachusetts Press, and Amanda Heller merit far more. Their patient professionalism and incisive input have made this a far better book than it was when they received it.

Of course I owe debts to many others, including two whose knowledge of the period is unsurpassed. L. Kinvin Roth, co-editor of John Adams's legal papers, provided valuable assistance when I was stumbling around the book's first few chapters, and Colin Nicolson, Governor Francis Bernard's biographer, shared useful ideas about researching the fascinating and turbulent times that were the 1760s.

Also not to be forgotten are the professionals at the numerous institutional repositories who were so helpful to me. The list is a long one, but heading it are the people at the Massachusetts Historical Society, the Huntington Library, the Mormon Family Library, the Massachusetts Archives and Commonwealth Museum, the American Antiquarian Society, the Houghton Library of Harvard University, and the San Diego County Library.

THE LAST
GREAT
COLONIAL
LAWYER

Introduction

In late October 1758, a young John Adams made the following entry into his diary:

> Went in the morning to Mr. Gridleys, and asked the favour of his Advice what Steps to take for an Introduction to the Practice of Law in this County. He answered "get sworn."
>
> [Adams]. But in order to that, sir, as I have no Patron, in this County.
>
> [Gridley]. I will recommend you to the Court. Mark the Day the Court adjourns to in order to make up Judgments. Come to Town that Day, and in the mean Time I will speak to the Bar for the Bar must be consulted, because the Court always inquires, if it be with Consent of the Bar.[1]

This is how most of us are introduced to Jeremiah Gridley, generally considered "the greatest New England lawyer of his generation."[2] As noted earlier, it is ironic that, in view of his standing, the fact is that we know very little about Jeremiah Gridley. More than anything else, his fame is a product of the fame of his students, most notably Adams and that fascinating tragic character James Otis Jr., he of the writs of assistance speech and thundering declarations about the fundamental rights of Englishmen.

The reason for this state of affairs is simple. Other than what John Adams has told us about him and a scattering of letters, the firsthand evidence pertaining to Gridley is sorely lacking. He left no diary, no letter books, no doting relative or descendant who recorded and collected material relating to his life. Even the portrait of him at Harvard Law School is of dubious authenticity.[3]

Still, Gridley was a public man—in some ways, more public than most. He was, of course, a lawyer, and the records of the Massachusetts courts yield valuable information as to the nature and extent of his practice. Gridley spent four years in the Massachusetts House of Representatives, whose journals and archives can be mined for worthwhile material on Gridley's role in provincial affairs.

Gridley also was the editor of two publications—the *Weekly Rehearsal*, a Boston weekly newspaper which appeared in the early 1730s, and the *American Magazine*, a monthly published in the mid-1740s—which provide useful insights into Gridley's thinking. So too does the catalogue of Gridley's large library found in the inventory of his estate that was filed with the Suffolk County Probate Court.

Gridley lived from 1702 to 1767. Reading through the sources pertaining to his life, one cannot but be struck by the light they cast on so many aspects of his time, a period that often is overlooked by historians. While there are some excellent studies of particular events and developments which occurred during that period, for the most part historians tend to focus on the years after 1760, when the colonies started down the road to separation from Great Britain.

Gridley shares some of that focus. In 1761 he represented the Crown in the writs of assistance case, which some view as the first step on that road. Both of Gridley's opposing counsel in that case, James Otis and Oxenbridge Thacher, were his former students. A few years later, Gridley joined with Otis and Adams in presenting arguments to the governor of Massachusetts in favor of reopening the province's law courts in defiance of the Stamp Act.

Yet Gridley's life touched and was touched by so much more that was integral to provincial Massachusetts. To be sure, it is impossible to study his life without addressing the increasing strains with Great Britain, as well as other major events including the wars with France and the Great Awakening. But there are occurrences and developments, such as the smallpox epidemic of the early 1720s, the currency crisis of the 1740s, the economic panic of the 1760s, the growing religious diversity in the province, and the lure of land speculation, which, if rescued from the footnotes of time, give added dimension to the era in which he lived. It is my hope that this study facilitates that rescue.

Although this book explores all aspects of Gridley's life, because he was first and foremost a lawyer, more particularly a litigator, its primary focus is on his cases, examining the law, facts, issues, and personalities involved. These cases illuminate the nature of Massachusetts society, touching on such diverse subjects as race, status, commerce, property, inheritance, and power. As a tool of historical research, litigation may be unique in this regard. Because they are inherently adversarial, lawsuits can cast a searching, unrelenting light on people, institutions, and values. Benjamin Lincoln Jr., an eighteenth-century Massachusetts lawyer from a later generation, put it this way:

> A lawyer is called to stand forth & in public plead the cause of justice. To do it effectively they are necessitated to lash the vices of mankind. They are a mirror hateful to the eyes of the bigger part of Society for it shows them all their deformities.[4]

CHAPTER ONE

Student, Teacher, Editor
(1702–1733)

Jeremiah Gridley entered Harvard College in 1721. At nineteen years of age, he was considerably older than most of his classmates. The reason for Jeremiah's late start may be found in his background. He was born in 1702 to Captain Richard and Rebecca Gridley.[1] Richard came from a line of moderately successful civic-minded artisans; his grandfather had become a freeman in 1634 and is listed as a "Brick maker" in the Boston town records. He served as a captain in the militia, held several minor town offices, and was a member of the prestigious Ancient and Honorable Artillery Company. According to the records, Captain Gridley was one of the "richer inhabitants" who subscribed to hire a master for the first free school in Boston.[2] His son Joseph Gridley also was a brick maker and a member of the artillery company.[3]

Joseph's son Richard, who was Jeremiah's father, was a leather currier. A man of some means, he owned several pieces of property in Boston, including a tract on School Street on which his house probably was located. Richard was a member of the Old South Church and, like his father and grandfather, belonged to the Ancient and Honorable Artillery Company. Between 1696 and 1710, he held various town offices including constable, surveyor of highways, clerk of the market, and tithing man.[4]

Richard Gridley died in 1714. That same year, his son Jeremiah entered the Boston Public Latin School, the school that his great-grandfather had helped to establish.[5] Under the direction of headmaster Nathaniel Williams, Boston Latin offered a seven-year curriculum of Latin, Greek, and then more Latin. Grounded in *A Short Introduction to the Latin Tongue*, which had been written by Williams's predecessor, Ezekiel Cheever, the young scholars learned to read, write, argue, declaim, and think in Latin. They read, translated, and memorized Hesiod, Juvenal, Persius, Lucius Florus, Erasmus, Ovid, Cicero, and Aesop.[6] It was all directed toward one goal: entry into Harvard College, which would not even consider an applicant who could not ex tempore read Greek, and read and write Latin.[7]

Boston Latin had earned a well-deserved reputation as Harvard's nursery, but in all probability Jeremiah never would have attended the college but for the determination and kindness of an older brother.[8] As noted, the year Jeremiah entered Boston Latin, his father died. In his will Richard Gridley had instructed his son John to "carry my trade on" and maintain Rebecca and "my four youngest children," one of whom was Jeremiah.[9] Perhaps John saw promising potential in his younger brother, or maybe he was carrying out his father's specific request, but in any event, John financed Jeremiah's college education. It may have taken John some time to accumulate enough money to do so, delaying his brother's arrival in Cambridge.[10]

The Harvard that Gridley entered in 1721 was a far different institution than it had been just a few decades earlier, but then, Massachusetts itself had undergone a series of significant changes. The colony had been founded as a community of like-minded Puritan believers, but this dream perished in the 1670s, when, despite strenuous, even brutal efforts to keep them out, Baptist and Quaker congregations opened meetinghouses in Boston.[11] In 1684 the Puritans lost their virtual monopoly of political power when the Crown revoked the Massachusetts Bay Charter and the commonwealth became a royal colony.[12]

Two years later, the colony's leadership faced a greater loss of power in an administrative restructuring which incorporated Massachusetts into the Dominion of New England. The Dominion's governor, Sir Edmund Andros, was given autocratic powers over the Bay Colony, the rest of New England, New York, and New Jersey. Along with the other colonial legislatures in the Dominion, the Massachusetts assembly was abolished and its powers given to Andros and a local council appointed by the Crown.[13]

Through Andros's efforts, an Anglican congregation was established in Boston in 1689, but that year also saw the end of the Dominion of New England, the departure of Andros, and a new royal charter for Massachusetts. The new charter provided for a governor appointed by and answerable to the Crown, and an elected assembly whose acts were subject to veto by the governor or the Privy Council in London. Still, Massachusetts got its legislature back, and although suffrage no longer was based on church membership, property owners still wielded a good deal of power. All things considered, the charter provided Massachusetts with needed stability.[14]

By 1720 the province had quieted down. Baptists and Quakers, while still considered theologically wrongheaded, had proven to be solid citizens and were left alone.[15] After becoming somewhat aggressive during the Andros regime, Boston's Anglicans had backed off, and more liberal Congregational ministers counted Anglicans among their friends. Even Increase Mather, a leader of Massachusetts orthodoxy, had kind words to say about some Anglicans. Asked for his opinion of Anglican archbishop John Tillotson, whom he had just met, Mather replied, "Why truly . . . I like him so well that if you had always had such ArchBishops[,] New England . . . never [would have] been."[16]

Harvard too had become a different place. The college's entering classes had expanded from an average of twelve students in the years 1706 to 1715 to an average of about twenty-nine in the ten years ending in 1725. Gridley's freshman class of forty-nine in 1721 was the largest in the school's history.[17] Moreover, the composition of the entering classes had changed. There still were the sons of clergymen and large landowners, but there also was a growing number of students from the rising merchant class, and a sprinkling of boys from less likely backgrounds. Jeremiah could count among his classmates the sons of a brewer, a weaver, a tanner, a mason, a housewright, and a brazier.[18]

The Harvard that Gridley entered bore the indelible stamp of its president, John Leverett. Chosen to head the college in 1707, Leverett was Harvard's first president who was not a member of the clergy. He had been a tutor at the college, a lawyer, a judge, speaker of the House of Representatives, a member of the provincial council, and Massachusetts's envoy to the government of New York.[19] In the words of Harvard historian Samuel Eliot Morison, Leverett "was liberal in his attitude toward religion, conservative in politics, and withal a man with an innate sense of government, a majestic manner of speech, and a deportment that 'struck an Awe upon the youth.'"[20] Although Harvard's curriculum remained essentially the same as it had been in the previous century, the approach and the emphasis were far different. By the time Gridley arrived, the college had largely abandoned the Aristotelian-scholastic approach in logic, metaphysics, ethics, and natural philosophy.[21]

While "perfectly orthodox" himself, Leverett heralded a trend at the college that looked to Cartesian reasoning and latitudinarianism for inspiration.[22] He encouraged the reading of new books and free discussion among the students. Soon after Leverett's appointment, Harvard began to reflect his influence. As early as 1712, Benjamin Colman, the liberal pastor of the Brattle Street Church, wrote to the dean of Peterborough, rejoicing in Leverett's impact:

> The *generous* Principles of an enlarged Catholic spirit cherished in me by my *Tutor*, Mr. *Leverett;* now President of *Harvard*—College:—And if I am able to judge, no Place of Education can well boast a more *free Air* than our little *College* may.[23]

It was during Leverett's tenure as Harvard's president that the ideas of Archbishop Tillotson became a significant influence at the college.[24] A liberal, Tillotson rejected strict Calvinist predestination, emphasizing virtue more than the necessity of Christ's redemption.[25] Henry Flynt, a tutor at Harvard from 1699 to 1754, idolized Tillotson.[26] Another tutor, the Reverend Thomas Robie, a member of the Royal Society and, perhaps, the leading scientist in New England, regularly relied on Tillotson in his sermons.[27] Harvard's liberalization was strengthened in 1722, when Edward Wigglesworth became the first Hollis Professor of Divinity. Although the orthodox clergy attempted to straitjacket him into their theological viewpoint, Wigglesworth went his own way. He challenged their view of Calvinism, encouraged a "deadly method of doubt and inquiry," and became "a prime favorite of Harvard students."[28]

Not everyone was favorably impressed by what was going on in Cambridge. Writing as "Silence Dogood" in his brother's *New-England Courant,* sixteen-year-old Benjamin Franklin turned his satiric wit on Harvard. He depicted "that famous Seminary of Learning" as a place attended by "Dunces and Blockheads," where "sat LEARNING in awful State," where "Madam *Idleness* and her Maid Indolence " ruled, and where graduates left "after [an] Abundance of trouble and Charge, as great Blockheads as ever, only more proud and self-conceited."[29]

Others were less willing to make light of the situation. Conservatives believed that the college was well on its way to perdition. They were led by Cotton Mather, rector of Boston's Second Church and the leading voice of religious orthodoxy in Massachusetts. Bitter about the dismissal of his father, Increase Mather, as president of Harvard in 1701, and disappointed in his failed efforts to obtain the office for himself, Mather despaired of what he saw as a school "betray'd by vile Practices," leaving it in "a very neglected and unhappy Condition."[30] He saw an opportunity to rescue his alma mater when, in August 1723, Harvard's overseers reacted to growing criticism of the school by appointing a committee to investigate the general conduct of the college and, in particular, its religious and moral condition.[31]

Although not a member of the committee, Mather presented it with an unsolicited list of "Suggestions on Points to be Inquired into Concerning Harvard College."[32] Among other complaints, Mather decried the alleged failure to use Latin, an increase in rote learning (especially "of insipid stuff and trash"), and, in a shot perhaps aimed at authors such as Tillotson, the want of due concern for the *"doctrines of grace,"* asking whether "some that have been Tutors . . . 'have set themselves to instill contrary principles.'"[33]

Warming to the subject, Mather intimated that "scholars have . . . their studies filled with books which may truly be called Satan's Library."[34] He claimed that behind their tutors' backs, undergraduates were devouring "plays, novels, empty and vicious pieces of poetry, and even Ovid's Epistles, which have the tendency to corrupt good manners."³⁵ The result, Mather warned, was that Harvard was robbing pious students of their piety to the extent that before Harvard graduates could take their place among the "excellent young ministers, who are the gifts of Christ in the service of our churches," they must "lay aside the sentiments which they brought from College with them."³⁶

The committee was not as pessimistic. Its October 9, 1723, report described an institution still basically sound, but one in which coercion often had been replaced by choice. Apparently, reading in divinity was no longer required or even recommended, and "students . . . read promiscuously, according to their inclinations, authors of different denominations of religion."³⁷ In fact, the committee found that the students acted "promiscuously" in many aspects of their college experience. According to its report, many of them were "too long absent from the college [without] allowance," spent too much time on Saturday evenings in one another's chambers, and "are seen in great numbers, going to town, on Sabbath mornings, to provide breakfasts."³⁸ The committee also acknowledged that while there were a "considerable number of virtuous and studious youth in the college . . . there has been a practice of several immoralities: particularly stealing, lying, swearing, idleness, picking of locks, and too frequent use of strong Drink."³⁹ Harvard's overseers took no direct action on the report.⁴⁰

Unfortunately, we know very little about what Jeremiah Gridley was doing at Harvard while all of this was going on. He may have been one of those students whom the committee found a bit too ready to engage in less than scholarly pursuits. Clifford Shipton, the biographer of Harvard's graduates, apparently thought so. He concluded that Gridley "was anything but sober and diligent," and in a "comparatively orderly class," the "violence and frequency of the lad's rebellion against college restrictions was notable."⁴¹

Shipton may have had it right, but Harvard's treatment of Gridley after he graduated in 1725 indicates otherwise. Apparently unconcerned about any bad influence he might exert on impressionable undergraduates, the college permitted Gridley to stay on campus while he studied for his M.A.⁴² Then, in October 1727, Gridley was hired as a tutor by his old school, Boston Latin.⁴³ To be chosen for this post, Gridley must have received very positive recommendations from the Harvard faculty.

The strong grounding in the classical languages that Gridley received at Harvard prepared him well for teaching at Boston Latin. But before we look at his tenure there, it is worthwhile to review some other aspects of Harvard's environment that probably played a part in Gridley's later careers as a lawyer and a journalist. While, in the 1720s, Harvard's curriculum did not include any courses on the English common law, and its library contained only seven volumes addressing it, there were parts of the curriculum that included subjects useful to a future lawyer.[44] The college emphasized logic and rhetoric.[45] Morison describes the goal of these two disciplines as follows:

> Through Logic . . . the freshman's mind was "broken in to keep thought's beaten track." Rhetoric, studied from classical texts, manuals, and collections of [figures of speech], and practised constantly by declamations in English and Latin, taught him how to speak and write with "clearness, force, and elegance."[46]

The ability to communicate logically "with 'clearness, force, and elegance,'" an obvious asset to a lawyer, is equally valuable to a journalist. Like law, journalism was not part of Harvard's curriculum, but the art of persuasive communication—so necessary to any successful journalist—was developed in the college's classes in logic and rhetoric. Moreover, the Harvard that Gridley attended was alive with would-be journalists. Several handwritten student-edited and authored journals circulated among the undergraduates. The best documented of these publications, *The Telltale*, appeared in 1721. Secular in tone, *The Telltale* was modeled after Joseph Addison and Richard Steele's journal *The Spectator*, a London satirical periodical which had been very popular a decade earlier. *The Telltale* featured collegiate attempts at humor such as an essay that recounted a dream in which "two fellows were quarreling about Mrs. Kate, one contending that she was more beautiful than Venus, the other that she was an antidote against Matrimony."[47]

English light literature was not taught at Boston Latin when Gridley became an "usher" there in 1727. His old headmaster, Nathaniel Williams, still was in charge, and Latin and Greek still dominated its curriculum. Williams, Gridley, and, after 1729, a second usher, John Lovell, shared responsibility for upwards of one hundred students. Their pupils included dozens of boys bound for Harvard, among them a covey of ministers-to-be, a future president of the college, and Oxenbridge Thacher and Samuel Adams, who, years later, would figure significantly in Gridley's professional life.[48]

Gridley taught at Boston Latin for a little over six years. In 1730, about halfway through his tenure there, he married Abigail Lewis. She was the daughter of Ezekiel Lewis, a grandson of Ezekiel Cheever. Abigail's father, who had himself once taught at Boston Latin, was a successful merchant and a member of the House of Representatives.[49] In 1731 Abigail gave birth to a daughter.[50] Fortunately, Jeremiah's salary kept pace with his growing financial needs. In 1728 Boston's town fathers had raised his compensation from £50 to £80 per year, and then in 1731 to £110 after he had petitioned for an increase because his present salary was "very insufficient for the necessary Charges of Life."[51]

Gridley had to work hard to earn that salary. Boston Latin, like most grammar schools at the time, relied heavily on rote learning. Gridley often spent most of a school day listening to students reciting Ovid, Cicero, or Virgil from memory.[52] This approach, to use the words of some of the school's critics, was a "tedious and burthensome method" for students and teachers alike.[53] John Adams, who taught in Worcester thirty years later, acknowledged that a day of teaching left "his spirits all exhausted." Writing to a friend after only one month in the classroom, Adams concluded "that keeping this school any length of time, would make a base weed and ignoble shrub of me."[54]

Gridley was not ready to allow the drudgery of teaching to numb his mental faculties. Apparently he found relief in that generation of English essayists who enlivened the public prints in the first three decades of the eighteenth century. The inventory of Gridley's library, compiled after his death, lists works by Addison and Steele, including two volumes of Addison's works (published in 1721), seven volumes of *The Spectator* (1712–1715), Steele's Whig periodical *The Englishman* (1713–14), and all fifty-five numbers of *The Freeholder* (1715–16), in which Addison defended the Hanoverian succession.[55]

The inventory also includes copies of Jonathan Swift's and Thomas Sheridan's journal *The Intelligencer* (1729), with its observations of economic, literary, and social subjects, as well as a year of *The Examiner* (1710–1714), the Tory newspaper that Swift edited. Another political periodical, *The Craftsman* (1731–1737), has a place in the inventory, as do two lighter papers—*The Censor* and *The Freethinker* (1722–1723), an imitator of *The Spectator*.[56]

Gridley's quest for intellectual stimulation was not a solitary pursuit. He belonged to a circle of young men who, like him, were interested in language and literature. Gridley joined a French conversation club whose membership included John Lovell, Gridley's fellow usher at Boston Latin, and Joseph Green, a 1726 graduate of Harvard.[57] Both men were considerably younger than Gridley. Both were to earn reputations in Boston's literary world—Lovell as "a witty and elegant writer," Green as "the most famous wit" of his generation.[58] But now, only recently graduated from college, they were just two aspiring authors in search of an outlet. Gridley shared their ambition. The three pooled their resources and, with Gridley taking the lead, set out to establish a literary newspaper.[59] The history of earlier such efforts in Massachusetts did not bode well for their endeavor.

Newspapers were still relatively new to the province, only arriving on the scene with the debut of the *Boston News-Letter* in 1704.[60] All newspapers had to be licensed by the General Court, the colonial assembly, a fact that dampened their editors' enthusiasm for controversy and innovation. So too did the fact that Boston's postmaster was always selected from among the town's newspaper editors. This was an important appointment. As postmaster, an editor was in an advantageous position to gather news about other colonies from his fellow postmasters. He also got first look at the mail, including English newspapers, and could distribute his paper for free through his mail carriers.[61]

The tractability of Boston's newspaper editors also stemmed from their view of the appropriate role of their publications.[62] The editors saw their primary purpose to be the distribution of information, not opinion or entertainment. Typically, these weekly papers included items from England and the continent, provincial legislation, executive pronouncements, and notices of sailing arrivals and departures. They paid little attention to local affairs or the daily concerns of ordinary citizens, and made virtually no attempt at what might be considered creative writing.[63]

This all changed with the smallpox epidemic that swept Massachusetts in May 1721, and the attendant controversy over the advisability of inoculation which racked the province. On one side, favoring inoculation were most of the Congregational clergy led by Cotton Mather.[64] On the other were those who opposed the practice, including most of the province's medical community.[65] It was a gloves-off, bitter fight. Inoculation opponents branded Dr. Zebdiel Boylston, the only local physician who advocated inoculation, an "illiterate," "ignorant," and "dangerous quack," engaged in a "Wicked and Criminal Practice."[66] Their clerical adversaries argued that God was on their side and "that the known Children of the Wicked one are generally fierce Enemies to Inoculation."[67]

In the midst of all this, a new voice was heard—the *New-England Courant*, published and edited by James Franklin. Born in Boston, Franklin had learned the newspaper business in the London of Addison and Steele and their imitators.[68] Four years after returning to Boston and printing jobs for others, Franklin launched his own newspaper, one unlicensed and independent. He intended his *New-England Courant* to be Boston's version of *The Spectator*, providing a vehicle for a band of contributors who would bring wit and literary sophistication to the town.[69]

The inoculation controversy made the times propitious for something new in print. The dispute gave Franklin's paper much to talk about, and it was talk about some of the province's most prominent men. Franklin began churning out waspish attacks on Cotton and Increase Mather, other pro-inoculators, and the province's establishment in general. But this was only a momentary episode which gave the fledgling *Courant* much-needed impetus, notoriety, and readership. The newspaper was not intended to be an organ of high-octane popular dissent. As noted, the *Courant*'s primary goal was to provide an outlet for Boston's young, somewhat pretentious literary set who sought to poke fun at arrogance, pedantry, incompetence, foppishness, and romance.[70] In 1722, after the inoculation controversy died down, that is what Franklin attempted to do.[71]

It worked for a while. The *Courant*'s "sassy pseudonymous" essays satirically commenting on local habits, events, and personalities and tweaking the establishment were new, interesting, and unique.[72] But it did not last. In September 1723, James Franklin's younger brother Ben, the *Courant*'s most gifted writer, broke his apprenticeship indenture with James and left Boston to seek his fortune elsewhere.[73] Readership declined. The simple fact was that Boston, with its population of about twelve thousand people, did not have enough interested readers to support a colonial *Spectator,* and the *Courant* did not have enough talented contributors to make for consistently interesting reading.[74]

There also was the problem of government scrutiny. James Franklin was arrested twice for offending church and state, and although he avoided serious punishment and toned down his jibes at authority, the threat of prosecution was always there.[75] Finally, in June 1726, Franklin shut down the *Courant,* packed up his press, and departed for Newport, Rhode Island.[76]

The demise of the *New-England Courant* left a void in Boston's newspaper scene. To be sure, the remaining papers droned on, but any reader seeking something a bit more creative looked in vain. But not for long. On March 27, 1727, less than a year after the *Courant*'s last issue, the first number of the *New-England Weekly Journal* appeared. It contained, according to its masthead, news of "the most Remarkable Occurrences Foreign and Domestick."[77]

As surprising as the quick birth of the *Weekly Journal* was the identity of one of its founders: twenty-year-old Mather Byles, the grandson of Increase Mather and the nephew of Cotton Mather. Byles had been bitten by the literary bug at Harvard but had a good deal more talent than most of his schoolmates. Eschewing their collegiate attempts at journalism, he had become a contributor to Franklin's *Courant,* which, although it had attacked his family during the inoculation dispute, was the only literary outlet in town.[78]

When the *Courant* died, Byles, Cambridge schoolmaster Samuel Danforth, budding historian Thomas Prince, and several of their friends persuaded a Boston printer to publish the *Weekly Journal* while giving them editorial powers.[79] The *Journal*'s initial issue promised "regular schemes for the Entertainment of the ingenious Reader, and the Encouragement of Wit and Politeness," and its editors proved to be as good as their word.[80] Each issue of the *Weekly Journal* included an essay, perhaps a humorous letter to the editor, and occasionally a poem.[81] These literary efforts dominated the paper, usually taking up the entire first page and often spilling over to the second. Byles's forte was verse. Poems such as his "Verses written in Milton's Paradise Lost" and "A Congratulatory Poem" to the province's new governor, William Burnett, earned the young poet praise and notoriety.[82]

Nevertheless, Byles's career as a journalist was a brief one. With Increase Mather for a grandfather and Cotton Mather for an uncle, it was preordained that Byles would be ordained. He remained a poet—one of the best in colonial America—but by 1729 he was a poet looking for a pulpit, which, after a few setbacks, he obtained in November 1732.[83] The *Weekly Journal* went on without him, but as its printers became involved as its editors, the paper's literary content soon disappeared.[84]

With the *Journal* now a traditional newspaper, James Franklin in Rhode Island, and Mather Byles writing sermons, there seemed yet another opportunity for a literary newspaper if someone was inclined to seize it. Jeremy Gridley and his friends were so inclined. The *Weekly Rehearsal* made its debut on September 27, 1731. Printed on a half sheet of small paper, it was only two pages long. But the little newspaper had big aspirations.[85] According to a statement on the first page, "the Design of the Present Undertaking . . . is to be useful or entertaining." Art, nature, history—every subject was to be fair game, "circumscribed by nothing but Discretion, Duty and good Manners."[86]

Acknowledging up front "the exceeding and almost insuperable difficulty of being an original in this known and polite age," the *Rehearsal* made it clear that it would be "in the general Course . . . derivative," drawing from "an Infinity of Sources."[87] Still, the editor understood that at times, "entertained with some appropriate Cast of [thought] and Turn of Humor," the paper might "venture" into the "Character of an original author" so as to shed a different light on a subject.[88]

Jeremiah Gridley was the de facto editor of the *Weekly Rehearsal* for about a year. During that time, despite its pretensions, the *Rehearsal* was similar in many respects to other Boston newspapers. Its columns included the requisite "shipping news" of inbound and outbound sailings. In addition, it regularly carried stories from England and the rest of the British Isles, as well as items from all over the world, from Seville to Moscow. There even was a story datelined St. Petersburg about an earthquake in China "with an account of 36,000 persons perished therein."[89]

Except for those of special interest to the Massachusetts, such as a proposed act to prohibit the importation of French sugar into the northern colonies, the items from England that the *Rehearsal* published rarely contained hard news. The newspaper had a tabloid-like penchant for the violent and the unusual. For example, in its November 15, 1731, issue, the *Rehearsal* reported that Lord Stafford's lunatic brother, who claimed that "all the Devils in Hell" were spinning wheels in the chambers above him, had been indicted for murdering a porter who "gave him saucy language."

Gridley's *Rehearsal* included news reports from Massachusetts with an occasional item from New Hampshire, New York, Pennsylvania, or Connecticut. While there were some accounts of legislative and executive actions, these were far less frequent and usually much less comprehensive than what appeared in the other Boston newspapers. The *Rehearsal* also carried its share of local interest items. Thus, in the February 21, 1732, number, readers learned of an accused counterfeiter who successfully escaped from jail by calmly walking out in his wife's clothing, the sinking of a ship bound for Salem, and the death of a gristmill operator who was "killed by the wheels" when a co-worker inadvertently "set the Mill a-going."

All Boston newspapers carried advertisements, but unfortunately for its backers, advertisements accounted for relatively little space on the *Rehearsal*'s pages. Some issues carried only one or two ads, some none at all. Usually running only a few lines, the advertisements hawked everything from ships to salt, to "very good Port Wine," and (sadly) to "A Negro Man about Thirty Years of Age."[90] The paper also was a forum for public announcements including those concerning decedents' estates, public lotteries, lost property, and runaway servants, some of whom absconded with "sundry valuable goods of said Masters."[91]

With such advertisements and notices, as with its coverage of local and foreign news, Gridley's *Rehearsal* was similar to its competitors.

What set it apart was what Gridley had intended to set it apart: literary content. Occasionally there were poems, such as the melancholy "Poem by Mr. H. on his only Daughter, who died aged 14," and the romantic "on a Lady singing . . . inserted at the Request of a Friend, who says they are the Production of a young Gentleman in the Country."[92] Usually, however, the paper's literary efforts were essays on polite subjects. In its early numbers, the *Rehearsal* included essays on conversation ("the Ligament of Society"), virtue ("makes the Man of honour"), love of novelty ("the parent of fashion"), life span ("full sufficient"), and the like.[93] It is highly unlikely that Gridley or any of his associates authored many, if any, of these essays.[94] Most were taken from London magazines without attribution.[95]

While Gridley was its editor, the *Rehearsal* did not reflect the views of the political or religious establishment. If anything, the paper had a liberal slant with a mild emphasis on the power of reason. Thus, an essay in the February 7, 1732, issue downplayed the direct role of God in daily happenings, arguing "there can be no Occasion of recurring to supernatural Causes, to account for what may be very easily accounted for by our Ignorance of natural Ones." In recommending a young gentleman's reading, a *Rehearsal* essay advised that when reviewing religious works, "give not your Belief implicitly to any of their interpretations, but follow your own Reason in the last Resort."[96] Another piece addressing "Liberty . . . the Darling of a true *Briton*" emphasized that "the noblest part of Liberty is . . . the Liberty of free Enquiry & Speculation, and religious Practice."[97] The writer maintains that "some People still are mighty timourous, and apprehensive of the ill Consequences of Liberty."[98] They fear "Toleration," but in his opinion, "Toleration" is essential "to the Strength and Security of our Constitution."[99]

None of this was very contentious. Perhaps with the memory of the divisiveness of the previous decade in mind and the example of James Franklin still fresh, Gridley's *Rehearsal* spoke softly and moderately. Apparently that approach reflected Gridley's view of the role of the press. An essay titled "To Writers" extolled "the useful, valuable and praise deserving Writer" who "employs his Pen to inform the Judgment, to amend the manners, and promote the Happiness of

Mankind."[100] It had little use, however, for the other, less "valuable" types of writers. While freedom of the press was

> the most effectual Preservative of our religious & civil Rights . . . I would not, methinks have this Liberty turned into a wild and licentious Wantonness, and employed, as it is too frequently, in the Service of Prophaneness and Immorality; neither would I have it made the Means of dispensing Calumny, blowing up Civil Discord, or sowing Sedition amongst the People.[101]

Throughout its existence, the *Rehearsal* was strapped for cash. Receipts from its sales barely covered the cost of production.[102] Before long the newspaper began to change, and these changes became increasingly substantive. In August 1732, when the *Rehearsal*'s printer resigned, his successor apparently took a financial interest in the paper and began running the show. The *Rehearsal* started to turn away from a literary to a more traditional format.[103]

The change became official with an announcement in the paper's April 2, 1733, number that "the Gentleman who first set up and [had] hitherto been interested in this Paper, [has] now resign'd all his Right and Interest therein." In 1735 the paper's name was changed to the *Boston Evening-Post,* and the *Weekly Rehearsal* faded into history.[104] But Jeremiah Gridley did not. Destined for bigger things, by 1733 he had found the road to get there.

CHAPTER TWO

Gridley's Law Practice

The First Ten Years (1732–1742)

In February 1732, while he was still teaching at Boston Latin and editing the *Weekly Rehearsal*, Jeremiah Gridley was admitted as an attorney by the Massachusetts Superior Court.[1] He left no record of how he arrived at this pass. His father-in-law, Ezekiel Lewis, may have played a role in his decision. He too had left teaching at Boston Latin for another profession, and although he became a merchant and not an attorney, Lewis must have had some affinity for the law. Appointed a justice of the peace in 1731, and a special justice of the Supreme Court two years later, he was remembered as a "distinguished lawyer."[2]

Gridley may have considered the ministry before settling on law.[3] One source has it that Gridley actually "began to preach," but either failed to find "a parish which suited his views, or thinking his lofty and fastidious feelings would often be wounded in this profession, or that he should not bear the cross with true christian meekness, he turned his attention to law."[4] While there is no authority for the first two of these assertions, there is no doubt that Gridley eventually "turned his attention to law."

During the colonial period, some aspiring lawyers prepared for their future career by clerking with an established attorney, but in the 1730s this was not nearly as common a practice as it later became.[5] Gridley did not follow this route. With a family to support, giving up his position at Boston Latin to clerk in a law office was not a practical option. He could ill afford to lose his annual teacher's salary, let alone come up with the fee required to pay a lawyer to train him. As it was, Gridley did not leave his teaching job until a year after he was admitted to the bar. This probably was a difficult time for him. Years later he advised John Adams "not to marry early," warning that it would "obstruct your Improvement" and "involve you in Expence."[6]

With no other viable alternative, Gridley had to teach himself the law.[7] He had an inspiring role model. John Read, the most prominent lawyer in Massachusetts, was self-taught. Acquiring his "knowledge of the law," he reportedly said, "cost me seven hard years [studying] in that great chair."[8] Read's was not an isolated case. Professionally speaking, there often was no great gap between lawyers who had taught themselves the law and those who had clerked with an attorney. From a pedagogical point of view, however, the latter could leave much to be desired.

Although a clerkship sometimes provided an environment in which legal education was a total and many-faceted experience, too often clerks spent far too much time tending to the menial tasks of a law office, including countless hours copying routine documents by hand.[9] With legal fees set low by law and their income directly related to their volume of business, it was not surprising that some attorneys were remiss in educating their clerks.[10] A generation later, John Adams complained that his mentor James Putnam's neglect disadvantaged him, even going so far as to blame Putnam for the dismissal of his first writ.[11]

Gridley's primary means for educating himself in the law were observation and reading. What he observed were court proceedings. Living in Boston, the provincial capital, he was able to audit a range of judicial venues, from proceedings before justices of the peace to trials in the Massachusetts Superior Court and the Court of Vice Admiralty. Moreover, Boston was home to the best lawyers in the province, including William Shirley and Robert Auchmuty, who had been educated at the Inns of Court; William Bollan, who had studied with Auchmuty; and of course the redoubtable John Read.[12]

Under the best of circumstances, reading for the law in the eighteenth century was, in John Adams's words, "a dreary ramble."[13] Doing it on your own was an especially daunting task, especially in New England. As Gridley explained to Adams:

> [Unlike] a Lawyer or Gentleman of the Bar in England . . . a Lawyer in this Country must study common Law and civil Law, and natural Law, and Admiralty Law, and must do the duty of a Counselor, a Lawyer, an Attorney, a solicitor, and even of a scrivener, so that the Difficulties of the Profession are much greater here than in England.[14]

In 1758, when Adams came to Boston to practice law, Gridley took him under his wing and recommended books that the young lawyer should study. There is no record of what Gridley himself read in preparing for the bar, but if, as a student, he challenged himself in the same manner that he later advised Adams to do, Gridley's studies would have been comprehensive. He advised Adams to "conquer the Institutes," recalling that he "began with Co. Litt. and broke thro."[15] Gridley was referring to the first volume of Sir Edward Coke's *Institutes of the Laws of England, Commentaries on Littleton*.[16] Gridley must have studied Coke on Littleton because, for most of the eighteenth century, every aspiring lawyer in the English-speaking world studied Coke on Littleton.

Adams voiced the popular view when he referred to Coke as the "Oracle of the law," and maintained that "whoever is master of his writings is master of the laws of England."[17] First published in 1628, Coke's commentary contained a wealth of common law knowledge at a time when there was no good comprehensive study of English law. In addition, Coke dealt with real property and pleading, which in the eighteenth century were the prime concerns of law students on account of the underdeveloped state of the law of business and personal relations.

Mastering or even getting through Coke was no easy task. Lord Eldon compared it to a mountain from whose summit one could view the whole world of law, but generations of law students often doubted whether the view was worth the climb.[18] John Quincy Adams agreed that Coke was analogous to a mountain, but one "rugged, dangerous and almost inaccessible."[19] Daniel Webster admitted that he read the book completely "without understanding a quarter of it."[20] It reduced future Supreme Court justice Joseph Story to tears.[21]

Much of the difficulty with Coke on Littleton stemmed from the nature of the book itself.[22] The core of the work was Sir Thomas Littleton's study of land tenures, first published in 1481 or 1482. A legal classic, this "little excellent treatise," as William Blackstone called it, was the first great book on English law neither written in Latin nor influenced by Roman law.[23] Written in the professional law French of the day, it demonstrated that the common law was not just a collection of rules of practice and pleading, but rather possessed principles of its own, scientific in their exactness, yet practical because they were founded on the actual problems of daily life. Littleton described land law as it existed at the end of a period of continuous development by the common lawyers of the Middle Ages. This created a problem for later students because the legal doctrines and origins with which Littleton dealt, although understood by the lawyers of his day, had lost all meaning by the seventeenth century. They stood only on the weak basis of a priori reasoning. Consequently, much of the book had to be accepted blindly, without any real understanding.

Coke's commentary was an attempt to bring Littleton up to date by illuminating its various aspects. Unfortunately, the venerable chief justice could not stay his pen. He went to great pains to explain in depth every word, every doctrine, every institution. Coke's thoroughness was matched by his lack of proportion and organization. The most esoteric technicalities shared the same page with basic legal principles. There was no index to light the way, no abstract to ease the pain. Coke on Littleton was "a legal encyclopedia arranged on no plan, except that suggested by the words and sentences of Littleton."[24]

As much time as it demanded, Coke on Littleton was only one of the books that Gridley had to study. There were many others that he apparently had read and later recommended to Adams. One was Thomas Wood's *Institute of the Laws of England,* a book Adams deemed so significant that he vowed to "read, over and over again."[25] Published in 1720, Wood's treatise was an attempt to provide an updated methodical book on English law. Although it failed to supplant Coke, it proved quite popular and went through many editions.[26] Gridley also suggested, and no doubt had studied, Sir Matthew Hale's *History and*

Analysis of the Common Law of England, which was first published in 1713 and is regarded as the first general history of English law.[27]

In addition, Gridley's recommended reading included older common law classics including Glanville's *Tractatus de Legibus* (ca. 1187–1189), the first treatise on the English common law; Bracton's *De Legibus & Consuetudinibus Angliae*, which replaced Glanville in the thirteenth century and strongly influenced fifteenth- and sixteenth-century legal writers; and Bracton's two most significant imitators—*Fleta* (ca. 1290), which was first printed in 1647, and *Britton* (ca. 1300), which, as the first great treatise written in law French, was popular among practicing lawyers for centuries. Sir John Fortesque's *In Praise of the Laws of England* (ca. 1470), with its lucid explanation of some common law basics, also was on Gridley's list.[28]

Advising Adams to do so, Gridley must have included yearbooks in his legal studies. These annual volumes were reports of cases, the building blocks of the common law.[29] In the mid-sixteenth century, they were replaced by unofficial court reports by named reporters. Gridley recommended two of these to Adams. One was Plowden's Commentaries, which reported cases from 1550 to 1580 and was considered highly authoritative.[30] The other was Sir Edmund Sanders's Reports, which probably was the best of the late-seventeenth-century law reports, becoming a classic textbook on pleading.[31]

Along with books on common law, Gridley also advised Adams to study works on civil and natural law. It was a "maxim which he inculcated on his pupils . . . 'that a lawyer ought never to be without a volume of natural or public law, or moral philosophy, on his table or in his pocket.'"[32] Gridley urged Adams to read three such books that Gridley had in his library: *Corpus Juris Civilis, Corpus Juris Canonici,* and Johannes van Muyden's *Compendiosa Institutionum Justiani Tractato: In Usum Collegiorum,* a treatise on civil law, specifically Justinian's Institutes.[33] Gridley also recommended Arnold Vinnius's commentaries on Justinian's Institutes, and Giovanni Paolo Lancelloti's *Institutiones Juris Canonici* (1563), a study of canon law modeled on the Institutes.[34]

In addition, Gridley directed Adams to two French civilian writers—Jacques Cujacius (or Cujas) (1520–1590), whose *Paratitla* distilled parts of the Justinian Code into clear, short axioms;[35] and Jean Domat (1625–1696), the author of a multivolume legal digest, *Lois civiles dans leur ordre naturel* (1689–1707), in which he attempted to found all law on ethical and religious principles, and *Legum Deteclus* (1700), a selection of the most common laws in the collections of Justinian.[36]

As to natural law, Gridley advised Adams that he would "do well" to read Hugo Grotius and Samuel Pufendorf, as "they are great writers."[37] In his own legal studies, Gridley must have done so. His library included two volumes by Grotius, *Mare Liberum*, which formulated the new principle that the sea was international territory, and *Jure Belli ac Pacis Libres Tres*, a study of the legal status of war;[38] and two by Pufendorf, *Law of Nature and Nations*, which developed the concept of secularized natural law derived from human reason, and its summary, *De Hominis et Civis*.[39]

Gridley's legal studies probably included other treatises in addition to most of those just mentioned. The inventory of his estate lists over 149 law books that were in print when Gridley was preparing for the bar. Their subjects include criminal, civil, and canon law, as well as wills, trusts, commerce, and admiralty. There are also books of forms, statutes, and reports of decisions and trials.[40]

Gridley's was not unstructured reading. Apparently he kept a commonplace book, a well-established learning device used by law students and lawyers for centuries. It was a digest or collection of court decisions, legal maxims, and principles arranged by subject matter, area of law, or some other criterion.[41] Gridley thought a commonplace book so important to law students that he gave Adams a copy of Lord Hale's "Advice" on the mechanics and merits of maintaining a commonplace book,[42] removing it from his own.[43]

With only his commonplace book and no mentor to guide him, Gridley's exploration of the law must have been a lonely and somewhat frightening quest. As in Josiah Quincy's description of the law student's experience before the advent of law schools, and even more than most, Gridley "was left to find his way by the light of his own mind, and obliged to take possession of the wilderness upon which he had entered, as one of our backwoodsmen take possession of an American forest."[44] Nevertheless, in whatever manner he studied, Gridley must have done the right thing because, as noted, he was admitted to the bar in 1732. No doubt Gridley was aided by the fact that, in the 1730s, there were no formal educational or proficiency standards required for admission to the practice of law in Massachusetts.[45]

It was a good time to be a lawyer in Massachusetts. The province's citizens were suing one another as never before. Between 1710 and 1730, the number of lawsuits filed in the Massachusetts Superior Court increased by over 700 percent, and the rate of lawsuits per one thousand people increased by almost 350 percent.[46] Not only was there a growing demand for lawyers, but also there was an increased need for those lawyers to be skilled practitioners. This was due in part to a marked improvement in the caliber of the justices on the province's highest and most important court. In 1710 there had been no lawyers on the Massachusetts Superior Court. The chief justice was a physician, and his colleagues on the court included a minister, a soldier, and two merchants. Only one justice was a college graduate.[47]

In contrast, in 1732, when Gridley was admitted to its bar, the Superior Court's chief justice, Benjamin Lynde, was a Harvard graduate who had attended the Inns of Court, as had Justices Addison Davenport and Paul Dudley, also Harvard alumni. So too was Justice Edmund Quincy, who had fourteen years' experience on the high court. Justice John Cushing was not a college graduate, but by 1732 he had a combined total of thirty years' experience on the Superior Court and the Court of Common Pleas.[48]

In the early 1730s the court they sat on, the Superior Court of Judicature, Court of Assize and General Gaol Delivery, was the highest court in the Massachusetts judicial system. This system was little changed since the last decade of the seventeenth century, and would stay essentially the same for the remainder of the colonial period.[49] The base of this system was the courts held in each county by individual justices of the peace. Appointed, as were all of the province's judges, by the governor and council, these magistrates had jurisdiction over all cases in which the amount in controversy did not exceed forty shillings, except those involving title to land.[50] A justice of the peace also had jurisdiction of criminal matters involving "breakers of the peace, prophaners of the Sabbath, and unlawful gamesters, drunkards or prophane swearers or cursers."[51] He was empowered to order a guilty defendant whipped, pilloried, fined, or jailed up to twenty-four hours.[52] Appeals from his decisions in civil cases lay to the County Inferior Court of Common Pleas, and those in criminal cases to the County Court of General Sessions of the Peace.[53]

In addition to his judicial duties, a justice of the peace was entrusted with various notarial functions such as swearing deponents, taking depositions, witnessing signatures, and performing marriages.[54] Four times a year, all of a county's justices of the peace sat together as the County Court of General Sessions of the Peace.[55] It heard appeals in criminal cases from the courts of individual justices of the peace.[56] Every county also had an inferior court of common pleas which met concurrently with the sessions court.[57] The four judges who sat on each of these courts heard civil appeals from the courts of the individual justices of the peace and had original jurisdiction in actions involving amounts in excess of forty shillings and in cases concerning title to land.[58]

The chief justice and the other four justices who sat on the bench of the Superior Court had cognizance of all actions, personal, real, or mixed.[59] The court's original jurisdiction extended only to certain criminal cases and other matters in which the Crown was a party.[60] As an appellate tribunal, the Superior Court usually granted a trial de novo, but frequently the trial in the Superior Court was the first full-scale trial in the case.[61] In order to avoid two trials, litigants would often seek judgments on a technical point of preliminary pleadings in the Inferior Court of Common Pleas, and then seek a full-scale trial before the Superior Court.[62] This practice of securing a second judgment in the Superior Court led some to conclude that the Court of Common Pleas "generally serves, without much pleadings, only to transmit [actions] to the Superior . . . Court."[63]

After trial before the Superior Court, the losing party had yet another bite at the apple. He or she could bring an action for review, which afforded an opportunity for a second trial in the Superior Court.[64] The province charter permitted an appeal to the Privy Council in personal actions, but this required leave of the Superior Court, which often was denied. A party who had been denied leave could appeal directly to the Privy Council, but this usually was an empty remedy because the Superior Court did not recognize the legitimacy of such appeals and would refuse either to transmit documents to the Privy Council or to order execution on the council's final judgment.⁶⁵

Unlike the other judges in Massachusetts, the judge of the Court of Vice Admiralty held his commission directly from the Crown. Sitting without a jury in Boston, this court had jurisdiction, under the Crown's prerogative, over traditional general maritime actions and, by act of Parliament, in particular cases such as those involving the Acts of Trade. This mandate led to varying and conflicting interpretations.⁶⁶ From the 1730s through the 1750s, the Vice Admiralty Court's docket consisted primarily of seamen's actions, contracts for maritime services, disputes over prizes seized during wartime, claims against parties who cut protected timber in violation of the Naval Stores Act of 1722, and actions by customs officials against smugglers and other alleged violators of the Navigation Acts. Appeals from the Vice Admiralty Court lay to the Privy Council in London.⁶⁷

The bar that Gridley joined in 1732 was a bar in transition. The growing sophistication of the bench had been matched by an increasing number of educated, accomplished attorneys. Nowhere was this trend more advanced than in Boston, where Gridley began his practice. As noted, the courts in Suffolk County provided the arenas for the forensic exploits of John Read, William Shirley, William Bollan, and Robert Auchmuty. In 1734, according to the number of times that their names appear in the minute books of the Suffolk County sessions of the Superior Court, these four were the most active lawyers in that court.⁶⁸

Those minute books, however, also show that men named Lane, Hiller, and Marion also handled a significant number of cases. At the February 1736 session, only Read and Auchmuty were listed in more cases than Hiller and Lane, and in the next term, only Auchmuty's name appears more often than Hiller's.⁶⁹ Yet neither Lane, Hiller, nor Marion is mentioned in histories of the Massachusetts bar. Who were they? Lane was Andrew Lane, who, in the ten years before his death in 1750, was the busiest litigator of the three.⁷⁰ Hiller was Joseph Hiller, a notary public.⁷¹ Marion was Joseph Marion, another notary, who advertised himself as ready and able to furnish "all Instruments of

Conveyances, Sales, Contracts, Agreements, Merchants Affairs, as well as other Clerk-ship, with Fidelity and Dispatch."[72] None of these men was college-educated. None had formal training in law. None, like their better-educated colleagues, was going to step aside when Jeremiah Gridley entered the profession.

Given this competition, it was not surprising that Gridley's progress as an attorney was gradual at best. Of course, it must be noted that measuring any aspect of Gridley's law practice is difficult. No personal records pertaining to its extent have been uncovered. It is impossible to determine how much of his time was spent on the office side of his practice—drafting documents and consulting with clients. Fortunately, it is possible to gain insight into the public side of his practice—litigation. Though incomplete and at times ambiguous, some Massachusetts provincial court records document individual lawyers' involvement in litigation, making it possible to gain a general idea of the level of Gridley's activity in the Supreme Court's Suffolk County sessions, or at least how that activity compares with that of other attorneys.[73]

In the February 1734 session, the first time that his name appears in the minute books, Gridley is listed in eight out of 253 new actions. In contrast, Robert Auchmuty is listed in forty-five new actions, John Read in forty-four, William Bollan in thirty-seven, and William Shirley in twenty-two. Gridley ranks ninth out of the ten lawyers whose names are recorded, behind Lane and Hiller but ahead of Marion.[74] The available Suffolk County Superior Court minute books indicate that during his first decade in practice (1732–1741), slowly, haltingly, Gridley increased the volume of his caseload and raised his ranking among his peers. In 1736 he is listed in twenty-two new cases, in 1738 in twenty-five new cases, in 1739 in thirty-four, and in 1740 in thirty-one.[75] Gridley's best ranking in the period occurred in the August 1739 and February 1740 terms, in which he ranked fifth out of seventeen and fifth out of fifteen lawyers, respectively.[76]

It would appear that in the early years of his practice, Gridley did not follow the Superior Court on its circuit from county to county. Other than Suffolk, his home county, the only other Superior Court sessions in which his name is mentioned are Ipswich and Salem, in

Essex County, which is north of, and contiguous to, Suffolk County. Even there, his name appears only about twenty-five times, and not at all after the March 1739 session at Salem. His busiest term in Essex County was the October 1736 Salem session, in which his name appears five times.[77]

Of those of Gridley's clients who can be identified in the Suffolk and Essex County Superior Court records, many were merchants. One of them was his father-in-law, Ezekiel Lewis.[78] Others included Amos Wood, who advertised "Very good Bohea Tea at 30s Per Pound," and Jacob Griggs, whose merchandise included "A Variety of English and India Goods . . . at lowest Prices, Wholesale or Retail."[79] John Little, "Gardiner in Milk Street," retained Gridley to represent him, as did ship chandler Joseph Parsons, who advertised "very good white Oakum," and Anthony Brackett, who "kept a house of Public Entertainment in School Street."[80] Gridley's clientele also included his brothers Richard and Isaac, clergyman Joshua Gee, and mariners John Henderson and Othiel Beal.[81]

In his first decade of practice, most of Gridley's clients were solid middling sorts, but he did have some clients of considerable social standing. One was his father-in-law. Another was the aforementioned Joshua Gee, who succeeded Cotton Mather at the Second Church of Boston.[82] Clients William Brattle and Edmund Quincy were members of eminent Massachusetts families.[83] Given the relatively few cases that he handled in Essex County, Gridley had a surprising number of prominent clients there. In 1736 he represented a Benjamin Lynde, either the father or the son. Whichever, both were important men in the province. The elder Lynde was chief justice of the Superior Court, and his son was soon to become a judge on the Essex County Inferior Court of Common Pleas.[84] Gridley appeared twice at the 1736 session on behalf of John Wainright, who sat on the Essex Court of Common Pleas.[85] Two years later he represented Benjamin Pickman, a wealthy merchant who later was appointed to the Common Pleas.[86]

During his first years of practice, most of Gridley's cases were routine debt actions, but occasionally a truly unusual case came along. *Vassall v. Rogers* was one such case. On the surface, it was a simple action for battery, but there was a "principle" involved, and as every lawyer knows, when there is a "principle" involved, nothing is simple. The plaintiff in *Vassall v. Rogers* was William Vassall or, more precisely, Leonard Vassall, suing as William's "Father & next friend."[87] A teenager, William was too young to bring the action. His father, Leonard, was a very wealthy man with plantations in Jamaica. In 1717 he had moved his family from the West Indies to Philadelphia. Two years later they relocated to Boston, and then to Braintree.[88] William attended Harvard, where, because his father made a gift to the college and paid double tuition, William was a Fellow Commoner, entitling him to sit at the head table and enjoy certain minor privileges. But for a weakness for gambling, he does not appear to have been an especially troublesome student.[89]

Daniel Rogers, the defendant in the case, was an unfortunate individual. In 1733 he was a tutor at Harvard, having been appointed the previous summer. His appointment was limited to three years.[90] Harvard must have had its doubts about Rogers, and if so, with good reason. Daniel's grandfather had been president of the college, and his mother was descended from the sister of John Calvin, but Daniel showed none of the promise that might have been expected, given his lineage.[91] After graduating from Harvard in 1725, Rogers would not leave. He remained in residence as a Hopkins Scholar. He sought a pulpit with no success. In 1728 he lost his scholarship but stayed on campus. In 1730, with Rogers unemployed and now five years out of college, an aunt, Mary Saltonstall, insisted that her nephew receive the income from a fund that she had donated to Harvard for the benefit of some "student..., 'esteemed of bright parts & good diligence.'"[92]

Finally, in July 1732, perhaps concluding that if Rogers was going to hang around anyway, he might as well do something useful, the president and fellows of Harvard appointed him a tutor.[93] They soon had cause to regret their decision. On March 20, 1733, near the marketplace in Cambridge, Rogers clashed with young William Vassall. According to Rogers, Vassall "shewed ... contempt" for him when he "pass'd close by" the tutor without removing his hat. Then when Rogers "reproved [Vassall] for his Irreverent behaviour," Vassall "insolently stood before [Rogers] still keeping his hat on his head." So Rogers gave Vassall a "Box on the Ear."[94]

Enraged by Rogers's actions, William's father hired the best lawyer he could find. In May 1733, John Read filed suit against Rogers on the Vassalls' behalf in the Middlesex County Court of Common Pleas. Read's writ alleged that the defendant "on the body of [William Vassall] . . . an assault did make & then and there did strike & beat with force . . . & other Enormities did to him."⁹⁵ The Vassalls sought £100 in damages. Rogers also faced criminal charges for assault and battery.⁹⁶

Now, principle entered the picture. It had nothing to do with whether or not Rogers had struck young Vassall; everyone acknowledged that he had done so. The question was, at least as far as the Harvard Corporation was concerned, who should adjudicate the case. The corporation viewed the incident as an internal matter, and the Vassalls' lawsuit as "an Invasion of the Rights and Privileges of the College . . . likely to prove very hurtful to the Government of this society." It assumed Rogers's defense, voting that "a proper Attorney be procured to defend Mr Rogers wherein the Rights and Privileges of the College are concerned." Allocating £3 for his fee, the corporation hired Jeremiah Gridley, on the face of it an unlikely choice.⁹⁷

Gridley had been a member of the Superior Court bar for less than a year and had relatively little litigation experience. Moreover, he would be facing John Read, the best lawyer in Massachusetts. From this distance, it is difficult to say what was going on. It seems likely that Harvard's lawyer had to be a Harvard graduate, which eliminated attorneys like Hiller and Lane. It also could be that in a case against Leonard Vassall, no more qualified Harvard man was available, or would make himself available. Vassall was a rich and powerful man. He may have paid some lawyers "hush money" not to appear against him.⁹⁸

Of course, there are more innocent explanations. Perhaps some influential person promoted Gridley's appointment. His father-in-law, Ezekiel Lewis, is a possibility. In 1733 he was a member of the provincial council and, as such, a member of Harvard's Board of Overseers. Daniel Rogers, the defendant, also may have played a role in Gridley's selection. The two were Harvard classmates. It could be that Rogers expressed a preference for Gridley and, because Rogers was, after all, the named defendant and had an aunt who was a benefactor of the college, the corporation deferred to his wishes.

As per Harvard's concerns, Gridley argued jurisdiction. He did not take issue with the plaintiff's factual allegations but instead argued that the court "ought not to take cognizance of the plea." In a somewhat overwritten response that went all the way back to Charles I, Gridley argued that long before the incident in question, Harvard College had "made & published a Law . . . ordering . . . that all Students shall reverence the Fellows & Tutors by all Expressions of honour as uncovering the head & the like." He also contended that Harvard had long had a "Law ordering that if any Scholar break any Law of God or the College willfully or thru gross negligence . . . he shall be checked by the Severe punishments according to the president[']s or a Tutor[']s prudence." In view of all this, Gridley argued, Rogers was answerable for his acts only to the authorities at Harvard and "not elsewhere."[99] Gridley made the same argument in the criminal case in the Court of General Sessions. He lost in both courts. The juries in both found his client guilty. In the civil case, the jury awarded Vassall £5 and costs.[100] In the criminal action, the court fined Rogers five shillings and costs.[101] Still arguing jurisdiction, Gridley appealed both judgments to the Superior Court.[102] He won. Both judgments were reversed.[103]

Just how Gridley came to represent Harvard in the *Vassall* case is a question that could be asked with regard to most of his early cases. Some clients, like his brothers, were family. Some, such as Daniel Rogers and Nathaniel White, may have been college or Boston Latin friends or acquaintances.[104] Perhaps Gridley drew clients from among those who had been connected with, supported, or purchased space in the *Daily Rehearsal*, clients like Amos Wood, who had advertised his wares in the newspaper while Gridley was its editor.[105]

Then, there was networking. Gridley was a very social man, a joiner. In January 1737, he joined with about twenty others to found the West Church on Cambridge Street in the West End of Boston.[106] Subsequently he was active in the Fellowship Club, which was composed primarily of ship's masters, and the "Society for encouraging Trade and Commerce with the Province of Massachusetts Bay," whose membership included many merchants.[107] He also was a member of St. John's Lodge of the Masons, rising to grand master of the Masons of North America.[108]

Then as now, such involvement presented business opportunities for an ambitious man. Forty years later, John Adams advised one of his students to join some clubs because "Clubbs in Boston are the Nurseries of Statesmen Lawyers, Physicians . . . and the influence of them . . . is very great."[109] Networking may have played a role in Gridley's Essex County client list. It appears he had known Benjamin Lynde Sr. since as early as 1734, when the two had shared a stagecoach from Hingham to Boston.[110] Perhaps this is when Gridley so favorably impressed the chief justice that he or his son decided to retain the new lawyer.

At some point later on, Gridley became recognized as the "Head of his Profession."[111] It is impossible to say how early in his career his ability manifested itself, but it should be remembered that in 1732, when he was admitted to the bar of the Superior Court, Gridley was not a callow young man just a few years out of college. He was over thirty, with years of teaching school, editing a newspaper, and voluminous reading behind him. When he began his practice, Gridley probably hit the ground running and kept on running. After ten years of practice, he was well on his way to becoming one of the leading lights of the Massachusetts bar.

CHAPTER THREE

The Land Bank Crisis (1740–1742)

The strongest indicator of Gridley's growth in stature as a lawyer was the decision of the Massachusetts General Court, in 1742, to name him attorney general.[1] As with so many aspects of his life, it is not clear why Gridley was nominated for the post. It may be that he was something of a pawn, albeit a qualified pawn, in the latest round of an ongoing dispute between Massachusetts's House of Representatives and its governors, a dispute with a long and sometimes petty history, behind which lay a fundamental constitutional issue.

The controversy was over who, under the Massachusetts Charter of 1691, had the power to appoint the province's attorney general. As contested as it would later become, the issue lay dormant during the first twenty-five years of charter government. In 1692, pursuant to his instructions from the Crown, Governor William Phipps appointed the attorney general. When that appointee, Anthony Checkley, retired in 1702, Governor Joseph Dudley followed Article 35 of his instructions "to nominate a fit person to that trust" and selected his son Paul.[2]

While their instructions offered support for the governors' actions in this regard, the ultimate authority for those actions had to be found in the province charter, which, as a later attorney general of England explained, even the king "can't alter by his Instructions."[3] The governors looked to the charter provision which gave them the power to appoint, with the provincial council's advice and consent, "Judges . . . sheriffs . . . and other Officers to our Council and Courts of Justice belonging." They maintained that the last group of "Officers" included attorneys general because they were officers of the court.[4]

This position went largely unchallenged until 1715, when the House of Representatives argued that the General Court, not the governor, had the power to name the province's attorney general, subject only to the governor's veto. The House based its contention on the charter provision that gave the General Court "power and Authority to settle Annually all civil Officers" except those reserved to the Crown or to the governor. It rejected the counterargument that the office of attorney general was included in the phrase "other Officers to our . . . Courts of Justice belonging" on the grounds that the attorney general did not "belong" to any particular court, but was rather "a great civil officer" of the entire province.[5]

For then on, the House of Representatives regularly nominated candidates for attorney general. At first the council was reluctant to go along with the lower house. After, however, receiving a favorable opinion from Sir Edward Northey, England's attorney general, it dropped its objections. In 1716 Paul Dudley was elected attorney general, as were all of his successors. Although their instructions commanded that they, not the General Court, appoint the attorney general, none of the province's governors objected to allowing the legislature's nominees to serve—until 1729.[6]

In May of that year, soon after the election of a new House of Representatives, Governor Samuel Shute sent it a message in which he announced that only he, as governor, could name the province's next attorney general. Shute's declaration was based on a recent change in the royal instructions to Massachusetts governors which was specifically aimed at the General Court's claim to a right to appoint the attorney general:

> [You] are with all convenient speed to nominate with the advice and consent of the council . . . a fit person [to be attorney general]. *And whereas we have been informed that the general court have taken upon them to name this officer, you are therefore to signify to them that we conceive that*

nomination to be our undoubted right and you are not to suffer any person to act in that station but shall be nominated by you as aforesaid.[7]

The council refused to approve John Read when the House nominated him to be attorney general, siding with the governor, who appointed John Overing to the office.[8] There followed a strange dance in which, year after year, the General Court nominated an attorney general (usually John Read), only to have the governor reject the candidate on the grounds, as Governor Jonathan Belcher (1730–1741) put it, of "John Overing, Esq; being at present in that Office according to the Direction of the Royal Charter."[9] This happened and these words were used even when Overing was the legislature's choice, just to make the point that the House had no role whatsoever in the appointment to the office.[10]

In 1741 William Shirley replaced Jonathan Belcher as governor of Massachusetts. Belcher's departure presented the legislature with a fresh opportunity to assert its "right" to name the attorney general. There was a desperate need for change. The province was suffering from a serious financial crisis which affected all segments of society and was fraught with legal complications. Understanding that crisis requires a brief look at the economic situation in the years leading up to it.

From its very beginning, Massachusetts never had enough money in circulation. The province imported more than it exported, and because its foreign creditors demanded payment in specie, there was a constant drain of gold and silver from the province's economy.[11] Over the years, the Massachusetts legislature experimented with various methods to increase the local monetary supply, always under the skeptical eyes of creditors worried about being paid in depreciated currency and the Board of Trade in London concerned about protecting the interests of English merchants.[12]

After 1690, the provincial government annually issued paper money in the form of bills of credit to pay public debts and serve as a medium of exchange. To give the bills value, the statutes authorizing their issuance provided for taxes to be imposed after a set term of years when the bills could be used in payment of taxes or redeemed with general funds. Unfortunately, in response to ever-increasing demands for more currency, the provincial government issued more and more bills of credit and postponed their scheduled redemption. This led to uncertainty in the marketplace and decreased the value of the bills in circulation, which in turn led to a demand for even more currency. The cycle of increasing inflation meant that debtors could pay off their obligations with cheap money.[13]

Unhappy about the situation, in 1737 the Board of Trade instructed Governor Belcher to see to it that all outstanding bills of credit were redeemed by 1742. As taxes were increased and bills returned in an effort to achieve this goal, the Massachusetts economy struggled and commerce suffered. In 1739, desperate to find a solution, the House of Representatives invited propositions for currency reform.[14] One such plan, the Land Bank and Manufactory Scheme, called for subscribers to borrow £150,000 in bills (known as manufactory notes) from the Land Bank, which they would pay for (with interest) in twenty yearly payments of manufactory notes or enumerated commodities. These loans were to be secured by realty or, in some cases, personal property. In September 1740 the Land Bank began issuing bills, in the hope that they would circulate freely and facilitate commerce.[15]

The Land Bank was immensely popular, and the number of its subscribers grew, but many of the province's merchants regarded it as an anathema. Some of them publicly agreed not to accept Land Bank notes. Some established a competing venture (the so-called Silver Scheme), which issued silver-backed banknotes that they agreed to accept. Governor Belcher also opposed the Land Bank and carried out a campaign of harassment and intimidation against the company's subscribers and supporters. Despite these efforts, the Land Bank's popularity continued to grow.

The Land Bank's adversaries turned to Parliament, where their lobbying efforts were decisively rewarded in the spring of 1741 with "An Act for the restraining and preventing several unwarrantable schemes and undertakings in America."[16] In what amounted to a legislative sleight of hand, the act appropriated the "Bubble Act" of 1720, which, by its terms, did not apply to the colonies, and retroactively extended it to the Land Bank, and to the Silver Scheme, and made each void as of the date of its creation (*ab initio*).[17]

In so doing, the act voided all contracts relating to the two enterprises. Significantly, it authorized anyone who held a note from one of the ventures to seek immediate judgment for the face value of the note not only from the company but also from any subscriber or anyone else "engaged or interested in" the companies.[18] The act provided for treble damages unless every demand were met and the schemes wound up by September 29, 1741.[19] All of this promised extreme hardship for the Land Bank's subscribers. Many of them advocated aggressively resisting the measure. In fact, anti-British sentiment ran so high that, writing three decades later, John Adams maintained that "the act to destroy the Land Bank scheme raised a greater ferment in this province than the Stamp Act did."[20]

Cooler heads prevailed. On September 28, 1741, the Land Bank's directors declared it out of business and attempted to persuade the company's subscribers "with all possible Dispatch, to bring in their Proportion of the Manufactory Bills . . . to redeem them."[21] Unfortunately, there was a hard core of Land Bank subscribers who either could not or would not make an effort to redeem the notes that they had received, which created a very difficult situation for their former partners who remained personally liable for all of the notes still outstanding.[22]

William Shirley, who had replaced Belcher as governor, was painfully aware of the "Consternation and Distress" occasioned by Parliament's action against the Land Bank:

> The Act has destroyed the Agreements and Contracts, which pass'd between the Directors and partners . . . , and has subjected every person concerned . . . to the Demands of the Possessors of the Bills; by which means it has happen'd that the honester part of [the company], who have comply'd with the Directions of the Act by bringing in their Quotas of the Bills . . . [,] still remain exposed to the Demands of the Possessors of the Outstanding Bills, and all remedies against the knavish partners, who obstinately refuse to redeem their respective Quotas of 'em, taking advantage of their Bonds and other securities for that purpose being annull'd and made void by the Act.[23]

Deprived of the power to compel their obstinate colleagues to redeem their share of Land Bank notes by the very act that required those notes be redeemed, the "honester" members of the company entreated the governor and legislature for relief.[24] Their pleas were heard. On March 31, 1742, the General Court, which was dominated by Land Bank supporters, passed an order calling for the appointment of a committee with the authority "to demand, sue for, and recover" from all directors and partners "or others all such Bills, Notes, Sums of Money, Goods & Effects" that belonged to the company, and "to require and have immediate payment from the Directors and Partners of all such Sums and Effects . . . found due from them respectively."[25]

Though sympathetic, Shirley believed that he had no choice but to reject the bill because "the Remedy proposed by it is at the Bottom founded upon the supposed . . . mutual Agreements . . . made at first between the Directors and Partners . . . which are declared by the Act of Parliament to be . . . void abinitio."[26] About the same time, note holders began filing suits against members of the Land Bank.[27] There was pressure on the governor to deal with the problem by instructing the attorney general to prosecute recalcitrant subscribers, but he believed that the 1741 act did not permit him to do so.[28]

This was when the newly elected legislature decided to name Gridley attorney general.[29] In an attempted end run around their reluctant governor, the House of Representatives and the council sought to put their own man in the office of the province's chief prosecutor. They wanted someone there who would do as they instructed and initiate proceedings against Land Bank holdouts.[30] If, however, the General Court believed that Shirley would approve Gridley's nomination, they were mistaken. Like Belcher's, his instructions were clear and unequivocal as to the course he should follow, and he followed them.[31]

Shirley rejected Gridley's nomination, retaining Overing as attorney general. Nevertheless, the legislature's plan pushed the governor to take action.[32] He ordered Overing to

> prosecute such of the Partners who shall contumaciously stand out In Defiance of the Act of Parliament and the Orders of the Government, I shall use my Endeavour to enforce it, and have the Edge of the Act turn'd against such as shall still persist in their Obstinacy and Contempt of the Law; and to save as such shall shew an Obedience to it as far as they are able.[33]

The legislature's decision to select Gridley as their agent in this political maneuver defies easy explanation. In his favor, no doubt, was the fact that although his brother Richard had subscribed to the Land Bank, and his brother Isaac to the Silver Scheme, he himself had not participated in either.[34] There is no evidence of Gridley's attitude toward the bank, but if he showed a readiness to prosecute its "knavish partners," this in itself would not have singled him out from most other lawyers. The need to secure payment from those Land Bank subscribers who failed to redeem their fair share of outstanding notes was a position on which almost everyone in the province could agree.

Gridley's ability coupled with his availability may have led to his appointment. If the legislature was going choose its own attorney general to institute prosecutions that the governor opposed, it needed someone it could trust to do the job effectively. By 1742, Gridley had earned a favorable reputation as an attorney who had a respectable practice with some high-profile clients. Moreover, while not the most prominent or successful attorney in the province, arguably he was the best one available.

In 1741 Gridley ranked only eighth in the number of cases in which attorneys were noted in the Superior Court of Suffolk County minute book, but none of those with more was better suited to be attorney general.[35] John Read, the perennial candidate, now sat on the provincial council.[36] Andrew Lane and a newcomer named Joseph St. Lawrence both lacked the appropriate academic credentials. Benjamin Kent, a controversial defrocked minister, handled so many unpopular causes that he was referred to as "the Chimney Sweeper of the Bar."[37] Robert Auchmuty was the judge of the Vice Admiralty Court, William Bollan was a close ally of Governor Shirley, and John Overing, of course, was the attorney general whom the legislature sought to replace.[38]

Gridley simply may have been the most able available attorney who was willing to take the job. That willingness was important. Although it carried a measure of prestige, the office had its drawbacks. It was not a full-time position, and its incumbent received a "pittance of Salary or Pay," which he often had to beg the House of Representatives to vote him.[39] Consequently, any appointee had to maintain a private practice, which presented a dilemma: an attorney general's unpopular prosecution "must prejudice him in his other Business."[40] And that was in the best of circumstances.

Whatever the reason for his selection as attorney general, however political and, in the end, however ineffectual that selection was, it was a clear indication that, by 1742, Jeremiah Gridley's career was on an upward trajectory. Five years later, this ascent was confirmed when Governor Shirley named Gridley a justice of the peace and, as such, a member of the Suffolk County Court of General Sessions of the Peace.[41]

This was a significant appointment. There was money to be made. Justices' fees could amount to a tidy sum. The amount of this sum depended in part on a justice's ability to draft documents and deal with other legal business in a more satisfactory manner than his colleagues. A skilled lawyer like Gridley had a marked advantage in attracting business over justices who were laymen. In addition, a justice of the peace received fees for sitting with his fellow justices in the sessions court, and he received these fees even if he occasionally departed the bench to argue a matter before it.[42]

The prestige associated with the office of justice of the peace was at least as important as the fees that went with it. Always aware of such things, John Adams saw the office as "a great Acquisition in the Country."[43] Most of a justice's prestige stemmed from his seat on the County Court of General Sessions, a body of surprising power and influence. As a judicial tribunal, it heard appeals in criminal cases from courts of individual justices of the peace. But it was as the governing body of the county that the sessions court exercised the most power. The court was responsible for apportioning taxes and appropriating public funds. It built and repaired jails, courthouses, highways, and bridges. It licensed innkeepers, tavern owners, and coffee sellers. To protect the interests of the consuming public, the court appointed agents, such as wine gaugers and leather sealers. The court's decisions in administrative matters could be appealed to the province's legislature, but such was its influence that its decisions seldom were overruled.[44]

When Gridley sat on the sessions court, he was sitting with some of the most important men in the county. Because that county was Suffolk County, where Boston, the province's political, economic, and intellectual center, was located, those men were some of the most influential men in Massachusetts. His colleagues included Thomas and Eliakim Hutchinson, members of the powerful and politically connected Hutchinson family of wealthy Boston merchants.[45] Samuel Waldo also sat on the court, as did John Jeffries and George Rogers, all wealthy merchants, and Thomas Hubbard, who had made a fortune in land speculation.[46]

Not only did his appointment provide Gridley with the opportunity to interact with such influential men, but it also it placed him in a nearly unique position to impress them with his legal acumen. Gridley's appointment in 1746 was different from most because he was appointed a "justice of the peace and quorum."[47] Under Massachusetts law, the Court of General Sessions was to be held by three or more justices, including at least one "justice of the quorum." Very few of Gridley's fellow justices held this commission, and far fewer possessed anything approaching his professional expertise. Gridley filled a crucial role and this made his appointment atypical. In contrast to most of his fellow justices, who owed their appointments to their wealth, family, or politics, Gridley did not. Apparently he was selected as "a means of bringing his great legal knowledge to the aid of the judges with whom he sat on the County Court."[48]

CHAPTER FOUR

The American Magazine (1743–1746)

In the years following his departure from the *Weekly Rehearsal,* Jeremy Gridley never lost his appetite for editing. In 1743, less than a year after the General Court's unsuccessful attempt to name him attorney general, Gridley returned to journalism. While still actively practicing law, he became the editor of a literary magazine—the *American Magazine and Historical Chronicle*—the first true magazine in the American colonies to last more than six months.[1]

In addition to Gridley, four others presided at the *American Magazine*'s birth. It was printed by Gamaliel Rogers and Daniel Fowle of "Queen Street, near the Town House."[2] Among other jobs, Rogers and Fowle printed books for two Boston booksellers, Samuel Eliot and Joshua Blanchard, a relationship that probably led to the idea that became the *American Magazine.*[3] Soon after its first issue, Eliot and Blanchard became the magazine's sole proprietors.[4] To judge from their earlier efforts, they seem an unlikely pair to have published a literary magazine.

Samuel Eliot sold a variety of books and other merchandise from his shop on Cornhill Street.[5] He had begun publishing books in 1737, and by 1742 had published about forty titles. All were on religious subjects, the vast majority of them sermons. There was not one book of essays, poetry, history, or literature. Eliot's partner in the *American*

Magazine, Joshua Blanchard, seems a bit more likely to have become involved in a literary periodical. Although all seven of the books that he had published from his shop at the Bible and Crown in Dock Street had religious content, two of them were written by poets: an edition of Ralph Erskine's popular *Gospel Sonnets* (1720) and one of Elizabeth Singer Rowe's *Devout Exercises of the Heart* (1737).

At some point—perhaps from the beginning—Gridley became involved in the *American Magazine.* It may even have been his idea, but if not, when the others began looking for an editor, Gridley was a logical choice. He had what no one else in Boston had: experience in editing a literary publication and an interest in doing it again.[6] In January 1743 Gridley and his associates put their plan before the world with an advertisement in the *Boston News-Letter.* Their notice announced "Proposals For Printing by Subscription, the *American Magazine and Historical Chronicle;* for all the British Plantations."[7] According to the announcement, the new magazine promised a varied content. On the mundane side, there were to be summaries of proceedings in Parliament, "an Abridgment of the Laws enacted in the respective Provinces and Colonies," current prices, births and deaths, new books, and the "Monthly Chronologer containing an Account of the most remarkable Events, Foreign and Domestick."[8]

Then it got more interesting. Along with "poetical Essays on a variety of Subjects" and "moral, civil, political, humorous and polemical" essays, the *American Magazine* would include "select pieces, relating to the Arts & Sciences, *viz.* speculative and practical Mathematics, astronomical, mechanical and experimental Philosophy, Physick, Surgery, Chymistry, Oratory, Musick, Painting, Architecture, Husbandry, Gardening, *etc.*"[9] If this were not enough, the proposal assured prospective subscribers that the new publication would provide its readers with "A view of the Weekly and Monthly Dissertations, Essays, *etc.* selected from the publick Papers, and Pamphlets, published in *London* and the Plantations." In sum, the public was promised a first-class magazine. "No Care shall be wanting, or expence spared," to make the *American Magazine* "as Entertaining and Useful as Possible," all for the price of forty-eight shillings a year.[10]

In January 1743, when they first announced the creation of the *American Magazine,* Gridley and his associates saw a clear field in front of them. There was no colonial competition. Both Andrew Bradford's *American Magazine* (1741) and Benjamin Franklin's *General Magazine* (1741) had been published briefly and perished.[11] Then suddenly, in March 1743, the *American Magazine* had two competitors—both weeklies, both published in Boston. One of the two, *The Christian History*, did not present a direct threat. Edited and published by Thomas Prince Jr., the son of Reverend Thomas Prince, the magazine's first issue appeared on March 5, 1743. It dealt exclusively with religious topics.[12]

The *Boston Weekly-Magazine* was another story. The new publication's advertising threw down an undeniable challenge to the *American Magazine*:

> Wednesday March 2d was published, No. 1. *The* BOSTON MAGAZINE, to be continued Weekly: In which, besides the more remarkable Passages of News, will be contained from Time to Time, Originals, and the best Collections upon the most entertaining and useful Subjects, Essays of Wit and Humor, Poetry and polite Learning; and so as to make the whole a Piece of valuable Furniture in the Library of a Gentleman.[13]

The initial issue of the new magazine featured five essays, two poems, and some local news.[14] At first blush this would appear to be simply a situation in which, coincidentally, a competitive publication had chosen the same time to enter the same market targeted by the *American Magazine*, but there was more to it than that. Some of the same individuals who were involved in the *Boston Weekly-Magazine* also were involved in the *American Magazine*. Both periodicals were printed and sold by Rogers and Fowle.[15] "Subscriptions and Letters" for the *Boston Weekly-Magazine* could be taken at the Bible and Crown in Dock Square from one Joshua Blanchard, who was one of the founders of the *American Magazine*.[16]

Jeremiah Gridley's reaction to the appearance of the *Boston Weekly-Magazine* deepens the mystery. He sent a strange commentary on the appearance of the rival publication to the *Boston News-Letter*.[17] After accusing those behind the *Boston Weekly-Magazine* of "copying our Title, and pursuing our Scheme," Gridley charged that this Weekly Paper owes its hasty and immature Production, not only to a desire of hindering Subscriptions to the [*American Magazine*], but also from a Suspicion that the Compilers [Gridley et al.] would not be so hearty and zealous in promoting and maintaining Religious Controversies of the Present Day as it was imagined the Exigencies of the Case required.[18]

Then Gridley launched into an explanation of the position of the *American Magazine*'s "Compilers" on the matter. He declared that originally they had "had some Tho'ts of wholly omitting" religious disputes, "chiefly because many think we had eno' of them." Because, however, some might think them "remiss" if the *American Magazine* did not address "the Disputes of the present Day," the "Compilers" had agreed "to appropriate three or four Pages for that purpose," giving equal space to both sides.[19]

What is curious about Gridley's commentary is that while the *Boston Weekly-Magazine* never contained anything relating to theological disputes, not very much earlier two of his colleagues at the *American Magazine* had enthusiastically participated in "Religious Controversies" arising from the Great Awakening. Reaching Massachusetts in the early 1740s, this revivalist movement split Congregationalists between those who supported the movement ("New Lights") and those who opposed it ("Old Lights"). In the year prior to the inauguration of their *American Magazine*, Joshua Blanchard and Samuel Eliot had become embroiled in the dispute between the Old and New Lights.

First, Blanchard had unleashed a blistering attack on Andrew Croswell, the revivalist minister of the Second Church of Groton, accusing him of acting "in a base outrageous manner, not as becomes a Christian or a Gentleman."[20] A few months later, Samuel Eliot engaged in an unseemly, very public dispute with the *Boston Gazette* over its editor's purported unwillingness to publish the views of the Reverend Jonathan Ashley, who was critical of the revivalist movement.[21]

How these incidents—Blanchard's involvement in the Croswell dispute; Eliot's role in the Jonathan Ashley dustup; the appearance of the *Boston Weekly-Magazine;* the relationship of Rogers, Fowle, and Blanchard to that publication; and Gridley's attack on it—relate to one another is unclear. It appears that there had been a dispute among the group putting together the *American Magazine* which aligned Gridley against his colleague Joshua Blanchard and perhaps Eliot as well. Apparently the disagreement related to whether or not their new magazine should feature religious polemics.

Gridley seems to have opposed such inclusion, and Blanchard, who was an active partisan in at least one religious dispute, may have favored it. It could be that Blanchard promoted the rival magazine to pressure Gridley into changing his position. If so, Blanchard's scheme worked. As noted, in his submission to the *Boston News-Letter,* Gridley announced that the *American Magazine* would dedicate several pages to "the [religious] Disputes of the present Day."[22] The *Boston Weekly-Magazine* then vanished as quickly as it had appeared, and, once again, the *American Magazine* had the field to itself.[23]

The first issue of Gridley's magazine made its debut in the autumn of 1743.[24] In his "Introduction," Gridley described what the new publication was all about:

> a Collection of the best and most approved Pieces publish'd in *Great-Britain* and the Plantations, with summary Rehearsals and Quotations from the best Authors that of all Parts of polite and useful Learning; with such Originals as we have, or shall from Time to Time be furnish'd with from Gentlemen of Ingenuity and Erudition.[25]

Although it had been soliciting subscriptions for about nine months, Gridley acknowledged that the magazine "has not yet such a number of subscribers as are sufficient to support it." His hope was "that if the Design be well executed, further Encouragement will arise hereafter."[26] That "Design" was definitely English. The first issue, and all thirty-nine subsequent issues of the *American Magazine,* imitated the *London Magazine, or Gentleman's Monthly Intelligencer* in both appearance and format. Where, on its title page, the English publication had a large cut of London, the *American Magazine* had one of Boston. The pages of both were the same size and laid out in two columns.

Each issue of the *American Magazine* consisted of about fifty pages. Like another London periodical, *The Gentleman's Magazine,* Gridley's was divided into two sections, as described by its full name, the *American Magazine and Historical Chronicle.* The "Historical Chronicle" usually consisted of the last six pages or so of each issue. Essentially, it was a monthly newspaper collecting items from the colonies, Great Britain, and the rest of the world. In the first year and a half of its life, the "Historical Chronicle" included a fairly wide variety of stories, from fires in Boston to the war raging in Europe. Beginning in the summer of 1745, however, the pages of the "Chronicle" were dominated by two events: the siege and capture of the French fortress of Louisbourg in Canada by provincial troops, and the progress and defeat of the Jacobite uprising under Bonny Prince Charlie.

The location of the "Historical Chronicle" in the back pages of Gridley's magazine duplicated its location in its English prototype but also made good sense. There was little that was unique in the "Chronicle." Because the *American Magazine and Historical Chronicle* was published monthly, while most colonial newspapers were published weekly, many of the "Chronicle" stories had appeared elsewhere before the *American Magazine* reached its subscribers' hands. Given this fact, it is logical to conclude that most of its readers bought the *American Magazine and Historical Chronicle* for its first section—the "American Magazine." Constituting about 80 percent of the publication, this portion included essays, poems, and biographies, as well as items on religion, geography, science, medicine, and world events, some by a remarkable collection of authors including Voltaire, Joseph Addison, Henry Fielding, Benjamin Franklin, John Locke, and Alexander Pope. There was little in the way of belles-lettres.

The most frequent feature in the magazine was something titled the "Journal of the Proceedings and Debates of a Political Club of young Noblemen and Gentlemen established some time ago in London." Borrowed from the *London Magazine,* this recurring satire on English politics and politicians led off twenty-two issues of the *American Magazine* between 1744 and 1746, accounting for about a dozen pages of each issue. The mainstays of each number, however, were literary essays covering a wide range of subjects, especially human traits and behavior. In 1746, for example, there were pieces condemning inconsistency, flattery, cunning, haughtiness, and cursing.[27] At the same time, gaiety, good humor, and mirth received a good deal of attention, as did happiness, pleasure, and, of course, love, be it "Virtuous Love" or the "Passion of Love" or "Education and the Power of Love."

The January 1745 issue of the magazine was somewhat typical. In its pages the reader was warned about "The Mischiefs of Avarice" and "Prating" (chattering), while being advised on "How to Enjoy Life."

Gridley seems to have delighted in such tension, with the same issue dividing space between an essay titled "Reflection on Death" and "An Essay on Happiness," or "Of Style and Elocution" and "Great TALKERS Exposed," or, my personal favorite, "The Form of a Modern Love Letter, drawn up by a Set of Pretty Fellows" and "A Caution against the ATTEMPTS of LIBERTINE WITS."[29]

Usually each issue included a description of a country, a city, or an institution. The geographic reach was far-ranging, from China to Greenland.[30] The institutional descriptions also varied. One issue discussed the government of the United Provinces, another the London College of Physicians, and a third Edinburgh Castle.[31] About half of the science articles that appeared in the *American Magazine* dealt with physics, especially astronomy. There were three pieces on comets alone.[32] Included also were treatments of biological and geological subjects, as well as essays on telescopes and microscopes. Medicine was largely neglected. After including four medical articles in the magazine's first four numbers, Gridley made room for only five in the remaining thirty-six issues, four of which dealt with Bishop George Berkeley's experiments with tar water as a universal cure-all.[33]

In its forty issues, the *American Magazine* included about a dozen biographical essays. These were abbreviated affairs, many borrowed from Pierre Bayle's *Historical and Critical Dictionary* (1695–1697; 1702), the first modern biographical dictionary. Along with names that still resonate today—names like Newton, Locke, and Milton—the magazine included subjects now somewhat obscure, such as Thomas Sydenham (1624–1689), the "English Hippocrates," and John Jewel (1522–1571), whose *Apologia Ecclesiae Anglicanae* (1562) was the first methodical statement of the Church of England's position against the Roman Catholic Church.[34]

The October 1743 issue of the *American Magazine* included a poem titled "A Charge to the Clergy," which ridiculed ministers whose oratorical inadequacies showed "only that a man, at once, may be a scholar and a dunce." A poem in another issue took aim at believers "of sour temper . . . who think it a sin to take any Pleasure," while "The Church: A Religious Satire" castigated some of the faithful as an "ungodly presumptuous train."[35] Despite items of this nature and the generally secular, sometimes irreverent tone of the magazine, serious religious pieces regularly appeared at the rate of about one an issue.

While a few of the religious items, such as "On the Immortality of the Soul" and "An Essay on Divine Judgments" dealt with academic theological subjects, most were of more interest to the general reader.[36] Articles such as "An Apology for Religious Zeal," "Hypocrisy in Religion exposed," and "The Folly and Absurdity of Atheism" were typical of this genre.[37] Although Gridley had indicated in his response to the publication of the *Boston Weekly-Magazine* that the *American Magazine* would "appropriate three or four Pages" to religious disputes, he rarely did so.[38]

The magazine section of Gridley's periodical included a sprinkling of political items. By far the most common of these were speeches by colonial governors to their legislatures. The governors of Connecticut, Barbados, Pennsylvania, New York, and Massachusetts were represented. Not surprisingly, Governor Shirley of Massachusetts received the most ink. All of this changed with the *American Magazine*'s January 1746 issue. Beginning with that number, the monthly's magazine section, like its "Historical Chronicle," became awash in pieces about the Jacobite rebellion. The January issue alone had ten articles on the subject.[39] Throughout 1746, each issue stuck to this focus, reflecting the course of the dramatic events an ocean away. Thus it went from "On the possible reign by the Pretender" in the January number, to "On the Rebellion, and its unexpected Progress," to "Peers to the King on the Victory over the Rebels," to "Of Punishing the Rebels," to November's "Account of the Scotch Rebels executed."[40] The Scottish rebellion also invaded the *American Magazine*'s poetry section, with at least a dozen poems devoted to the subject.

These poems represented a significant departure. Typically, the monthly collection of "Poetical Essays" contained a wide variety of verse, some serious, some humorous, some dealing with religion or virtue, or vice, death, science, love, or the "fair sex"—especially the "fair sex." Every issue included at least one poem devoted to the subject. Perhaps the June 1745 issue was the most infatuated. It included poems to ladies "very frightened of Thunder," who "had ill-Luck in the Lottery," and who had "a Withered Rose," as well as "Verses sent to a LADY on May-Day, with a Nosegay," and a poem that sought to describe "The Furniture of a Woman's Mind."[41]

The *American Magazine* generally lived up to its advance billing, presenting varied and interesting fare. Ironically, given the fact that Gridley was a lawyer, the magazine was virtually devoid of the parliamentary summaries promised in its "Proposals," and never included "an Abridgment of the Laws enacted in the respective Provinces and Colonies," as had been advertised. Not only did Gridley fail to include colonial statutes, he also all but ignored anything to do with law or lawyers. With a few exceptions such as the brief accounts of the trial and execution of two sailors from HMS *Wager* who had "assaulted and mortally wounded" two sailors from a provincial sloop, the *American Magazine* contained no crime reports, a staple of colonial journalism that had appeared often in Gridley's *Weekly Rehearsal*.[42]

No lawyers or jurists were profiled in the biographies included in the *American Magazine*. Gridley nodded to his profession but once, publishing a poem about every law student's nemesis. In "Written in a Gentleman's COKE upon LITTLETON," the poet promises this "precious volume" an "undisturb'd . . . sleep" if it would be his guide:

> Thro' labyrinths of law;
> Direct my steps thro' paths untry'd,
> From error free and flaw.
> Assist to keep unturn'd my head,
>
> While I the maze explore:
> Teach me thro' doubt's dark fear to wade
> And touch the golden shore.[43]

In the magazine's September 1744 number, Gridley included a short essay titled "Of Liberty and Government," which analyzed the extent to which government is entitled to encroach on liberty and inviolable rights. It is the type of piece that frequently appeared in English periodicals of the day, but one of only a very few of that genre published in the *American Magazine*. Moreover, unlike his counterparts in England, who often included ad hominem political attacks in their magazines, Gridley demonstrated a marked aversion to them.[44]

As discussed earlier, much of the *American Magazine*'s appearance and configuration were copied from the *London Magazine*, but the similarities were more than skin-deep. One historian has concluded that "except for the imprint, it might have been printed in London."[45] There was a simple reason for this: most of the *American Magazine*'s copy was taken from other publications, the vast majority of them English.[46]

Such "borrowing" was neither untoward nor unusual. Gridley had made it clear from the outset that he would include "Essays, *etc.* selected from the publick Papers and Pamphlets, published in *London* and the Plantations."[47] Moreover, other similar publications, including those from which he took material, did the same thing. In fact, some of the items that Gridley borrowed, he took from periodicals that had taken them from another publication.[48]

The December 1746 issue of the *American Magazine* was its last. Its demise may have stemmed from the same economic realities that had killed its precursors. By its very nature, a colonial magazine was an iffy proposition. The colonies simply were not yet ready to support such a periodical.[49] Each of the *American Magazine*'s Philadelphia predecessors—both published in a larger market by shrewd businessmen—had failed to last a year.[50] Its immediate successor in Boston, the *New-England Magazine,* did not appear until 1758, was published sporadically, and soon was gone.

Loss of a key man also may have played a role in the decision to cease publication. Sometime in 1745, Samuel Eliot died. He was the more experienced half of the team of Eliot and Blanchard, the magazine's proprietors. If Gridley and Blanchard did, in fact, have problems with each other, Eliot's death may have removed the buffer necessary for the two men to work together effectively. Then again, Gridley may have been the "key man" who was lost. Perhaps he had too many other things to attend to. Along with his legal practice, he had embarked on a number of financial endeavors that now demanded his attention.

CHAPTER FIVE

Iron and Land

As his legal practice flourished in the late 1730s and early 1740s, Jeremiah Gridley's income increased accordingly. In 1743 he purchased a new house in Boston, large enough for his growing family, which now included three young daughters.[1] Gridley also looked for promising business opportunities in which to invest his disposable income. Such an opportunity came Gridley's way through his longtime friendship with Peter Oliver, the youngest son of one of the wealthiest men in Massachusetts.[2] In about 1737, Oliver left the mercantile partnership that he had formed with his brother in search of something different, something more to his liking. He found it about forty miles south of Boston in the small town of Middleborough, where his family held real estate, and where there was an infant iron milling industry and plenty of waterpower to support its expansion.[3]

Seeing a future in the iron business, Oliver mortgaged much of his property in Boston to raise capital, moved to Middleborough, and formed a partnership with Gridley. Apparently, Oliver supplied most of the vision and probably most of the money, while Gridley provided the legal expertise necessary for an ambitious program of acquisitions which formed the basis of their iron milling operations.[4] During the next seven years, the partners made over twenty real estate purchases on, and in the area of, the Nemasket River. These included dams, forges, gristmills, sawmills, and, most important, a slitting mill with tools, forges, and attendant buildings.[5] It appears that Gridley took the laboring oar with regard to these transactions, sometimes retaining James Otis Sr. as his man in the field to deal face-to-face with the sellers. Fearful of inflated prices if their identities became known, Gridley instructed Otis, in negotiating with some sellers, to "conceal Mr. Oliver's & my name till we desire you to mention them."[6]

By about 1750, after significant repairs, development, and expansion, the slitting mill, forges, and foundry were in operation, manufacturing hollowware, nails, cannon, mortars, howitzers, shot, and shells. A combination of factors soon made it a profitable operation. Slitting mills were becoming increasingly important in the colonies because the rolled rod iron they produced was used in making nails, for which there was a growing demand.[7] Probably because of the expense of building them, there were only a few slitting mills in Massachusetts, which gave Gridley and Oliver's mill a ready market.[8] Their position was further enhanced by Parliament's passage of the Iron Act of 1750. In an attempt to protect English manufacturers of finished iron products, the act prohibited the future erection in the colonies of any "mill or other engine for slitting or rolling of iron," but allowed such colonial mills then in existence to continue operation.[9] This, of course, gave the operators of such mills, like Oliver and Gridley, protection from future competition.[10]

Soon, thanks in part to Oliver's political connections, the ironworks received a huge boost from military contracts during the French and Indian War.[11] Oliver estimated that during the war, the operation was netting between £400 and £500 per year.[12] By then, however, Gridley was no longer associated with the venture. He sold out to his partner in 1758.[13] This probably was a mutual decision. Unlike Oliver, who had made his home in Middleborough and was deeply involved in the day-to-day operation of the ironworks, Gridley found his role diminished once the acquisition stage was over, and apparently had no desire to move so far from Boston or to become an industrialist.

Gridley's investment in his friend's iron mill was, for its time, somewhat unusual. In mid-eighteenth-century Massachusetts, there were not many investment opportunities for a relatively small capitalist like Gridley. There were no private banks.[14] Joint stock companies typically had few members, each of whom had made a significant investment.

Underwriting maritime insurance presented a potential avenue for investors, but at the time, it was still a fledgling industry that had to compete with established English insurers, and while it could produce large returns, the vagaries of seaborne commerce in a world at war made it far too risky for investors with little margin for error.[15] While industries such as commerce and shipbuilding were tolerated and even encouraged by British law, to protect domestic English manufacturers, others, including clothing fabrication, hat making, and sugar refining, either were forbidden or were restricted by British statutes, royal edicts, or informal trade practices.[16] The want of skilled workers and the lack of inexpensive labor in general also inhibited colonial business opportunities.[17]

In the face of these obstacles, many Massachusetts entrepreneurs looked to Maine and New Hampshire, where there were thousands of acres of undeveloped land. This untapped resource, coupled with a growing population pent-up on the seaboard, and a provincial government willing to grant the land on very liberal terms, was an enticing lure to which Gridley was not immune.[18] He invested in at least three townships in New Hampshire. Of the three, Peterborough is the best documented and the most interesting because it offers, in microcosm, a view of the dangers, problems, and legal complications attendant on so many of these ventures.

It began in 1721, when forty-nine men and one woman petitioned the Massachusetts General Court for a grant of yet "unapportioned" province land. Apparently the legislature had "voted in favor" of the petition, "but the Indian War then breaking out," the petition had been "dropped."[19] Sixteen years later, most of the same petitioners were back, in their words, having "kept to their first intention, of settling together," which was, "as they conceive, laudable in itself, and conducive to the public good."[20] On December 6, 1737, the House of Representatives granted the petition and appointed a committee to recommend a "suitable place . . . six Miles square" for the petitioners to locate a settlement.[21] Two days later, the House voted to accept the committee's recommendation and ordered the petitioners to have the land surveyed with provision for sixty-three lots of equal size, two of which were to be set aside for clergy and one for a school. A second committee was named to admit "grantees or settlers," each of whom had to swear that he or she had not received a land grant in the last three years and post a £40 bond to ensure compliance with the conditions of the grant.[22] Governor Belcher approved all of this on January 16, 1738.[23]

The list of grantees announced by the legislative committee on March 17, 1738, was different from the list of original petitioners. There were twenty new names. About half of these filled additional spots that had been created to bring the number of grantees to the required number. This group included Gridley's brother Isaac. The other new grantees, who included Gridley's brother Richard and brother-in-law Ezekiel Lewis Jr., had purchased the interests of original petitioners.[24] This trend gathered momentum. By the first meeting of the proprietors in July 1738, the majority of grantees had sold out. Soon there were only four proprietors—Jeremiah Gridley, John Hill, John Fowle Jr., and Peter Prescott—not one of whom had been a petitioner or an original grantee.

Much of this had occurred within nine days of the governor's approval in January 1736, a period during which these four had purchased most of the grantees' interests at prices between £1 and £5 each. Gridley's total of sixteen purchases included the interests of his two brothers and his brother-in-law.[25] It is very likely that these developments were part of a prearranged plan orchestrated by Hill and/or Fowle, both active land speculators. Between 1730 and 1739, Hill became a grantee or a proprietor of eight towns in the Massachusetts–New Hampshire border region. Fowle was the sole or part owner of six in the same area. It also seems probable that Hill, who practiced law in Boston and was active in public affairs there, had invited Gridley to participate.[26]

The partners set about dividing up the township's land and preparing it for sale to settlers. After laying out sixty-three fifty-acre home lots, their surveyor divided the rest of the township into lots not exceeding two hundred acres. The lots then were divided among the proprietors, with each one receiving a five-hundred-acre "farm" as well. Perhaps to compensate him for his legal work with regard to the purchase of the grantees' interests, Gridley's farm included the most valuable acreage.[27] The proprietors sought out prospective settlers to purchase plots in the new township and were ready to deal in order to do so. For example, one of their advertisements promoting the sale of "Seven Thousand Acres of Land" offered to sell the property "upon very reasonable terms" in "such Quantities or Parcels as the Purchaser shall see meet." Even more, it noted that they did not insist upon payment in "money" but were willing to accept payment in "goods."[28]

In another effort to attract settlers, Gridley and his associates offered an agreement to the Reverend William Johnston, a Presbyterian minister who was preaching on a temporary basis in Windham while awaiting a contract there. The proprietors promised Johnston that if he would settle in Peterborough and bring a sufficient number of settlers with him, they would sell each settler one hundred acres of land for ten shillings an acre. In addition, they would pay Johnston £25 a year for four years as the town's first minister as well as £200 if he stayed for one year and another £200 if he stayed a second. Johnston turned down the deal and accepted a permanent position in Windham.[29]

The proprietors' failure with Johnston was not unique. Gridley and his partners found their path to the establishment of a viable settlement slow going. Circumstances conspired against them. Always a dangerous place, the Massachusetts frontier became all the more so when war broke out in the early 1740s between the English and the French and France's Native American allies. Years later, the proprietors reported that before the war "broke out," they had built bridges and a mill, and that "there were 50 families settled there," but all of them moved out.[30]

There can be no doubt that the threat of attack forced people to leave Peterborough and kept others from moving there, but that was not the only reason for its lack of settlers. Perhaps even more important was the fact that for many years, the territory in which Peterborough was situated was the subject of a dispute between Massachusetts and New Hampshire over which province had the better claim to it. In fact it may well be that the 1738 Peterborough grant was part of a plan on the part of Massachusetts to solidify its claim to the area by planting as many towns there as possible.[31]

Finally, in 1741 the Crown ruled against Massachusetts and in favor of New Hampshire, giving it over seven hundred square miles more than it had ever requested.[32] Peterborough was now in New Hampshire, but the title to it held by Gridley and his three partners was based on a grant from Massachusetts. This called into question all ownership claims to land in Peterborough, from those of its proprietors to those of anyone who bought land from them. Understandably, settlers were reluctant to buy land with the title in doubt.

Unless the Peterborough proprietors could find a way to solidify their claim, any return on their investment in the town was threatened by the cloud of uncertainty that hung over the title to it. Ironically, that cloud was lifted when another claim to the land, one long thought moribund, was given new life. More than one hundred years earlier, Captain John Mason had received grants of huge swaths of land in what was now much of New Hampshire.[33] Mason died in 1635, devising his claim in entail, which meant that, on the death of its owner, the land could descend only to his oldest surviving male heir. What this meant was that, although the owner could convey the property to a third party, that party held an interest only so long as the owner was alive. When the owner died, the property reverted from the third party back to the owner's heir.[34]

Captain Mason's efforts to settle New Hampshire had been unsuccessful, and his heirs fared no better. Finally, in 1691, the captain's great-grandsons had had enough and sold their claims to New Hampshire to Samuel Allen, a Boston merchant. To give Allen clear title, the entail attached to the title had to be eliminated. This was accomplished in the English Court of Common Pleas through an arcane legal process known as fine and recovery.[35] For the next twenty-five years, Samuel Allen, and after Samuel's death his son Thomas, attempted to assert their rights in New Hampshire against those who trespassed on their title. They had little success, alienating the population, and after Thomas died in 1715, the Allen claim was largely unenforced.[36]

It was during this period that John Tufton Mason revived the Mason claim, asserting that the attempt to sever the entail from the New Hampshire grant when Allen had purchased it was invalid, and that he, as the captain's eldest male descendant, had inherited title to the land in question. His timing could not have been better. The turf war between New Hampshire and Massachusetts was before the Privy Council for final decision, and each side was looking for an edge. Both believed that Mason could give them one.[37]

Massachusetts acted first. Its agents contacted Boston attorneys John Read and Robert Auchmuty for a legal opinion. They supported Mason's position that the attempt to eliminate the entail was invalid because it had resulted from a proceeding in a court in England rather than one in New Hampshire, which clearly had jurisdiction over the land in question.[38] Massachusetts then attempted to purchase Mason's interest but so bungled the effort that he turned to New Hampshire. The parties had a deal on the table, but the province could not pull the trigger. Finally, after effectively eliminating the entail in a New Hampshire court, Mason sold his interest in New Hampshire to a group of prominent New Hampshire citizens, who became known as the "Masonian Proprietors."[39]

Like the Allens, the new owners of the Mason grant faced the problem of townships on their land which had been established pursuant to grants from either New Hampshire or Massachusetts. Peterborough was one of those grants. Learning from their predecessors' mistakes, the Masonian Proprietors did not attempt to evict the squatters in viable towns. Instead they quitclaimed their rights to the property, giving up all of their claims against the squatters.[40] As yet unsettled townships with Massachusetts grants like Peterborough were dealt with on an individual basis, but with an eye toward resolving the situation with as little acrimony as possible. Gridley and his associates entered into negotiations with the Masonian Proprietors which lasted for several years. Finally, in January 1748, after formally recognizing that their township "falls within your claim," the Peterborough proprietors officially petitioned the Masonian Proprietors for leave to "settle under your claim."[41]

The Masonians were agreeable, granting "all their Right Title Estate Interest & property of in unto [that tract of land called and known by the name of Peterborough] and Quit their Claim unto . . . [Jeremiah Gridley et al.]" with three significant caveats. The Masonians reserved to themselves 3,400 acres of land "as [the grantees] shall think most convenient for promoting the said Settlement." In addition, they required that all trees fit for masts in the Royal Navy be preserved from destruction, and that the grantees "settle forty Families on said tract of land within four years."[42]

Peterborough's proprietors had no difficulty in meeting this third requirement. Within ten years, over fifty families had settled in the town and its population numbered in excess of three hundred people. Even a new war with France did not stem the tide. The very increase in numbers increased the settlers' sense of security and encouraged others to join them.⁴³ The only aspect of the Masonian Proprietors' requirements that proved problematical was their retention of 3,400 acres of land. Peterborough was surrounded by property held by the Masonian Proprietors. They sliced off 3,400 acres of some of Peterborough's best land in the west to add to their own holdings and compensated the town by adding 3,400 acres of rocky mountainous terrain in the east, which they had cynically reserved to themselves according to the quitclaim deed. The Peterborough proprietors found this sleight of hand difficult to accept and refused to agree to it. The dispute simmered for over fifteen years until finally, in 1765, the Peterborough proprietors acknowledged the inevitable and accepted the status quo.⁴⁴

Apparently, this disagreement did not poison the relationship between the Peterborough proprietors and the Masonian Proprietors, who in fact seem to have been well disposed toward Gridley and his associates, especially Gridley. In 1753, while the Peterborough land dispute was as yet unresolved, the Masonian Proprietors granted Gridley, Hill, and Fowle "title, right, and possession of the property of Dantzic," now Newbury, New Hampshire, which is about forty miles north of Peterborough.⁴⁵ About a year later, they granted Gridley a one-sixth interest in a township contiguous to Dantzic named Hereford.⁴⁶

This second grant may have been somehow related to some legal work that Gridley had done for the Masonian Proprietors. If it was, it would not have been unusual. According to a Masonian internal document dated January 3, 1753, Gridley had drawn up "a State of Masons Title." To reward him for this service and "for his further Encouragement as a retaining Fee," they granted Gridley "the Right & Title of the Property in So much of the lands adjoining on the north & east of Peterborough . . . as he shall think best."⁴⁷

It appears that from then on, Gridley represented the legal interests of the Masonian Proprietors on a somewhat regular basis. In the same letter in which he thanked the proprietors for their "Generous" gift to him, Gridley discussed his efforts to convince Benjamin Lynde Jr., one of the proprietors of the township of Salem-Canada, "upon the Goodness of your title."⁴⁸ This was a reference to the final stages of a four-year dispute between the Masonian Proprietors and the proprietors of Salem-Canada, who, like those of Peterborough, had received a grant from Massachusetts only to find their claim in New Hampshire challenged by the Masonians. Gridley's efforts proved successful, and the dispute was settled on terms very favorable to his clients.[49]

Gridley's defense of the Masonian claim was a major and deeply researched project. It revolved around the argument that John Tufton Mason inherited his family's right to New Hampshire because the attempt to cut off the family's entail rights with a decision in an English court was ineffectual. It will be recalled that John Read and Robert Auchmuty had provided an opinion to this effect, but apparently, when the Masonian Proprietors attempted to assert Mason's claim ten years later, their opinion was repeatedly challenged.[50]

Such challenges probably explain Gridley's letter to Nicholas Fazakerley in late 1753 or early 1754 in which he requested that the eminent English barrister answer a series of pointed questions relating to John Tufton Mason's grandfather's attempt to cut off his progeny's claims to New Hampshire. Gridley's first question was typical: "Whether a fine for recognizance, etc. levied at Westminster, of lands lying in New-England, by fiction, supposed to be in England, will bar the heir in tail by common or statute law?"[51] Fazakerley's answer to that question ("the heir in tail will not be barred or affected thereby"), like his answers to Gridley's other three questions, all supported the Masonians' claims to lands in New Hampshire. It appears that Gridley may have partnered with another well-respected Boston lawyer, Benjamin Prat, in drafting the defense of the Mason claim, a defense that proved effective year after year.

For example, in 1773, the Masonian Proprietors were confronted with a claim by Samuel Lauchlen based on a "right & Title to a large tract of land in [New Hampshire] which is thought to have regularly descended from Grandfather Samuel Allen, Esq. to his Mother." Lauchlen maintained that, seeking to "avoid the disagreeable necessity of a Law Suit," his mother was "willing to quit claim all of her right on Condition of having a Township allowed on which will instantly settle thirty families."[52] The proprietors responded that they did not question the facts behind Lauchlen's claim, "but from the Authority of Mr. Gridley and Prat and other good lawyers are fully convinced that no Title under [A]llen can be held after the decease of the person [Robert Tufton Mason] who conveyed to [A]llen, the Premises being an Estate in tail."[53]

Gridley's familiarity with proprietary dealings led to his retention by others embroiled in land controversies. This was true in central Maine, then a part of Massachusetts, where land companies battled one another as well as settlers over land claims and titles. The biggest dog in the fight was the Kennebec Proprietors, known as the Plymouth Company because its claims were based on a long-dormant patent from the Plymouth Company which encompassed the territory extending fifteen miles on either side of the Kennebec River.[54] Founded in 1741, this group of powerful Boston investors aggressively promoted their somewhat questionable rights against other land companies and settlers with titles based on equally vague grants or Native American deeds. Reluctant to risk the validity of their claims in court, the companies often resorted to extrajudicial means to achieve their purposes, intimidating settlers and forcing them to recognize their claims.[55] Although its methods were not unique, the Plymouth Company was the worst offender. Its tactics were described in a pamphlet circulated by one of its rivals, the smaller Clark and Lake Company:

> [The Plymouth Company has] used actual Force in taking and retaining some Possessions, and have destroyed the Finest Part of the Timber. They have also used many methods to persuade and oblige the poor Settlors . . . to acknowledge their claim and hold under them.[56]

On the basis of grants in Native American deeds, Clark and Lake long had asserted an interest in territory claimed now by the Plymouth Company and was not about to give up without a fight.[57] Clark and Lake brought a suit against one of its adversary's most aggressive agents for trespassing on some of the land in controversy and, in June 1753, was awarded damages by the Superior Court sitting in York County. When the Plymouth Company paid the judgment rather than appeal, Clark and Lake told the world this was proof its claim was the valid one and warned that it would sue if the Plymouth Company challenged that claim.[58] As could be expected, the larger company scoffed at Clark and Lake's defiance, threatening to "convince them sooner than they desire, that they are under a Mistake" if the firm continued to spend money attempting to "establish their Claim."[59]

Within two years, the Plymouth Company found itself in court defending itself against a suit by Clark and Lake which involved some of the defendant's most prized acreage. In June 1756 the parties agreed to submit their conflicting land claims to a committee of five referees. Each party had the right to choose one of the referees, with the other three to be selected by agreement between the parties, and if that proved impossible, by order of the court. Benjamin Prat was one of the referees, apparently selected by the Plymouth Company, for which he had done extensive work in the past. Clark and Lake chose Oliver Wolcott of Connecticut, a descendant of one of its founders. Two prominent lawyers from western Massachusetts, John Worthington and Joseph Hawley, were picked, most likely as disinterested parties.[60]

The fifth referee who was selected, either by choice of the litigants or by the court, was Jeremiah Gridley. He must have been considered unbiased, but if so, it was in spite of the fact that apparently two years earlier he had represented the Plymouth Company in a suit in Falmouth, Maine, over land claims against the Pejepscot proprietors.[61] Be that as it may, the referees ruled in favor of Clark and Lake.[62] For his efforts, Gridley received £30 plus expenses, an impressive amount in an era of very low fees.[63]

In the early 1760s, Gridley represented Silvester Gardiner, the most aggressive member of the Plymouth Company proprietors, in several lawsuits in Maine. He also represented Samuel Waldo Jr., the son of one of Gridley's early clients, who, on his father's death, had inherited 40 percent of the Waldo Patent, which held claims to land between the Muscongus and Penobscot rivers, including much of the shoreline of Penobscot Bay.[64] He also probably represented other clients in land disputes. It is entirely possible that the amount of money that Gridley made in fees arising from disputes involving other proprietors exceeded what he made from his own proprietary interests.

Unfortunately, documentation relating to this issue is woefully incomplete, but there are some clues. On the basis of his study of the internal documents and public records relating to the Peterborough proprietorship, probably Gridley's most successful proprietary venture, one of its historians concluded that "it is doubtful if [Gridley] made very much out of the enterprize."[65] He noted that while Gridley's initial investment—the £48.5s that he paid grantees for their interests—was relatively small, the expenses incurred in settling the township were not. The proprietors had to pay for newspaper advertisements, sales representatives, and other costs of promoting their enterprise. More daunting were the costs of development—surveys, roads, bridges, and mills, and, most likely, houses, barns, and fences for the more impecunious settlers. Most of these usually were routine, one-time expenses with which virtually all proprietors had to deal, but Gridley and his partners had to do so twice.[66]

As noted, settlers began moving to Peterborough in 1740, but this emigration abruptly ceased with the outbreak of the Indian War, and those living in Peterborough quickly exited the town. For years it stood deserted, subject to the vagaries of the elements and the depredations of marauding Native Americans. When the war ended, the whole process of developing the site and attracting settlers had to be repeated, once again at the proprietors' expense. When these costs are added to those incurred in fighting, and then settling, the claims of the Masonian Proprietors, it seems likely that at least the Peterborough proprietorship, and most likely all of Gridley's ventures into land speculation, left Gridley little richer for his efforts.

Chapter Six

Fletcher v. Vassall (1752)

In the spring of 1816, John Adams and Thomas Jefferson, correspondents in their old age, were engaged in a long-distance philosophical discussion about the relationship of pleasure to pain. In making a point, Adams cited the opinion of one of his "old friends and clients"—William Vassall—"a man of letters and virtues, without one vice that I ever knew or suspected, except garrulity."[1] Adams's choice of the word "garrulity" in describing William Vassall was strikingly appropriate. It was Vassall's "garrulity"—the man's propensity to talk too much—that led to one of Jeremiah Gridley's most high-profile cases, one that involved a huge amount of money and sent shock waves that rattled the windows of many stately homes in Massachusetts.

William Vassall was the wealthy undergraduate whose father sued Harvard tutor Daniel Rogers over Rogers's treatment of young William. Gridley, then newly admitted to the bar, represented Rogers in the case.[2] Fifteen years later, William Vassall was still wealthy, living off of his sizeable inheritance.[3] Although Vassall did not choose to work for a living, he was not an indolent man. His was an inquiring mind. He corresponded with Benjamin Franklin in Philadelphia about the spread and treatment of smallpox, and the two exchanged books on philosophical subjects.[4]

Vassall also wrote to the Anglican bishop of Durham about slavery. Vassall's wealth was built on the backs of the slaves on his family's Jamaican plantations, and evidently that fact bothered him. Although the bishop assured him that the scriptures justified slavery, Vassall was less than convinced.[5] Apparently he wrote to Thomas Chubb, the English deist, for advice.[6] It was not William Vassall's mind, however, but rather his mouth that got him into trouble. Still as brash as he had been in college, Vassall used some very offensive language in denouncing William Fletcher, and Fletcher sued him for defamation.

Born in Boston in 1716, William Fletcher was a merchant of some means.[7] According to his brother Thomas Fletcher, who sometimes managed William's businesses, at the time he brought suit against Vassall, William was worth about £4,000, not including his house in Boston, a farm in Cambridge, and other real estate.[8] As with many colonial merchants of his time, Fletcher's business was multifaceted.[9] He bought, transported, and retailed merchandise. He also traded in ships, often buying and selling part interests in the vessels to third parties.[10] He underwrote maritime insurance.[11] In these undertakings Fletcher relied on credit, the lifeblood of Massachusetts maritime commerce. With no banking system to supply needed capital, the Boston mercantile community funded their endeavors on a personal level.[12]

Fletcher dealt with a large circle of lenders, including some of the more prominent men in the province, such as Thomas Cushing, Thomas Hubbard, and Edmund Quincy.[13] He also did business with Thomas and Adrian Hope of Amsterdam, Ralph Carr of Newcastle, and other merchants abroad.[14] Fletcher often borrowed money on nothing more than his good name and his promise to pay, but sometimes he gave collateral in the form of goods or property.[15] One common form of security Fletcher used was "bottomry"—a maritime contract by which the owner of a ship pledges the ship or its cargo as security for the repayment of money advanced or lent.[16] In such cases, the creditor can recover the money lent only if the vessel arrives safely at its destination. If the ship founders, the lender has no rights against the ship's owner personally unless he can show that the vessel was unseaworthy from the start, or that negligence or malfeasance was involved in its loss.[17]

In 1745 Fletcher's prospects had taken a dramatic turn. Great Britain was at war with France and Spain. Facing depredations from the French and their Native American allies to the north, the New England colonies launched an amphibious assault on the French fortress of Louisbourg on Cape Breton Island. Massachusetts purchased several vessels for use in this expedition, including the *Boston Packett,* a brigantine commanded by William Fletcher's father.[18] In August 1745, while patrolling outside Louisbourg harbor, Captain Fletcher captured a valuable prize: a French ship carrying over £300,000 in Peruvian gold and silver.[19] The captured vessel was declared "a prize of the fleet," and every captain who had been in sight of the capture (and some who were not) claimed a share of the prize money.[20] The case came before the Lords Commissioners for Appeals in Prize Cases, where it dragged on for years.[21] The matter was still pending when Fletcher brought his suit against Vassall.[22]

William Fletcher and William Vassall were about the same age, and the two were once close enough to go in together in the purchase of lottery tickets. Vassall fronted the money. Fletcher was slow to pay him the £10 he owed for the tickets. According to Vassall, by the time Fletcher finally did come up with the money, deflation had depreciated the currency's value to the point where the amount Fletcher paid him was not fair recompense for what Vassall had spent.[23]

Vassall and Fletcher also had a second, more complicated dispute. Fletcher held notes from Andrew Hall at a time when the two were adversaries in several unrelated lawsuits. The two agreed with each other and with William Vassall that Vassall would hold the notes in trust and release them to Hall only if Hall won judgments from Fletcher totaling at least £8,000. Otherwise, Vassall would return them to Fletcher.[24] When decision time came, Vassall mistakenly calculated the amount due Hall from Fletcher as more than £8,000, and delivered the notes to Hall. Fletcher was outraged and, as he later acknowledged, "could not help saying that *Mr. Vassall was a——ignorant Fellow, and did not know the difference between Six and Eight.*"[25] Vassall believed that, in responding to his good faith mistake in the manner that he did, Fletcher "had treated him very ill, notwithstanding all the pains he had taken in it."[26] Vassall went on the offense against Fletcher—with his mouth.

Many of Vassall's verbal attacks on Fletcher were nothing more than epithets, often strung together. Fletcher was a "rogue," a "scoundrel," a "villain," a "rascal," and a "man of no honor."[27] He told one friend that Fletcher was a "tricky shuffling fellow," and another that Fletcher was "not fit company for any Man and those who kept Company with him were as bad as he."[28] Vassall cast aspersions on Fletcher's financial condition. He spread it about that Fletcher was unable to pay his debts, owed more than he was worth, and was "not worth a groat."²⁹ Vassall repeatedly brought up the lottery tickets, which, one witness recalled, "Mr. *Vassall* . . . gave as an Argument of said Mr. Fletcher's Unfairness and Dishonesty."³⁰

Perhaps Vassall's most serious allegations related to Fletcher's ships. He claimed that Fletcher had wrecked one of his ships knowing that, by law, the bottomers, who had lent money with the ship as collateral, would receive nothing, and that he would not be obligated to them for anything.³¹ More disturbing, Vassall accused Fletcher of plotting the death of one of his brothers. According to the Reverend Jonathan Mayhew, while he was a guest at Vassal's home, his host announced

> that . . . Mr. *Fletcher* had sent one of his own Brothers to Sea in an old rotten, leaky, or condemned Vessel or Ship, with an Intention that she should be cast away or lost; . . . Mr. *Fletcher's* End and Design in casting the said Vessel away . . . [was] that said Mr. Fletcher might get his Brother's share of some Money that was likely to come to his brother's heirs, or the Family.³²

Some of Vassall's other guests confirmed Mayhew's account; nor was this an isolated incident.³³ On another occasion, Vassall loudly declared:

> What a Villain was that *Fletcher* to send his Brother to Sea in an old condemned Ship which he bought to drown him in? and if it had been in his Power, I believe he would have *sent the whole Family in her*, if he could have got any Thing by it.³⁴

Vassall seems to have been ready to disparage Fletcher to anyone within earshot. At least ten different witnesses testified that they had heard Vassall malign Fletcher. Many heard him do so on more than one occasion. For example, Mayhew witnessed Vassall's anti-Fletcher statements at least three times that he could recall with certainty, and in addition, he said, he had

> *diverse Times* . . . heard Mr. *Vassall* speak of said Mr. *Fletcher* as being a great Rogue, a Scoundrel, a Villain, a Rascal, a tricking shuffling Fellow, a base ungrateful Fellow, a Fellow of no Honour or Honesty,

all of which Expressions I have, to the best of my Remembrance, heard Mr. *Vassall* in Company use concerning said Mr. *Fletcher*.[35]

Vassall also showed no reluctance in disparaging Fletcher to Fletcher's business associates. One of Fletcher's creditors heard "*Vassall* declare . . . that said *Fletcher* . . . was a *damn'd Scoundrel, and was not worth a Groat, and that he would never come back* [from England] *again.*"[36] Another of Fletcher's creditors was present when Vassall announced that "*Fletcher* was not able to pay his Debts, and . . . sent a Ship that was lost with a Design to defraud some Gentlemen."[37] Thomas Cushing, who had posted a £200 bond for Fletcher, heard Vassall, "utter divers Expressions concerning Mr. *Fletcher* tending greatly to hurt his Character and Reputation."[38]

In October 1751, in the Suffolk County Inferior Court of Common Pleas, William Fletcher brought suit against William Vassall for defamation.[39] He sought £8,000 in damages. In an apparent attempt to avoid costs and forward the matter to the Superior Court as quickly as possible, Fletcher did not respond to Vassall's answer to his complaint and produced no witnesses.[40] Of course he lost and appealed to the Superior Court. It granted him a second trial and heard the case, which again was "committed to the Jury, without any Witnesses being produced." The jury found for Vassall and confirmed the "former Judgment." Fletcher "review'd the Case to the next Superior Court" for yet another trial. This was his last chance. The parties geared up for a fight.[41]

Both were well represented. Fletcher's attorneys were Edmund Trowbridge and Colonel James Otis. Born in 1709, Trowbridge graduated from Harvard in 1728, studied law, and was admitted as an attorney to the Superior Court. In 1749 Trowbridge was appointed attorney general of Massachusetts, a position that he was to hold for almost twenty years.[42] He was a very good lawyer, long remembered as "one of the most learned lawyers in Massachusetts, and, withal, one of the most devoted students of the law."[43] His contemporaries shared this view. John Adams acknowledged that Trowbridge had an "extensive" knowledge of the law and "commanded the practice in Middlesex and Worcester and several other counties."[44] Trowbridge's status was such that he "had the power to crush, by his frown or his nod, any young lawyer in his county."[45]

Trowbridge's co-counsel, Colonel James Otis, was cut from different cloth. After riding from Taunton to Milton with him, John Adams described Otis as "vastly easy and steady in his Temper. He is vastly good humoured and sociable and sensible. Learned he is not But he is an easy and familiar Speaker."[46] Adams's assessment of Otis's intellectual capabilities was a bit harsh. While Otis was not college educated, he was an intelligent man with learning enough to advance himself as a merchant, lawyer, and politician. Otis was born in Barnstable on Cape Cod in 1702. His father, a successful merchant and ship owner who was one of the richest men in the county, represented Barnstable in the General Court and later sat on the provincial council.[47] Unlike his two older brothers, who went to Harvard, James was designated for the family business and spent a "long apprenticeship" in his father's store, but he did not remain there.[48] According to tradition, Otis "got himself such books as were then to be obtained—Coke's Institutes, Brownlow's Entries and Plowden's Commentaries and Reports, and commenced *reading and practicing [law]*."[49]

However it happened, Otis became a lawyer and, in 1731, was admitted to the bar of the Superior Court. Although he remained a merchant, and in fact grew the family business, Otis became a very busy lawyer.[50] Adams acknowledged that at one time, Otis "reigned in three southern Counties," and the numbers bear this out.[51] In July 1744, for example, he represented almost half of the litigants at the Superior Court session in Barnstable.[52] He also rode the Superior Court circuit, which took him to other counties, including Suffolk County, where the court met twice a year in Boston.[53]

In his later years, Otis was ridiculed by loyalist lawyers for his supposed "Ignorance of Law," but there is evidence that he could hold his own at the bar.[54] Even while jabbing at Otis's lack of learning, Adams noted that "he is an easy and familiar speaker," an attribute that probably played well with provincial juries. That his forensic ability was acknowledged by his legal colleagues is evidenced by a letter from a Dartmouth attorney beseeching Otis never to oppose him in a case, and another by Samuel White, a Harvard-educated lawyer, insisting that Otis defend one of White's clients.[55]

Otis had another thing going for him: he was politically wired. He represented Barnstable in the House of Representatives from 1745 to 1756, during which time he was appointed a justice of the peace and attorney general of the province (1748).⁵⁶ More important, he was one of Governor Shirley's floor managers in the House of Representatives with the ear of the province's chief executive.⁵⁷

William Vassall's attorneys also were an interesting pair. At age fifty, Gridley was a respected institution at the bar. He knew Vassall well enough to have been a guest at his home. In fact, according to Jonathan Mayhew, Gridley was with him "at the house of said Vassall" when their host cut loose with one of his angry diatribes accusing Fletcher of "Unfairness and Dishonesty."⁵⁸ Gridley's co-counsel was Colonel Otis's son. At the time of the trial, James Otis Jr. was twenty-six years old, new to the Superior Court bar, and still finding his way as a lawyer. In contrast to his father, whose early exposure to books was largely limited to account ledgers, young James received an education that was, in John Adams's opinion, "the best his country afforded."⁵⁹ After being tutored by a clergyman uncle, Otis attended Harvard, where he was an "indefatigable student."⁶⁰

Adams had fulsome praise for Otis's intellect and learning: "He was a gentleman of general science and extensive literature. . . . He was well versed in Greek and Roman history, philosophy, oratory, poetry, and mythology. His classical studies had been unusually ardent, and his acquisitions uncommonly great."⁶¹

Upon graduating from Harvard in 1743, Otis did not begin to prepare for a career, which must have created something of a family crisis:

> After graduation . . . young Otis did little but read literature in preparation for the traditional second degree. If he had been allowed to follow his own wishes James probably would have devoted his life to the study of the classics. However, his father intended that the law should be his career. It was a sure road to influence and power.⁶²

The colonel sent his son to his old friend Jeremiah Gridley to read for the bar. Again, James's devotion to his studies evoked comment. Richard Dana, a lawyer who observed him on a daily basis, noted "that he had never known a student in law so punctual, so steady, so constant and persevering."⁶³ At his father's "suggestion," Otis began his law practice in Plymouth.⁶⁴ It did not go well. After Cambridge and Boston, Plymouth was less than stimulating. Otis's practice suffered accordingly. At the May 1749 session of the County Court of Common

Pleas, while most other lawyers averaged over a dozen filings, James Jr. filed just one.[65] The next year, Otis moved back to Boston. In May 1750, he was admitted to practice before the Superior Court as an attorney. A year later, he joined his mentor in defending William Vassall.[66]

None of the five justices who presided over the trial of *Thacher v. Vassall* had been members of the Superior Court two decades earlier when Gridley had been admitted to practice before it.[67] While the caliber of the bar had improved significantly in twenty years, arguably that of the bench had declined. In 1732 the Superior Court included three justices who had studied at the Inns of Court. In 1752 there were none. In fact, although there were two justices who had read some law, not one of the five was a lawyer. Chief Justice Stephen Sewall was one of the two justices who had studied law. He had been a tutor at Harvard College before his appointment in 1739 as an associate justice of the Superior Court and generally was regarded as a learned man who "gave universal satisfaction to the people of the province."[68] Justice Chambers Russell, who also was judge of the Vice Admiralty Court, was remembered as a man of "great Ability and unsullied Integrity."[69]

After these two, there was a definite drop-off in ability. Benjamin Lynde Jr. succeeded his father on the court in 1746. He had studied law but never practiced. The best that could be said about Lynde was that "his record on the bench was only ordinary."[70] The same was true of his colleague Richard Saltonstall, a country squire who had never studied law and had no judicial experience when he took his seat on the high court.[71] John Cushing, the court's fifth member, was its only justice who had not attended college. Emory Washburn, who wrote about the early bench and bar of Massachusetts and usually could come up with something positive to say about everyone, had difficulty with Cushing: "He was undoubtedly a respectable magistrate, but I can learn little of his qualifications for the place of Judge, which he filled for twenty four years."[72]

Fletcher's case came before the Suffolk County term of the Superior Court in Boston on November 14, 1752. His declaration included a comprehensive description of Vassall's allegedly defamatory statements and how they had allegedly injured him.[73] James Otis Jr. filed Vassall's response. It disputed Fletcher's allegations and preserved all of the legal "Exceptions" that Vassall had raised in the previous two trials.[74] The most significant of these was the argument that because Fletcher had never replied to Vassall's response to his declaration, the issue in the case had never been joined, and therefore the Superior Court should not "proceed to Tryal upon [Fletcher's] plea."[75] Like the others, this exception was not successful. For the third time, a jury was empaneled. On December 27, 1752, the matter went to trial.

Fletcher presented thirty-seven witnesses. The first dozen or so recounted episode after episode in which Vassall had disparaged Fletcher in the manner described earlier.[76] Many of these witnesses were Vassall's friends, three of them—Joseph Scott, Thomas Gray, and Jonathan Mayhew—his "intimate Companions."[77] Two witnesses, Mayhew and Dr. Ebenezer Miller, were men of the cloth, and Belcher Hancock was a tutor at Harvard.[78] The testimony of all of the witnesses was consistent, believable, and devastating.

The next wave of witnesses "were produced by Mr. *Fletcher* to support his Character, and to prove what special Damages he had suffered by Means of Mr. Vassall's injurious Treatment."[79] A long line of solid citizens—merchants, shipwrights, tradesmen, a distiller, and a mariner—testified to Fletcher's good name, his honesty, and his fair dealings. Men of business like Edmund Quincy and Stephen Greenleaf also spoke to Fletcher's sterling reputation and the way in which the negative rumors about him had caused them to doubt his solvency and to seek security for the money he owed them.[80] Finally, there were witnesses who were familiar with the ship that had been lost with Fletcher's brother on board. They testified that the vessel was *"strong enough to go to any part of the World, and a good Ship, and had not some uncommon Accident happen'd to her . . . would have lasted some years."*[81]

According to the only account available (which is Fletcher's), the testimony elicited from the witnesses whom Vassall produced did not help his case. The basic problem was that Vassall actually had made most of the defamatory comments attributed to him, most of those comments were untrue, and many had been injurious to Fletcher's reputation. While showing that Fletcher was carrying a rather heavy load of debt, had manipulated the mortgage on his house, and had some difficulty paying some of his creditors, Vassall's witnesses did little to damage Fletcher's case.

Gridley and Otis Jr. had hopes for more, but it did not work out. After Fletcher's brother Thomas had provided his testimony, they sought to ask him whether some of his brother's goods had been seized by customs officials as illegal imports.[82] Fletcher's attorneys objected to the question, arguing that it was "impertinent to the Issue, and tending to charge the Plaintiff with an Offence against which he was not prepared to defend himself."[83] The court was divided on the issue. To judge from their comments, Justices Saltonstall and Russell thought the question a proper one. Sewall and Lynde apparently felt otherwise. The fifth justice, Cushing, said nothing. Some persuasive arguments must have been made in chambers, because in the end, "it was ruled by the whole Court, that the witness should not be put to answer the Question."[84]

After all of the witnesses had testified, either in person or by deposition, the court permitted the parties to do something that, by present-day trial norms, seems extraordinary. The parties were given the opportunity to make a statement, apparently without being subject to cross-examination. William Vassall spoke first. He read from a text that he had "committed to Writing in his leisure hours" so, as he explained (apparently without a hint of irony), "that he might not say any Thing rashly, or that was not agreeable to the truth."[85] Two of his points were familiar ones. Vassall described how Fletcher "had wronged him" with regard to the lottery tickets, and "treated him very ill" after he had miscalculated the amount that Fletcher owed Andrew Hall.[86] Then, "in order to prove Mr. Fletcher a Man of bad Character," Vassall repeated a story he claimed to have heard about how Fletcher had supposedly cheated Harrison Gray out of a beaver hat by rigging a wager so that Gray would lose.[87]

Fletcher's response was a bit more comprehensive and much more to the point. With regard to the allegation that he had defrauded bottomers, Fletcher produced copies of an agreement that he had with the bottomers and the decision of three prominent arbitrators which ruled in his favor against them.[88] He maintained that his brother's doomed vessel "was a strong good Ship" and that "there was no room to suspect but that she met with some uncommon Disaster at Sea, as thousands of new ships had done before."[89]

Responding to Vassall's other allegations, Fletcher stated that the only reason why he had refused to pay Vassall for the lottery tickets was because of "said Vassall's abusing him on account" of them.[90] He asserted that "he had good reason to blame Mr. Vassall as he did" for the defendant's error regarding the amount that Fletcher owed Andrew Hall because it was an "Ignorant mistake."[91] Fletcher explained that the stakes in his "bantering Wager" with Harrison Gray had been a bowl of punch, that he had tricked Gray as a joke, and that he "did not remember the Punch was ever paid."[92]

After the parties had had their say, "Mr. *Gridley* for the Defendant, and the King's Attorney *Edmund Trowbrige*, Esq., for the Plaintiff closed the Case."[93] Unfortunately, there is no account of what the attorneys said; but at some point in the proceedings, apparently before the closing arguments, James Otis Jr. made the case for Vassall:

> "He strenuously insisted . . . *that there was not one single word in the Writ that was actionable in this Country,* and after saying *a Great Deal of that Nature, he finish'd what he had to say* . . . with some indecent Reflections upon the Plaintiff.[94]

Because Vassall's alleged defamation involved oral statements, the rules of the law of slander applied to the case.[95] These rules required Fletcher to prove that Vassall had made at least some of the statements attributed to him and that those statements had injured Fletcher's reputation.[96] Yet there was an exception to this requirement which lightened Fletcher's burden of proof. While he did have to prove to the jury that Vassall had said what he was accused of saying, Fletcher did not necessarily have to prove that the words had injured him in his reputation. The law considered certain classes of statements so obviously injurious that they were deemed inherently defamatory. If a court ruled that the defendant's statements fell into one of these classes, the plaintiff was not required to prove actual damages to prove defamation.[97]

Two categories of such statements were relevant to Fletcher's case against Vassall: words that imputed the commission of a crime, and words that prejudiced the plaintiff in his office, profession, or employment. With regard to a merchant, this latter category included words relating to the plaintiff's integrity, knowledge, skill, diligence, and credit, especially credit. Once the court had ruled alleged statements defamatory per se, all the jury had to do was to reach agreement on how much in damages to assess.[98]

Given the amount of uncontradicted evidence of instances in which

Vassall had maligned Fletcher to others, the jury must have had no difficulty in finding, as a matter of fact, that Vassall had made many of the statements in question. Among other accusations, Vassall had asserted that Fletcher had committed the crimes of murdering his brother and defrauding his investors.[99] He also had asserted that Fletcher was "a scoundrel" who was unable to pay his debts and was "not worth a groat," all of which prejudiced Fletcher in his business.[100] Therefore, the court must have found it relatively easy to rule, as a matter of law, that certain of these statements were defamatory per se. That left it up to the jury to determine how much Fletcher had been damaged. It was quite a bit. The jury found "for the plaintiff . . . two thousand pounds lawful money Damage."[101]

Two thousand pounds was a very large amount of money in 1752 Massachusetts. According to Vassall's subsequent filings, "such Damages . . . have never been given in any Action for Words in any of the *British* Plantations."[102] James Otis Jr. considered it excessive even in comparison to damage awards in England.[103] Gridley may never have been associated with another case involving so much money. For example, in those cases heard by the Superior Court in Suffolk County from August 1751 to August 1759 for which information is available, the £2,000 awarded in *Fletcher v. Vassall* was by far the largest judgment in any case in which Gridley is listed as one of the attorneys.[104] The next largest was £478.1.6.[105]

Given the size of the judgment and Vassall's personality, it came as no surprise when he moved to appeal the decision to the Privy Council, a motion that the Superior Court granted. At Fletcher's insistence, however, the court refused to stay the judgment. It ordered Vassall to pay Fletcher £2,000 and required Fletcher to post bond for that amount.[106] Then the court record was forwarded to England and everyone awaited word from London. As with all such appeals, Vassall's was heard by the Committee for Hearing Appeals from Plantations, a subcommittee of the Privy Council, where it was argued by English lawyers.[107] Like Gridley, Vassall's English counsel attacked the manner in which the case had finally made it to a full-blown trial with witnesses and evidence on the third try via a writ of review.[108] Their brief contended that Massachusetts law required that civil actions should be "originally heard and tried" in the Court of Common Pleas and that the trial there "should be a real Tryal, on the Part of the Plaintiff, upon Evidence, and not a mock trial, without so much as an offer of Evidence by the Plaintiff."[109]

The brief argued further that Fletcher's

> attempt to try his Cause, in the First Instance, upon Evidence by Surprize, which the defendant could not be prepared to answer in the Court of Review, the [court of last resort in Massachusetts], ought not to be tolerated, as it totally inverts the Order of Appeal in the Province; for this last Court had really, and in Fact, nothing at all to review; the Hearing before them being an original Hearing in the First Instance.[110]

Vassall also contended that a "great Part of the Evidence on which the verdict was founded was illegal and improper"; that he had been "denied Liberty to cross-examine and put such Questions to [Fletcher], and his own Witnesses, as he apprehended material and conducive to the bringing out of Truth"; that Fletcher had failed to prove special damages; that the action was barred by the province's two-year statute of limitations on actions for defamation; and that the amount of the verdict was excessive.[111]

Fletcher's brief was far briefer. It argued that Vassall's alleged statements clearly were actionable, that it was proven that he actually had made the statements, and that his statements had caused "the greatest Damage to [Fletcher's] Credit and Reputation, as a Trader."[112] The brief also maintained that the damages had been awarded by "a Jury acquainted with the Circumstances of both the Parties," and as Vassall had never moved the Superior Court to set them aside as excessive, "they cannot be deemed so here."[113]

On January 31, 1754, in accordance with the report of its Committee of Appeals, the Privy Council reversed the judgment of the Massachusetts Superior Court on the ground that the court never should have heard the case a second time because Fletcher "gave no evidence in either of the former trials on which the case could with any propriety be reviewed by a jury, and was therefore not entitled to a writ of review."[114]

The decision had a far-reaching ripple effect in Massachusetts. William Vassall had scores to settle. His first target was William Fletcher.

Vassall was angry with Fletcher for many reasons. First, Fletcher had £2,000 of Vassall's money, had had it for over a year, and, despite the Privy Council's order, would not pay it back. Then there was past history. Vassall could not forget the "ill treatment" that he believed he had received at Fletcher's hands with regard to the lottery tickets and the Fletcher-Hill dispute.[115]

Of course, the litigation between the two had made matters worse. Vassall was furious at Fletcher for bringing the suit and for demanding high bail, which twice landed Vassall in jail while he attempted to raise the money to pay it. Vassall viewed Fletcher's failure to produce evidence in the first two trials as an underhanded ploy designed to unfairly surprise him in the third trial with a full-blown presentation including dozens of witnesses for which he was not prepared.[116] During the trial itself, Vassall had suffered the embarrassment of having some of his closest friends testify against him in front of an overflow crowd of his fellow citizens. Finally, as his appeal to the Privy Council had argued, Vassall believed that he had not received a fair trial and that the jury's award to Fletcher was excessive.

Vassall's attempt to get his money back was beset by obstacles. In 1753, and again in 1754, Cambridge had elected William Fletcher to the House of Representatives, a development that complicated everything.[117] On May 30, 1754, James Otis Jr. appeared before the Superior Court on Vassall's behalf seeking a writ of execution against Fletcher to recover Vassall's money. Citing the fact that it was short a justice, the Superior Court refused to act.[118] Even when a replacement finally was appointed, the justices still refused to proceed, believing that the court could not act against Fletcher so long as he was a member of the legislature.[119]

Finally, on November 14, 1754, the Superior Court ordered that execution issue on Vassall's judgment against William Fletcher. Execution issued, but to no avail.[120] Fletcher had fled to Dutch Surinam, beyond the reach of Crown law.[121] Unable to lay his hands on Fletcher, Vassall ordered Gridley and Otis to go after John Tudor and Edmund Quincy, who had posted bond for Fletcher, in effect, promising to pay back the judgment if Fletcher lost in the Privy Council (which he did) and did not pay it back himself (which he did not).

Tudor and Quincy were an incongruous pair. John Tudor, who had testified at the trial to Fletcher's "Honour and Honesty," was a baker and a man of limited means.[122] Edmund Quincy, by contrast, was the senior partner in Edmund Quincy and Sons, a prominent commission merchant firm, which in 1748 had made a fortune when one of its privateers had captured a Spanish ship loaded with silver and gold.[123] Unfortunately, Edmund Quincy "was not overly gifted with business ability."[124] Quincy and Sons had become somewhat notorious for making bad investments. In fact, describing how decrepit was the ship in which Fletcher allegedly had sent his brother to sea, Vassall reportedly had said that it was "Such a Vessel as [even] *Edmund Quincy* would not venture or would refuse to send to Sea."[125]

Initially, Vassall's efforts to collect from Tudor and Quincy went nowhere. In the Superior Court, Gridley moved for writs requiring the two to make good on Vassall's rights under their bonds. At the Superior Court's February 1755 term in Boston, the court quashed the writs. It also denied Gridley's motions for leave to appeal to the Privy Council.[126] But Vassall had the time and the money to keep trying, and finally he succeeded. In February 1756, the Superior Court awarded Vassall a judgment against John Tudor in the sum of £2,398, an amount far beyond Tudor's ability to pay.[127] Fortunately, his friends came to his aid with bonds in small amounts.[128] Tudor then sued Quincy. Vassall also sued Quincy and Sons on a £1,500 note from Fletcher to Vassall which it had endorsed.[129] The claims proved too much for Quincy's firm, already overextended, having sold too many of its bills.[130] On December 31, 1757, Edmund and his two sons were declared bankrupts.[131] The collapse of a firm generally "reckoned" to be "very considerable merchants . . . worth one hundred thousand pound[s]," was "a financial disaster which Boston remembered for generations."[132]

Vassall went after everybody he thought had wronged him. Incensed because they had jailed him pending bail in Fletcher's proceeding against him, Vassall sued the sheriffs of Middlesex and Suffolk counties for £7,000 and £6,000, respectively.[133] Apparently this was too much for Gridley. In January 1753, when the actions were about to be instituted, Gridley told James Otis Jr. that he would not join Otis in filing them.[134] When the writs abated in the Court of Common Pleas, Otis drafted new ones, confessing to Vassall that he "should have been glad of Mr. Gridley's assistance . . . but he utterly refused to be concerned."[135]

CHAPTER SEVEN

The House of Representatives

War, Influence, and Opportunity Lost (1755–1757)

Jeremiah Gridley's refusal to continue representing William Vassall may have resulted from substantial changes in Gridley's life. His wife had died, and, early in 1755, Gridley moved from Boston to Brookline.[1] Although it took him just five miles from Boston, the move meant a dramatic change from the sophisticated atmosphere of the provincial capital with its fifteen thousand inhabitants to a bucolic town of about five hundred.[2] Gridley left no explanation for his move to Brookline, but it seems likely that he, a currier's son, shared "the ideal of landed gentility that haunted the provincial imagination."[3] If that was it, his new property was a suitable choice. Described as "fit for a Gentleman's Seat," it included a "large elegant dwelling house," set on about "30 acres of rich land."[4]

Relocating to Brookline significantly affected Gridley's involvement in provincial government. Although he was a man of respected ability who had occasionally served as town counsel, Gridley had never been elected one of Boston's representatives to the provincial legislature and "did not enjoy many public honors."[5] Appointment to the "committee of dignitaries which visited the public schools" was the best he could do.[6] This changed with Gridley's move to Brookline. Recognizing that they had a big fish in their small pond, Gridley's fellow townsmen often elected him moderator of the town meetings.[7] More important, Brookline, which had not sent a representative to the General Court in a decade, elected its new resident to the House of Representatives in 1755, the year he arrived, and again in 1756 and 1757.[8]

The House of Representatives to which Gridley was elected was one of the two houses of the Massachusetts General Court, the province's legislative body. Every year, each town with eighty or more qualified voters was required to send a representative to the House or pay a fine.[9] There were two exceptions: Boston was entitled to send four representatives, and Cambridge two.[10] The House elected the members of the General Court's second chamber, the governor's council.[11] The role of the council as an executive body was to advise the governor, assist in carrying out the laws, and approve or disapprove executive appointments.[12]

In its legislative capacity, the council, together with the House of Representatives, had three principal functions: to dispose of public lands, levy taxes, and enact laws.[13] The actions of the legislature were subject to approval by the governor, the chief executive officer of the province. Appointed by the Crown, he was charged with implementing British colonial policy in Massachusetts. It was not an easy task. Although the governor could veto legislation and appoint provincial judges, executive officials, and militia officers, the General Court controlled the purse strings, including the governor's salary.[14] All of this infused provincial administration with politics, but this was politics without parties.[15] In the middle of the eighteenth century, Massachusetts politics was a collage of ad hoc coalitions, shifting alliances, and personal agendas. That is not to say, however, that there were not those who shared common interests.

Boston merchants usually supported commerce and hard money, with those who were smugglers favoring relaxed customs enforcement. Residents of the coastal communities outside Boston typically advocated depreciated currency and increased trade.[16] Facing depredations from Native Americans, settlers on the western frontier and in Maine supported strong defensive measures. Maine land speculators wanted their timber and property interests protected from interlopers. Congregationalists had their interests, as did Anglicans, Quakers, and every other religious group. Family also played a role. As family relations changed, so did political alliances.[17] Although they differed in significant respects, the competing factions shared some commonalities. None of them was stable. Their makeup was ever fluctuating as individuals sought personal advantage, preference, and place. Whether it was a government contract, a patronage position, or an advantageous marriage, the search was relentless.

In order to achieve the British ministry's and his own personal objectives, the governor had to build a coalition out of the various factions in the province. He had money and honors to distribute, but always had more supplicants than resources, and most of those whose support he sought cared only about their own selfish interests and were jealous of one another.[18] The governor's was a balancing act requiring a great deal of political acumen, not to mention personal charm and favorable circumstances. Some governors were quite adroit and fortunate. Others were not.

Jonathan Belcher, who was governor of Massachusetts from 1730 to 1741, fell into the latter category. Beholden to interests in London, he appointed members of English families to lucrative provincial posts, depriving provincials of the positions. When he did appoint locals, he exercised patronage so ruthlessly in favor of his friends that it left him with a growing number of bitter enemies. Many of his political allies, whom he was unwilling to cross, were smugglers, which undermined Belcher's authority as the province's chief law enforcement officer.[19]

Belcher's personality made matters worse. A man who "felt himself surrounded by enemies," he could be "a vicious partisan" one minute and "afraid to act" the next.[20] Belcher's "fierce temper," "indiscreet statements," and penchant for inflating minor difference into major issues alienated many who owed their places to him.[21] Finally, his ineffectual response to the monetary crisis that occurred during his governorship and his arbitrary, despotic measures against Land Bankers lost him the support of hard money and paper currency men alike.[22] Belcher's successor, William Shirley, had three advantages that Belcher lacked: an understanding of the province's political dynamic, the ability to use that understanding to his advantage, and a war.

Prior to his appointment, Shirley had been astute enough to avoid taking sides in the monetary squabbles that deeply divided

Massachusetts.[23] When he became governor, his attempts to alleviate their hardships earned the support of the Land Bankers, who, together with Belcher's enemies, provided the early nucleus of Shirley's administration.[24] Shirley's early opponents included many of Belcher's former supporters, especially Boston merchants who had chafed under the tough anti-smuggling regime that Shirley had advanced when he was the Vice Admiralty's advocate general. Shirley worked to win them over. After 1743, the number of smuggling prosecutions declined. Although this meant that Shirley lost some revenue from the seizures to which he was entitled as governor, it gained him adherents among the merchant community.[25]

King George's War (1740–1748), however, was the most important agent for change in the political landscape during Shirley's tenure. With the French threatening the province's frontiers and seaborne commerce, defense became the order of the day. There were troops to muster, supplies to purchase, warships to build, commissaries to appoint, and officers to commission. Presented with an unprecedented opportunity to enlarge and solidify support for his administration, Shirley doled out patronage where he thought it would do him the most good.[26] His adroitness in this respect, together with the province's general wartime prosperity and its capture of the French bastion of Louisbourg in 1745, provided Shirley with a strong coalition of supporters. Even former political foes, who now were benefiting from government contracts, could be counted among his allies.[27]

Then it all began to unravel. Stories of the suffering of the supply-starved colonial occupation force at Louisbourg, together with reports of war profiteering and the highhanded acts of Royal Navy press gangs operating at the direction of Shirley's appointees, damaged his standing. A projected invasion of Canada never came off, and then the war and the days of free spending were over. Little had been accomplished. The treaty in 1748 that ended the war returned Louisbourg, purchased with provincial blood and enterprise, back to the French. When the smoke cleared, the French and their Native American allies remained a threat poised to attack the Massachusetts frontier, and that threat soon became a reality. By 1752, the French had refortified Crown Point at the southern tip of Lake Champlain, and in the early spring of 1754, there were reports of French incursions into northern Maine. Once again, Massachusetts had to defend itself.

Directly or indirectly, the war with France dominated the proceedings of the House of Representatives when Brookline elected Gridley to it in May 1755. Soon after taking his seat, Gridley was named to a committee to report on two lawsuits filed against the speaker of the House, Thomas Hubbard, as well as the House messenger and the town jailer.[28] Brought by the *American Magazine*'s former printer, Daniel Fowle, the more important of the two suits arose out of Fowle's imprisonment for his alleged involvement in the publication of a satirical pamphlet titled *The Monster of Monsters,* which savaged the General Court for passing an excise tax intended to raise money for the war.[29] Fowle claimed that his incarceration was "without Cause or lawful authority" and sought £1,000 in damages.[30]

On June 11, 1755, Gridley's committee presented its report to the House. Signed and most likely authored by Gridley, the report recognized that the suits probably would raise the question of "the Right of Commitment by the House of Representatives . . . for Breach of their Privileges."[31] Then it posited the following:

> That this Power of committing has often and for a long Time been exercised by many former Houses of Representatives; that the House of Representatives . . . are the Indisputable Judges of any Breach of their Privileges, and have an Authority to arrest, commit, and examine for such Breaches, not only their own Members, but others.[32]

Gridley maintained that "it was the indispensable Duty of the Speaker . . . to issue his Warrants . . . , and of the Messenger of said House, and Keeper of said Goal to execute them." He condemned the lawsuits as "an Attempt against the Rights of the People of this Government, in the Authority of this House to commit for Contempt to their Representative Body, and to frustrate all Effect of this Authority, and to introduce Disorder and Confusion."[33] The "Privileges" to which Gridley referred were a "bundle of rights" that, historically, the House of Commons and the House of Lords had claimed and exercised.[34]

These rights included the right to be free from arrest, the right to freedom from molestation, the right to freedom of speech, and the right to punish both members and nonmembers for violation of the privileges.[35] In varying degrees, all of the American colonial legislatures had adopted the parliamentary privileges. While in some colonies the assembly usually made a formal request for them, in Massachusetts they were taken for granted.[36]

With regard to *The Monster of Monsters*, the particular privilege at issue was the right to freedom from molestation, which could be violated by physical acts against members of the legislature, as well as verbal offenses: "These included words and phrases, whether written, printed, or orally Spoken, tending to deny the assembly's authority, reflect upon its honor, or, singly or collectively, slander its members."[37]

In England, adverse reflections on the House of Commons or its members, written or oral, amounted to seditious libel and were subject to prosecution by the House itself. The procedure was arbitrary with few of the protections offered by the common law courts. The accused was examined in a summary fashion and, if found guilty, compelled to apologize to the House, often on his knees or in some other demeaning fashion. The offender could be imprisoned until the end of Parliament's current term, and then ordered to pay costs. If a writing was involved, it was burned by the public hangman.[38]

Adopting Parliament's model, the colonial legislatures were quick to drag printers before them "to answer for 'affronts,' 'breach of privilege,' 'impudence,' 'indignities upon authority,' and 'libels.'"[39] The most significant prior instance in Massachusetts occurred in 1722, when a piece critical of the province's anti-piracy efforts in his *Boston Courant* had landed James Franklin before an angry council, which sent him to jail.[40] Daniel Fowle's offense also was a piece of satire. Unfortunately for him, the Massachusetts legislature still had no sense of humor.

Gridley's report recommended that the speaker, the messenger, and "the Keeper of the Prison" should "be defended . . . and that a Committee of the House be appointed to attend and take Care of the Defence."[41] The House adopted the recommendation and appointed Gridley, Edmund Trowbridge, and James Otis Sr. to represent the speaker and the other defendants.[42] Gridley was the lead attorney. On October 7, 1755, he filed a response to Fowle's complaint in court.

After describing the events leading up to Fowle's arrest and jailing, Gridley prayed for judgment on the grounds that the "taking Custody and Imprisonment," as described in his response, "is the same assault and Imprisonment and detention . . . whereof . . . [Fowle] above complains."[43] In essence, Gridley argued that the facts spoke for themselves, and given what the House believed Fowle had published, the defendants' actions against him were justified.

In reply, Fowle's attorney claimed that Gridley's plea was "Insufficient in law to preclude . . . [Fowle] from having his action aforesaid."[44] Gridley pointed out that Fowle had not denied the facts as detailed in the defendants' plea and moved to dismiss.[45] The Suffolk County Inferior Court of Common Pleas granted the motion and dismissed Fowle's action. He appealed.[46] The Superior Court ruled against him, holding that his "action be barr'd and Thomas Hubbard, William Baker & Alexander Young recover against the said Daniel Fowle Cost of Courts Taxed at £6."[47]

Gridley also was actively involved in critical issues more directly relating to the war with the French. Together with Trowbridge and Otis Sr., he was given the job of drafting a bill aimed at preventing the export of provisions and warlike stores from Massachusetts.[48] The same three were assigned the task of preparing a message to the governor regarding war expenditures, and presented that message to the chief executive.[49] In February, Gridley was appointed a member of a committee assigned to report on what should be done to protect the inhabitants of "Number 4," a settlement on the frontier that was in danger of enemy attack.[50]

In April, he served on a committee that was instructed to interrogate a Native American prisoner "relating to the Situation and Disposition of the French & Indians on the Western Frontier of the Province."[51] The next month, the speaker put Gridley on one committee which addressed the need for seamen and another charged with raising a regiment of light horse.[52] He served on a committee to review the role of Quaker public service in the war.[53] He also was a member of a committee "to take under consideration some Proper Method for the better Security of the Fishery and trade of the Province."[54]

Two projected campaigns against the French fort at Crown Point occupied the House's attention for most of Gridley's first year there. The first expedition, Governor Shirley's brainchild, had been approved by General Edward Braddock, who had recently arrived as commander in chief of British forces in North America. The undertaking was to be part of a four-pronged attack against the French. The other three prongs were an attack on Fort Duquesne in western Pennsylvania by General Braddock, the subjugation of the French fort at Beauséjour in Nova Scotia, and the reduction of Fort Niagara in western New York. The Niagara foray was to be led by Shirley, who was appointed a major general and second in overall command to Braddock.[55]

It was an ambitious plan and suffered the fate of many ambitious plans.[56] Except for success in Nova Scotia, it failed miserably. On July 9, 1755, Braddock's advance on Fort Duquesne became an inglorious rout after he and much of his army were slaughtered by French regulars and their Native American allies in the backwoods of Pennsylvania.[57] The Niagara campaign stalled at Fort Oswego for want of provisions. After fighting off an enemy attack on the shores of Lake George, learning that the French were receiving reinforcements, and finding himself short of supplies and military ardor, Major General William Johnson of New York called off the Crown Point expedition.[58]

Undaunted, Governor Shirley, who, on Braddock's death, had become commander in chief, pushed for another campaign against Crown Point. He attempted to convince the Massachusetts legislature that Parliament would assist in financing the endeavor, and promised to appoint John Winslow, an experienced Massachusetts officer, as major general in command. The General Court agreed to raise three thousand men as Massachusetts's contribution to the total force of 7,500 provincials.[59]

In the first half of 1756, Gridley spent much of his time and effort in the House of Representatives on matters relating to Crown Point. February 23 saw his appointment to a committee to encourage "Officers and Soldiers . . . to engage in the proposed [Crown Point] Expedition."[60] In April, he brought his legal knowledge to the war, sitting on a committee considering what the General Court should do with regard to "Articles of War, and a Court-Martial in the Army now raising for the intended Expedition against *Crown-Point*."⁶¹ In May, Gridley, recently reelected to the House, was a member of two committees addressing the lack of Massachusetts recruits for the Crown Point expedition.⁶²

By then, however, the project was on life support. On June 25, 1756, Governor Shirley was informed that he had been relieved as commander in chief.⁶³ On July 23, the Earl of Loudoun, Shirley's successor, landed in New York. A few weeks later, the French overwhelmed Fort Oswego, leaving the British force at Fort William Henry on the southern tip of Lake George exposed to attack. Loudoun ordered the troops at Fort William Henry to cease preparations for the move against Crown Point and to strengthen their defenses.⁶⁴ They would need them.

The end of active campaigning in the autumn of 1756 brought with it the question of where to house thousands of soldiers who had to be fed and sheltered through what promised to be a typically harsh northeastern winter. Provincial troops could go back to their homes, but the British regulars would need billets provided them. The problem of quartering troops and the issues that it raised were an integral part of English constitutional history. From the eleventh century on, questions of how and where to billet armies on the move had plagued the country and its property owners.⁶⁵ During the reign of Charles I, soldiers tramping around England on their way to his wars in Europe so aggravated the situation that Parliament took action.

The Petition of Right (1628) recognized the right of Englishmen to be free from quartering "against their wills," declaring the practice to be "against the laws and customs of this realm."⁶⁶ Fine words, but the practice continued, reaching epidemic proportions during the English Civil War (1642–1651), and then, after the Stuart restoration in 1660, during the Third Anglo-Dutch War (1672–1674).⁶⁷ In 1679, in another attempt to outlaw the practice, Parliament promulgated a statute that prohibited involuntary quartering at any time, in any place. James II ignored the law, which only added to the grievances against him leading to his downfall in the Glorious Revolution in 1688.⁶⁸

When the smoke cleared, the Declaration of Rights (1689) put future sovereigns on notice of those actions that would not be tolerated from an English monarch. Included in the list of the ways in which James II had endeavored "to subvert and extirpate the Protestant religion and the laws and liberties of this kingdom" was the quartering of soldiers "contrary to law."[69] Nevertheless, when William and Mary ascended to the throne, and most of the rights listed in the Declaration of Rights were included in the Bill of Rights (November 1689), the right to be free from coerced billeting was not. It also was omitted from the initial Mutiny Act of 1689, which governed certain aspects of raising and disciplining a standing army.[70]

That omission was rectified in 1690. Section 17 of the Second Mutiny Act permitted the compulsory quartering of soldiers on English soil, in "Inns Livery Stables Alehouses Victualing houses and all houses selling Brandy Strong Waters Cyder or Metheglin," but specifically recognized the protections afforded by the Petition of Right. Section 17 made it clear that the quartering it authorized was due to the exigent circumstances resulting from a "Rebellion in Ireland and a Warr against France," and that it would be permitted only "for and during the continuance of this Act and noe longer." The act allowed quartering in "noe Private Houses whatsoever."[71]

The Mutiny Act, which stood for the proposition that quartering required statutory authorization, was reenacted annually, sometimes with modifications. The quartering section in the 1757 version contained language regarding the Declaration of Rights similar to that in the 1690 version, but watered down the rationale for quartering from immediate threats to the rather vague "[when] there is and may be Occasion for the marching and Quartering of [troops], in several Parts of this Kingdom."[72] Like all of its predecessors, however, the 1757 version of the Mutiny Act retained the ban on quartering soldiers in private houses.[73]

Thus, by the beginning of the French and Indian War, the rules regarding quartering in England had been in place for nearly seventy years, and quartering was not much of an issue there. In British America, however, the question was as alive as ever. And it was a complicated one. First, the hard facts: there were thousands of British troops in need of food and shelter, only a handful of barracks in the colonies, and far fewer public houses than in England. Next, the law: despite changes that made some of its provisions applicable to the American colonies, the Mutiny Act's quartering provisions did not apply there.

Attempts to reach a solution to the problem were undermined by the differing agendas of the parties involved. On the one hand, there was the British military, intent on doing whatever it believed necessary to win the war. On the other, there were the provincial legislatures jealous of what they saw as their rights and careful with their money. Finally, there were strong personalities on both sides, most significantly that of John Campbell, the fourth Earl of Loudoun.

A Lowland Scot, Loudoun was in his early fifties when he became commander in chief of the British forces in the American colonies. Although he was a career soldier, his military credentials were relatively modest. His service as aide-de-camp to George II in 1743, and his performance in the Scottish Rebellion of 1745, in which he raised a loyalist regiment, were the strongest items on his résumé. Loudoun was one of a dozen officers considered for the American post. Given the fact that he was one of the sixteen representative peers of Scotland on whose vote the ministry always could count, it seems likely that he owed his appointment as much to his political connections as to his martial achievements. It also may have been thought that his title and lineage would earn him respect in the colonies.[74]

Loudoun's reputation has suffered at the hands of his American contemporaries and later historians. John Adams recalled that when Loudoun arrived in Massachusetts, his behavior "gave us no great esteem of his Lordship's qualifications to conduct the War and excited gloomy Apprehensions."[75] In 1758, the Reverend Samuel Davies of Hanover, Virginia, wrote of Loudoun's "imperious Insolence in authority."[76] Historian Francis Parkman described him as "a rough Scotch lord, hot and irascible."[77] This was not completely fair. Loudoun was neither a tyrant, a fool, nor a lout. After the battle of Culloden, when bloody retribution was the order of the day, he was almost alone in his humane and honorable treatment of surrendering Highland rebels.[78] Loudoun's friends described him as "amiable."[79] He was an amateur botanist and a fellow of the Royal Society.[80] But Loudoun was neither a diplomat nor a lawyer nor a politician. He was above all else a soldier and an aristocrat, and it showed in the manner in which he dealt with the quartering issue in America.

At the beginning of the war, the British government knew that quartering in the colonies would be a problem, and that it was essentially a constitutional issue. Nevertheless, during Loudoun's tenure as commander in chief, nothing was done to define a viable legal basis for it. The Mutiny Acts were no help because, by their terms, their quartering provisions did not apply to the colonies.[81] Loudoun was given no direction with regard to quartering.[82] Likewise, the secretary of state had instructed the provincial governors to quarter such troops as the commander in chief desired, but did not specify what those quarters should be, how much should be paid for them, or who should foot the bill.[83] Well aware of the weakness of his position on the quartering issue, Loudoun repeatedly requested the ministry to come up with a parliamentary remedy.[84] None was forthcoming. Left to his own devices, Loudoun shifted from one quartering rationale to another, finally resorting to the claim that he had the right to do whatever he believed necessary for the good of the service, even if this meant forcible billeting in private homes without statutory authority, an anathema to all true Englishmen.

Loudoun's first challenge was Albany, a predominantly Dutch frontier town which served as a staging area for British forces while, at the same time, carrying on a brisk trade with the French. In late August 1756, after he had called off the Crown Point expedition, Loudoun demanded that Albany provide quarters for two regiments of regulars. When the town's mayor refused to comply, the general ordered the troops into the town and compelled private homeowners to billet them.[85] The quartering issue then moved with Loudoun down the Hudson River to New York. As in Albany, the city's mayor refused to quarter Loudoun's soldiers. It was only when the general threatened to move three or four battalions into the town to take quarters by force that New York's governor signed a law calling for the billeting of soldiers in public houses and, if those proved insufficient, in private homes.[86] By Loudoun's lights, New York, he said, had "given every thing I demanded."[87] Philadelphia would prove more difficult.

In late October 1756, Loudoun demanded that that city provide quarters for a battalion of the Royal American regiment. The Pennsylvania assembly responded with an act that basically adopted the Mutiny Act's provisions for the compulsory quartering of troops in public houses, inns, and livery stables, but not in private houses. It was not enough.

When Colonel Henry Bouquet and five hundred regulars arrived in the city, not nearly enough public space could be found to house them all. Moreover, Bouquet demanded a hospital for soldiers stricken with smallpox.[88] After a three-week, four-cornered dispute among the legislature, the governor, the city, and the army which left the soldiers out in the cold, Loudoun warned the governor, "If the number of troops now in Philadelphia are not sufficient, I will instantly march a number sufficient for that purpose and find quarter [for] the whole."[89] He made his point. Pennsylvania turned over a nearly completed hospital to the army, billeted enlisted men in public houses, and provided officers with stipends for room and board.[90]

In Massachusetts, the situation was markedly different. The year before, confronted with the need to provide housing for two regiments, the General Court had built barracks on Castle Island in Boston Harbor, and Governor Shirley had drawn on Crown funds for beds, firewood, and barracks utensils.[91] Shirley had issued warrants to officers which enabled them to pay for quarters, drawing down Crown money to fund them.[92] Both the barracks and the warrants were expensive solutions which clearly limited their use, especially if Massachusetts were called upon to house any more regulars. For the time being, however, quartering was not an issue in Massachusetts. Lord Loudoun's arrival changed that.

A joint legislative committee met with Loudoun in an attempt to ascertain what the general expected of Massachusetts.[93] After informing the committee that the province needed to supply the regulars housed at Castle William with bedding, candles, and firewood, Loudoun dropped a bombshell. He told the committee that, in certain circumstances, he was ready to billet soldiers in private homes, by force if necessary, adding (pointedly) that the houses of "people even of quality are not exempted."[94] While it is unclear why Loudoun made this threat, it seems very likely that it was not spontaneous. At least as early as the quartering dispute in Albany the previous year, Loudoun had been aware of what was at stake. He had noted the "good deal of trouble" that his demand for quarters was creating, "but as this year will be Precedent for future times, I shall spare no pains to settle it right."[95] Then, of course, when nothing else worked, he had forcibly billeted some of his soldiers in the homes of Albany's citizens.[96]

Moreover, especially after Philadelphia, Loudoun fully understood that the colonials were impervious to appeals to practicality, humanity, and patriotism. He had learned that they were capable of prolonged opposition, complete with political maneuvering, technical legal arguments, and emotional appeals to the rights of Englishmen for which he now had no patience whatsoever.[97] He also was painfully aware that his quiver of legal arguments was empty. Whereas, early on, he had attempted to rely on the Mutiny Act in making his demands, by early 1757, he recognized that

> the manner of Quartering in England as in time of Peace, on Publick Houses only, will in no way answer the interest, in this Country; for here, there are few Public Houses. . . .
>
> Whilst the War lasts, Necessity, will Justify exceeding that Rule; as Troops must be under cover, in the Places where it is necessary to post them, for the Security of the Country, and carrying on the Service, . . . the only remedy that occurs to me at present, is adopting the method of Quartering in Scotland, *where*, . . . they are by Law, Quartered on private Houses.[98]

Loudoun's threat to quarter troops in private homes ignited a firestorm when it was reported to the Massachusetts House of Representatives, with some members moving to challenge the general's right to seize quarters.[99] Apparently, Jeremiah Gridley put out the fire, or at least, tamped it down for a while. According to a letter he wrote to Gilbert McAdam, one of Loudoun's aides-de-camp, "knowing [his fellow legislators'] incapacity to determine such [a] Point," Gridley "moved . . . that ye members who had begun ye motion might be appointed a Committee to consider it and report."[100]

If, as has been suggested, Gridley offered his solution in the hope that the troops at Castle William would be quickly supplied and the members of the more conservative council would be reluctant to question Loudoun's right to quarter, he was badly mistaken.[101] Neither happened. The House did pass a bill calling for the provisioning of Castle William, but the council refused to concur. Gridley had argued too well for committee review. "Instead of acting upon the vote," Gridley wrote McAdam, the council "appointed Mr. Hutchinson & the Chief Justice a Committee to be joined with [a committee] of ye house to consider what was requisite."[102]

The "Chief Justice" was Stephen Sewall, chief justice of the Massachusetts Superior Court, and a man revered for his temperament and erudition.[103] "Mr. Hutchinson" was Thomas Hutchinson, who was one of the most powerful men in the province, a leader in the council, and the "prime figure" in Governor Shirley's administration.[104] When Shirley left for England in what turned out to be a futile effort to save his job, Hutchinson became the de facto spokesman for Massachusetts.[105] Perhaps the most important person to whom Hutchinson spoke was Lord Loudoun. The two had met in November 1756 in Albany, where Hutchinson was attending to province business. Impressed with Hutchinson, Loudoun asked him to ghost-write a speech that the general presented to the New England war commissioners.[106] For the next six months, until Shirley's successor, Thomas Pownall, arrived, Hutchinson clandestinely briefed Loudoun on developments in Boston.[107]

It appears, however, that Hutchinson was not Loudoun's only source of information about what was happening in Massachusetts. He also had Jeremiah Gridley. There is evidence that this relationship stemmed from the two men's membership in the Masons. Loudoun had been familiar with Gridley's lodge since 1736 when, as grand master of the Masons in England, he had sent a letter to the lodge appointing its new grand master.[108] In 1757 Gridley was the grand master of North America. On January 31, 1757, perhaps even before Loudoun officially entered the town, three members of his staff were inducted as Masons at a meeting of Gridley's lodge at Boston's Royal Exchange Tavern.[109] Later, everyone, including Loudoun, attended a fete given by the lodge at which "the day was spent in a very agreeable manner."[110] All three of the new inductees were there, including Loudoun aide Gilbert McAdam, who was soon to become Gridley's primary contact within the general's inner circle.[111]

Between the end of February 1757 and the middle of March 1758, Jeremiah Gridley regularly wrote to Loudoun or to Loudoun's associates about the political situation in Massachusetts. These letters demonstrate that Gridley was an active supporter of the commander in chief's policies, and that his support played a significant role in determining the assembly's response to them. Nowhere was this more apparent than in the February 1757 conference between the House and council committees to discuss the appropriate response to Loudoun's quartering demands.

Gridley had been appointed chairman of the House committee. When it met with its counterpart from the council, he was handed a document. As Gridley recounted in a letter to McAdam, "Mr. Hutchison & [Sewall] had . . . drawn up a report, the Substance of which was a Protest against his Ld Ships Demand . . . asserting their right as Englishmen & by Charter."[112] Gridley "opposed ye report, & incurr'd ye Displeasure of Mr. Hutchinson and ye Chief Justice."[113] Sewall was especially offended, and "with great warmth and Sputtering began to catechize me about English rights."[114]

Gridley did not back down. Noting that Hutchinson's report "tended to nothing but to bring ye right of Quartering into question," he advised against making trouble when there was no need to do so.[115] Loudoun, Gridley contended, knew the law as well as they did and had not "demanded" quarters but rather had "requested" them. Moreover, inasmuch as the province had provided quarters at Castle William in the past, "was it not natural for my Lord to suppose his hon'r & ye Council would provide for others in the same manner?"[116] Gridley won the day. Although Sewall "adhered to his own opinion," Hutchinson "retreated" and agreed with Gridley, as did a majority of the joint committee.[117] Their report supported Loudoun's position. The General Court voted to provision the regulars billeted at Castle William, but the quartering issue was not dead.[118] It would arise anew.

In the meantime, there was growing friction between civilians and British regulars. There never had been any love lost between the two sides, and increased contact aggravated the situation. It started at the top. Loudoun had little use for provincial governments or provincial soldiers. Among "Provincial Troops," he found "little appearance of their obeying his Majesty's Commands," with the "Gentlemen from Massachusetts . . . the principal Opposers."[119] Provincial governors, Loudoun concluded, are "Cyphers," and the "backwardness of the

People in this Country, to give any Assistance to the Service is incredible."[120] Lieutenant George Cottman probably summed up the feeling of many of his brother officers when he concluded that "the whole Country are Against the Regulars."[121] He was right. Colonial soldiers and civilians viewed regular officers of all ranks, from Loudoun on down, as merciless and haughty.[122] This arrogance was institutionalized in the British army's Rules and Articles of War, which provided that "provincial field officers [majors and above] serving in conjunction with regulars lost all rank as such and were reduced to the status of junior captains."[123]

"Respectable" colonials were particularly offended by the regulars' recruiting methods, especially before those methods became more strictly regulated in mid-1756.[124] The British army's enlistment practices were so notorious that the recruiting sergeant had become a familiar character of contemporary folklore. He was, according to the Irish soldier-playwright George Farquhar, the "Sum Total" of "Canting, Lying, Impudence, Pimping, Bullying, Swearing, Whoring, Drinking and a Halbard."[125] Recruiting "was always carried on in an alcoholic haze, which when dispelled usually found the prospective recruit safely enlisted in His Majesty's service."[126]

For many a recruit, that "service" was a demoralizing combination of bad food, harsh discipline, sickness, danger, and public opprobrium.[127] Not surprisingly, many soldiers deserted. It was no small problem. Loudoun complained that "desertion and *Drunkeness* are the diseases of the Country."[128] The situation was aggravated by the fact that many provincials were more than ready to assist soldiers who did not wish to be soldiers anymore.

In Massachusetts, the situation was as serious as in any of the colonies. In a letter to Loudoun, Gridley described the hostile response to recruiting in Massachusetts:

> Recruiting, my Lord, is an unfavour'd Cause, unless for the Royall American regiment, and even there if any native of the Province enlists, the Enlistment is critically examined, every imaginary flaw is made a real one, and the Desertion of such a person encouraged. This is ye popular temper, & the Magistrates, always in some shape or other dependent upon the people, are in my opinion too complaisant.[129]

The "popular temper" in the province rendered efforts to recover deserters a difficult, occasionally dangerous pursuit. Friends and neighbors often came to the aid of the deserter, giving him shelter and assaulting the soldiers sent to apprehend him. Provincial magistrates were slow to offer their assistance to the army, and juries were quick to rule against the military whether the suit was against the deserter and his abettors or against the soldiers for some alleged impropriety.[130] One frustrated regular officer put it this way:

> The Jury consist generally of Men whose greatest merit is a rigid adherence to the old Charter Privileges, everything that has the appearance of infringing them is an unfavour'd Cause. . . . I have just Reason to believe that the lower Class of Men here will swear to the greatest Untruths rather than that the Military shall escape.[131]

Anyone who assisted the regulars in their efforts to apprehend deserters or represented them in related legal proceedings made himself, in Gridley's words, "obnoxious" to a large segment of the public.[132] Gridley spoke from experience. In June 1757, Lieutenant Shaw of the Royal American Regiment was escorting a captured deserter in Boston when a mob rescued the prisoner and carried him away in triumph.[133] It soon became public knowledge that the deserter had taken refuge at the house of Caleb Dana, attorney Richard Dana's brother. After consultation with Gridley, a search warrant was obtained and Lieutenant Shaw was dispatched to Caleb Dana's house to apprehend the fugitive.[134] Things did not go well. In the dead of night, one of Shaw's squad "knocked gently" at the window of the room in which the deserter supposedly was sleeping and "called him by his Name." Upon receiving a reply, Shaw demanded entrance. When the soldiers were not admitted, they "forced the Door open." A small melee ensued, during which a man thought to be the fugitive was wounded. He turned out not to be the fugitive. That individual was nowhere to be found.[135] Then came the lawsuits.

Retained to prosecute Caleb Dana under the "Act for the better recruiting of his Majesty's forces on the American Continent," Gridley charged him with rescuing and concealing a deserter.[136] He sought the penalty provided under the act to penalize those who "harbour, conceal, or assist any Deserter."[137] "To balance," Richard Dana, suing on behalf of his brother, "brought a heavy charge of Trespass against the whole party that apprehended the Deserter."[138] Dana also included as defendants "the two Soldiers, who were the only witnesses of [the deserter's] Inlistment, in order to deprive us of their Evidence [as interested parties]."[139] Apparently, Dana's ploy and his suit failed. Gridley put in this way: "God who gives curst cows short horns, had not endow'd them with understanding to accomplish the Design. Accordingly it came to naught."[140]

Around this time—June 1757—about twelve thousand soldiers, with Loudoun in command, were miles away from Boston, in Halifax, impatiently awaiting British warships long overdue. The men constituted an invasion army. Loudoun's target was a familiar nemesis: Louisbourg. To put the force together, the general had stripped frontier garrisons of every available soldier, but now they sat idle, waiting for their escorts. When the British men-of-war finally dropped anchor on July 10, they were followed by alarming news. Countering British lethargy with their own alacrity, the French now had three squadrons of fighting sail in Louisbourg harbor, and had reinforced the garrison. On August 4, 1757, confronted with a superior naval force, a well-entrenched enemy, and the coming of autumn's uncertain weather, Loudoun ordered his men back to New York.[141]

The aborted Louisbourg campaign had consequences far beyond a lost opportunity in Canada. When Loudoun drained troops from the New York and New England frontier for the expedition, he presented the French with an opportunity of their own. In late July 1757, the Marquis de Montcalm, with over seven thousand men, including two thousand Native Americans from as far away as Iowa, moved out from Fort Carillon (Ticonderoga), south down Lake George toward Fort William Henry. They invested the fort and began a heavy artillery barrage. On August 9, the outnumbered garrison capitulated. The French terms of surrender were honorable, but those terms were not honored. Montcalm's Native American allies fell upon the withdrawing British, slaughtering many men, women, and children.[142]

Just around the time that Massachusetts was receiving the horrifying news about the fall of Fort William Henry, the quartering problem returned to the province, and this time it got nasty. It did not start that way. In early August, Loudoun informed Thomas Pownall, who had just taken the reins as governor of Massachusetts, that he needed billeting for a battalion of Scots Highlanders.[143] Seeking to avoid a confrontation, Pownall convinced the General Court that it was better to address the army's needs than to leave it up to the army to impose a solution. On August 31, the legislature voted to enlarge the barracks at Castle William to accommodate one thousand officers and men and "to provide necessary Articles usually allowed for Barracks."[144]

The legislators would go no further. When Pownall proposed an act "to empower and require magistrates to "take up and assign quarters" to regulars so that the troops "might be well accommodated, and the province be as little burdened as possible," the General Court balked. The House of Representatives and the council informed the governor that the barracks and supplies at Castle William "were all the provision proper to be made by the province."[145]

The assembly's stubbornness soon was put to the test. In early November, recruiting officers from two British regiments asked Pownall where they could billet their men. They explained that Castle William, situated as it was in Boston Harbor, was not convenient for recruiting purposes. The governor referred the officers to the local justices of the peace, who refused to do anything, maintaining that "they had no power by Law to proceed any further in quartering Men."[146]

When Pownall explained the need for quarters to the speaker of the House and the representatives from Boston,

> their answer was, that . . . [t]hey had provided Barracks & supplied them with all necessaries and were willing & disposed to do everything in their power that the Service could require. That as it is an Essential right of the Subject that no one could be quartered upon, unless by Law and as there was no Law directing such or indemnifying those who should attempt to do it[,] No Magistrate they thought would venture to do it.[147]

On November 4, 1757, Pownall wrote to Loudoun seeking his "further pleasure and Directions" on the matter.[148] He received outrage and a knowing misrepresentation of the law. Loudoun declared that the Mutiny Act extended to the colonies, making any provincial act unnecessary. He warned Pownall that unless the Boston authorities recognized his right to demand quarters and quartered his men within forty-eight hours, he would dispatch three battalions of regulars to Boston to make sure that they did so.[149] When Pownall delivered Loudoun's message to the General Court, the legislators responded with uncommon dispatch. Insisting that a provincial law was necessary before any British troops could be legally quartered, they met over the weekend and drafted "An Act Making Provision For The Quartering And Billeting Recruiting Officers And Recruits," which Pownall signed into law on December 1.[150]

Loudoun remained outraged—not with the law itself, but with the fact that the General Court had effectively denied his authority to quarter troops in the absence of such a law. He repeated his threat to march troops into Boston. On December 16, a House committee adopted a somewhat conciliatory tone, but recommended that the statute remain in place and "reminded the general . . . that the 'inhabitants of this Province are intitled to the Natural Rights of English born Subjects.'"[151]

Pownall wrote to Loudoun defending his approach.[152] According to Thomas Hutchinson, this letter, "or perhaps further consideration upon the subject, abated the resentment of the general, and caused some change of sentiments."[153] Apparently Loudoun believed that he had won the test of wills, but the General Court remained unbowed.[154] In a message to Pownall, the legislators avowed their readiness to acknowledge the "authority of all acts of parliament which concern the colonies, and extend to them," but reiterated their position that because the quartering provisions of the Mutiny Act "did not reach the colonies," they had no choice but to pass a law "to regulate quarters as the circumstances of the province require."[155]

All of these developments—the bitter quartering disputes, the animosity between regulars and provincials, the defeats of British arms in the field—made it a tough sell when Loudoun came looking to Massachusetts to commit troops for his projected 1758 offensive. Gridley was one of the general's floor managers in the House of Representatives. He found it rough going. Governor Pownall's political clumsiness did not help matters. When he had asked Gridley to present a motion in the House "for ye rangers Lord Loudoun wrote for," Pownall had assured Gridley that he would line up support for the measure.[156] Yet when Gridley "consulted the principal members" about raising the troops, he found them "averse."[157] Pownall had not "spoken to a man of them." In the end, convinced that "ye motion at present would have no other effect than to hurt ye cause in future," Gridley dropped the whole thing."[158]

Frustrated by the legislative wrangling, Gridley complained that Pownall had "embroiled himself with the house of Representatives" over where to send a "scouting party," claiming that the House's actions were "an invasion of his Authority."[159] Pownall prorogued the legislature in late January. Little had been accomplished toward raising troops for the next offensive. Disheartened, Gridley observed that the "Aspect of things is frowning."[160]

When the legislature reconvened on March 2, 1758, the "Aspect of things," was even worse. February had seen violence send recruiting officers to the hospital.[161] Pownall spent the next week or so laboring to raise troops for Loudoun's proposed offensive, with the House of Representatives, in Pownall's view, contributing nothing "but Difficulties and Objections, Diffidence in the Plan, Objections against the Number as a Quota."[162] In particular, there was an unwillingness to support a joint force of provincial and regular troops as long as provincial officers were discriminated against in rank.[163]

Then everything changed. On March 12, 1758, Pownall read two letters to the General Court that he had received from Secretary of State William Pitt. One announced that Major General James Abercrombie would replace Loudoun as commander in chief of the king's forces in North America.[164] The other letter, addressed to the governors of the New England colonies, New York, and New Jersey, announced the king's plans "to repair the Losses and Disappointments, of the last inactive, and unhappy Campaign."[165]

In a tone of cordiality and collegiality, this letter called for an ambitious campaign against Canada. It requested the governors to use their "utmost Endeavors and Influence" with their respective legislatures to raise a total of twenty thousand men, whom the king would furnish with arms, ammunition, and a "sufficient train of artillery."[166] In addition, Pitt healed a festering sore by promising that "all officers of the Provincial Forces" would retain the rank of their "respective Commissions," and not only up to the rank of captain as had been the prior practice.[167] The letters melted legislative resistance. The Massachusetts House of Representatives voted unanimously to supply seven thousand troops to the invasion effort.[168] The mood was exuberant. Pownall was so elated that he wrote to General Abercrombie offering to take the field with the Massachusetts troops "to give a Spring to this good Measure."[169]

Gridley reported to the now former commander in chief, Lord Loudoun, on what had happened. He began his letter by reminding Loudoun that he had "attended the house all Saturday last" in "obedience to your Lordship's earnest commands that I should do my utmost for the Services proposed by his Majesty to this Government."[170] Gridley took credit for the House's unanimity in its vote for troops and for the large number of troops it had agreed to supply:

> The previous question, whether the Government would raise a suitable number of men to join with his Majesty's regular forces against Canada, came on in the morning and continued some time: the Question was put, and there was a large majority in the affirmative: with which I was not contented, and observed to the Speaker of what consequence it was to the Spirit of such an Expedition, if possible, unanimous. We eas'd the Difficulties of the dissenting members and obtained a unanimous vote in a full house for it. Then I made the motion that seven thousand should be raised by this Province, and in a short time it was voted.[171]

In closing, Gridley thanked Loudoun "for animating me so warmly to my Duty in this Matter," and, again, subtly reminded the general of all he had done for him.[172]

Gridley's readiness to educate Loudoun on his efforts on the general's behalf was part of a pattern. The March letter was reminiscent of Gridley's letter to Loudoun's aide, Gilbert McAdam, a year earlier. In that letter, Gridley had taken sole credit for quashing any attempt to challenge the general's request for quarters and for guiding the quartering bill though the House.[173] Similarly, in writing to Loudoun in June 1757 about his defense of regulars in lawsuits arising out of their attempts to apprehend deserters, Gridley had made certain that

Loudoun understood that he had acted at great personal risk. "I had like to have lost my Election this Year by the Insinuations of Mr. Dana," Gridley wrote, adding, "[My] Engagements in prosecuting these affairs where my Townsman is the deserter will certainly deprive me of my Election next Year."[174]

Gridley was writing with purpose. No doubt he sincerely attempted to do his best for Loudoun and the war effort, but Gridley was an eighteenth-century British politician. Seeking private preferment was viewed almost as a public duty. Moreover, for a fifty-five-year-old lawyer with an outstanding reputation, Gridley had relatively little to show for it compared to some of his contemporaries at the bar. Edmund Trowbridge, James Otis Sr., Timothy Ruggles, and Samuel White were admitted to practice in Massachusetts at about the same time that Gridley was. By 1757, Trowbridge had been attorney general for eight years. Otis too had served as attorney general and was a colonel in the militia. Ruggles, also a colonel, was a judge of the Worcester County Court of Common Pleas, and White had just been appointed to the Bristol County Court of Common Pleas.[175]

All of these lawyers had been members of the House of Representatives, and, arguably, each owed his offices, at least in part, to services performed and connections developed there. This could not have been lost on Gridley. Finally, as a member of the assembly, he saw his relationship to Loudoun as a ticket to advancement. In his letter describing how his efforts on behalf of accused English regulars threatened his reelection to the assembly, Gridley asked Loudoun, still commander in chief at the time, to make a "recommendation to Mr. Pownall" for a militia command.[176]

Gridley's request did not stem from a desire to take the field against the enemy:

> It is not a Place of any Profit, but a Command that will place my Townsmen in a Dependency upon me. . . . It does not require any great Skill in military affairs to command a regt here. Your Lordship may depend upon my Veracity for ye Truth of these things. And tis no unusual thing for a man to command a regt here per saltum [without ever holding a lower rank].[177]

Gridley was not shy about noting the quid pro quo involved: if Loudoun would procure him the commission, the general would retain a supporter in the legislature, or, as Gridley put it, "[I will] have it in my Power whilst your Lordship presides here, to sit in the Genl Assembly of my Country."[178]

In what may have been his last letter to Loudoun, his March 12, 1758, letter dealing with the House vote to raise seven thousand troops, Gridley closed somewhat sentimentally, assuring the general, "I shall always remember your Lordship with the highest Pleasure & Gratitude."[179] But even then, Gridley could not resist requesting that "your Lordship be so kind as to remind Mr. Kilby of some Employment this year wherein I can be serviceable to him in his Department."[180]

In the end, Gridley's efforts came to naught. He had bet on the wrong horse and came away with nothing. Kilby did not find "some Employment" for Gridley in his "Department." The militia colonelcy that he thought would "place my Townsmen in a Dependency on me" did not materialize. Worst of all, his dire forebodings came to pass. Gridley was not reelected to the House of Representatives. On May 22, 1758, Brookline elected Samuel White moderator and voted "Not to send a Representative This Year."[181]

CHAPTER EIGHT

Gridley's Law Practice in the 1750s and 1760s

During the 1750s, Jeremiah Gridley's law practice was essentially what it had always been: a diverse collection of mundane civil actions, typically with relatively little money at stake. In terms of the amount involved, the Vassall case was an exception, but Gridley's representation of rich and powerful clients like William Vassall was not. The Suffolk County Superior Court minute books for the 1750s list Gridley as counsel for some of the most influential men in Massachusetts. For example, in February 1754, Gridley successfully represented Jacob Wendell, a prosperous merchant who was a colonel in the Suffolk militia and had served on the provincial council since 1738.[1] He was one of the group of "powerful men" who, as close advisers to Governor William Shirley, helped shape government policy, and made fortunes from military contracts generated by the war with France.[2] Others in Shirley's inner circle also chose Gridley as their lawyer. One of them, Charles Apthorp, held the lucrative posts of paymaster and commissary to the British troops during the war.[3] The money these positions brought him only served to augment the sizable fortune of a man who, "in his day, ... was called the richest man in Boston."[4]

Samuel Waldo had been a client of Gridley's since at least 1742, and that relationship continued into the next decade.[5] Until his break with

Shirley in 1748, Waldo had been a close adviser to the governor, a position that had brought him an appointment as a brigadier general of provincial troops and a fortune in government contracts. Even the after that estrangement, Waldo remained a wealthy and powerful man with interests in land and enterprises from Rhode Island to Nova Scotia.[6] In the 1750s, Gridley also represented Chief Justice Stephen Sewall and two members of the powerful Hutchinson family: Lieutenant Governor Thomas Hutchinson and Eliakim Hutchinson, chief judge of the Suffolk County Court of Common Pleas.[7] The Superior Court minute books also list Gridley as attorney for Benjamin Hallowell in two cases in Suffolk County.[8] Hallowell was a man of considerable wealth, whose mansion "was acknowledged to be one of the finest in the town."[9]

By the early 1760s, Gridley had been an attorney for about thirty years. These three decades had seen notable changes to the practice of law in Massachusetts. The volume of litigation had continued to increase. Between 1759 and 1763, the number of new filings in the Superior Court rose from 434 to 791, an increase of about 82 percent.[10] The Suffolk County docket books recorded about a 70 percent jump in the number of new filings, but the greatest changes were in Bristol County, which experienced an increase of close to 300 percent, as did the western counties of Hampshire and Berkshire.[11]

The 1760s also witnessed halting steps aimed at enhancing the stature of the province's bench and bar. In what may have been an effort to increase the prestige of the Superior Court, the new chief justice, Thomas Hutchinson, introduced gowns, bands, and wigs for the court's justices and lawyers.[12] To John Adams's critical eye, the "scarlet and sable robes" that the justices wore were "showy," "shallow," "theatrical," and "ecclesiastical."[13] He found their "enormous tie wiggs, more resembling fleeces of painted merino wool than anything natural to man."[14]

Adams was more ambivalent about another of Hutchinson's changes: the creation of an elite group of lawyers whom the chief justice designated "barristers."[15] Looking back after fifty years, Adams questioned whether Hutchinson had the "legal authority to establish a distinction between barristers and attorneys."[16] Authority or not, at the August 1762 Superior Court term at Boston, twenty-six lawyers, including Gridley and Adams, were "called by the Court to be Barristers at Law."[17] It is not clear how *their* rights and privileges as barristers differed from those of other lawyers. There is evidence that they alone were permitted to manage actions in the Superior Court and argue to the court and jury.[18] Yet there also is evidence which indicates that if such was the rule, it was not always enforced. For example, Josiah Quincy Jr., who never was named a barrister, recorded how, at the Superior Court's August 1769 term in Charlestown, "I proceeded . . . at this Court to manage all my Business . . . though unsanctified and uninspired by the Pomp and Magic of—the Long Robe."[19]

Most lawyers probably were less concerned about robes and titles than they were about competition for clients. Despite legislation and court orders designed to discourage them, unsworn practitioners carried on a flourishing legal business, taking clients away from sworn attorneys and, as far as the bar was concerned, bringing dishonor on the profession. Writing in January 1759, John Adams complained in his diary that "Deputy Sheriffs, petit Justices, and pettifogging Meddlers . . . attempt to draw Writts, and draw them wrong oftener than they do right."[20] This concern probably was behind the bar's attack on unlicensed practitioners in the 1760s.

In February 1763, on behalf of the Suffolk County bar, Jeremiah Gridley proposed several rules to the Suffolk County Court of Common Pleas. The lawyers requested the court to order that (1) no general powers of attorney be granted; (2) no attorney's fee be taxed, unless the declaration was drawn by the plaintiff or a sworn attorney; (3) no fee for attendance be taxed unless the plaintiff or sworn attorney attended personally; and (4) only sworn attorneys be permitted to practice before the court.[21] The plan failed when James Otis Jr. rose to his feet, raging that he had never agreed "for any such Rules as these, for they were vs. the Province Law, vs. the Rights of Mankind, and he was amazed that so many wise Heads as that Bar was blessed with could think them practicable." All "schemes to suppress Pettyfoggers," he thundered, "must rest on the Honor of the Bar." The court declared that it could do nothing unless the bar was unanimous.[22]

Otis's colleagues were outraged by his behavior.[23] The next year, plans were afoot for a meeting of the Suffolk bar to "advise Proper

Measures for the Supporte of the Honour of the Barr, and to prevent Irregular admissions in the Future."[24] In 1765, they obtained an order from the Superior Court that only attorneys admitted to practice before it could secure blank writs.[25] By July of the next year, Adams was pleased to note that the Boston bar had "at last introduced a regular Progress, to the Gown, and seven years must be the State of Probation."[26] Those seven years probably consisted of three years of legal study, two years as an inferior court attorney, and two more as an attorney in the Superior Court.[27] The bar established this time frame to improve the quality of the profession, but also to limit competition from new attorneys, who, Adams complained, "swarm and multiply."[28]

Thanks to better sources, the 1760s provide us with a more comprehensive and detailed picture of Jeremiah Gridley's litigation practice than do earlier decades. Josiah Quincy Jr.'s accounts of cases heard by the Massachusetts Superior Court between 1761 and 1772 are the earliest American law reports. First published in 1865, they recently have been republished in a valuable two-volume edition, carefully edited with insightful analysis by Daniel R. Colliquette.[29] *Quincy's Reports* include at least eighteen cases in which Gridley played an active role.[30] The other important source for Gridley's litigation practice in the 1760s are the Adams papers, especially the *Legal Papers of John Adams*, edited so well by L. Kinvin Wroth and Hiller B. Zobel. These three volumes include at least eight cases in which Gridley was involved.[31] The discussions that follow are drawn from these sources. They provide a useful sample of some of Gridley's more significant nonpolitical cases, and a feel for Gridley the working lawyer and the kinds of issues that he was called upon to address and to argue.

Dudley v. Dudley (1762)

Born in 1731, Abigail was the eldest of Jeremiah Gridley's three daughters.[32] She married Joseph Dudley, a lawyer who had graduated from Harvard in 1751 and been admitted to the Superior Court as a barrister in 1762. Abigail probably came to know her future husband when he was studying law with her father.[33] That mentoring relationship continued after Dudley's admission to the bar. Dudley was a member of the Sodalitas, "a little Clubb" founded by Gridley and attorney Samuel Fitch in 1765. For a brief period, this "private Association," which also included John Adams, met "for the Sake of Sociability, literary Conversation and reading new publications as well as the Classicks in concert."[34]

Gridley's son-in-law had been born into an illustrious family. His great-grandfather was Thomas Dudley, who had come to Massachusetts on the *Arbella* in 1630 and had served four terms as the colony's governor between 1634 and 1651.[35] Joseph's grandfather and namesake also had been governor, as well as chief justice of the Superior Court.[36] William Dudley, our Joseph Dudley's father, had been a judge on the Suffolk County Inferior Court of Common Pleas, a colonel of the Suffolk militia, speaker of the House of Representatives, and a member of the provincial council.[37] When he died in 1743, despite his years as a legislator and a judge, William Dudley died intestate—without a will.[38] He should have known better.

William's unsettled estate led to a dispute between Abigail's husband, Joseph Dudley, together with his sisters on the one hand, and their older brother Thomas on the other.[39] Ironically, although their father, William, had left no will, the dispute among his children centered on testamentary language in a will—that of Governor Joseph Dudley, William's father and the warring siblings' grandfather. To understand the nature of the dispute, it is necessary to understand the law involved, the words that the governor had used in his will, and what he had intended in using those words. First, the law, which, while not entirely free from confusion, was fairly straightforward.

In mid-eighteenth-century England and Massachusetts, there were various types of ownership in land (estates) which could be transferred by a will. Two of the most important of these were a fee simple estate and a fee tail (or entail) estate. In general, a fee simple estate "is the largest estate known to law," giving the person who receives it ownership of the land without limitation, and with an unconditional power to sell it or give it away.[40] In contrast, a fee tail estate gave the recipient no such power. His or her ownership of the land was subject to a fixed line of inheritable succession limited to direct descendants of the original owner's bloodline (heirs of the body), and transfer to anyone else was prohibited.[41]

In England, if a person died without a will (intestate), his or her lands were governed by the law of primogeniture, by which the eldest son inherited all of the decedent's real property.[42] Massachusetts did not follow this rule. In a significant departure from the common law, a 1692 statute provided that if a man died without a will, one-third of his personal estate went to his wife,

> *and all the residue of the real and personal estate, by equal portions, to and among his children, . . . [e]xcept the eldest son then surviving . . . who shall have two shares or a double portion of the whole.*[43]

In his will, Governor Dudley left his younger son, William, the father of Gridley's son-in-law, his "new Farm in the Woods in Roxbury," his "Farm of 1000 Acres at Manchaug," and "Three Hundred Pounds toward building him a House."[44] In addition, the governor stated:

> *And my Will is that my Lands descend after the Manner of England forever; to the Male Heirs first, and after that to the Females. If either of my Sons die without Male Issue, his Brother and his Male Issue shall inherit the Lands herein bequeathed.*[45]

This then was the question: Did these words mean that the governor intend to give William a fee tail or a fee simple estate in the Manchaug farm? If the governor intended a fee tail, he gave William the land with strings attached. When William died, with or without a will, all one thousand acres of the farm could be inherited only by the governor's eldest male descendant, who was Joseph's older brother, Thomas. Alternatively, if Governor Dudley intended to bequeath the farm to William in fee simple, he gave William an unlimited right to the land, which meant that if William died without a will (which he did), the Massachusetts statute of 1692 kicked in, and the property would be divided equally among all of William's children, with Thomas receiving a double portion.

Interpreting his grandfather's will as giving his father a fee tail and himself the right to all of the Manchaug property, Thomas Dudley "entered on the premises."[46] Joseph and his sisters brought a "plea of partition" to divide the land in accordance with the statute of 1692.[47] In the initial hearing before the Superior Court, they persuaded Justices Cushing, Oliver, and Lynde to rule in their favor "against ye opinion" of Chief Justice Stephen Sewall and Justice Chambers Russell.[48] Their older brother, Thomas, filed for review. The Superior Court, which heard his action at its August 1762 term in Boston, was different from the one that had heard the case earlier. Justices Cushing, Oliver, and Lynde were still there. Gone were Chief Justice Sewall, who had died in September 1760, and Justice Russell, who was on temporary leave. Thomas Hutchinson now presided as the new chief justice. Samuel Danforth, chief judge of the Middlesex County Court of Appeals, sat in for Russell.[49]

Jeremiah Gridley and James Otis Jr. represented Gridley's son-in-law and his sisters. Thomas Dudley retained Edmund Trowbridge, Benjamin Kent, and Robert Auchmuty.[50] All of the attorneys emphasized the need to interpret the will so as to give effect to the governor's intent, but this emphasis only begged the question because the language of the governor's will was unclear.[51] Older brother Thomas based his claim to sole ownership of the farm on the language of his grandfather's will, which began *"And my Will is that my Lands descend after the Manner of England forever,"* claiming that this language created an entail, and at his father's death, the farm had reverted to him as the eldest son.[52]

Gridley and Otis argued that because entails were unknown at common law, they could be created only by the use of unambiguous language, and the language used in the governor's will was anything but clear. Moreover, and this became the key issue in the case, the governor's language bequeathing the farm to his son demonstrated an intent to create a gift in fee simple.[53] To show this, Gridley had to find language in the governor's will indicating that he intended for William to be freely able to dispose of the Manchaug property, which he could do only if the property was given to him in fee simple.

Gridley found it in the governor's bequest to William of "Three Hundred Pounds toward building him a House." He argued that the referenced "House" was to be built in Roxbury, the Dudley family seat, and that £300 was not nearly enough money to build a suitable house there. Therefore, the governor must have *intended* that William be free to sell some of the Manchaug farm to raise money to build the house in Roxbury, and, to give William the freedom to do so, the governor must have intended that the gift of the farm to William be in fee simple.[54]

Thomas Dudley's attorneys attacked Gridley's assumption that the referenced "House" was to be built in Roxbury. They pointed out that there was nothing in the governor's will that indicated where the "House" was to be built, and that at the time the will was drawn, his son William—Joseph's father—was building a house in Roxbury which most likely would have been completed before the governor died. They contended that, if anything, the "House" in question was to be in Manchaug, where it could easily be built for £300, the amount given to William in the will.[55] Gridley countered that the possibility that William's house in Roxbury might be finished and paid for before his father passed away was irrelevant. He argued that if the house was still under construction when the governor died, the gift of £300 and money from the possible sale of the Manchaug land was intended "to finish it." If the house had been completed, the gifts were to "reimburse" William."[56]

The lawyers presented their arguments at two different sessions of the Superior Court. At some point during the first day, Thomas Dudley's counsel moved "that they might be heard again before Judgment." The court, "thinking it a Matter of Nicety and Consequence, desired further Argument, and continued it to the next Term for Judgment."[57] Trowbridge made good use of the break. He wrote to William Bollan in England requesting him to secure an opinion from Randle Wilbraham, an acknowledged expert on the rules of descent.[58] Wilbraham agreed with Thomas Dudley's position: the Manchaug farm had been left in fee tail.[59]

Wilbraham's opinion in hand, Trowbridge was optimistic about "Opening the Eyes of those Judges who . . . gave ye last Judgment."[60] He had good reason for optimism. Based as it was on assumptions and speculation, Gridley and Otis's argument in favor of fee simple seems weak. Samuel Quincy and Daniel R. Coquillette, the two editors of *Quincy's Reports,* conclude that Governor Dudley intended to give William an entailed estate.[61] Thomas Dudley should have won. He did not. After hearing the second round of arguments at the February 1763 term in Boston, the *"Chief Justice delivered the Judgment of the Court in Favour of Fee Simple."* This meant that the farm at Manchaug, which passed intestate from William Dudley, did not go in its entirety to his son Thomas, but rather was divided up among all of William's children as mandated by the provincial statute of 1692.[62]

The court did not explain its decision.[63] Coquillette theorizes that the court might have been "seizing on the draftsman's incompetence to strike a bold stroke for the presumption of partibility."[64] This would have been consistent with the Massachusetts law of intestacy, which mandated partibility rather than primogeniture as was the rule in England. There also may have been something else at work here, something that made Gridley's argument about William's house in Roxbury less speculative than it appears. Some justices may have known for a fact exactly what Governor Dudley had intended in devising the Manchaug farm to William, or at least what William and his older brother Paul believed their father had intended.

The social elite in provincial Massachusetts was composed of a relatively small group of families who regularly interacted economically, politically, and socially with one another. The Dudleys were members of this elite, as were the Hutchinsons, the Lyndes, and the Cushings. Therefore, when the question of Governor Joseph Dudley's testamentary intentions came before the Superior Court, that question was addressed by men some of whom knew the governor's sons personally and may have been privy to their views on the subject.[65] Quincy's notes on the hearing provide some support for this hypothesis. While arguing in support of fee tail, Trowbridge conceded that £300 was not enough to build a house in Roxbury, but contended that "perhaps and most probably" the governor had intended the house be built "on the Farm at Manchaug."[66] Chief Justice Hutchinson then interjected, "The words are build *him* an House; not an House simply, but *him, one whom he knew was to live at Roxbury.*"[67]

To the critical ear, it appears that the chief justice may have known facts not in evidence. Be that as it may, according to Trowbridge, Hutchinson sided with him as did Justice Danforth, both believing that the Manchaug property was *not* devised in fee simple.[68] Unfortunately for Trowbridge and his client, nothing "could open ye Eyes of . . . Lynd Cushing & Oliver," a majority of the court, who held that William Dudley took "by force of his Father's will an Estate in fee Simple."[69]

Dudley v. Dudley was an important milestone on colonial America's journey away from the aristocratic and sexist property laws of England.[70] It also places Jeremiah Gridley in an interesting light. Here we find him on the more liberal side of the law, arguing against fee tail when the language of the will seems to point in that direction. Moreover, in his argument Gridley repeatedly cited differences between the law in Massachusetts and that in England. When his adversaries claimed that the governor's will used language that created an entail, Gridley responded that "the Law of this Province forbids his giving it as the Law of England."[71] In dealing with the will's use of the word "descend," Gridley stressed the fact that the word had a different meaning in Massachusetts because "in this Country we make our Real Estate almost Personal Estate."[72]

Later, Gridley expanded on that difference, explaining why the restrictive English rules of property were impractical in land-rich Massachusetts, and why large hereditary estates were much rarer in the province than in England:

> We must consider of our Country and Real Estate here: To a Person unacquainted with our Estate, this might seem strange, but to us who know Real Estates are liable for the Payment of Debts, and are by Act of Parliament made Chattels Real, for the Payment of Debts, that they are almost the only Things we have to trade upon, and that they continue in a Family scarce over three Generations, 'tis not strange they should be put on the same Footing with Personal Estate.[73]

Given his role in *Dudley*, one might conclude that, at least when it came to the law of estates in land, Gridley had liberal leanings. Yet his advocacy in two other cases that also involved ambiguous testamentary language cuts against such a conclusion. In *Elwell v. Pierson* (1763)[74] and *Banister v. Henderson* (1765),[75] Gridley was on the "conservative" side, arguing against fee simple and in favor of fee tail. Gridley was not alone in his "inconsistency." The fee simple/fee tail test simply is not a reliable indicator of a Massachusetts colonial lawyer's liberal or conservative proclivities even with regard to estates in land. The colony's bar showed no consistent affinity for one position or the other. Robert Auchmuty, who argued in favor of fee tail in *Dudley*, argued for fee simple in both *Elwell* and *Banister*. Similarly, James Otis Jr., who advocated fee simple in *Dudley*, took a conservative position in the case of *Baker v. Mattocks* (1763).[76]

Baker was an important entail case. It involved the question whether a fee tail estate could be split among all of the children when there were no "heirs of the body," and land reverted back to the original donor, or whether it reverts to his eldest son in England.[77] The Superior Court ruled three to two in favor of primogeniture, but Gridley presented a persuasive argument in favor of a more "egalitarian" interpretation.[78] He contended it was axiomatic that an estate of fee tail must be cut out of the larger estate of fee simple, and therefore, in a reversion situation, the rules of fee simple should apply. In England, Gridley asserted, those rules call for primogeniture, but in Massachusetts, the statute of 1692 governed fee simple and should cover fee tail as the smaller part, requiring apportionment among the heirs.[79] As noted, Gridley lost.

But Gridley won the *Dudley* case. He won a victory for his son-in-law and his daughter. No doubt the two of them rejoiced in their victory, but unfortunately, their celebration was short-lived. Indeed, Joseph was short-lived. On Friday, September 25, 1767, he "departed this Life in the 35th Year of his Age."[80] He left Abigail a childless widow and, as the most promising Dudley of his generation, a family in decline.[81] Abigail subsequently married John Gray, a Boston rope maker.[82]

Dunn v. Scollay (1763)

In October 1756, sailing from Newcastle to Boston with a cargo of "coals and other goods," the brigantine *Peggy* was captured by a French privateer.[83] Captained by Isaac Freeman and owned by John Scollay and Thomas Fletcher of Boston, the ship had been consigned to John Sitwell in London.[84] After surrendering to the French ship, Freeman and the privateer's captain reached an agreement that allowed the *Peggy* to go on its way in return for a "ransom bill" which bound John

Sitwell to pay five thousand livres to the owner of the French ship. At Freeman's "request and direction," John Dunn, the *Peggy*'s first mate, went with the French as a hostage to be held until the bill was paid. Freeman and the *Peggy* then disappeared over the horizon.[85]

The *Peggy* was an unlucky ship. She was seized again by another French ship and taken to Bordeaux, where Captain Freeman died in prison. Meanwhile, John Dunn, the mate he had left behind, ended up imprisoned in Nantes. Sick and destitute, Dunn waited for his ransom to arrive. Months turned into years. Nobody wanted to foot the bill.[86] Stilwell, the consignee on whom the bill was drawn, looked to the insurance underwriters to pay the ransom. Scollay denied any responsibility for Dunn's situation, maintaining that Captain Freeman had no authority to ransom the ship. He insisted that either the insurance carrier or Freeman bore the burden of paying for Dunn's release. Six years went by.[87]

Finally, Dunn was released. He crossed the channel to England. In a letter to Scollay, Sitwell described the circumstances of Dunn's liberation and what lay ahead:

> Jno. Dunn . . . has at length obtained his Discharge. His friends compounded ye Affair for about £200. . . . I thought the Affair would have ended here, but his Friends are of Opinion yt ye Owners are liable to make good all Damages, & have advised him to get over & endeavor to recover it. They have taken ye Opinions of some of ye best Counsel here, wch are in his Favour.—How your Courts may determine this Affair, if it should come to Tryal, I know not.[88]

Dunn took his friends' advice. He went to Massachusetts and hired two of "ye best Counsel" there—Jeremiah Gridley and Robert Auchmuty, the advocate general of the Massachusetts Vice Admiralty Court.[89] In January 1763, the two filed libels in the admiralty court on Dunn's behalf against John Scollay and Thomas Fletcher.[90] It is not clear why they decided to bring the suit in admiralty. With a sympathetic client like Dunn, who had such a compelling story to tell, most plaintiff's attorneys would prefer a jury trial, but there were no juries in the admiralty court. Unlike the province common law courts, admiralty was a prerogative court. Its judge received his authority directly from the Crown and served at the sovereign's pleasure. He alone determined both the facts and the law of a case.[91]

Auchmuty may have preferred admiralty because, as the advocate in admiralty, he was very familiar with the court, its judge, and its procedures. Or it could be, as Coquillette has suggested, that the choice stemmed from both lawyers' conservatism and mistrust for common law courts.[92] They also may have believed, given English precedents, that the admiralty court was the appropriate forum for this type of case.[93] Whatever their reasons, as soon as Gridley and Auchmuty brought suit in admiralty, the owners' attorneys, James Otis and Oxenbridge Thacher, petitioned the Superior Court for a writ of prohibition. They sought an order dismissing the suit in admiralty on the ground that the admiralty court had no jurisdiction over either the matter at issue or the owners of the ship.[94] On February 12, 1763, the Superior Court granted a temporary writ of prohibition subject to further review.[95]

Directed to the judge of the Vice Admiralty Court, the Supreme Court's order was unequivocal:

> We . . . Command and firmly Enjoin you that you meddle not further in the said Plea or Cause, not molest or cause to be molested the said John Scollay and Thomas Fletcher or either of them in the Cause aforesaid in the said Court of Vice Admiralty neither attempt or presume to attempt anything more therein: Until our said Justices have advised and consulted therein at our Superiour Court . . . to be holden at Boston on [February 15, 1763].[96]

Just as the decision to bring Dunn's suit in admiralty seems a bit strange, the defense attorneys' attempt to get the case dismissed from that court also appears counterintuitive. In all probability, if the case were dismissed, it would end up in a common law court with a jury likely sympathetic to the plaintiff. Perhaps, in contrast to their counterparts, Otis and Thacher, as "Whig lawyers," were wary of prerogative courts, always opting for common law courts when given the opportunity to do so.[97] They also may have believed that procedural maneuvering might wear Dunn down to the point where he would settle on the cheap.[98]

Four justices—Chief Justice Hutchinson and Justices Lynde, Oliver, and Cushing—convened to determine whether the temporary writ of prohibition would stand.[99] The issue before the court was whether or not the admiralty court had jurisdiction of Dunn's action against the *Peggy*'s owners. In England, admiralty jurisdiction was limited, in theory, to actions in tort arising on the high seas, and actions on contracts made upon the high seas or to be performed upon the high seas. Actions in admiralty could proceed only *in rem*, that is, against the vessel liable for the obligation sued upon and not against its master or owner.[100]

There were significant exceptions to these rules. The most notable of these were actions by seamen for wages in which the admiralty court allowed them to recover against the vessel, its master, and its owner.[101] Admiralty jurisdiction also had been extended to cases in which a master in foreign parts pledged the ship, freight, and cargo for ships' "necessities," that is, whatever was necessary to enable the ship to continue its voyage.[102] The Massachusetts Vice Admiralty Court not only recognized these exceptions but also, in general, exercised more extensive jurisdiction and followed more flexible procedures than the court in England. Apparently it was not unusual for the Massachusetts admiralty court to decree recovery against a ship's owners personally, and not against the vessel.[103]

Arguing in support of admiralty jurisdiction, Gridley contended that if admiralty had jurisdiction over the "Principal," meaning the vessel, then it also had jurisdiction over whatever was "incident" to it, such as the "Person[s]," in this case the owners of the *Peggy*.[104] He pointed out that admiralty jurisdiction attached to disputes about subjects such as seamen's wages because they were "necessary for the Support of the Voyage," and with regard to such necessaries, the "Vessell, Master and Owners are all liable."[105] He argued that, by analogy, the defendants were liable for the ransom to retain the *Peggy* because the ransom was "necessary for the Support of the Voyage" and, therefore, within admiralty jurisdiction.[106] Apparently, Chief Justice Hutchinson agreed with Gridley's position that admiralty could have personal jurisdiction over the owners, but, he concurred, only if Captain Freeman's ransom agreement with the French privateer could be deemed "the Contract of the Owner."[107] Auchmuty argued that it could be deemed the owners' contract because "Masters may make Contracts that bind Owners."[108]

Defense counsel disagreed. Thacher contended that the owners had not authorized Freeman to enter into such an agreement, and that they did not have to "answer in their Persons for the Act of the Master at Sea, of which they were utterly unknowing."[109] Citing Molloy's *De Jure Maritimo et Navali*, "probably the chief source on the substantive maritime law in the colonies in the eighteenth century," Otis argued that the master of a vessel could bind the owners only so far as their interests in the vessel.[110] "It is now settled," he asserted, that if a captain acts without authority to the detriment of the ship's owners, the "Owners shall not be liable . . . further than the Ship and the Freight."[111] Therefore, while the admiralty court might have had jurisdiction over the *Peggy* and its cargo, it had none over its owners.[112]

To judge from his comments, Justice Oliver believed that the admiralty court had personal jurisdiction over the *Peggy*'s owners, and apparently Justice Cushing agreed.[113] Lynde and Hutchinson saw it differently. While acknowledging that an "Affair of Ransom is a maritime matter upon the sea," Lynde believed that admiralty had jurisdiction over the ship and cargo only, not of the owners.[114] Hutchinson reasoned that, as between the master (Freeman) and the hostage (Dunn), the matter was maritime, but as between the master and the owners, "it does not appear to be a Contract upon the High seas."[115] The chief justice was troubled by what he considered a lack of authority supporting admiralty jurisdiction, and "where it is doubtful, I think 'tis a Rule that common [law] Jurisdiction ought to be maintained."[116] Hutchinson's vote left the four justices divided: two in favor of admiralty jurisdiction and two against it. A tie—and in appeals, ties preserve the status quo. The writ of prohibition stayed in place.[117]

Gridley "then claimed an Appeal to the king and Council."[118] The success of his motion depended upon the Superior Court's interpretation of the provision in the Massachusetts charter which authorized such appeals. That provision provided in pertinent part:

> We judge it necessary that all our subjects should have liberty of Appeal . . . in Cases that may deserve the same[.] We do by these presents . . . Ordain that in case either party shall not rest satisfied with a [judgment] . . . in any Personal Action wherein the matter doth exceed the value of three hundred Pounds Sterling that he or they may appeal to us . . . in our . . . Privy Council.[119]

Gridley's motion raised two questions. First, were the two clauses of the provision independent—the first giving the court *discretion* to grant appeals in cases that "may deserve it," and the second *requiring* it to do so when the matter exceeded £300—or did the second clause modify the first, requiring that, even in those cases deserving an appeal, the "matter" must exceed £300? The second question was whether the £300 threshold required an actual judgment of at least £300, or was a claim of at least that amount sufficient? Gridley argued that "the Charter should be liberally construed in Favour of Appeals."[120] Dunn's was "a Matter that deserved Appeal," and therefore, given what Gridley saw as the discretion granted by the first clause of the charter provision, an appeal should be granted.[121]

In rebuttal, Scollay's attorneys emphasized the charter provision's second clause, which, Thacher claimed, "seems evidently explanatory of the first, the Matter in Difference only is what is to be considered in giving Jurisdiction, and not the Suggestion of Damages."[122] To Otis, "by the plain Construction of the Words of the Charter, the Matter in Difference must necessarily be £300." He claimed that courts had consistently denied appeals "where there has been no Judgment for more than that Sum."[123] Gridley would not concede that an appeal must be denied unless there was a judgment in excess of £300. To him, that position made no sense: "The Construction, the Gentlemen on the other Side would give, seems to be providing Appeals only for the Defendant; upon their Principles, a Demurrer being to the Declaration, and Judgment against the Plaintiff, how can he ever appeal."[124]

All of the justices agreed that for an appeal to lie, the amount in controversy had to exceed £300. Oliver and Cushing seemed sure that the amount did not, and voted against appeal.[125] Lynde was "doubtful" as to the actual amount that could be considered in dispute, "but as I am in general against Appeals, I am against it in this case."[126] Hutchinson may have favored an appeal, but he was somewhat opaque on the point: "As for this case, whether it exceeds £300 or no, there is Difficulty. I am considering the Allegations, etc. in Favour of Appeal."[127]

If Hutchinson did favor appeal, he was alone. Dunn's motion was denied, but he and his attorneys did not go away.[128] They filed suit in the Suffolk County Court of Common Pleas. A jury awarded Dunn £700 for his troubles, a verdict that could not have come at a worse time for John Scollay[129] He already had more than enough problems. A successful merchant with "the Character of an honest Man," Scollay traded in ships and merchandise from his shop "near the Town-Dock."[130] From 1756 on, his fellow townsmen regularly elected him a Boston selectman, and the trust in him was such that he often was appointed a manager of public lotteries.[131] When Thomas Pownall left for a new post, Scollay was among a dozen or so other notables selected to wait on the former governor with a letter of gratitude.[132]

Then it all fell apart. In a diary entry dated January 19, 1765, merchant John Rowe noted a "very bad" day, "Mr. John Scollay shut up."[133] A victim of a financial crisis that gripped Massachusetts, Scollay, who, in James Otis's words had "over traded himself," went bankrupt.[134] Subsequently, Scollay's business and personal property were sold to pay his debts.[135] Now there was the need to appeal Dunn's jury award to the Superior Court. Fortunately for Scollay, the appeal went his way. As before, the primary issue was whether or not Captain Freeman's hostage ransom agreement bound the *Peggy*'s owners.[136] Apparently the first jury had believed that it did, but, on appeal, Dunn's judgment was reversed.[137] He left the courtroom with nothing but a bill for costs. Perhaps like many of you, John Rowe, who had been called to testify as a witness, "was very sorry the jury dismissed Capt. Dunn's action & think he has been vilely used."[138]

Jenny Slew v. Benjamin Whipple, Jr. (1766)

In *Slew v. Whipple*, Jeremiah Gridley found himself on the wrong side of history. John Adams's diary entry of November 5, 1766, described what was at stake in the case:

Attended Court [and] heard the Tryal of an Action of Trespass brought by a Molatto Woman, for Damages, for restraining her of her Liberty. This is called suing for Liberty: the first Action that ever I knew, of the Sort tho I have heard there have been many.[139]

The "Molatto Woman" was Jenny Slew of Ipswich in Essex County, a woman of mixed race in her fifties. In March 1765 she had bought suit in the county Court of Common Pleas alleging that on January 29, 1762, "John Whipple, Jun., of said Ipswich, Gentleman[,] . . . with force and arms, took her . . . , held and kept her in servitude as a slave in his service . . . from that time to the fifth of March last . . . without any lawful right & authority so to do." Slew sought £25 in damages.[140] The suit was something of a long shot. Jenny Slew was a poor black woman. Her adversary was a white man with money. John Whipple Jr. was a "Gentleman" from a family with Essex County roots dating back to the 1640s. A man of some means, Whipple retained Gridley and Edmund Trowbridge to defend him.[141]

Slew's lawyer was Benjamin Kent, the former clergyman who was nothing if not irreverent. It was his "delight," observed a young John Adams, "to tease a Minister or Deacon with his wild Conceits, about Religion."[142] Adams concluded that Kent "is for fun, Drollery, Humor, flouts, Jeers, Contempt. He has an irregular immethodical head."[143] But an older and (in 1759) wiser man, Benjamin Franklin, saw Kent's public persona as a kind of "inverted" hypocrisy, "with which a man is not so bad as he seems to be."[144] To Franklin, Kent "was an honest man and had his virtues."[145]

Kent often represented the poor, the outcasts, and the powerless—people like Jenny Slew.[146] His ability as a lawyer is an open question. There is no contemporary critique available. Perhaps it is significant that Adams—never shy about finding flaws in others—had nothing negative to say about Kent as a lawyer. In his *Sketches of the Judicial History of Massachusetts* (1840), however, Emory Washburn wrote that Kent "was not greatly distinguished in his profession."[147] There is, of course, another measure of Kent's competence. Did people hire him? As inexpensive and available as a lawyer may be, if he fails to get positive results, people will stop retaining him. This did not happen to Kent. Even Washburn acknowledged that Kent "acquired considerable popularity as an advocate and practiced with good success."[148] Court records bear this out. Kent "practiced with good success" for a long time. In 1738, when Gridley ranked eighth in the number of new actions in which an attorney's name was listed at the Boston sessions of the Superior Court, Kent ranked sixth. Twenty years later, in 1758, in the same court in Boston, Kent ranked fourth. In 1766, the year of the *Slew v. Whipple* case, Kent ranked fifth.[149]

In representing Jenny Slew, Kent had an advantage enjoyed by few other lawyers in the province: in 1752 he had represented a slave named Pompey in an action for his freedom against Benjamin Fanueil. In that case, Kent had convinced a jury of twelve white men that Fanueil had "unjustly" taken Pompey and "held [him] in servitude against his free will." The jury awarded Pompey his freedom, £180, and costs, but the case was reversed on appeal.[150]

In Jenny Slew's case, Kent's client had lost in the Court of Common Pleas, but it was a meaningless defeat. Apparently the parties sought to avoid the cost and delay of a trial before the inferior court, and acted to facilitate a quick appeal to the Superior Court.[151] On November 5, 1766, the matter came up for a pretrial hearing before the high court (with John Adams in attendance).[152] Arguing on Whipple's behalf, Gridley contended that Slew's complaint should be dismissed because it identified her as "Jenny Slew of Ipswich . . . , Spinster," but there was "no such person in nature as Jenny Slew of Ipswich . . . , Spinster."[153] Jenny had been "married" at least twice before, both times to slaves.[154] Citing precedent "that a Married Woman could not call herself Spinster," Gridley asserted that, in view of her marriages, Slew's complaint, which identified her as a "Spinster," was defective.[155] But he had a problem.

"An Act for the Better Prevention of a Spurious and Mixt Issue," a 1707 Massachusetts statute, made it illegal for whites to marry "any negro or molotto," while allowing marriage between a "negro" and "one of the same nation," that is, another "negro."[156] The problem was that Jenny Slew was of mixed parentage. She was neither a "white" nor a "negro" within the terms of the statute. She was a mulatto, and although Massachusetts law often treated blacks and mulattos the same, it also recognized a distinction between the two.[157] No doubt Gridley was aware of the 1707 statute and the difficulties that it presented if the court considered it in determining Slew's marital status.

If, for purposes of the statute, the court found Slew's race to be white, then her marriages to slaves were void, she was indeed a "spinster," and her complaint was not defective. Moreover, the finding also would entitle her to a judgment in her favor because, with the possible exception of convicted felons, people legally ruled to be white could not, under Massachusetts law, be held as slaves.[158] Therefore, Gridley stayed away from the provincial statute and looked instead to natural law, declaiming that "Marriage is the Law of Nations. Justinian extends it, even to the Brutes."[159] Gridley probably was relying on *Liber Primus,* Title 2, *De Juris Naturali, Gentium et Civill* of Justinian's *Institutes,* which states that the male-female union "which we term matrimony" is part of natural law, "which nature teaches to all animals," and animals other than humans "are considered as having knowledge of this law."[160] In essence, Gridley argued that although lower on the scale than whites, nonwhites were higher on that scale than animals, and according to natural law, even animals were capable of marriage. Therefore, Slew's relationships with two slaves, whatever their status might be under Massachusetts law, were marriages under natural law, and she was not a "spinster," the complaint was defective, and it must abate.

Four justices sat on the Superior Court that day to hear Jenny Slew's suit for freedom and Gridley's motion to dismiss her complaint.[161] "The writ did not abate," Adams noted, "2 judges for Abatement and 2 against it. So being divided could not abate."[162] Gridley next raised the question of whether the plaintiff had pleaded a sufficient action for trespass. He argued that Jenny Slew had never been free, and therefore, in enslaving her, Benjamin Whipple could not have forcibly deprived her of freedom:

> Shall Trespass be maintained? Shall not the Plaintiff who sues in Trespass for Goods be compell'd to prove his Possession and that it was by force taken out of his Possession. She has never been in Possession of her Liberty, she has been out of Possession of it for 50 years.[163]

Responding, Kent took the high ground. Using a classic forensic technique, he introduced a technically irrelevant argument by attacking the morality of slavery while, at the same time, maintaining that he was not going to address the subject:

> I shall not enter into the right of some men to enslave others. This Right in some Places seems established. Not indeed a Right to Life [or death], tho this is assumed in [the] West Indies to the shame of Human Nature.[164]

Moving on, Kent disputed Gridley's claim that Slew had never been free. He cited "evidence that Jenny Slew was commonly reputed to be the Child of Betty Slew a white Woman by a Negro Man."[165] Then he asked for proof that Jenny had been a slave, referencing an earlier case "where they pleaded in Bar that [a party] was a slave, and produced a bill of sale. Why did they not do so here?"[166] Kent's argument convinced the court. "This is a Contest between Liberty and Property—both of great Consequence," observed Justice Peter Oliver, "but Liberty [is] of most importance of the two.[167] Justice John Cushing found that Slew's color raised only a "presumption" of slavery, and that presumption was rebutted if she could show that her mother was white, because "Partus sequitur ventrem" ("the child follows the mother," that is, the child takes the mother's status).[168] In his opinion, "if a person is free he may bring Trespass at any Time."[169]

Jenny Slew's case survived Gridley's motions to dismiss. It went to the jury, which found in her favor.[170] The Superior Court reversed the lower court's judgment and held "that the said Slew recover against the said Whipple the sum of four pounds lawful money of this province Damage & costs taxed at £9.9s.6d."[171]

CHAPTER NINE

The Writs of Assistance
(1760–1761)

On Friday morning, September 12, 1760, Thomas Hutchinson encountered Jeremiah Gridley on a Boston street. The two men discussed the recent death of Stephen Sewall, the chief justice of the Massachusetts Superior Court. In the course of their conversation, according to Hutchinson's diary, the man he described as "the first lawyer at the Bar" unexpectedly told Hutchinson that Hutchinson "must be [Sewall's] successor." This suggestion "caused [Hutchinson] to think seriously upon it, for it was an employment which nothing but a diffidence of his qualifications for it would render unwelcome to him."[1] Although Hutchinson always maintained that after Sewall's death, "several gentlemen spake to me and told me they hoped the Governor would nominate me for his successor," he never mentioned Gridley by name.[2] Identifying Gridley as one of those "gentlemen" would have strengthened Hutchinson's claim to the judicial post, but Hutchinson, a man not insensitive to such things, may have been reluctant to expose the venerable lawyer to the clamor that followed his appointment as chief justice.

That clamor came from several sources. The province bar, increasingly self-conscious of its professionalism, was increasingly intolerant of lay judges.[3] While Hutchinson was a learned man with a great deal of judicial experience as a justice of the peace, judge of probate for

Suffolk County, and a judge on the Suffolk County Inferior Court of Common Pleas, he had no formal training in the law, and that was a problem.[4] Jeremiah Gridley may have believed that Hutchinson's lack of legal training did not disqualify him from the position of chief justice, but some of Gridley's fellow lawyers disagreed. Even before Hutchinson was named to the post, John Adams was fretting over the prospect of Hutchinson or any other nonprofessional rising to the highest judicial position in the province. Among his diary entries in the autumn of 1760, there is a draft of a letter to a newspaper in which Adams emphasized the necessity for a candidate educated in the law from "early youth" to fill the recent vacancy on the Superior Court:

> A Man whose Youth and Spirits and Strength, have been spent, in Husbandry Merchandise, Politicks, nay in science or Literature will never master so immense and involved a science [as law]. . . . Youth is the only time for lay[ing] the Foundation of a great Improvement in any science or Profession and that an Application in advanced Years, after the Mind is Crowded, the Attention divided, or dissipated, and the Memory in part lost will make but a tolerable Artist at best.[5]

Adams's attitude was shared by attorney Oxenbridge Thacher. In a pamphlet arguing against appointing Superior Court justices to the provincial council, Thacher sniped at the judges' lack of legal training. With mild sarcasm, he argued that if the justices sat on the council, they would have little time to study law. Every citizen had a right to expect a bench well versed in the law. It was mere foolishness to claim that the judges of the high court knew "so much law that they [could] not increase their knowledge."[6] Not all of the disgruntled lawyers were as indirect as Thacher. Seldom a man to mince words, James Otis Jr. thundered that if all the judges of the province were taken together, "they would not make one half of a common lawyer."[7] But then Otis had an axe to grind. His father, Colonel James Otis, had long aspired to a seat on the Superior Court but had lost out to Hutchinson.

When Stephen Sewall died in September 1760, Francis Bernard, the man charged with appointing Sewall's successor, had been in Massachusetts less than a month after arriving to replace Thomas Pownall as governor. A somewhat scholarly provincial English barrister,

Bernard sought a position in the colonial service as a means of meeting the financial needs of his large family.[8] His wife's uncle, the politically powerful Viscount Barrington, had used his influence to secure Bernard the governorship of New Jersey in 1758 and, two years later, that of Massachusetts. Bernard was no politician. More important, he had no understanding of the intricate, shifting political landscape of provincial Massachusetts.[9] That landscape became all the more unsettled and complicated whenever a new governor took the reins of power. Individuals, families, and interest groups jockeyed for favor with the new man, who was as yet an unknown quantity. His first political appointments were scrutinized as indications of the course the new governor might follow. Moreover, at any time the appointment of a new chief justice was an important one. It was a rare opportunity. There had been only three chief justices in the last thirty-two years. Now, after less than four weeks on the job, Governor Bernard had to deal with the politically sensitive task of appointing one.[10]

Bernard did not look to the Superior Court for Sewall's successor. Of the four remaining justices, Benjamin Lynde Jr. would have seemed the most obvious choice.[11] Fifty-nine years old, Lynde was the court's senior associate justice, having been appointed in 1746. Nevertheless, it appears that Lynde never was in the running, perhaps because, as noted earlier, the consensus was that he was a man of "slender" ability.[12] Justice John Cushing, a twelve-year veteran of the Superior Court, had a similar reputation.[13] Justices Chambers Russell and Peter Oliver were more highly regarded than their colleagues, but neither seems to have been considered for chief justice.[14] Both men were forty-seven, an average of fifteen years younger than every man but one previously appointed to the post.[15]

Among those practicing lawyers who had sufficient experience to merit consideration for the high court, there was only a limited selection. Apparently Gridley was never a possibility. Although well respected for his legal knowledge, he was a man of humble origins who had no judicial experience save as a justice of the peace, had never held a provincial office, and had only three years of service in the House of Representatives as a member from a relatively inconsequential community.[16] Most of the other senior members of the bar had equally disqualifying backgrounds.

Richard Dana not only wanted for judicial experience but also lacked a reputation for legal acumen.[17] As noted earlier, Benjamin Kent often represented unpopular clients and unpopular causes. Benjamin Prat was recognized as one of the province's leading lawyers, but he had no judicial experience and may have been too closely identified politically with Thomas Pownall, whom Bernard had replaced.[18]

Qualified or not, there were two well-known lawyers who actively sought a seat on the Superior Court: William Brattle and James Otis Sr. Although Brattle usually is mentioned as one of the aspirants, little is known of his pursuit of the appointment.[19] It was but the latest of Brattle's many pursuits. Upon his graduation from Harvard in 1722, this son of a prominent (and wealthy) Cambridge clergyman tried preaching. When that did not work out, Brattle turned to the practice of medicine with the same results. He then became a member of the bar, but was a mediocre lawyer.[20] By this time, however, he was achieving success in yet another pursuit. Brattle was a very good soldier. At age twenty-three he had been made a major in the militia. Four years later he published a manual on military drill, formations, and tactics.[21] Promotions followed—culminating in 1760 with his appointment as brigadier general and commissary.

Probably because of the value placed on military expertise in a time of war, Brattle was elected to the House of Representatives and then, in 1756, to the council.[22] Despite these achievements, Brattle was not widely respected and was sometimes the object of ridicule. On occasion his behavior could be quite strange. His "oddities, of mind," as Governor Jonathan Belcher termed it, led Belcher and others to consider Brattle "a queer fellow."[23] Many viewed him as a shallow intellect, and a contemporary probably summed up a common perception when he referred to Brattle as "a man of universal superficial knowledge."[24] Given all this, Governor Bernard was not about to waste political capital by making such a man chief justice of the Superior Court.

Nobody considered Colonel Otis "a queer fellow," but his candidacy also was problematical. Repeatedly elected by Barnstable to the House of Representatives, Otis had tirelessly promoted Governor Shirley's unpopular war measures. Through it all, Otis had been a strong political ally of Thomas Hutchinson, whom he considered a close personal friend.²⁵ Otis longed for a seat on the prestigious provincial council, or perhaps the Superior Court, but when he approached Shirley about it, the governor advised patience. Otis was too valuable in the House. He soldiered on. In 1756, when Shirley appointed Peter Oliver to the seat on the Superior Court left empty by the death of Richard Saltonstall, Otis accepted it with good grace and what he took as a promise that the next vacancy would be his.²⁶

The next year, however, Shirley was replaced as governor by Thomas Pownall. In the spring of 1757, while Massachusetts awaited Pownall's arrival, Otis relinquished his seat in the House of Representatives and made a concerted push for a place on the council. It failed. The House refused to elect him.²⁷ Then it got worse. When Otis went to Hutchinson for an explanation of what had happened, his erstwhile friend broke his heart. According to Otis's memorandum of the conversation, Hutchinson told the colonel that he was no longer of any use, because when Pownall arrived, wrote Otis,

> Hutchinson and Mr [Andrew] Oliver would Be [Pownall's] advisers and . . . they had a Bad opinion of my Conduct and . . . Mr Hutchinson . . . said that I never Did Carry things while in the [General] Court By any merit But only By Doing Little Low Dirty things for Governor Shirley such as Persons of . . . worth Refused to medle with and . . . Shirley made use of me as a Tool for his Purposes.²⁸

Otis blamed Hutchinson for his failure to obtain a council seat. His disaffection spread to Oliver, Shirley, and most of the old Shirley faction. He aligned himself with Shirley's enemies and sought Pownall's favor.²⁹ So did Hutchinson. Both had limited success. Pownall approved Hutchinson's appointment to replace the deceased Spencer Phips as lieutenant governor but kept him at arm's length. The governor approved Otis as speaker of the House, and promised him the next open seat on the Superior Court, but the colonel was nowhere nearer to the council, and before there was an opening on the court, Pownall left Massachusetts to be governor of South Carolina.³⁰

The court's next open seat, Chief Justice Sewall's, became available in September 1760, but there was an obstacle: Thomas Hutchinson.

Soon after Sewall's death, Colonel Otis's son James Jr. called on Hutchinson to discuss the vacancy on the court. What happened next became the subject of a controversy that raged for years. According to Otis, he informed Hutchinson about his father's desire to be appointed to the court, not as chief justice but as "the youngest Judge on the Superior Court." Otis told Hutchinson that he had heard that "it was a settled point" that the lieutenant governor would be the next chief justice, and if that was so, the Otises would not "expect his Honor's assistance." Otis claimed that Hutchinson had replied that while it was true that he had been approached about the appointment, "he had no Thoughts nor Desire of the Office." Then, again according to Otis, Hutchinson assured him "that Col. *Otis* had the best pretensions to be Judge" and "promised his Interest."[31]

Sometime after he had met with Hutchinson and before Bernard announced his final decision, Otis Jr. reportedly made a statement that has become part of the folklore of this period. Otis, so the story goes, declared that "if his father was not made a Judge, he would thro the Province into flames if it cost him his Life."[32] Tales of the purported incident gained immediate and widespread currency. Conservatives embraced accounts of the alleged threat, repeating them again and again. Hutchinson cited it in explaining why he could not support Otis Sr. for the Superior Court.[33] Attorney General Edmund Trowbridge and Governor Bernard repeated it in letters to London.[34] Justice Peter Oliver complained to John Adams that "for that one Speech, a Thousand other Persons would have been indicted."[35]

Years later, Otis attempted to disavow the statement, but his denial, printed in the *Boston Gazette* in 1763, was less than convincing. He did not unequivocally state that he never said the words attributed to him. He asserted instead, "I have not the least Remembrance of having ever used such Expressions in my life; nor do I believe I ever did."[36] Moreover, the purported statement sounds like something that Otis could have said. He was susceptible to such outbursts. Although the madness that destroyed his future did not fully manifest itself until years later, even in the early 1760s Otis was prone to unstable behavior. Andrew Oliver angrily observed to John Adams that Otis "will one Time say of [Thomas Hutchinson] that he had rather have him than any Man he knows . . . and the next Hour will represent him as the greatest Tyrant, and most despicable Creature living."[37]

It was not just Otis's enemies who were offended by his erratic conduct. After Otis unexpectedly and angrily sabotaged the bar's effort to restrict unsworn competition, his friend and political ally Oxenbridge Thacher was totally disgusted, advising his colleagues that "whoever votes for [Otis] to be any Thing more than a Constable let him be Anathema maranatha. I pamphleteer for him again? No. [I'll] pamphleteer against him."[38]

It is impossible to say how much this drama influenced Governor Bernard in choosing Thomas Hutchinson to be the new chief justice. In retrospect, the choice seems a bit surprising. One would think that, as a lawyer himself, Bernard would have opted for a member of the legal profession, and in fact, years later, Bernard expressed regret that he had selected a man "'not . . . bred to the law.'"[39] Nevertheless, there is no indication that, at the time when he made the decision, the governor had any qualms about it. Indeed it seems probable that Bernard had his eye on Hutchinson all along and that he never seriously considered James Otis Sr.[40]

Bernard may have seen Hutchinson as perfect for the job. Although Hutchinson lacked a formal legal education, he had served on the Suffolk County Court of Common Pleas, had a well-rounded education, wide-ranging experience in mercantile affairs, and a searching intelligence. To a governor new to Massachusetts, Hutchinson offered more than twenty years of unrivaled experience in provincial politics and "knew more about the dynamics of royal government that anyone else in the province."[41] In addition, the lieutenant governor was linked by class, family, and interest to some of the most powerful men in the province, men whom Bernard could ill afford to alienate.[42] Moreover, on a personal and intellectual level, unlike the less urbane Otis, Hutchinson was a man to whom Bernard could relate, with whom he could discuss literature and science over a glass of port by a fireside on a winter's evening.[43]

There also was the money. Bernard's salary as governor, which was controlled by the legislature, was not nearly enough to satisfy his needs and expectations. The real pot of gold was a product of the enforcement of the Navigation Acts. By law, the governor was entitled to a share of all moneys realized from the sale of seized contraband goods. Thus, it was in Bernard's best interest that the smuggling laws be strictly enforced. To accomplish this, a reliable hand on the tiller of the Superior Court was a necessity. With his firm commitment to the best interests of the empire, Hutchinson would provide that hand.[44] This motive was not lost on contemporaries. John Adams maintained that Bernard "appointed Hutchinson, for the very purpose of deciding the fate of the writs of assistance, and all other causes in which the claims of Great Britain might be directly or indirectly implicated."[45]

The validity of those writs, of course, was the subject of a hearing in 1761 which has been called "one of the greatest of all pre-revolutionary legal cases," a case that "may have been the most important legal event leading up to the American Revolution."[46] Jeremiah Gridley was there representing the Crown. The newly minted chief justice presided over the hearing in which the son of his rival, James Otis Jr., launched into an argument that "made [his] reputation."[47] Legend has it that Otis was "a flame of Fire" whose oration sent a "great crowd of spectators . . . away absolutely electrified."[48] In John Adams's words, "Then and there the child of Independence was born."[49]

What is curious about this iconic event is the amount of confusion that surrounds it. Questions abound. What exactly were these "writs of assistance," or even, whatever they were, was "writs of assistance" the proper name for them? How did the case get to trial? If Otis said some really significant things, what specifically did he say? How much of the language attributed to him actually was spoken by him, and if any, was it spoken by him at the hearing? Finally, there is Jeremiah Gridley's role. He represented the Crown, but was Gridley really working at cross-purposes to his client?

The writ of assistance was an important enforcement tool in the British colonial system. This system was based on a rather commonsense premise: England's colonies should benefit the mother country. That benefit might be strategic, as with outposts like Gibraltar; political, as a holding area for potential troublemakers like separatists; social, as a dumping place for convicts and debtors; and, most important, economic. To derive economic benefit from its colonies, England relied on the Acts of Trade, a "coherent body of legislation, enacted between

1660 and the American Revolution, which regulated the flow of colonial trade, laid duties on some aspects of it, and established a system of enforcement."[50] Designed to benefit English merchants and shipbuilders, these acts provided that only English- or colonial-built, owned, or manned vessels could engage in the colonial trade, that certain "enumerated" colonial goods could be shipped only to England or another British colony, and that most foreign goods shipped to the colonies had to originate in English ports. Prior to 1764, in keeping with this design, the duties levied in Massachusetts and the other British North American colonies were intended not to raise revenue but rather to encourage colonial production of certain commodities and to promote trade with England.[51]

Violations of the trade regulations could bring a wide range of penalties. Noncompliance with administrative rules brought relatively small fines. Violations of more substantive statutory requirements could result in the forfeiture of ship and cargo. While in England the Court of Exchequer had jurisdiction of such offences, in Massachusetts, the Vice Admiralty Court had jurisdiction of many of them.[52] In 1760, the enforcement of the Acts of Trade in the northern mainland British colonies was entrusted to a surveyor general, who was answerable to the commissioners of the customs in England. There were two customs districts in Massachusetts: Boston and Salem-Marblehead. In addition to support personnel, the Boston district was composed of a collector, who had full responsibility for enforcing the Acts of Trade and Navigation; a controller, who acted "as a check on the activities of the collector" by keeping his own set of books; and a surveyor-searcher, who was responsible for actual inspection and control activities. Salem-Marblehead had only a collector.[53]

Parliament provided the customs officers with search powers to carry out their duties. The Act to Prevent Frauds and Concealment of his Majesty's Customs of 1660 gave them authority to search for offending goods without risking an action for trespass. The act required the customs officer to swear on oath that no duty had been paid on the goods in question.[54] The warrant that then issued enabled the officer, with the assistance of a local magistrate or other peace officer, "to enter any House in the Day-Time where such Goods are suspected to be concealed, and in case of Resistance to break open such Houses, and seize and secure the same Goods so concealed."[55] In practice, the 1660 act proved unsatisfactory. The customs officers had no way of compelling reluctant peace officers to assist them, and, more significant, complying with the procedure required to obtain the search warrant gave ample time for the contraband to be relocated.[56]

Parliament addressed these drawbacks in Section 5(2) of the Act of Frauds of 1662, which provided in pertinent part:

> And it shall be lawful to or for any Person or Persons, authorized by Writ of Assistance under the Seal of his Majesty's Court of Exchequer, to take a Constable . . . or any other publick Officer . . . , in the Daytime to enter . . . any . . . House . . . or other Place, and in Case of Resistance to break open Doors, Chests, Trunks and other Package, there to seize . . . any Kind of Goods or Merchandise whatsoever, prohibited and uncustomed.[57]

Three things should be noted about Section 5(2). First, it refers to a "Writ of Assistance." There has been scholarly debate over whether the writ in question is more accurately termed a writ of *assistance* or a writ of *assistants*. Although the statute and most eighteenth-century Englishmen referred to them as writs of "assistance," Jeremiah Gridley insisted that "this is properly a Writ of Assist*ants*, not Assistance."[58] He probably was right. Apparently, "assistance" was an archaic form of "assistants"—a body of official helpers.[59]

Second, contrary to many accounts, the writ of assistance authorized by the 1662 act was not a search warrant.[60] The writ itself did not give a customs agent authority to search anything. The writ merely referred to such power given elsewhere, in particular, in Section 5(2) of the 1662 act.[61] The writ of assistance ordered peace officers, if so requested by a customs officer, to assist him in making a search, including, if necessary, forcibly entering buildings and seizing goods. In practical terms, however, this was a distinction without a difference. Like a warrant, the writ put the law's imprimatur on the custom man's search, and made any attempt to resist that search unlawful.[62]

Finally, Section 5(2) of the authorizing statute was silent as to the requirements to obtain a writ of assistance, its limitations, and its duration.[63] Did it require a sworn statement showing probable cause? Was it limited to specific items in a specific location? Was it "returnable," that is, did it require a showing from the customs officer of what had happened as a result of the search? These questions were the ones that triggered opposition to the writs of assistance and led to the battle in the Massachusetts Superior Court as to the propriety of that court's granting them.

The Superior Court had done so before. Beginning in 1755, it had routinely granted writs of assistance to customs officers as part of a general plan to tighten up a system that was leaking like a sieve.[64] Smuggling and other illegal trading were rampant.[65] Too many customs officers were apathetic or corrupt. In Boston, smuggling was a common and respected business. For decades, the officials there who were charged with enforcing the Navigation Acts were allied with merchants in finding the most effective way to evade those laws (to the benefit of all concerned).[66] In the mid-1750s, however, this began to change. The transformation resulted from a combination of changes in thinking, institutions, and personnel. Some of these alterations occurred at the imperial level, others locally. Perhaps the most significant development was the recognition in London that the system simply was not working the way it was supposed to work. This recognition was coupled with one even more significant: colonial trade with France and Spain, which was merely unlawful during peacetime, amounted to treason when Britain was at war with those nations.[67]

The shift in attitude in London would take years to result in concrete reforms, but change was in the wind and this became apparent in Boston.[68] The power of the Vice Admiralty Court, which tried cases without a jury and was quick to order forfeitures for customs violations, was increased. Historically, the court's power to try customs cases had been limited by the province's common law courts through their use of the writ of prohibition, which commanded the admiralty court to surrender jurisdiction.[69] This crippled customs enforcement because the juries in these courts, often sympathetic to the accused smugglers, seldom convicted them. Governor Shirley set out to keep more cases in that court, and thus strengthen customs regulation and better secure the sale of seized ships and cargos from the proceeds of which he was entitled to a share as governor. In 1752 he appointed Chambers Russell to a seat on the Superior Court, and elevated Justice Stephen Sewall to chief justice. Russell, who was the judge of the Vice Admiralty Court, could be expected to protect that court's jurisdiction from writs of prohibition, and the well-respected and evenhanded Sewell would make sure that juries received instructions that limited their ability to nullify the effect of the Navigation Acts.[70]

Customs enforcement in Boston also changed when, in 1752, Charles Paxton became surveyor and searcher.[71] Paxton was a man on the make, and the way to make it in the customs department was through the sale of seized contraband. The more contraband that Paxton seized, the more money he received. Paxton was very effective at his job.[72] He developed an extensive web of spies and informants who supplied him with information about which vessels were violating the law and where contraband might be stored.[73] Writs of assistance enabled him to seize the goods without the usual common law procedure.[74] Obtaining a writ from the Superior Court was merely a matter of asking for it. A sworn statement as to purpose, time, location, and probable cause was not required.

For example, when Paxton applied for a writ from the Superior Court in June 1755, he merely stated that he was the surveyor of the Port of Boston and could not "fully Exercise said Office in such Manner as his Majesty's Service and the Laws in such Cases Require Unless Your Honours . . . will please to Grant him a Writ of Assistants."[75] The writ that the court granted Paxton, like all writs of assistance, was effective until six months after the sovereign died and was general in form. It commanded "all and singular Justices of the Peace, Sheriffs, Constables" and "all other officers and subjects" to permit, aid, and assist Paxton and his deputies

> from Time to time at his or their Will as well in the day as in the Night to enter and go on board any Ship, Boat or other Vessel. . . . And also . . . to enter and go into any Vaults, Cellars, Warehouses, Shops or other Places to search and see whether any Goods, Wares or Merchandise . . . are or shall be there hid or concealed.[76]

As a result of Paxton's vigorous prosecution of the Navigation Acts and the increased jurisdiction of the Vice Admiralty Court, the amount of merchandise seized and sold by Boston customs increased significantly in the late 1750s.[77] No one was exempt. In April 1760, customs officials seized the brigantine *Sarah*, which belonged to John Erving, a wealthy member of the council.[78] What made it worse for Boston smugglers was that their competitors in Rhode Island were subject to no such impediments. There was nobody like Paxton among Providence's customs officers. Content to live in peace with the mercantile community, they rarely bestirred themselves to search out contraband. In the few instances when they did so, they did not employ writs of assistance, and the malefactor usually escaped unscathed because, in Rhode Island, such cases were heard not by a judge in admiralty but by sympathetic juries in common law courts.[79]

Boston's merchants needed a champion. They got two of them. The first was one of the oddest characters in early American history. Benjamin Barons was an English merchant who, in 1750, saw one of his ships confiscated by Boston customs officials for trade regulation violations. Nine years later, through the wonders of English patronage, Barons arrived in Boston as the collector of the port's customhouse, the head man, the officer charged with enforcing English trade regulation laws.[80] Like Bernard and Paxton, Barons saw his public office as a road to wealth but differed in the manner in which that road should be taken. Barons believed more could be gained by working with the merchant community than by working against it.[81] As he put it, "I don't want to distress the people here" but would "rather be upon such Terms with them, as that [I] might at any time when [I] pleased go and drink a Glass of wine with them."[82]

Barons had no use for the "devilish and Confounded" Vice Admiralty Court, and he loathed Charles Paxton, who he thought was unethical, especially when it came to dividing the fruits from the sale of contraband.[83] This last put Barons on a collision course with Paxton and his chief supporter, Governor Bernard. Under the Navigation Acts, the receipts from the sale of forfeited contraband usually were divided three ways: a third to the customs officer, a third to the governor, and a third to the Crown. The Molasses Act of 1733 was an exception. Under this act, which levied a duty on foreign molasses, the Crown's share went to the province.[84] Sometime in the late summer of 1760,

Barons discovered documents which showed that the admiralty court routinely deducted the costs of Paxton's informers and other administrative expenses solely from the province's third and not equally from all three shares.[85] Instead of dealing with this information internally, Barons "carried the same copies all over Town Shewing them to the merchants of the Town with his remarks upon them to inflame the Minds of the people against [Paxton]."[86]

On December 17, 1760, a group of merchants signed a petition to the General Court demanding that suit be brought against Paxton to recover the money wrongfully taken.[87] James Otis Jr., who had resigned or was about to resign as advocate general of the Vice Admiralty Court, was at the meeting. The merchants had their second champion.[88] They selected Otis to present their petition to the House of Representatives. The House approved a lawsuit against Paxton, the council agreed, Governor Bernard reluctantly signed off, and the province treasurer filed a complaint against Paxton.[89] Meanwhile, on February 17, 1761, many of the same merchants filed a petition in the Superior Court, requesting a hearing on their objection to the writs of assistance. And that is how the writs of assistance case was initiated—or was it?

Like so many aspects of the case, its origin is unclear. According to John Adams, who is the primary source for most of what is known know about the case, it did not begin in February 1761 in Boston. In his autobiography, written about forty years after the fact, Adams maintained that the case began three months earlier at the Superior Court session in Salem, Massachusetts:

> An inferior Officer of the Customs in Salem whose Name was Cockle petitioned the Justices of the Superiour Court, at their Session in November for the County of Essex, to grant him Writs of Assistants. . . . Some Objection was made to this Motion and Mr. Stephen Sewall, who was then Chief Justice of that Court, and a zealous Friend of Liberty, expressed some doubts of the Legality and Constitutionality of the Writ, and the Power of the Court to grant it. The Court ordered the question to be argued in Boston, in February term 1761. In the mean time Mr. Sewall died and Mr. Hutchinson . . . was appointed . . . Chief Justice.[90]

Adams repeated this account, with slight variations, for the next fifteen years, and many historians have accepted it as generally accurate.⁹¹ It probably is not. There is no documentary evidence to support it. The records of the Superior Court mention no such application in Essex County in the autumn of 1760.⁹² Moreover, the account is riddled with inaccuracies. James Cockle was not, as Adams would have it, an "inferior Officer of the Customs in Salem." He was collector of customs for Salem and Marblehead, that is, the highest-ranking customs officer in those ports.⁹³ More significantly, Adams contended that when the issue came up before the Superior Court in November 1760, Chief Justice Sewall continued the matter to February 1761. Sewall could not have done this in November 1760. He died in early September of that year.

All things considered, it seems most likely that the writs case arose in February 1761. King George II died on October 25, 1760. Existing writs were good only until six months after the date of his death, news of which reached Boston on December 27, 1760. Paxton probably applied for a new writ at the February session of the Superior Court in Boston.⁹⁴ When the merchants learned of this, encouraged by Otis and Barons, they filed a petition with the court on February 17, 1761, that "they may be heard . . . upon the subject of Writs of Assistance."⁹⁵ In response to the merchants' petition, Thomas Lechmere, the surveyor general of customs for the northern colonies, filed a memorial requesting to be heard "upon the same Subject: And that Writs of Assistance may be granted to him and his Officers, as usual."⁹⁶ As the editors of the *Legal Papers of John Adams* concluded, the "proceeding seems to have gone forward as a hearing on these petitions, rather than on the application of any single officer."⁹⁷

Before we move on to that hearing, it should be noted that although Adams's assertion that Chief Justice Sewall first heard the application for the writs in Salem probably is inaccurate, his statement that Sewall "expressed some doubts of the Legality and Constitutionality of the Writ" may be correct.⁹⁸ While there is no evidence as to whom Sewall expressed these "doubts," apparently he did not keep them to himself. According to Thomas Hutchinson, in February 1761, when James Otis requested time to argue against the writs, his motion "was the more readily complied with, because it was suggested, that the late chief justice, who was in high esteem, had doubts of the legality of such writs."[99]

James Otis represented the merchants in the writs of assistance case. There is evidence that they turned first to Benjamin Prat, a brilliant lawyer.[100] Prat refused their request. He also declined that of the customs office.[101] At the time, Prat was under consideration for an appointment as chief justice of the province of New York. Most likely he did not want to diminish his chances by being identified with either side in such a contentious dispute.[102] Otis had no such reservations. In giving up his position as advocate general, Otis had abandoned, in Adams's opinion, "a sure road to the highest favors of government in America."[103] Adams claims that when the Boston merchants offered Otis "rich fees; he engaged in their cause, but would accept no fees."[104]

On February 17, 1761, when he appeared in court to do battle, Otis was not alone. He was joined by Oxenbridge Thacher. Because they took the same side of the case, Thacher and Otis have been referred to as "co-counsel," but that may not be quite accurate. According to Adams, Otis appeared for "the inhabitants of Boston," and "Mr. Thacher was joined with him at the desire of the Court."[105] Moreover, Thacher began his presentation by saying, "In obedience to the Order of this Court I have searched with a good deal of attention all the antient Reports of Precedents."[106]

In *The Writs of Assistance Case,* W. H. Smith notes that Thacher's opening leaves the "impression . . . that Thacher was not so much spokesman for the petitioners as *amicus curiae* [friend of the court], whose function was less to argue on one side or other than to help the court with his learning."[107] Smith contends that this role "would have been consistent with a lay bench, embarrassed by doubt, wishing to have the writ of assistance researched by a professional."[108]

Perhaps, but it is unlikely that the Superior Court justices viewed themselves as a "lay bench." Among the five of them, the justices had more than seventy years of judicial experience.[109] Moreover, it is difficult to think of the formidable Chief Justice Hutchinson as "embarrassed by doubt" over any intellectual problem, legal or otherwise. It seems probable that Hutchinson was the one who made the decision to enlist Thacher, and that he may have done so for political reasons.

The chief justice must have been aware of the charged atmosphere surrounding the writs case, and the fact that many viewed him as a partisan who would not permit a fair hearing on the writs and would ignore the law in order to reach a decision favorable to the Crown. It could be that Hutchinson tapped Thacher in the hope of disarming these critics. No doubt Hutchinson considered Thacher an able lawyer capable of doing a solid job in researching "all the antient Reports of Precedents," but it was more than that.[110] Thacher held something of a unique position. While some "considered" him "on the side of government," nevertheless his fellow Bostonians regularly elected him to responsible municipal offices.[111] Adams probably was not grossly overstating the situation when he gushed that "this gentleman was universally beloved for his learning, ingenuity, every domestic and social virtue, and conscientious in every relation of life."[112] In sum, nobody could accuse Hutchinson of appointing a toady. Moreover, even if Thacher argued against the writs, it did not matter. Whether he was going to decide the case solely on the merits or blindly support the Crown, Hutchinson was going to do what he was going to do, but in choosing Thacher to take part, the chief justice invested the proceedings with a needed air of credibility.

Jeremiah Gridley was the third member of the trio of lawyers who appeared before the Superior Court at the February hearing. First option or not, Gridley was a solid choice. In 1761 he generally was recognized as the dean of the Suffolk County bar.[113] Like all of the prominent attorneys in Boston, Gridley listed many merchants among his clients but had displayed conservative leanings. It was not that long ago that Gridley had been one of Lord Loudon's strongest supporters in the House of Representatives.

There is no official record of the February 1761 writs of assistance hearing, but John Adams was present in court and took notes. Adams was young, he was excited, and his contemporaneous scribblings reflect that youth and excitement.[114] They are incomplete, often cryptic, and sometimes inaccurate. Fortunately, Adams recognized these failings. Two or three months after the hearing, with time to collect his thoughts, he wrote another account of the hearing. This "Abstract," as he styled it, contains information that cannot be found in his notes, and is a far more finished product in both style and content, a fact not lost on his friends.[115] Upon reading it, Colonel Josiah Quincy chided Adams for his account of Gridley's presentation:

> Did you take this from these Gentlemen as they delivered it? You can do any Thing! You can do as you please! Gridley did not use that Language. He never was Master of such a style. It is not in him.[116]

M. H. Smith speculates that the "improvement" of Adams's "Abstract" over his notes may be due to the fact that Otis and, perhaps, Gridley reviewed those notes and suggested, or even drafted, changes to them.[117] That seems unlikely. In the spring of 1761, the twenty-five-year-old Adams held both Otis and Gridley in esteem verging on awe. Adams promised himself, "with steady Resolution and an aspiring Spirit," to win their "Applause and Admiration."[118] If, in fact, Gridley and Otis contributed to his "Abstract," it is curious that Adams made no mention of their involvement in either his diary, his autobiography, or his numerous letters about the writs case. It seems most likely that Adams was guilty of taking his own "artistic license" with regard to any embellishment of his account.[119]

The writs arguments began on Tuesday, February 17, 1761, and likely continued for several days.[120] It appears that Gridley went first, presenting the government's brief for the legality of the writs.[121] Then Thacher and Otis had their say, and Gridley spoke again in rebuttal. Adams took few notes on Gridley's opening argument, giving his rebuttal much more comprehensive treatment. His "Abstract" seems to meld the two together.[122] To judge from these sources, Gridley's argument was well organized and straightforward. He noted that it had been the regular practice of the Court of Exchequer in England and the Superior Court in Massachusetts to grant writs of assistance such as those at issue in the instant case. To Gridley, this practice and the merchants' petition raised two questions: First, was it legal for the Exchequer to issue the writs, and second, if it was legal for the Exchequer to do so, was it legal for the Superior Court to do the same?[123]

Gridley argued that the act of 1662 "established this Writ almost in the words of the Writ itself," making it lawful for any person *"authorized by Writ of Assistance under the seal of his Majesty's Court of Exchequer"* to enlist public officers to search any place and seize prohibited goods.[124]

He asserted that by the 1660 and 1662 acts, "all the powers in the Writ of Assistance mentioned are given, and it is expressly said, the persons shall be authorized by Writs of Assistance under the seal of the Exchequer."[125] Therefore, it was clear that the English Court of Exchequer had "a power by Law of granting these Writs" and, Gridley contended, the Act for preventing Frauds of 1696 gave revenue officers in the British colonies the same powers "as provided for the Officers of the Revenue in England."[126] While acknowledging that writs of assistance under the seal of the Court of Exchequer "will not run here," Gridley maintained that they could be granted by the Superior Court pursuant to the province statute which gave that court cognizance of all pleas and other matters to the same extent "as the Courts of King's Bench, Common Pleas and Exchequer."[127]

Finally, Gridley addressed the issue that was the crux of the opposition to the writs: that they were so easy to procure, and so expansive in scope and duration, that they took away "the common privileges of Englishmen." While acknowledging that this was "true," Gridley observed that it was not unique. Englishmen lost such privileges "in Cases of Crime and fine."[128] Unfurling the Union Jack, he proclaimed that such a deprivation was necessary for the good of the nation:

> Tis the necessity of the case and the benefit of the Revenue that justifies this Writ. Is not the Revenue the sole support of the Fleets and Armies abroad, and Ministers at home? Without which the Nation could neither be preserved from Invasions of her foes, nor the Tumults of her own Subjects. Is not this I say infinitely more important, than the imprisonment of Thieves, or even Murderers? Yet in those Cases 'tis agreed Houses may be broke open.[129]

Gridley concluded by reminding the court that such powers were not alien to Massachusetts. Province law permitted a tax collector to seize the property of a suspected delinquent, or when there was no property, to imprison him until the matter could be adjudicated. "The necessity of having public taxes effectually and speedily collected," he argued, "is of infinitely greater moment to the whole, than the Liberty of any Individual."[130]

The Writs of Assistance (1760–1761)   145

Thacher followed Gridley. According to Adams, Thacher argued with his "usual Sobriety, Ingenuity, and Fluency."[131] Nevertheless, Adams did not give him much copy. This probably was because Thacher limited his presentation to the Superior Court's power to issue the writs, which he called the "most material question." Thacher claimed that in a previous case, the Superior Court had "renounc'd the [Chancery] Jurisdiction which the Exchequer has in Cases where either party was the King's Debtor."[132] He also asserted that the situation in Massachusetts differed from that in England, where customs officials were officers of the Court of Exchequer "under the eye and Direction of the Barons and so accountable for any wanton exercise of power." In Massachusetts, however, customs officers were not answerable to the Superior Court, the court that issued the writs. With no provision for judicial review, customs seizures amounted to "wanton exercises of power."[133]

James Otis was next. His argument is so clouded in myth—much of it created by John Adams—that there is no way of knowing with certainty what he said or how well he said it. The confusion begins with Adams's "Abstract," about a third of which has little to do with the writs at all. It is all about Otis's self-declared patriotism in opposing "the worst instrument of arbitrary power, the most destructive of English liberty, and the fundamental principles of the constitution."[134] Curiously, the Otis depicted in the "Abstract" seems aware of this anomaly when, after expressing his willingness "to sacrifice . . . life itself" for his country, he says, "In the mean time I will proceed to the subject of the writ."[135] Finally!

Otis's argument hinged on the differences between special warrants, which required application under oath and were limited as to duration, place, and objective, and the writs of assistance, which required no oath and included no such limitations. To Otis, an Englishman's right to be secure in his home was one of "the Fundamental Principles of Law," which could be encroached only in "Cases of great public Necessity."[136] Nevertheless, and here Otis cited the act of 1660, such encroachment could be only by

> *special writs, directed to special officers, . . . to search certain houses . . . [granted] upon oath . . . by the person, who asks, that he suspects such goods be concealed in* THOSE VERY PLACES HE DESIRES TO SEARCH.[137]

Because the writs of assistance were general, not "special writs," their use to invade the sanctity of a man's home violated the English constitution.

Otis maintained that while the older authorities, to which Gridley had alluded, might contain precedents for general warrants, "in more modern books, you will find only special warrants . . . and you will find it adjudged *that special warrants only are legal*."[138] Then Otis went further. Where fundamental rights were concerned, legal precedent, even statutory mandates, were irrelevant. "Had this writ been in any book whatever it would have been illegal," Otis declared. "ALL PRECEDENTS ARE UNDER THE CONTROUL OF THE PRINCIPALS OF THE LAW."[139]

Otis dramatically laid out the Superior Court's duty:

> No Acts of Parliament can establish such a writ; Though it should be made in the very words of the petition it would be void. "AN ACT AGAINST THE CONSTITUTION IS VOID."
>
> It is the business of this court to demolish this monster of oppression, and to tear into rags this remnant of Starchamber tyranny.[140]

When the attorneys had concluded their presentations, the Superior Court was confronted with two different arguments against the writs of assistance, based on different premises and requiring different relief. Thacher had attacked the writs on the ground that the court lacked the power to issue any writ, general or special, and that any search using that writ was invalid. Otis's argument was directed only at writs of assistance as general writs, which, he contended, violated the fundamental rights of Englishmen and thus were invalid. Theoretically, given Otis's position, the court could issue special writs of assistance that would be valid, but no matter. Given the "cumbersome" procedure required for its issuance, and its limited scope, a special writ of assistance would not be worth the effort to obtain it.[141]

Otis understood this fact and so did Hutchinson. The chief justice perceived that the problem of special writs went beyond just the added effort to procure them. Requiring such writs would destroy Paxton's network of spies and eliminate the element of surprise so necessary for effective customs enforcement. Special writs, Hutchinson observed, "would rarely, if ever, be applied for, as no informer would expose himself to the rage of the people."[142] In view of this reality, the chief justice was troubled by Otis's claim "that the late practice in England was that . . . [writs of assistance] issued upon special information only."[143] The rest of the court shared Hutchinson's concern. The efficacy of the entire customs system in Massachusetts was threatened. According to Hutchinson, some of the justices seemed to "doubt whether such [general] writs were still in use in England," and if the court had decided the case then and there, "it is uncertain on which side it would have been."[144]

After some debate, the chief justice "prevailed" upon his colleagues to "suspend" judgment while he endeavored "to obtain information of the practice in England."[145] Hutchinson requested William Bollan, the province's agent in London, to ascertain "whether such writs of assistance were issue[d] from the exchequer except upon special information, & confined either to particular houses or to particular goods of which information is made."[146] On June 13, Bollan sent Hutchinson "a copy of the writ of assistance taken out of the court of exchequer."[147] The writs used in England were not specific as to place or occasion and were provided "out of course" to customs officers "without any affidavit, or order of the court."[148]

Apparently Bollan's letter and its enclosure gave Hutchinson the ammunition necessary to persuade his fellow justices that the Superior Court should issue the writ. He also may have shown the copy of the English writ to the House of Representatives and the council.[149] All of this made the second hearing something of an empty exercise with the result a foregone conclusion. By the time the matter came up before the court on November 18, John Adams, who had so eagerly chronicled the February hearing, took no notes. In fact, he may not even have been there. Four days earlier, "upon a motion made by Jeremy Gridley, Esqr.," Adams had been sworn in as an attorney of the court, an event he dutifully recorded in his diary. There is nothing in there, however, about the second writs hearing.[150]

Fortunately, Josiah Quincy, Jr., then a student at Harvard, was in court that day and recorded some of what transpired. Unfortunately, Quincy's notes reflect the fact that he was "absent . . . most of the Time" while Otis was speaking. All that can be gleaned from them about the man who apparently dominated the first hearing were Otis's references to English history and his claim that "this writ . . . is generally illegal" and never was constitutional in England, "much less here."[151] When his turn came, Thacher returned to the argument that the Superior Court lacked the power to grant any writ whatsoever, again asserting that, in a previous case, the court had "in the most solemn manner disclaimed the Authority of the Exchequer." He contended, as he had in February, that even if the Superior Court had the power of the Court of Exchequer, it did not, like that court, control the officers who used the writ or try the cases they brought.[152]

Then Thacher added something new. Attempting to make a case for "non-use," he maintained that although the Act for preventing Frauds (1696) had been around for sixty years, writs of assistance had not been applied for or granted in Massachusetts until 1756, and that such nonuse "is a great presumption that the law will not bear it." Hutchinson cut him short on this one. He pointed out that prior to the application to the Superior Court for the writ in 1756, the governor had frequently granted customs house applications for it. "Therefore," the chief justice concluded, "though [the governor] had no power to grant it, yet that removes the Argument of Non-user."[153]

The first attorney to speak for the Crown was new to the case. Robert Auchmuty had joined Gridley in presenting the brief supporting the writs. Auchmuty probably owed his involvement to his recent appointment as acting advocate general in admiralty, an appointment soon to become permanent.[154] His role was a small one. Briefly addressing Thacher's arguments, he asserted that no matter how their situations differed, the law invested the Superior Court with the same power as the Exchequer, and the court "must follow Law." He gave Thacher's nonuser argument short shrift: "That ends whenever the Law is once executed; and this Law has been executed in this Country."[155]

Gridley closed the Crown's case. He returned to the essence of the writ. It did not, he stressed,

> give the [customs] Officers a greater Power, but [served] as a Check upon them. For by this they cannot enter into any House, without the

Presence of the Sheriff or civil Officer, who will be always supposed to have an Eye over and be a Check upon them.[156]

Gridley mocked Otis's repeated references to passages in Rapin's *History of England:* "Quoting History is not speaking like a Lawyer."[157] Finally, he cited the 1696 "Act for preventing Frauds and regulating abuses in the Plantation Trade" for the proposition that if the writ "is Law in England, it is Law here," and the province law that "gave this Court Authority to grant it."[158]

"The Justices," Quincy wrote, "were unanimously of Opinion that this Writ might be granted, and some Time after, out of Term, it was granted."[159] The Crown had won. Gridley had won. Adams, who had witnessed much of Gridley's performance, gave him high grades for it. Writing a half century later, Adams described Gridley as arguing his brief "with his characteristic learning, ingenuity, and dignity and said everything that could be said in favor of [the writ]."[160] Historian M. H. Smith disagrees. In *The Writs of Assistance Case,* Smith maintains that "the case for the crown was not presented too effectively."[161] His criticism is not directed at Gridley's treatment of the question of the Superior Court's power to issue the writs, the question on which Thacher spent so much effort and some, especially in England, believed was the crucial issue in the case.[162] Smith grudgingly conceded that on this question, "the argument [Gridley] conjured forth was not without neatness."[163]

Smith's problem with Gridley's "case for the crown" was Gridley's linkage of the Statute of Frauds of 1662, which gave customs officers the power to request writs of assistance, with the earlier act of 1660, which required a sworn affidavit to acquire a search warrant and that the warrant be specific as to time and place. Smith sees this linkage as "wrong both in law and history."[164] Moreover, in his opinion, it played into Otis's hands. Smith contends that Otis's objective in his attack on general writs was to establish that the statutory power of entry identified with Section 5(2) of the 1662 Statute of Frauds (which introduced writs of assistance) was available "for the one sworn and specific occasion only, by dint of suitably regulated issuance of the writ of assistance it was contingent upon."[165] To do this, Otis had to convince the court that Section 5(2) should be regarded "as one" with the customs search warrant act of 1660, "in particular, the 1660 regime of issuance of warrants on sworn statements as to specific place and occasion should be fastened on to the 1662 writs of assistance."[166]

Smith considers this connection a "highly disputable proposition" for Otis to establish, but argues that when Gridley himself linked the two acts, he made Otis's task much easier. Otis was quick to take advantage of this "gift" when he pointed out Gridley's linkage to the court.[167] Smith may be right. Gridley's linkage may have provided Otis with a needed assist. That being said, it is easy to overstate its importance. The relationship of the two acts was a natural area of exploration. Whether Gridley pursued it or not, the ordinary rule of statutory construction which calls for statutes dealing with the same matter (*in pari materia*) to be construed together probably would have led the court to consider the relationship between the act of 1662 and the act of 1660.[168]

Whatever the proper statutory interpretation, even if Otis could show that general writs violated England's constitution, it did not matter. The writ that Bollan sent to Hutchinson graphically demonstrated that in England, writs of assistance were general in form and did not require sworn applications. There was no way that a provincial court in Massachusetts was going to overturn the interpretation of a statute sanctified by practice in England.[169] As the editors of the *Legal Papers of John Adams* explain, Otis's appeals to the "English constitution" were an attempt to limit the power of Parliament by applying seventeenth-century concepts that had been used in attempts to limit a despotic monarchy and, as such, came a century too late:

> By 1761, the doctrine of absolute parliamentary sovereignty, which is today the foundation of the British Constitution, had become generally accepted in England. As Blackstone said in 1765, "if the parliament will positively enact a thing to be done which is unreasonable, I know of no power that can control it."[170]

Not content with attacking Gridley's competence, Smith also questions his integrity. Smith argues that "Gridley's failure to come to grips with Otis's position . . . had more behind it than mere error as to what the writ really was."[171] Smith claims that Gridley's presentation made it appear likely that there was a "conscious equivocation in his attitude to the custom house brief."[172] Gridley's argument, Smith would have us believe, involved "a calculated lack of impact," a refusal to "pull out all the stops."[173] In boxing parlance, Gridley "took a dive." This claim cannot withstand scrutiny. The idea that Gridley would agree to present the Crown's brief in such an important case, and then act to sabotage it, is completely at odds with everything that Gridley was. He was a man ever in search of place and favor, never about to cross anyone he deemed to be in a position to advance his interests. Double-crossing the Crown had no upside for him. He simply would not have done it.

Yet Smith argues that that is exactly what Gridley did, and that Gridley did so because his sympathies "had always been broadly whig," and he believed that the writs were illegal.[174] The failure of Smith's hypothesis begins with its premise—that Gridley was "broadly whig." To support his position, Smith cites only the fact that in 1742, Gridley was nominated to be attorney general by the House of Representatives during the Land Bank controversy.[175] That this nomination necessarily made Gridley a "whig" in 1742 (or in 1761) is highly questionable, given the complicated issues involved in his nomination.[176]

Everything else Smith says about Gridley's politics cuts against his claim that Gridley was a "whig." Conceding, as he must, that Gridley's "['whig'] affiliations had been rendered suspect by his being 'the chief supporter of Loudon's war measures,'" Smith excuses this support because, according to Smith, Gridley was a colonel in the militia.[177] This was not so. At the time of the writs case, Gridley held no rank in the militia. He was not appointed a colonel until 1767, about a decade after Loudon had been relieved of command.[178] Moreover, Gridley's support of Loudoun's war measures included acting as the general's point man on the issue of forcibly quartering troops in the province, a question of constitutional dimensions. How far he was from being a "whig" on this issue is clear from his heels-in opposition to Thomas Hutchinson and Chief Justice Sewall, who had drawn up a protest "against his [Loudoun's] Demand . . . asserting their right as Englishmen & by Charter."[179] Finally, it is difficult to understand why, if Gridley was so "broadly whig," the customs office selected him to represent its interests in the writs case. Either no one took notice of what Smith sees as Gridley's obvious "whig" proclivities or no one cared about them. Neither possibility makes sense.

Smith concedes that Gridley's justification of general writs of assistance on the ground that the collection of taxes was necessary to pay for the defense of the nation is not one that a "whig" would make. In fact, Smith acknowledges that Gridley's conclusion that "the necessity of having public taxes effectually and speedily collected is of infinitely greater moment to the whole, than the Liberty of any Individual," appears to be "high toryism" of a "gross order."[180] One would think this an admittedly "strange sentiment . . . from a man of Gridley's [supposed] whiggish orientation," which might lead Smith to conclude that perhaps Gridley was not so "whiggish" after all, but no—Smith comes up with an explanation that is as unpersuasive as it is convoluted.[181]

Smith argues that these "out-of-character" statements did not reflect Gridley's true "whig" sentiments. Gridley did not really mean them. They were intended to be ironic.[182] Citing Gridley's statement that the revenue safeguarded by the writs of assistance was "the sole support of Fleets and Armies abroad . . . without which the Nation could . . . [not] be preserved from . . . the Tumults of her own Subjects," Smith contends that Gridley knew that this argument "might have seemed a doubtful benefit to colonists already apprehensive" that British troops would remain in America after the war was over, but used it to mock the Crown's justification for the writs.[183] This is nonsense. If Gridley was a "whig" seeking to torpedo the writs and resorted to this kind of irony, he was a fool. Irony always is a dangerous tool, especially in the superheated atmosphere of a courtroom during a controversial case. Too often the judge or the jury does not get the "joke" and takes what is said literally.

Gridley was not engaging in verbal gymnastics but, like any prudent lawyer, was saying exactly what he meant. Take the "Fleets and Armies" comment. It may be that colonists did not appreciate the need to fund the armed forces, but Gridley did. He was a firm advocate for the British military, supported Loudoun, had no use for deserters, and aggressively prosecuted colonists who sheltered them.[184] He was not being ironic.

Smith's claim that Gridley believed that the writs were unconstitutional is equally flawed. It is based on the statements of a Boston customs officer, Robert Temple, which were given in the suit that had been brought against Benjamin Barons, Boston's renegade collector of customs. In his deposition, Temple testified that Barons declared "that in his Opinion the Customs house Officers were not entitled to the writs of Assistance ... and that Mr. Gridley his lawyer was of the same opinion."[185] Thus, Smith was taking Temple's testimony about what Barons said that Gridley said as proof of what Gridley believed. Temple's statement about Barons's comment is classic hearsay and, like most hearsay, it is inherently unreliable. We do not even know for certain what it was that Gridley allegedly said. Temple himself acknowledged that he "doth not pretend to set forth the exact words said but only the meaning and purport of them as nearly to the words used as he can remember."[186]

The unreliability of the supposed comment is aggravated by its source. Benjamin Barons was far from a trustworthy one. Bernard claimed that he had never met a man so "wonderfully wrong-headed & so wantonly mischievous."[187] Even if Gridley actually said something like the words that Barons allegedly attributed to him, it is impossible to know what Gridley meant without knowing the context in which they were spoken. Furthermore, if Gridley told Barons that he did not believe that the customs officers were entitled to the writ, that does not mean that he would present the Crown's case with any less effort. He may have been merely leveling with Barons—a duty every lawyer owes to his client, even a loose cannon like Barons.

Smith concludes his attack on Gridley with the observation that a year after the writs case, the town of Boston appointed him to the school committee and asks, "How came it, the popular side of the writs of assistance case having been defeated, the advocate responsible seemed to have suffered no ill consequences."[188] Smith's conclusion: "Gridley himself could have put it around in private conversation that his advocacy of the writ of assistance was not all that it might seem."[189] Not likely. Gridley never would have "put it around" that he had not done his professional best in the case, first, because it was not true, and second, because it would have destroyed his reputation as a lawyer.

The reason that he "suffered no ill consequences" from his role in the writs trial was that, in 1761, Massachusetts was not yet the strongly divided, partisan place that it would soon become. Gridley's decades of honorable service had earned him the respect of his fellow citizens, who realized that in arguing in favor of the writs, Gridley was "simply doing his duty as the duly appointed attorney for the crown."[190]

Finally, if it was true, as Smith contends, that Gridley was "broadly whig," that he intentionally failed to represent the Crown in the writs case to the best of his ability, and that he broadcast this malfeasance all over Boston, why, in 1767, when Governor Bernard needed all the loyal support that he could muster, did he appoint Gridley attorney general?[191] The answer is simple: Smith's cynical speculation is baseless. John Adams had it right: "Mr. Gridley was incapable of prevarication or duplicity."[192]

Chapter Ten

Sugar and Stamps
(1762–1766)

Some regard the writs of assistance case as the first step on the path toward the American Revolution. It may have been that, but at the time, neither the participants, the provincial government, nor Massachusetts society in general seemed aware of its portent. As noted earlier, the divisions within the colony had not yet reached the point where partisanship was all-consuming. Nowhere was this more apparent than in the case of James Otis Jr., whose contentiousness with regard to the writs, John Adams believed, could have earned him the "vengeance" of the government.[1] Otis had attacked the writs with such inflammatory language that it was reasonable to assume that he and his family would have found themselves barred from future patronage. That did not happen.

In May 1762, only about six months after the Superior Court's decision in the writs case, Governor Bernard approved the election of Otis's father to the council.[2] This move was part of Bernard's plan to deal with some uncomfortable realities. Even before the second writs argument in November 1761, it was clear that the Otises, father and son, had become a powerful political force. The previous May, after the first hearing on the writs, James Jr. had been elected overwhelmingly to one of Boston's seats in the House of Representatives. His father was the House speaker, and their ally William Brattle, another disgruntled Superior Court aspirant, led the popular party in the council.³ A dispirited Thomas Hutchinson wrote to William Bollan that these three seemed "to carry all before them."⁴

The triumvirate took revenge for the parts played by the chief justice and his allies in the writs case. Angry at the Superior Court for its ruling, they piloted a bill through the General Court reducing the justices' salaries.⁵ Angry at Bollan's role in the court's decision, they engineered his replacement by Jasper Mauduit as the province's agent.⁶ Angry at the writs decision itself, the Otises introduced a bill that would have required an officer requesting a writ of assistance to identify the informer and the place to be searched.⁷ Bernard sought to woo the Otises into taking a less anti-administration position. Hutchinson believed that the governor "flattered himself" in his thinking that through cooperation and patronage "he should be able to reconcile to him, both [Otises] father and son."⁸ The governor, however, saw this as a necessary effort not only to improve his ability to get administration measures through the legislature, but also to lessen his dependence on the Hutchinson faction and diminish its power by using the Otises as a counterweight.⁹

For a while the strategy seemed to work. Bernard approved the reduction in the justices' salaries and, although he had a "good opinion of [Bollan's] Abilities & integrity," consented to the agent's dismissal.¹⁰ For its part, the Otis-dominated legislature readily passed the governor's supply bill, and none other than James Otis Jr. "appeared in favour of a grant, made by the assembly to the governor, of the island of Mount Desert," in "consideration of . . . his extraordinary services."¹¹ Bernard viewed this as "evident proof" that, he wrote, there was no "personal opposition to me."¹² Then, as noted, in May 1762, Colonel Otis was elevated to the council, leaving his son to manage the House of Representatives.¹³

This transition proved to be disastrous. Gone from the lower chamber were the colonel's years of political sagacity and readiness to compromise.¹⁴ In their place was his son's almost pathological hatred of Thomas Hutchinson, coupled with a growing emotional and political instability. The result was the younger Otis's alienation not only of the

Hutchinson faction but also of the governor. Otis and Bernard's administration soon seemed to be at odds about everything. First it was the governor's veto of Otis's writs of assistance bill with its stringent application requirements.[15] Then, when the General Court was in recess and Bernard unilaterally allocated money to increase the crew of the province warship in response to a petition from fishermen intimidated by French warships, Otis accused him of "annihilating one branch of the legislature."[16] The two also butted heads over who would replace the new province agent, Jasper Mauduit, should the ailing Mauduit resign.[17]

Jeremiah Gridley was not involved in any of this skirmishing. He did, however, play a small role in an interesting dispute. Israel Williams was a man so powerful in western Massachusetts that he was called the "Monarch" of Hampshire County.[18] In the spring of 1762, Williams requested a legal opinion from Gridley and the prominent New York attorney William Smith as to Governor Bernard's authority to grant Williams and some of his friends a royal charter to establish a college in Hampshire County. Like many in the Connecticut River Valley, he had grown frustrated with Harvard College. It was too far away and too close to Boston, "where Luxury and Wickedness . . . prevail'd."[19] Moreover, Harvard held "liberal religious views" that were unacceptable to the hard-headed Calvinists in the west.[20]

Gridley and Smith advised Williams that "a charter from Mr. Bernard under the Massachusetts constitution would not be good" because, in the province charter, the king had granted such powers to the General Court. They recommended that Williams present the matter to the legislature.[21] He did so, and it became a political football. James Otis Jr. knew that the issue would put his sworn enemy Thomas Hutchinson in a bind, because while the lieutenant governor was "ye idol of ye clergy," most of whom opposed the new college, he also was "in strict alliance" with his classmate and good friend Williams, who supported it.[22] Otis hoped to defeat the college, discredit Hutchinson, and win the backing of the Boston clergy, whose support Otis had been courting.[23]

In February 1762, the House of Representatives approved a bill to establish a college in Hampshire County. The council, every member of which was an ex officio member of Harvard's Board of Overseers, rejected the measure.[24] The council maintained that "the province could not support two universities, they would interfere with one another."[25] The council's, Gridley's, and Smith's opinions to the contrary, Governor Bernard signed the charter. He believed that "he had a right to give [the charter] as the King's Representative, and it was a royal right reserv'd to the Crown, which the [province] Charter the King had never given away."[26]

Charging that Bernard's actions in signing the charter constituted "an Infraction upon the Constitution," Otis persuaded a majority of a thin House to vote to inform the governor of its "desire" that he not "give [Williams] a Charter at present, if he had not done it."[27] But this alone did not defeat the charter. According to Oxenbridge Thacher, the "overseers of our college waked" and sent a remonstrance to Bernard, who "[gave] a gracious answer promising to vacate the charter."[28] Actually, he went a step further. As Quincy's *History of Harvard University* has it, Bernard promised "he would suspend the issuing of the obnoxious charter, and should not assist any application for a similar charter elsewhere."[29]

Throughout this period, James Otis Jr. and his allies repeatedly attacked Hutchinson and Bernard in the press.[30] Otis forcefully implied that Hutchinson had taken steps "to make the people of England look upon us in a very bad light, forward attempts to alter our constitution, and have a tendency to procure a standing army, to dragoon us into passive obedience."[31] Otis's violent attacks on Bernard and Hutchinson proved counterproductive, serving only to drive the two closer together. In addition, his railings against the threat of imminent tyranny failed to resonate with the public, which, now that he had lost all chances of Bernard's support, was essential to Otis if he hoped to be an influence in provincial politics. In the May 1763 elections, Hutchinson's partisans, newly strengthened by Bernard's patronage, won a resounding victory over Otis's "country Party" for control of the assembly.[32]

May 1763, however, brought news much more significant than the results of the provincial elections. The May 23 number of the *Boston Evening Post* carried the following notice:

> We also hear, that it has been proposed to lower the duties from French Molasses, from 6d. to 2d. per Gallon, in order the more Effectively to

secure the Payment; which was thought would be carried through before the Rising of Parliament.[33]

There was a good deal of contentious political history behind this seemingly innocuous news item, and despite its forecast of lower taxes, an even more turbulent political future lay ahead of it. It was all because of sugar. By the early decades of the eighteenth century, Europe had developed a sweet tooth, and the continent's demand for sugar had become almost insatiable. The sugarcane planters in the British, French, and Dutch West Indies did their best to fill this demand (and their pockets). In England, where they usually lived as absentee landlords, the British West Indian planters' wealth made them a political force with power hugely disproportionate to their numbers.[34] They were prepared to use that power, and not just against their French and Dutch competitors.

They also faced competition from their fellow British subjects in New England and the central colonies, where sugar cultivation was impossible. There, rum was the problem. It was made from molasses, and molasses was a byproduct of the eighteenth-century sugar-refining process. With as many rum distilleries as there were sugar plantations, the British West Indian plantations produced thousands of gallons of rum, most of which was profitably sold to thirsty colonials on the mainland.[35] Given such a lucrative market, it was inevitable that some of those thirsty colonials would turn to importing molasses and distilling their own rum. All they needed was a ready source of inexpensive molasses, and they found it.

To protect domestic brandy production, the French government prohibited French sugar planters from making rum. Eager to realize at least some money from the molasses created by the sugar-refining process, the French planters shipped it at a low price to Massachusetts and other British colonies where it became rum to compete with the British West Indian product.[36] Faced with this development, the English planters flexed their political muscle.[37] In 1733, Parliament enacted the Molasses Act, which placed a duty of sixpence per gallon on foreign molasses imported into British dominions.[38] Convinced that they could not make a profit if they paid the duty, most of the distillers in New England and the other northern colonies did not do so.[39]

Through the incompetence, indifference, or corruption of local customs officers, the duty was evaded on a wholesale basis, and by 1763, the Molasses Act had become all but a dead letter.[40]

But now this comfortable situation was threatened. The Molasses Act was due to expire in the spring of 1764, and Great Britain needed money.[41] The recent war with France had been very expensive, and some costs would continue, including an estimated £200,000 a year to maintain British regulars in the thirteen colonies to protect them from possible Native American attack.[42] The situation was aggravated by the fact that traditional sources of revenue were tapped out. It seemed logical to George Grenville, the new First Lord of the Treasury, to look to the colonies to foot at least some of the bill for their own defense. A revised Molasses Act seemed one way to do it.[43] The plan was simple: lower the duty on molasses to an amount that colonial importers would be willing to pay while increasing enforcement efforts to a level that left those importers with no viable option but to do so.

While the ministry debated what the new duty should be, it also began taking steps to tighten existing restrictions on colonial trade.[44] The enactment of "An Act for the further enforcement of His Majesty's Revenue of Customs" (1763) was a step in this direction.[45] To raise the price of bribery and encourage customs officers to enforce the law, the act significantly increased the officers' share of the amount netted from the sale of seized ships and contraband goods.[46] It also called for the employment of men-of-war off the coasts of the American colonies, and incentivized naval officers to hunt down smugglers by providing that all officers and crew of a ship that seized smuggled goods were entitled to a "Part of all and every Seizure."[47]

In a July 1763 circular letter to colonial governors, the secretary of state directed them to use the new act vigorously to prevent all illicit practices.[48] Nonresident colonial customs collectors who resided in England were ordered to their respective stations in America,[49] with instructions to enforce "in the strictest manner the strictest attention to their duties."[50] Local customs houses issued notices advising all masters of foreign ships carrying rum, sugar, and molasses that once they entered port, "proper Officers will be put on board such Vessels, to see that the [Molasses Act] be . . . fully carried into Execution."[51]

The ministry's efforts had an impact. "The publication of orders for the strict execution of the Molasses Act," wrote Governor Bernard in January 1764, "has caused a greater alarm in this Country than the taking of Fort William Henry did in 1757." The merchants, he noted "say there is an end of the trade of this Province; that it is sacrificed to the West Indian Planters."[52]

Meanwhile, the colonists still faced the fact that Parliament was preparing to modify the Molasses Act. As early as April 1763, the question of what could be done to protect colonial interests with regard to these modifications was the primary topic of discussion at a meeting of the Society for Encouraging Trade and Commerce within the Province of Massachusetts-Bay. Although predominantly composed of merchants, the society's membership was open to "others concerned in Commerce and . . . any other Persons of Ability and Knowledge in Trade who may be desirous to encourage the same."[53] Jeremiah Gridley was an active member.[54] While his involvement probably was a natural product of his penchant for joining and the fact that many of his clients were merchants, he also appears to have had a genuine interest in maritime commerce, as well as a concern for the safety and security of ships and the men who sailed them.

For example, in 1754, at the request of a group of ship captains, Gridley had obtained a charter from Governor Shirley incorporating their club as the "Marine Society" and wrote its bylaws.[55] According to its charter, "the principal ends of said Society are to . . . make navigation more safe" and "to provide for members and their families in poverty" or other "adverse accidents in life."[56] Turning his legal talents to the study of marine casualty law, Gridley advised provincial merchants and shipmasters to insure their ships and cargos in Boston rather than in England.[57] It was a good idea, but one ahead of its time. There simply was not enough ready capital in the colonies to cover potential losses. Even the relatively few colonial underwriters who offered marine insurance usually covered only a portion of the value of a ship or cargo and, acting as brokers, placed the remainder of the business in London.[58]

But back to the April 1763 meeting of the Society for Encouraging Trade and Commerce. At that meeting, the society appointed two members to draft a "State of the Trade," describing the burdens that the current Molasses Act imposed on the commerce of Massachusetts.[59] Loaded with statistics and written in a remarkably even tone, the completed analysis did just that.[60] In January 1764 the society sent a copy of the "State of the Trade" to the Massachusetts legislature and to merchants in other colonies.[61] The next month it sent the analysis, together with a cover letter, to William Bollan, the society's regular correspondent in London, and to 250 merchants in London with instructions for distribution.[62]

Given his active participation in the Society for Encouraging Trade and Commerce, his interest in things maritime, and his legal expertise, it is tempting to conclude that Jeremiah Gridley must have played some meaningful role in the society's efforts to influence the trade debate in London. This does not appear to be the case. He seems not to have been a member of the committee responsible for the "State of the Trade," and there is no evidence to indicate that he played a role in the document's creation.[63] This was not a coincidence. Doubtless by design, the "State of the Trade" contained no legal arguments, no appeals to the English constitution, and no citations to the province charter. It was authored by two merchants, and its argument was economic, in the belief that an appeal to Great Britain's commercial interest was the better way to go. It was all for naught. On April 10, 1764, when William Bollan received the society's letter, the "State of the Trade" was not enclosed.[64] But this was a loss without consequence. Five days earlier, on April 5, the American Revenue Act (commonly known as the "Sugar Act") had become law.

Although colonial attention was focused on the Sugar Act's treatment of the molasses duty, the act had much more to it than that. It was a comprehensive revision of the trade acts covering everything from pimentos to lumber to Asian textiles.[65] The act was aimed at "extending and securing the navigation and commerce between Great Britain and dominions in America" and "improving the revenue of this kingdom."[66] And there was more to come. Among the proposals that Grenville presented to Parliament for inclusion in the Sugar Act was one denoted "Resolution Number 15." It provided that "towards further defraying ... Expenses, it may be proper to charge certain Stamp Duties in said Colonies and Plantations."[67] The House of Commons approved the resolution, but a stamp tax was not included in the Sugar Act.

It is not clear why Grenville opted against its inclusion. Reportedly he told the Commons that he delayed because he was "desirous, as he expressed himself, to consult the Ease, the Quiet, and the Goodwill of the Colonies."[68] Later, while informing some colonial agents that he considered the stamp tax "an indispensable duty" which he would "certainly bring in" to Parliament, Grenville left the door slightly ajar. He told the agents that in the upcoming year he "should leave it to each province to signify their Assent to such a Bill in General; or their requests about any particular modifications of it as they should think fit."[69] Seizing upon this comment, the colonists ignored Grenville's obvious determination to levy a stamp tax, as well as the implications of his refusal to provide them with the information necessary to come up with an alternative. Instead, they convinced themselves that Grenville would consider proposals that would permit the colonies to tax themselves, an idea that he had specifically rejected in his meeting with the agents, and to which he never would have agreed.[70]

The colonial assemblies ordered their agents to, as Thomas Cushing instructed Jasper Mauduit, "oppose most strenuously any Stamp Duty."[71] The agents mobilized those English merchants active in the colonial trade against the proposal. They also inundated Parliament with petitions drumming on the colonists' rights as Englishmen and attacking the tax as an unconstitutional abuse of power.[72] For its part, however, the Massachusetts General Court acted cautiously. Cushing wrote to Mauduit, saying that the legislature

> expressly asserted their exclusive right of Taxing themselves and ... endeavored to prove that the Subjects have ought not to be taxed without their Consent either in person or by their Representative; They have not been so full and explicit upon this Head in their Petition least they should give offense to so respectable a Body as They are now applying to.[73]

This approach represented a grudging compromise between the House of Representatives, who "were clearly for making an ample and full declaration of the exclusive Right of the People of the Colonies to tax themselves," and the council, which, in language authored by Thomas Hutchinson, claimed only "the liberties and privileges which English subjects claim, of being taxed by their representatives" rather than "a right which exempted them from the authority of parliament."[74]

Their moderation made no difference. Parliament refused to consider any of the colonists' petitions.[75] Grenville was irrevocably committed to the stamp tax, and with only a few exceptions, Parliament shared that commitment. They were not convinced by the arguments of English merchants that the colonists could not afford the tax and that it would cause trade to suffer. They were incensed by colonial claims that the act was beyond parliamentary power. The act passed easily with no meaningful opposition.[76] It was signed into law on March 22, 1765, to take effect on November 1, 1765.[77]

The Stamp Act touched nearly every aspect of colonial life. It provided for taxes on ships' clearing papers, college diplomas, appointments to public office, bonds, grants and deeds of land, mortgages, indentures, contracts, bills of sale, apprenticeship articles, liquor licenses, dice, playing cards, pamphlets, almanacs, and fifteen classes of court documents. While most fees under the Stamp Act were lower in the colonies than their English counterparts, the £10 tax on attorneys' licenses was almost double the similar tax in England.[78] According to Thomas Whately, the act's chief architect, the higher fee in the colonies was intended "to keep mean persons out of those situations in life which they disgrace."[79]

From the ministry's point of view, the beauty of the tax was that it was virtually self-enforcing. Colonials either purchased and used the revenue stamps on documents that required them or those documents were invalid. There was no need for informers, revenue agents, searches, trials, or the rest of the elaborate administrative apparatus and procedures that bedeviled the collection of custom duties. In fact, all that was required was a stamp distributor and a few deputies for each colony.[80] Grenville took the selection of these distributors very seriously. To mollify the colonists, he opted for Americans to fill (and profit from} the posts.[81] The treasury chose men of integrity and stature in their communities. For Massachusetts, Grenville selected

Andrew Oliver, the province secretary and brother to Peter Oliver, Gridley's good friend. The choice pleased Thomas Whately. "I have always heard a great character of him," Whately commented. "I was glad that the office was given to so very respectable a person."[82]

News of the Stamp Act's passage reached Boston in early April 1765.[83] The collective psyche of the Massachusetts that received the news was somewhat fragile. The province's relationship with England had changed dramatically in the preceding years as the ministry endeavored to assert its authority after decades of benign indifference. The "Act for the further Improvement of his Majesty's Revenue" was being enforced with alacrity, and the province's attempts to forestall the passage of the sugar and stamp acts had failed ignominiously without its agonizingly crafted petitions even being considered by Parliament. Domestic politics had reached a new low in partisanship. It seemed that almost any issue could become a heated political dispute, and it was politics with a malicious edge. Vituperativeness had become the order of the day, especially on the opposition side. Newspapers and pamphlets teemed with overheated rhetoric and personal attacks. Never before had provincial authority found itself subject to so much abuse and disrespect. The very holding of a government office was attacked as unpatriotic.

Other circumstances added to the tension. Boston was still feeling the effects of a disastrous fire five years earlier. Raging for over ten hours, the conflagration had destroyed 150 houses, as well as warehouses, shops, stores, and ships.[84] Damage estimates ranged as high as £100,000, and more than a thousand people were left homeless.[85] Four years later, smallpox had revisited Massachusetts. While it was not nearly as severe as the outbreak in the early 1720s, there were a number of deaths and a very real fear of what might happen. Those who could left Boston for the country. Merchants relocated their shops. Harvard College closed. The General Court retreated across the Charles River to Cambridge.[86] As one commentator put it, the "general discontent of the people was never greater than it is at present in this town. . . . [O]ur lives are threatened by a pestilence."[87]

Fear again gripped Massachusetts just months before news of the passage of the Stamp Act reached the province. This time the fear was economic. The conclusion of a war with the French brought with it an end to lucrative military contracts. A deep depression gripped Massachusetts.[88] Early in 1765, Nathaniel Wheelright stopped payments on his obligations.[89] A merchant heavily involved in war contracts, Wheelright had "acquired such an undue Credit that he became next to the Treasurer, Banker General for the province."[90] His financial failure triggered that of many others, including John Scolley, the defendant in Gridley's suit for John Dunn, the first mate who had been taken hostage.[91]

James Otis described the impact of Wheelright's bankruptcy with classic Otis hyperbole, comparing it

> to nothing but the late Earthquake at Lisbon, such was the Consternation . . . that people appeared with pale Horror and Dread, and When a little recovered run about the City. Widows and Orphans that are ruined can only bewail their fate.[92]

Their "fate," like the fate of the rest of Massachusetts, now included the Stamp Act. Boston's initial response was subdued. In April, May, and June, its newspapers carried descriptions of the act and the details of its passage without comment.[93] The Massachusetts House of Representatives, however, did have something to say. On June 8, 1765, it resolved to send a letter to the assemblies of each of the other mainland colonies inviting them to send representatives to a congress to discuss an appropriate response to the imposition of the Stamp Act.[94] The conference would take place sometime in the future on a date and at a place to be determined, but Massachusetts could not wait. Events in Virginia stirred the province into action.

On July 1, 1765, the *Boston Gazette* published the "Resolves of the Virginia Assembly, on debating the Stamp Act." The Resolves, as published in the *Gazette*, denied that the people of Virginia had a duty to obey "any Law or Ordinance whatever, designed to impose any Taxation whatsoever upon them, other than the Laws and Ordinances" of their own legislature, and that anyone who claimed that any person or persons other than that legislature had the right or power to tax Virginians "shall be deemed an enemy to his Majesty's Colony."[95] Some in Massachusetts were taken aback by the temerity of the

Virginia Resolves. James Otis publicly declared them "treasonable," but that reaction was not shared by everybody.[96] When John Adams asked Oxenbridge Thacher whether he had seen the Resolves, Thacher replied: "Oh yes—they are men! They are nobler spirits! It kills me to think of the lethargy and stupidity that prevails here."[97]

Thacher may have been the author of an anonymous comment that appeared in the July 8 issue of the *Boston Gazette:*

> The people of Virginia have spoke very sensibly, and the frozen Politicians of a more northern Government say they have spoke Treason: . . . Pray Gentlemen, is it Treason for the Deputies of the People to assert their Liberties, or to give them away? Dare any of these Sycophants to say that the American Subjects are not entitled to British Liberties? I hope the Times will not bear it.[98]

For the next two months, the *Gazette* harped on the injustice of the Stamp Act, praised the Virginia legislature, denounced the "mercenary hirelings" in Massachusetts, and lauded examples of resistance to government oppression such as the "Commotions" in England in which thousands of unemployed weavers violently sought relief.[99] Its August 12 issue carried an article about a planned meeting in Providence, Rhode Island, at which the town's freemen, "those sons of *Liberty*," would, the *Gazette* hoped, "serve as an Example to other Towns, to exert themselves at this Crisis, and to *remind* them that they are entitled to all the Privileges of *British* Subjects."[100]

That issue of the *Gazette* also included a sermon on the words of Psalm 105: "Touch not mine anointed, and do my prophets no harm."[101] The author maintained that although "the tools of power may . . . disparage the people and stigmatize them with the opprobrious names of *Mob* and *Rabble*," the "anointed" were the people to whom all rulers owed a duty to act for the public good.[102] In encouraging the people to take action when their rulers breeched this duty, the sermon appeared to give biblical sanction to mob action.[103] Two days later, all hell broke loose.[104]

As dusk fell on August 14, after a tumultuous day of looking for ways to vent their anger against the Stamp Act and, perhaps, against authority in general, a crowd ended up at Andrew Oliver's mansion. Forewarned by the sheriff, who was "apprehensive that the Person of the Stamp-Master and his family might be in Danger," the Olivers had fled, leaving a few of their friends to protect the house.[105] Those inside "committed some small Indiscretion," which so "enraged" those outside that they attacked the house full force and "searched about for Mr. Oliver, declaring they would kill him." Finding that their quarry had left, the mob set about vandalizing the house and grounds.[106] About eleven p.m., "the mob seeming to grow quiet," Thomas Hutchinson showed up with the sheriff in tow and demanded that the crowd disperse. Answered by a volley of stones, the "two Gentlemen narrowly escaped thro' favour of the Night, not without some bruises."[107] Soon after, the crowd dispersed "at their own Time, which they did about 12 o'clock."[108]

The events of August 14 in general, if not in detail, were anything but spontaneous, a fact obvious to many[109] Andrew Eliot expressed a common view when he wrote that "the attack on Secretary Oliver . . . was under the direction of some persons of character."[110] Those "persons" were members of a secret group known as the "Loyal Nine," a collection of radical merchants, mariners, tradesmen, and shopkeepers who had decided that the most immediate way to effectively oppose the Stamp Act was through physical intimidation, which would go largely unchecked.[111] They were right. The official response to the August 14 riot was tepid. An attempt to mobilize the militia died aborning.[112] When Governor Bernard ordered the colonel of the Suffolk County regiment

> to beat an Alarm; he answered that it would signify nothing, for as soon as the drum was heard, the drummer would be knocked down, & the drum broke; he added, that probably all of the drummers of the Regiment were in the Mob.[113]

The next evening, "a great Number of the Inhabitants . . . of both Sexes" returned to Oliver's, determined to "level his House."[114] The mob left the scene, however, after

> having been told of Mr. Secretary's resigning up his Stamp office as dangerous for him or any Man to accept; and that he had wrote Home, that it would endanger the Life of any that did it, being contrary to the Rights and Privileges of Englishmen.[115]

The mob left, but many did not go home. Acting on a rumor that Thomas Hutchinson "had forwarded the Stamp Act, by recommending it as an easy Method of gulling the People of their Liberty and Property," they surrounded the lieutenant governor's house.[116] The mob demanded that he appear on the balcony and "declare that he had not written in favour of the act, and they would retire quite satisfied."[117] Considering this "an indignity to which he would not submit," Hutchinson refused to answer.[118] Tensions increased until a neighbor declared that he had seen Hutchinson leave earlier for his estate in Milton.[119] Apparently satisfied with this fabrication, the crowd dispersed.[120] Hutchison's respite was short-lived.

After dusk on August 26, a group of what the *Boston Gazette* later described as "Rude Fellows" gathered on King Street, built a bonfire, and "quickly began to be very noisy."[121] A crowd gathered. There was some drinking. As night fell, the assemblage, whose numbers "made a very formidable appearance," split into two groups.[122] One group seriously damaged the house of William Story, the register of the Vice Admiralty Court, destroying official documents.[123] The other "furiously attacked" and "did great damage" to the house of Benjamin Hallowell, the comptroller of customs. After "heating themselves with Liquors" from Hallowell's "cellar," this second group united with the first, and the mob turned its attention to Thomas Hutchinson's mansion.[124]

The lieutenant governor was at supper with his children "when somebody ran in and said the mob was coming."[125] He ordered his children "to fly to a secure place," but his eldest daughter refused to leave without her father. Reluctantly, Hutchinson left with her. Minutes later, the mob's axes split open the doors of the house. Shouting, "Damn him, he's upstairs, we'll have him," the intruders raced all over the house searching for Hutchinson.[126] He escaped "through yards and gardens to a house more remote," where he remained until four a.m., when it was safe to return to his home.[127]

When he arrived there, Hutchinson found only bare walls and floors:

> Not content with tearing off all the wainscot and hangings and splitting the doors to pieces, they beat down the partition walls; and . . . they cut down the cupola . . . , and they began to take the slate and

boards from the roof. . . . The garden was laid flat, and all my trees, etc., broke down to the ground.

Besides my plate and family pictures, household furniture of every kind, my own, my children's, and servants apparel, they carried off about £900 sterling in money, and emptied the house of everything whatsoever, except a part of the kitchen furniture, not leaving a single book or paper in it, and have scattered or destroyed all the manuscripts and other papers I have been collecting for thirty years together, besides a great number of public papers in my custody.[128]

The vehemence of the mob's destruction aside, there were other aspects of this incident that made it all the more disturbing. One was the fact that the rampage was witnessed by men in authority who did nothing to stop it. Describing what happened, Hutchinson wrote that Boston "was under awe of this mob; many of the magistrates, with field officers of the militia, standing by as spectators; and nobody daring to oppose, or contradict."[129] Another alarming aspect was that the terror did not end for Hutchinson and his family even after they left Boston. As they headed into the countryside, the Hutchinsons encountered "two or three small parties of the ruffians," he reported, "and my coachman hearing one of them say, 'there he is!' my daughters were terrified and said they should never be safe, and I was forced to shelter them that night at the Castle."[130]

On the next day, August 27, 1765, when the Superior Court opened in Boston, Hutchinson took his seat as chief justice. He was a mess. Josiah Quincy Jr., who was in attendance, described Hutchinson's "look" as "big with the greatest Anxiety . . . with Tears starting from his Eyes, and a Countenance which strongly told the inward Anguish of his Soul." After apologizing for his dress—"indeed I had no other . . . no other Shirt—no other Garment, but what I have on"—the chief justice noted the "distress of a whole family around me" and declared that he never "was aiding, assisting or supporting, or in the least promoting or incouraging . . . the STAMP ACT." He pleaded that "all will see how easily the People may be deluded, inflamed, and carried with Madness against an innocent Man."[131] Touched by Hutchinson's "distress," Quincy concluded that the "compassion" of all of those in the courtroom must have been "moved by what they knew [Hutchinson] had Suffered."[132] For a brief period, there was a wave of sympathy for the lieutenant governor and his family, but it quickly ebbed.[133] The battle over the Stamp Act soon was renewed. This time it was a war of wills.

Four months after the attack on Hutchinson's house, John Adams was an angry, frustrated, and worried young lawyer. As was his wont, Adams took the Stamp Act personally. "So sudden an interruption in my Career, is very unfortunate for me," he confided to his diary. I "had but just become known, and gained a small degree of Reputation, when this execrable Project was set on foot for my Ruin."[134] The "execrable Project," of course, was the Stamp Act, with its taxes on legal documents, which Hutchinson had predicted would "lessen the number of lawsuits" in Massachusetts, and so "greatly abridge the practice of law" that "there should be no such thing as a practicing lawyer" in America."[135] But in December 1765, it was not the possible long-term effect of the act that was troubling Adams. The problem was more immediate:

> Stamps are in the Castle. Mr. Oliver has no Commission. The Governor has no Authority to distribute, or even to unpack the Bales, the Act has never been proclaimed or read in the Province; yet the Probate office is shut, the Custom House is shut, the Courts of Justice are shut, and all Business seems at a Stand.[136]

The courts had been closed since November 1, when the Stamp Act went into effect. Judges, as well as customs officers and other government officials, faced a dilemma. As Hutchinson saw it, if, on the one hand, they proceeded without stamps, "all processes in law, all bonds, deeds, etc. would be considered as null and void, if the act should finally be enforced."[137] On the other hand, if the courts and government offices refused to operate without stamps, businesses requiring them would come to a standstill and "great numbers of people would be deprived of their [incomes]."[138] Courts and government offices kept their doors closed.

United in their frustration with the situation, the province's merchants were the first to take effective action. The customs office would not issue ships' papers without stamps, and without papers, ships could not depart the harbor. In the face of the merchants' unrelenting pressure, Boston's customs officers sought approval to issue unstamped papers. There then ensued a game of political "hot potato." John Temple, the surveyor general of customs, refused to authorize proceeding without stamps and referred the matter to Governor Bernard, who referred the matter to the attorney general, who begged off on grounds of illness.[139] Everything was complicated by the fact that although Andrew Oliver had declared that he would not take action as stamp master, he had never formally resigned the office.[140]

The Loyal Nine solved the problem. At noon on December 16, 1765, pursuant to an "invitation" from "The True-born Sons of Liberty," Andrew Oliver met with them under the "Liberty Tree" and executed the declaration that had been prepared for him."[141] It read in pertinent part:

> I do hereby in the most explicit and unreserved Manner declare . . . that I never will . . . make use of the said Deputation [as distributor of stamps], or take any Measures for enforcing the Stamp-Act in *America;* which is so grievous to the People.[142]

Two days later the Boston customhouse was open for business as usual.[143] The effort to persuade the courts to follow suit did not go as well. It was not for want of motive. The closed courts were having an adverse impact on the bar. John Adams was not alone in his dismay. Writing to his son in England, Richard Dana advised the young man, "[You] must have no further dependence on me for further supplies." Why? Because "[I] am now reduced to [depending] on my small income . . . for no law-business can be done, we shall all be aground."[144]

Moreover, there was considerable public sentiment in favor of opening the courts. Boston's newspapers were filled with stories from other colonies where courts were open for business.[145] For example, the *Boston News-Letter* and the *Boston Evening Post* reported that in Virginia and Maryland, "Business of all Kind is in Courts and Public Offices and would be carried on . . . as usual without Stamps."[146] The *Boston Gazette* included a bit of editorializing in such stories, adding, for example, in its item about the courts opening in Portsmouth, New Hampshire, "In the Name of Wonder, Why do they not go on here in the same Manner?"[147]

The problem was that the Massachusetts bar, the group most immediately affected by the closure, lacked leadership and unity. It had lost the two members who might have led any attempt to force the courts to open. Oxenbridge Thacher was dead, and James Otis was, well, James Otis—more inconsistent than ever. One minute Otis would assert that the colonists had an inalienable right to freedom from taxation without their consent, and the next he would be proclaiming "that the Parliament had a Right to tax the Colonies, and he was a d——d fool who deny'd it."[148]

Lack of leadership was only part of the problem. Despite the common hardship that many lawyers were experiencing, the bar was not united in its opposition to the Stamp Act.[149] Of course, there were lawyers who were against the measure and let their feelings be known. Some, notably John Adams, Oxenbridge Thacher, and (sometimes) James Otis, had taken to the Boston press to write against the tax. The actions of especially vocal lawyers, however, distort the picture of the bar's response to the Stamp Act. When the totality of that reaction is examined, the image changes from one of united, resolute opposition to one of divided, uncertain immobility.

While many of the attorneys who supported the ministry held their peace rather than risk the mob, others did not. Otis, of course, was a bizarre example, but there were others. Jeremy Gridley's nephew Benjamin Gridley, who was a lawyer, claimed to have written in Boston's newspapers in support of the ministry during the crisis of 1765–66. His "lucubrations," Benjamin later declared, were "a scourge to a numerous group of seditious Gazeteers and Pamphleteers who audaciously reviled King, Parliament, Ministry and Governors."[150]

Benjamin Gridley may have exaggerated his role, but there were other Massachusetts lawyers who were outspoken in their support of the ministry. John Adams had few kind words for them:

> [Daniel] Leonard says that [John] Lowell is a Courtier, that he ripps about all who stand foremost in their opposition to the Stamp Act,

at your Otis's and Adams's etc. and says no Man can scribble about Politicks without bedaubing his fingers, and every one who does is a dirty fellow. . . . Thus it seems that the Air of Newbury, and the Vicinage of [Daniel] Farnham, [John] Chipman etc. have obliterated all the Precepts, Admonitions, Instructions and Example of his Master [Oxenbridge] Thatcher, and have made him in Thatchers Phrase a shoe licker and an A—se Kisser.[151]

In the western counties of Hampshire and Berkshire, opposition to the Stamp Act was minimal.[152] The bar in these counties reflected this mood. With the notable exception of Joseph Hawley, a man "under the influence of Strong irregular Passions," no western lawyer vocally opposed the measure.[153] The acknowledged leader of the Hampshire bar, John Worthington, served on the committee which recommended that the House of Representatives call a Stamp Act Congress, but was no opponent of the ministry. He declined to serve when named one of the province's representatives to the conference, and later was listed as one of those representatives who should not be reelected because they had failed to oppose the Stamp Act.[154]

Divided and leaderless, the bar, in John Adams's opinion, "seem to me to behave like a Flock of shot Pidgeons" that "seemed to be stopped, the Net seems to be thrown over them, and they have scarcely Courage left to flounce and flutter."[155] Adams blamed "Cowardice" for the bar's failure to take action to open the courts, and too much "Respect (*and Regard*) to the Act." To Adams, it appeared "to be by Implication at least an Acknowledgement of the Authority of Parliament to tax Us."[156] Outside of the bar, there were many who felt the same way Adams did and moved to do something about it. On December 17, 1765, the Boston selectmen received a petition praying for a town meeting to consider "Measures to obtain redress . . . occasioned by the shutting up Courts of Justice . . . through the Province."[157]

At the meeting the next day, with James Otis in the moderator's chair, it was decided to address the situation in a memorial to the governor in council. After declaring that "the Law is the great rule of Right, the Security of our Lives and Property," the memorial requested that the governor "give such Directions to the several Courts and their Officers,

[that] ... we may be [no] longer deprived of this invaluable Blessing."[158] The petitioners also prayed "that they may be heard upon this most important Subject by their Council learned in Law."[159] Jeremiah Gridley, James Otis, and John Adams were selected for the task.[160]

Adams received news of his appointment in a letter delivered to his home in Braintree on the afternoon of December 19, and it came as a complete surprise. The letter informed Adams that he would not even see Boston's memorial until the next day, December 20, when he was expected to appear before the governor and the council.[161] Fortuitously, the previous evening Adams had jotted down some thoughts on the Stamp Act and the misfortunes resulting from the courts being closed. Typically, Adams reminded himself that he was "now under all obligations of Interest and Ambition as well as Honour, Gratitude and Duty, to exert the Utmost of my Abilities, in this important Cause."[162]

It is not known how or when Jeremiah Gridley was notified of his selection. The topic probably had been discussed with him prior to the December 18 town meeting. Unlike those of Adams, who was the author of Braintree's instructions to its representative, Gridley's views had to be ascertained before he could be publicly named one of the town's representatives. In addition, as a practical matter, there was no guarantee that Gridley could be counted on to act on short notice. He was, after all, a man in his sixties who lived some distance from Boston.

On December 20, after dining together in Boston, Gridley, Otis, and Adams were taken to the Town House, where they met with the town's committee to await Governor Bernard's summons. "About dark, after Candle Light," Samuel Adams, the chairman of the town committee, received a message from the governor that he and the council were ready to hear Boston's memorial "and their Council in Support of it. But that no other Person might attend."[163] Governor Bernard requested that Boston's three lawyers divide their argument among themselves, and that there be as little repetition as possible. Gridley stated that he was to speak last and would observe the rule. Otis followed, saying that he would speak second, and that he too would avoid repetition.[164] Whether this order of presentation had been agreed to in advance is not clear, but to judge from Adams's comments in his diary, he was caught off guard when it became apparent that he, the youngest and least experienced, would go first:

> Then it fell upon me, without one Moments Opportunity to consult any Authorities, to open an Argument, upon a Question that was never made before, and I wish I could hope it never would be made again, i.e. Whether the Courts of Law should be open, or not?[165]

In arguing that the Stamp Act "is utterly void, and of no binding force on us," Adams took the high road. Because it was passed when colonials had no representation in Parliament, the act ran against "our Rights as Men, and our Privileges as Englishmen." He asserted that the only reason why Parliament had power in England "was because they are elected by the People, who, if their Liberties are infringed, have a Check at the next Election." The colonists had no such "Check." They could not vote for Parliament. Therefore, "a Parliament of Great Britain can have no more Right to tax the Colonies than a Parliament of Paris."[166] Then came Adams's backup position: even if the Stamp Act was binding, because it was impossible to execute the act, Massachusetts was excused from obeying it. In closing, he applied a touch of histrionics: "The Necessities of Business, the Cries of the People, call for Justice."[167]

For his part, Otis was emotional. Reportedly, his eyes welled up with tears as he began his argument:

> It is with great Grief that I appear before your Excellency and Honors on this Occasion. A wicked and unfeeling Minister has caused a People, the most loyal and affectionate that ever a King was blessed with, to groan under the most insupportable Oppression.[168]

After a nod to Adams's contention that the Stamp Act was void, Otis argued that keeping the courts closed was an abdication of government. "Every subject," Otis declared, "had the same Right to his Life, Liberty, Property, and *Law*, that the king had to his Crown." Only war, invasion, rebellion, or insurrection could justify closing the courthouse doors. The fact that an unpopular act could not be enforced was not enough to "put a Stop to all Justice; which is *ipso Facto* a Dissolution of Society."[169]

Toward the close of Otis's presentation, which was studded with citations to authorities, Governor Bernard addressed him, apparently the only time that he interrupted the attorneys:

> The Arguments made Use of, both by Mr. Adams and you, would be very pertinent to induce the Judges of the Superiour Court to think the Act of no Validity, and that therefore they should pay no regard to it; but the Question with me is, whether that very Thing don't argue the Impropriety of our Intermeddling in a Matter which solely belongs to them to Judge of in their Judicial Department. And can it be proper for us to command them to act in any particular Way . . . especially, as from some of the very Authorities you have cited, it appears, that the Judges are to obey no Mandate, come it from whomever it will.[170]

Bernard's remark was telling. It was clear that, given the high stakes involved, the governor was not prepared to tell the judiciary what to do. Any further argument most likely would fall on deaf ears, but Otis had no choice but to continue. He cited authorities that held it improper to command courts "not to proceed" in support of the instant plea to open the province courts. These authorities, Otis contended, "shew that Justice is never to be stopped, but that the Law shall always have its own Course."[171]

Gridley took a different tack from those of his colleagues. Ironically, he, probably the most legally erudite of the three, talked about practical realities and what was best for Massachusetts. Emphasizing the importance to the province of its people's safety and the preservation of its government, Gridley maintained that shutting up the courts was "a Renuntiation of government," which would reduce Massachusetts "to anarchy and Confusion."[172] He reasoned that if the "Stamp-Papers had been destroyed by Tempest, or some other Casualty," the courts would have proceeded. Then Gridley attempted to draw a distinction between those who had terrorized Oliver into resigning as stamp master and the province's law-abiding citizens:

> Necessity demands Justice should have its Course. It is . . . no Default of ours, that the Act cannot be put in Force. The Innocent shall never be involved in the same Fate with the Guilty if it can be avoided. It is not in the Power of any one to obtain Stamp-Paper. A thing that is impossible is as though it were not. He who is a Citizen shall never be denied his Law.[173]

The council's response to these arguments was not long in coming, and, given Bernard's comments to Otis, quite predictable. As could be expected, the council was dissatisfied with the presentation because, as Bernard put it, Gridley and his co-counsel

> did not attend much to what was the main Question with the Council, whether it was the Business of the Governor & Council as having the executive Power to direct the Courts of Justice in their proceedings, upon this or any other occasion.[174]

On December 21, 1765, the council resolved that it was up to the courts to determine whether or not they would hear cases without stamped papers, and that it was inappropriate for the council to make any determinations or recommendations on the question.[175]

Frustrated, James Otis, Sam Adams, and Boston's other popular politicians were "warm to have the Courts opened." Gridley advised them "to wait for a Judicial Opinion of the Judges."[176] It was good advice. One by one, judges opened their courthouse doors. In January 1766, the Suffolk County Inferior Court of Common Pleas resumed civil proceedings, and the Vice Admiralty Court and most other courts did the same.[177] The Superior Court did not. John Adams fumed at the high court's "insolence And Impudence, and Chickanery," James Otis "pressed hard for judgments in his actions," and although some of his fellow justices wavered, Thomas Hutchinson stood ready to "hold out as long as possible."[178] He had resigned the lucrative post as probate judge of Suffolk County rather than open that court, and as chief justice of the Massachusetts Superior Court, he was not about to give in.[179]

In February 1766, responding to a House resolve that "the shutting up of the Courts of Justice . . . requires immediate redress," the council requested that the Superior Court advise on whether it would open at the next term. Hutchinson replied that such a determination would be "irregular, unprecedented and unwarranted." The court could commit only that if circumstances remained the same and the bar urged immediate action, "the court may be under a necessity of permitting it."[180] Choosing to construe this as an indication that "the Superior Court will at the next term be open and proceed as usual to do business," the council nonconcurred in the House resolution as unnecessary.[181]

When it came to the bar, Hutchinson knew with whom he was dealing. The Superior Court finally reconvened on April 29, 1766. Given the opportunity to test Hutchinson's implication that the court might operate without stamps if the bar urged it to do so, the lawyers got cold feet. After their few halfhearted attempts to present matters were met with the chief justice's blunt response that he did not believe it "regular nor prudent" to do so "at this critical juncture," the lawyers acquiesced to an adjournment until June.[182]

What made April 1766 the "critical juncture" to which Hutchinson referred was the fact that, by the spring of 1766, rumors were rampant that the Stamp Act would soon be repealed. The chief justice had played a game of delay, "unwilling that any . . . business should go on," in the hope that Parliament would repeal what he called the "fatal act" and the issue of opening the Superior Court would soon become moot.[183] The tactic worked. The Superior Court was still closed when, on May 19, 1766, news reached Boston that the Stamp Act had been repealed.[184]

CHAPTER ELEVEN

Death and Legacy

The bells welcoming the repeal of the Stamp Act had barely gone silent when the popular party moved to gain control of the Massachusetts legislature. With the May 1766 House elections at hand, radical writers in the Boston newspapers listed thirty-two current members of House of Representatives as "enemies of the country . . . whose name[s] should descend, with all the marks of infamy, to the latest times."[1] In the elections that followed, twenty-two of those listed were not returned to the House.[2] The radicals had won a sweeping victory. They could count about two-thirds of the House membership as their supporters.[3]

Flexing their muscles, the House majority elected James Otis Jr. as their speaker. In a somewhat dubious move, Governor Bernard vetoed Otis's election, forcing the House to fill the post with the more moderate Thomas Cushing.[4] That very afternoon, seeking revenge, the House struck at Bernard's allies on the provincial council.[5] They refused to reelect Lieutenant Governor Thomas Hutchinson, Secretary Andrew Oliver, Attorney General Edmund Trowbridge, and Justice Peter Oliver. Two of Bernard's other supporters on the council, Justice Benjamin Lynde and Judge George Leonard, "apprehensive of this slight," resigned before the election.[6] In their stead, the House elected six new councilors, including Colonel Otis. Bernard vetoed all six and requested that the House submit new names to bring the council up to its normal complement. The House refused to do so.[7]

Heated rhetoric on both sides poisoned the confrontation between the governor and the House of Representatives. In his opening address to the newly seated representatives, Bernard delivered what John Adams termed "a most nitrous, sulphureous Speech."[8] He accused the House of attacking the government and, in rejecting Hutchinson, Trowbridge, and the Olivers, of attempting "to deprive it of its best and most able servants, whose only crime [was] their fidelity to the Crown."[9] Bernard declared his intention "to exercise every legal and constitutional power to maintain the King's authority against this ill judged and ill timed oppugnation of it."[10] Insulted by Bernard's remarks, the House likened his "high and grievous charges" against it for exercising its "right to choose" as "little short . . . of a direct impeachment . . . of high treason."[11] In a section most likely written by James Otis Jr., it took a jab at Hutchinson and Peter Oliver, asserting that it

> [had] released those of the Judges of the Superior Court who had the honor of a seat at the Board, from the cares and perplexities of politics, and given them opportunity to make still further advances in the knowledge of the law.[12]

In such a toxic atmosphere it was inevitable that even the most innocuous matter could become heatedly partisan. As fate would have it, the first substantive issue to come before the House—compensation of the victims of the Stamp Act riots—was one loaded with divisive potential. The question had been percolating since the attacks. Although there was a consensus that the victims should recover something, there was no agreement on who should pay them and, as can happen only in such a partisan environment, in what spirit they should be paid. In a June 3 speech to the House of Representatives, the governor stated that the "justice and humanity" of compensation "is so forcible, that it cannot be controverted. The authority, with which it is introduced, should preclude all disputation about complying with it."[13]

The House took exception to Bernard's argument that "justice and humanity" required compensation. It contended that while members were "sensibly affected with the loss [that the riot victims] have sustained," because making up those losses "appears to this House, not an act of justice, but rather of generosity, they are in doubt whether they have any authority to make their constituents chargeable with, without their express consent."[14] There followed more than five months of bickering, stillborn proposals, legislative adjournments, evasions, constituent polls, and failed votes.[15] The underlying problem was summarized by two Boston merchants to their London factors:

> We are sorry that nothing has yet been done to make good the Loss to the Lieutenant Governor. It appears to be the general Design to have it done. The Difficulties arise in the manner of doing it; The People of Boston are Desirous of its being a Provincial Charge, but would esteem it a great Reproach as well as Injustice to have it thrown on them alone; the Country Deputies are fearful of offending their Constituents by bringing Part of the Charges on them.[16]

Finally, under increasing pressure at home and from London to do something, the House passed a compensation measure, but only after adding a provision granting blanket amnesty to those who stood accused, or who might in the future be accused, of unlawful activities during the Stamp Act disturbances.[17] Bernard was not happy with the legislation, but, faced with the probability that it was the only way that the riot victims would receive anything, he signed it.[18]

Meanwhile, an old familiar controversy made a brief appearance on the political stage. John Rowe recorded the triggering event in his diary:

> Nov. 26 [1766] . . . A Transport Ship arr'd bound from Halifax to Quebec but could not get up the River. She had seventy people belonging to the Royal Train of Artillery on board, forty-three women & nineteen children.[19]

Confronted with an immediate need to house these troops and their dependents, Bernard found himself in a situation that had confounded his predecessors almost ten years earlier, but since then, Parliament had addressed the problem. The Quartering Act of 1765 amended the Mutiny Act to require that British troops in the colonies be quartered and provisioned in barracks where available, otherwise in public houses, inns, or vacant buildings.[20] The Massachusetts House of Representatives was not in session when the transport arrived. Bernard and the council decided to house the soldiers in the barracks at Castle William and to provide them with candles and fuel.[21]

When the House reconvened and demanded to know by what authority the governor had taken this action, Bernard stated that he had done so in pursuance of the Quartering Act. The House asserted that his reliance on the statute to justify his actions rendered those actions "still more grievous." Like the Stamp Act, it amounted to taxation without representation: "Your Excellency and the Council, by taking this step, have unwarrantably and unconstitutionally subjected the people of the province to an expense without giving this House an opportunity of passing their judgment upon it."[22]

Although this represented a direct challenge to Parliament's authority, Bernard refused to take the bait, and the "House," according to Thomas Hutchinson, "having made a publick declaration of their sense of the [quartering] act . . . suffered the affair to drop."[23] The quartering issue may have faded so quietly because it had become overshadowed by another dispute involving Hutchinson himself. In a January 31, 1767, message to the governor, the House of Representatives took umbrage at the lieutenant governor's presence in a meeting of representatives with the governor in the council chamber. The House claimed that because he had not been elected to the council, Hutchinson had no right to be in attendance, and that his presence in the chamber was "repugnant to the constitution, and the letter of the charter."[24]

Bernard met the challenge head-on. He presented the House with a report prepared by Secretary Oliver. The report, as Bernard read it, established

> that ev'ry Lieut. Governor since the opening of the present Charter, but usually and frequently when not elected a Councillor sat in Council, until the time of Governor Belcher, [when the Council] excluded the Lieut. Governor from a seat in the Council, which he complained of as a grievance and submitted to with resentment.[25]

The House was not impressed. Its response reiterated that Hutchinson's sitting with the council was "repugnant" to the province charter, which made no provision for a lieutenant governor.[26] Therefore, the exclusion of the lieutenant governor from the council was not inappropriate but rather demonstrated "a due regard for the royal charter, and the Rights of the General Assembly."[27] The next month, the council informed the governor that while Hutchinson's presence for the opening of the General Court was "excusable," it had voted unanimously that he had no constitutional right under the charter to a seat on the council.[28] Hutchinson gave up his claim to sit with the council, and Bernard lost a powerful friend in that chamber.[29]

In view of the recalcitrance of the House of Representatives toward working with his administration and its readiness to do battle over almost anything, it was clear that the governor had to gain some leverage there. Bernard needed votes, and he employed all the means at his disposal to bring representatives into the administration's camp. His shameless use of patronage embarrassed even some of his allies, one of whom observed that Bernard was "gitting into office Scandalous and unfit persons and Throwing about Commissions and promising almost Everybody" something if they would support his candidates in the [May 1767 House] elections.[30] Increased numbers were fine, but given the legalistic nature of many of his controversies with the legislature and the forensic firepower that his opponents could muster there, Bernard needed more. He needed an advocate in the lower house whose knowledge of the law and standing at the bar gave the administration a respected voice on questions involving the province charter, the constitution, and parliamentary statutes. Bernard tapped Jeremiah Gridley.

In November 1766, Superior Court Justice Chambers Russell died while on province business in England.[31] On March 25, 1767, Bernard elevated Attorney General Edmund Trowbridge to Russell's seat on the bench and appointed Gridley to replace Trowbridge as attorney general.[32] About the same time, Bernard named Gridley colonel of the First Suffolk Regiment.[33] These were the first two steps of a three-step political maneuver. The third step came two months later. In the May 1767 elections for the House of Representatives, the town of Brookline, which had not elected a representative in ten years, sent Gridley to the assembly.[34] It seems probable that Brookline had chosen Gridley because Gridley, as part of his arrangement with Bernard, had asked to be chosen.

The governor now had his lawyer in the House of Representatives and crowed about his achievement: "The Government party has received some accession by Elections, particularly of one very able

Advocate, whom I have just now appointed attorney general."[35] It was a very brief triumph. Earlier, when Bernard had named Gridley attorney general, he had chosen Jonathan Sewall as "special Attorney to act in [Gridley's] absence."[36] This rather unusual move may have been taken because of concerns about Gridley's health. According to one contemporary, Gridley had "laboured" under "an ill state of health . . . for many years."[37] After attending a meeting of the Boston bar in July 1766, Adams had noted in his diary that Gridley "was not in Trim. I never saw him more out of Spirits."[38] The June 12, 1767, Brookline town meeting was adjourned "on Account of Jer. Gridley Esq'r Indisposition."[39] On June 24, his friend John Rowe noted in his diary that Gridley was too sick to attend a dinner meeting of the Masons.[40] On September 10, 1767, at eleven p.m., Jeremy Gridley died "of Consumption."[41] He was sixty-five years old.

Gridley's funeral service was held in the chamber of the House of Representatives.[42] The procession was an extravagant affair, with, according to John Rowe, "such a multitude of Spectators I never saw at anything before since I have been in New England."[43] The funeral procession included

> the Members of the Council, and the Judges of the Superior Court in Town, the Gentlemen of the Bar, the Brethren of the Society of Free Masons, of which he was Grand Master, the Officers of the first Regiment of Militia, of which he was Colonel, the Members of the Marine Society of which he was President, and a great Number of the Gentlemen of the Town.[44]

According to the *Boston Post-Boy*, Gridley had "sustained the painful Attacks of Death with a Philosophical Calmness and Fortitude, that resulted from the steady Principles of his Religion."[45] If so, it is not clear what that "religion" was. While it has been claimed that Gridley died "in full faith in the truth of the Christian religion, and in hope of glorious immortality," it appears that may not have been the case.[46] Gridley's religious journey had been a meandering one.

In 1737, Gridley had been a founding member of the West Church, a bastion of liberal Congregationalism, but at the time of his death, one rumor had it that he was a "finished learned American Deist."[47] Charles Chauncy doubted that Gridley "had any fixed principles of religion; tho, if he had," Chauncy added, "I believe they were those of the present free thinkers in England," who believed in universal salvation.[48] After Gridley's death, conflicting stories circulated as to how he had confronted his impending demise. Chauncy claimed that that he had been "assured . . . by one had it from his nurse, that the day before [Gridley's] death, . . . she several times heard him commit himself to the mercy of God *thro' Jesus Christ*."[49] Another report had it that as he lay dying, Gridley would "not let any Minister pray with him. Said he knew more than they could tell him—asked the News and said he was going where he should hear no News."[50]

Gridley left no financial legacy. Despite his preeminence as a lawyer, his important cases, his investments, his landholdings, his rich and powerful friends, Gridley died insolvent.[51] For months after his death, the Boston newspapers carried notices of the auction sales of Gridley's Brookline estate, his household items, his personal effects, and his beloved library.[52] The only thing of value that he was able to dispose of as he saw fit was his law practice, "recommending his Clients to [John Adams] with expressions of confidence and Esteem."[53]

Adams's diary relates that at their first meeting, Gridley advised him "to pursue the study of the Law rather than the Gain of it."[54] Perhaps it was this admonition that led some of Gridley's early biographers to maintain that Gridley's dismal financial condition resulted from the fact that he "despised wealth."[55] That may be, but it seems that Gridley did not despise the attributes of wealth. It appears that his insolvency was the result of a man with somewhat expensive tastes living beyond his means. He had a big house ("fit for a Gentleman's Seat"), an extensive library, and a readiness to speculate in land.[56] Yet, unlike some of his colleagues at the bar, Gridley came from humble roots. There was no family fortune. His income depended almost entirely on his law practice, and very few colonial lawyers became wealthy from their practices alone.

Most of Gridley's income came, as it did for almost all Massachusetts lawyers, in relatively small increments, from small fees, one case at a time. Typically the amount of money a lawyer made from his practice depended on the number of cases that he handled. To do very well, he had to keep very busy.⁵⁷ Apparently Gridley did not keep busy enough. Reviewing new filings in the Superior Court in the years 1757, 1758, and 1759 as a sample shows that Gridley handled fewer cases than most of his high-profile contemporaries. In that three-year period, Prat filed 55 percent more cases than Gridley, and Thacher filed 38 percent more. Even with regard to new filings in the Suffolk County sessions of the Superior Court for the years 1757, 1758, and 1759, Gridley ranked fifth, behind Prat, Otis, Thacher, and Kent.⁵⁸

Gridley's lower numbers probably stemmed, to some extent, from two somewhat contradictory causes, both related to Gridley's personality. He was a very social man, a joiner. He was active in the Masons and the Boston Marine Society, serving many years as grand master of one and president of the other. John Rowe's diary is peppered with references such as "Spent the eve'ng at the Coffee House with . . . Mr Gridley," and "Dined at Mr Greatons at Roxbury with Jer'y Gridley."⁵⁹ It was said that he "delighted" in "polite festivity and nocturnal luxury."⁶⁰ It could be argued that Gridley may have preferred the ambiance and good company of a taproom a bit more than that of a courtroom and his caseload reflected that fact.

Ironically, for a man who apparently enjoyed the company of others, Gridley was not the most personable individual. Even John Adams, who admired him, found Gridley "proud" and "lordly," which rendered him "stiff and affected."⁶¹ Charles Chauncy, who had few kind words for Gridley, put it more harshly:

> Haughtiness of spirit accompanied him [wherever] he went, and was all along in life a great dishonor and disadvantage to him. He might have got as much [money] as he would, could he but have made an approach to him, and converse [with] him, [easy] and pleasant. His air, and the manner of behavior were so haughty, forbidding and insolent, but that a few cared to have to do with him. To this it is owing, that he died, as is [thought] insolvent.⁶²

Gridley has come down to posterity as "the greatest New England lawyer of his generation."⁶³ Like much that we know about him, the primary source of Gridley's reputation is John Adams, who, in letters written fifty years after Gridley's death, extolled him as the "greatest lawyer... I ever knew at any bar."[64] But these were not merely the fond recollections of an old man. When Adams was a young man seeking admission to the Suffolk bar, the first endorsement he sought was from Gridley, a man he knew by reputation only.[65] Other contemporaries shared Adams's opinion of Gridley. His obituary in the *Boston Post-Boy* lauded him as "the Head of the Profession." Gridley's fellow lawyers agreed. When the Suffolk bar drew up rules for admission and practice, it chose Gridley to present them to the court.[66] That high regard extended to the bench. Chief Justice Hutchinson ranked Gridley "the first lawyer at the Bar," and Justice Peter Oliver considered him "the Head of [his] Profession."[67]

It is difficult to determine the extent to which Gridley's oratorical ability contributed to his prestige. Adams was somewhat ambivalent on the subject. While critical of Gridley as "too stiff" with "too little Command of the Muscles of his face," Adams thought his mentor had "a bold, spirited Manner of Speaking." His "words seem to pierce and search, have something quick and animating. He is a great Reasoner, and has a very vivid Imagination."[68] Nineteenth-century biographers were less charitable. They wrote of Gridley's want of "fluency," describing him as a "rough and ungraceful" speaker.[69]

Unlike estimations of Gridley's aptitude as a speaker, favorable opinions about his writing ability abound. In his *Biographical Dictionary* (1809), John Eliot described Gridley's "manner of writing [as] handsome, and his speculations ingenious."[70] Samuel Knapp, a lawyer himself, described Gridley as "one of the most eloquent and classical writers of his age."[71] Other biographers followed suit. Writing a generation after Knapp, Emory Washburn praised Gridley as "an easy and graceful writer, being imbued with the spirit of classical learning."[72] His reputation continued into the twentieth century. A note about Gridley for the Brookline Historical Society in 1903 quoted Knapp's plaudits and then added that Gridley's "writings were praised for clearness of expression and their literary style."[73]

These accolades probably are exaggerated, and perhaps unfounded. To the extent that they are not based on one another, most, if not all, appear premised on Gridley's stints as editor of the *Weekly Rehearsal* and, perhaps, the *American Magazine*.[74] Yet there was little in either publication that was original. It has been estimated that only six pieces in the *Weekly Rehearsal* may have been Gridley's work, and that none of these contained original ideas.[75] Gridley's contributions to the *American Magazine* have been denigrated as "largely derivative and not worthy of Knapp's praise."[76] Still, Gridley's writing skills cannot be dismissed lightly. Biographers like John Eliot (1754–1813) and Samuel Knapp (1783–1838) may have obtained information from Gridley's contemporaries, who, for whatever reason, deemed Gridley a gifted writer. And there is something else.

In 1765 the *Boston Evening-Post* published a series of essays that had been written by John Adams. According to Adams, the essays "were so little noticed or regarded here, that the author never thought it worth his while to give it either a title or signature."[77] The essays did, however, attract attention in London. When Thomas Hollis and John Almon published *The True Sentiments of America* (1768), they appended Adams's treatise, which they titled "A Dissertation on the Canon and the Feudal Law" and attributed its authorship to "Jeremy Gridley, Esq.; Attorney General of the Province of Massachusetts Bay."[78]

The editors of the Adams papers praise what became known as the "Dissertation on Canon and Feudal Law" as both "important and eloquent."[79] Liberal pastor Charles Chauncy declared, "I esteem that piece one of the best yt. has been wrote."[80] As could be expected, Thomas Hollis thought it "one of the finest productions ever seen from N. America."[81] And Hollis attributed it to Jeremy Gridley, "on the assumption that [Gridley] was the only New Englander capable of having written it."[82] This conclusion probably was based on the erudition reflected in the piece at least as much as its eloquence.[83] More than the size of his practice, his wins and losses, or his abilities as a speaker and as a writer, it was, as his obituary in the *Boston Post-Boy* put it, Gridley's "thorough Knowledge of the Civil and Common Law, which . . . justly placed him at the Head of the Profession."[84]

John Adams wrote that "Gridley's Grandeur consists in his great learning."[85] Even Chauncy, who sniffed that Gridley was "far from being an universal scholar," was forced to acknowledge that Gridley "was certainly a man of erudition" who "excelled" in his learning of the law.[86] One hundred and fifty years later, in his classic *History of the American Bar* (1911), Charles Warren concluded that Gridley was "the great legal scholar of the Century."[87] It was this reputation for legal knowledge that led bright young men to Gridley's door in search of what was perhaps the best legal education in New England.[88] These young men became Gridley's legacy, and an impressive legacy it is. The names of a surprising number of his students appear in the pages of American legal and political history.

First, there was Benjamin Prat, who studied with Gridley in the late 1730s and went on to become one of Boston's leading lawyers and chief justice of New York. Prat was followed by Oxenbridge Thacher and then James Otis Jr., whose leading roles in the events that stirred Massachusetts in the 1760s are well documented. Years after he clerked for Gridley in the early 1750s, William Cushing was appointed the first associate justice of the Supreme Court of the United States (1789). Of course, John Adams was Gridley's most famous student. Adams did not clerk with Gridley. He studied law with James Putnam of Worcester. But on the completion of those studies, Adams went to Boston, where he sought out Gridley, who presented him for admission to the Suffolk County bar.[89]

Gridley clearly was taken with the young man. The day after he first met Adams, Gridley lent him a book on civil law, and in the years that followed, the two spent a great deal of time together, with Gridley the teacher and Adams the student.[90] Adams's diary provides a partial record of this relationship. For example:

> [October 7, 1760] Waited on Mr. Gridley for his Opinion of my Declaration Lombard v. Tirell and for his Advice, whether to enter the Action or not. He says the Declaration is bad and the Writ, if Advantage is Taken will abate.
>
> . . . Mr. Gridley sent me to Otis's office to examine in Viner's Abridgement under the Title Rent, and in the Entries, i.e. Lilly, Mallory, Coke, and Rastal, Under the Title Debt, for some Authority to decide the Point whether the Exception was fatal, or not. I could find nothing in Viner, Lilly, or Mallorry, but Mr. Gridley shewed me

in Coke and Rastall the Distinction taken between a Declaration on a Parol and on a Written Lease.[91]

Adams's diary goes silent for the last half of 1763 and all of 1764, but Gridley's instruction of his young protégé continued.[92] In January 1765, Adams began a new notebook which bears the heading "SODALITUS, A CLUBB OF FRIENDS." Gridley's brainchild, the "clubb" was intended as "a Junto, a small sodality" composed of Gridley, Adams, a forty year-old Boston lawyer named Samuel Fitch, and Gridley's son-in-law Joseph Dudley, to "read in Concert the Feudal Law and Tullies orations."[93]

After an evening spent laying the ground rules for their "sodality," the group met on January 17, at Gridley's office. It was a busy meeting:

> [W]e . . . suffered our Conversation to ramble upon Hurd's Dialogues, the Pandects, their Discovery in Italy by Lotharius in 1127, in the Reign of Stephen, upon Lambard, de priscis Anglorum Legibus, in Saxon and Latin, upon Ld. Kaims [Kames], Mr. Blackstone &c. but we agreed to meet the next Thursday night at Mr. Fitch's, and to read the Three first Titles of the feudal Law, and Tullies oration for Milo.[94]

At the fourth meeting of the club, Gridley outlined his vision for its future:

> Our Plan must be, when we have finished the feudal Law, to read Coke, Littleton, and after him a Reign and the Statutes of that Reign. It should also be a Part of our Plan, to improve ourselves in Writing, by reading carefully the best English Writers, and by Using Ourselves to writing—for it should be part of our Plan to publish Pieces now and then. Let us form our Style upon the Ancients, and the best English Authors.[95]

That did not happen. There is no mention of another meeting of the Sodality in Adams's diary. Nevertheless, Adams took to heart Gridley's injunction to "publish Pieces now and then." Sometime in February 1765, Adams began jotting down thoughts for the essay that was to become "A Dissertation on Canon and Feudal Law," which, ironically, was attributed to his mentor.[96]

The Sodality may have owed its demise to the onrush of public events which ultimately divided Massachusetts and its bar.[97] In that division, many of Gridley's students played prominent roles in opposing the Crown. Adams, Otis, and Thacher are the most well-known examples, but there were others. Samuel Swift, who clerked with Gridley in the late 1730s, was one of the leading Sons of Liberty and a manager of the Boston Tea Party.[98] William Cushing kept his political views to himself but eventually threw in his lot with the rebellion, becoming the only royal Superior Court justice to be appointed to the high court established by the Revolutionary Council in 1775.[99]

It is difficult to say what role if any Gridley's influence played in developing liberal, even rebellious, attitudes in so many of his students. At least at the theoretical level, however, there was much in what Gridley emphasized that could have instilled or reinforced such inclinations. For example, Gridley esteemed the classical orator Marcus Tullius Cicero. He owned at least a dozen volumes of Cicero's works.[100] When he established the Sodality, he announced its avowed purpose as reading "in Concert the Feudal Law and Tullies orations."[101] Living at a time when Roman political and moral values were decaying, Cicero was a favorite of American revolutionary pamphleteers who analogized their times to his and borrowed his "vivid vocabulary" for their efforts.[102] Gridley's library also included other classical writers such as Plutarch and Tacitus, who often were cited or quoted in colonial antigovernment tracts.[103]

The catalogue of Gridley's library contains fourteen volumes of *The Craftsman*. He may have introduced his students to this London periodical, which had appeared continuously, weekly or biweekly, for ten years from 1726 to 1736. Drawing heavily from *Cato's Letters* (1721) by John Trenchard and Thomas Gordon, *The Craftsman* savagely attacked the Walpole administration, political and social corruption, and the threat of autocracy. In the colonies, Trenchard and Gordon were often quoted "as the most authoritative statement of the nature of political liberty and . . . as an exposition of the social sources of the threats it faced."[104]

James Otis's *Rights of the British Colonies Asserted and Proved* (1764) and his *Vindication of the British Colonies* (1765) include lengthy quotes from the Enlightenment authors Hugo Grotius and Samuel Pufendorf, whom Gridley recommended as "great Writers."[105] He had at least eight copies of their works in his library.[106] His library also included other authors who influenced revolutionary writers, including Locke, Voltaire, and Montesquieu, as well as two seventeenth-century critics of ministerial power, Francis Hutchinson and Algernon Sidney, whose *Discourses Concerning Government* (1698) has been called the "textbook of revolution."[107]

It may have been Gridley's enthusiasm for these authors that led John Adams to declare in 1820 that although Gridley "took no active part in the events, which led to American Independence ... it was known that he favoured it."[108] Like many of Adams's statements in his later years, this one must be read with caution. Nine years earlier, in making the point that "difference of opinion make no unnecessary alterations in private friendship," Adams had noted, "I have differed in sentiments, in religion and politics, from my ... master Gridley."[109] Moreover, contemporaneous opinions of Gridley, as well as a review of some of his actions, portray a less likely rebel than Adams remembered.

Ezra Stiles, a confirmed radical, saw Gridley as "a Courtier & an Anti-american in heart."[110] Lorenzo Sabine included Gridley in his sketches of American loyalists.[111] There is considerable evidence to support this classification. The Massachusetts quartering dispute of 1757 was a controversy of constitutional dimensions. On one side, General Loudoun demanded what amounted to a royal right to quarter troops in the manner he saw fit even if it required armed force to do so. In opposition, the Massachusetts legislature stood for the right of the people's elected representatives to determine how their constituents' money was spent and how much intrusion was permissible. This right was deemed so fundamental that Thomas Hutchinson, an ally of Loudoun's, and a strong supporter of the British Empire, opposed the general's quartering proposals.[112]

Gridley was on Loudoun's side. He acted as the general's agent in the House of Representatives, provided him with information on the opposition, and worked to defuse that opposition. Moreover, in his letters to Loudoun on the subject, Gridley appears somewhat contemptuous of the legislators' civil rights arguments. For example, he opposed the 1757 report drafted by Hutchinson and Chief Justice Sewall "asserting their right as Englishmen" and mocked Sewall, relating how "with great warmth and Sputtering [he] began to catechize me about English rights."[113]

Those rights, of course, were the primary issue in the writs of assistance case, in which Gridley again placed himself in opposition to what many of his countrymen believed were their fundamental rights. "Placed" is the appropriate word to use here. Gridley was under no obligation to argue the Crown's case. He was not a Crown attorney and held no admiralty office. At least one other attorney, Gridley's great contemporary Benjamin Prat, turned down the job. Moreover, given the fact that Otis was on the other side, Gridley must have known that the writs' constitutionality would become an issue in the case. Nevertheless, Gridley chose to stand at the bar in support of the legality of the hated writs.

In representing the Crown, Gridley did not merely go through the motions. As noted, John Adams recalled that Gridley "said everything that could be said in favor of the [writs]."[114] In addressing Otis's argument that the writs violated the rights of Englishmen, Gridley maintained that when it came to raising revenue, the good of the nation justified depriving Englishmen of their "common privileges." These were not the words of a liberal "whig" but rather, as one commentator has put it, "high toryism" of a "gross order."[115]

Then there was Governor Bernard's decision to appoint Gridley attorney general in March 1767, and Gridley's subsequent election to the House of Representatives two months later. Apparently Bernard had no doubt as to where he could expect Gridley to stand on the questions of the day. He saw the new representative as "one very able Advocate" who could be expected to speak on the part of the "Government party."[116] All of these examples arguably strengthen the case for Sabine's conclusion that Gridley would have been a loyalist, but there are other examples that cut the other way, and even the ones just cited are not definitive.

When Gridley joined with Otis and Adams to petition the governor in council to order the courts to operate without stamped documents, his argument stressing the need for the courts to be open to protect law-abiding citizens did not sound "radical." Yet, like his two colleagues, Gridley was calling for Governor Bernard to do something very radical—to, in effect, nullify an act of Parliament.[117] Moreover, Gridley's actions with regard to quartering and the writs of assistance could be viewed as less the acts of a conservative political partisan than of a man doing his duty when called upon to do so. Gridley's support of Loudoun on the quartering issue was consistent with his position that, in time of war, the people of Massachusetts had a duty to do whatever was necessary to assist those fighting on their behalf. Gridley's support of Loudoun's attempts to raise more troops and his prosecution of those who abetted deserters could be viewed in the same light.

Gridley's support of Loudoun, like his later willingness to become Bernard's lawyer in the House of Representatives in return for government appointments, also may have been less an ideological statement than the act of an eighteenth-century politician playing by rules that in Massachusetts were quickly becoming obsolete. Born a leather currier's son, without wealth or status, Gridley was not about to let himself die that way. He wanted the huge funeral procession that only civil and military honors could bring.[118]

Much of this, of course, is speculation, but then, attempting to determine as of 1767 where the political loyalties of any colonial would vest eight years later—when words came to bullets—inevitably involves speculation. During those years, many people made drastic changes in course. The Massachusetts bar was no exception. William Brattle, James Otis's ally in the General Court in the early 1760s, headed an anti-Hutchinson faction until about 1773, when he switched sides and became a loyalist.[119] Timothy Ruggles, who was one of Massachusetts's representatives to the Stamp Act Congress in 1775, raised a corps of Tories in 1775 and fled to Nova Scotia in 1783.[120]

By contrast, John Worthington was thought to be so strong a government supporter that he was named to the provincial council by the British military governor in 1774. He declined the appointment and, by 1778, was reconciled to the patriot cause.[121] Likewise, Barnstable attorney Shearjeshub Bourne joined other conservatives in signing the farewell address to Governor Hutchinson in 1774 only to later recant, join the opposition, and subsequently become a United States congressman.[122] It happened in Gridley's own family. His brother Richard, who had won accolades, land grants, and a commission in the British army for his service in the wars with France, joined the rebels. He designed the fortifications on Breed's Hill, was wounded in the Battle of Bunker Hill, became Washington's commander of artillery, and died an honored and revered patriot.[123]

Had he lived long enough, it seems unlikely that Jeremiah Gridley would have become an active partisan on either side of the issues that divided Massachusetts. He was a man who treasured reason, reflection, prudence, and gentility. Gridley was a remnant of a generation for whom the primary end of politics was personal advancement. Political adversaries were not enemies, and ideology was a shared view of what was, and still should be, the time-honored order of things.

Decades earlier, as the editor of the *Weekly Rehearsal*, Gridley had studiously avoided anything contentious. He praised the writer who "employs his Pen . . . to promote the Happiness of Mankind" and condemned those who would use the press as a "Means of dispensing Calumny, blowing up Civil Discord, or sowing Sedition among the People."[124] As editor of the *American Magazine*, Gridley had followed a similar course. At a time when the Great Awakening was fracturing New England society, and he was challenged to be "zealous in promoting and maintaining the Religious Controversies of the Day," Gridley refused to do so.[125] In addition, his magazine never published the kind of personal political attacks that were staples of the English periodicals that he imitated.

When, as an attorney or a legislator, Gridley found himself in situations in which basic rights were put at issue, and inflammatory rhetoric replaced thoughtful disagreement, his was a voice of moderation. Thus, in the quartering dispute with Loudoun, when his fellow legislators were ready to confront the general with angry assertions of "their right as Englishmen & by Charter," Gridley argued that Loudoun had only "requested," not "demanded," supplies for his troops, that there were quarters available, and that there was no need to raise the issue of constitutional rights.[126]

It was the same in the writs of assistance case. Otis fulminated against the writs, inflated the dispute to one about fundamental rights, and questioned the power of Parliament to pass laws binding on the colonies. Gridley ignored the challenge. While he acknowledged that, for the greater good, the writs might have to infringe on individual liberties, he refused to make the power of Parliament an issue. He would not raise the stakes by raising the case to one of fundamental constitutional dimensions:

> Gridley's position was clear-cut. Parliament, he argued, had empowered the Exchequer to issue "writs of assistance"; authority showed these to be general writs. Parliament had given colonial customs officers the powers of the English customs; and the [Massachusetts] Superior Court had the powers of the Exchequer; thus the writ could issue.[127]

When Gridley appeared with Adams and Otis before the governor in council to persuade him to open the courts without stamps, his two colleagues argued in terms of rights and privileges, that the Stamp Act was void because Americans had no representation in Parliament. Gridley again refused to raise the stakes. He did not attack the Stamp Act or Parliament's power to pass it. He argued the need for the courts to be open so as to protect the province's citizens and enforce the rule of law.[128] The threat to that supremacy, more particularly the unrestrained and unchallenged violence of the Stamp Act riots, must have appalled Gridley. The destruction went beyond vandalism. The tone of the attacks had a terrifying edge. There was a palpable threat of serious bodily injury or death. As they rampaged through Oliver's house in search of its owner, the invaders declared that "they would kill him."[129] When Hutchinson and the sheriff attempted to disperse the crowd, the mob bloodied them with stones.[130]

Later, attacking Hutchinson's house, the mob smashed open his doors with broad axes and frantically searched the house for him, shouting, "Damn him . . . we'll have him."[131] These, in the words of one Bostonian, were "perilous times . . . a man dars't speak a word in favour of ye act without running the risqué of having his house pulled down, his goods destroyed & pillaged or his life lost."[132] Boston was no stranger to mob violence. The town's history was checkered with regular fights between rival gangs and impressment riots.[133] From Gridley's perspective, however, the Stamp Act riots were different. They were personal.

This time the mob's wrath was directed specifically at men whom he knew and respected, and whose acceptance he sought. Andrew

Oliver, the secretary of the province, was the older brother of Peter Oliver, Gridley's longtime friend and business partner. He was a brother Mason, a member of St. John's Lodge in Boston.[134] Benjamin Hallowell also was a member of St. John's Lodge.[135] Gridley had represented Hallowell in cases before the Superior Court. Gridley's relationship with Thomas Hutchinson dated back to the time when, as young men, they had sought to master French together. Later they had served with each other on legislative committees and had spent countless hours in the same courtroom, one on the bench and one at the bar. Hutchinson had been one of Gridley's clients.

If he had lived and was faced with choosing sides, Gridley would have been subject to many of the same factors that influenced his old colleague Edmund Trowbridge in making his decision. Admitted to the Superior Court bar in the same year as Gridley, Trowbridge, like Gridley, was a learned, respected lawyer. He had served as attorney general and been a justice of the Superior Court. As Gridley probably would have, Trowbridge found the choice between rebellion and loyalty a difficult one. Theophilus Parsons, whose father had read law with Trowbridge, did not believe that Trowbridge

> felt very strongly on the questions of the day, and at the beginning of the contest he certainly sympathized with those who resisted the usurpations of the royal ministers. These he could see to be illegal. But he was a thoroughly educated technical lawyer, and had been the king's Attorney-General, and was then a Judge by the king's commission, and he was accustomed to consider and decide all questions of right or of conduct, under the light of precedent, and perhaps was unable to regard them otherwise; and he could discern no ground that was tenable, according to his views and habits of mind, for pushing resistance to the king's authority quite to rebellion.[136]

These words could have applied to Gridley, another careful lawyer of another era. So too could Parsons's explanation for why Trowbridge "remained inactive, perhaps neutral, through the contest." He was, Parsons contends, a "kind-hearted man, strongly influenced by social and family relations." Trowbridge's wife died in 1772. He had no children, and his only close relative was a sister. His three "nearest connections"—Richard Dana, who was married to that sister; Francis Dana, who was their son; and William Ellery, who was married to Trowbridge's wife's sister—"were so strongly committed to the cause of independence, that they held him in check."[137]

Gridley would have been in a similar situation. His wife was dead, and although he had three daughters, Gridley's "nearest connections" were other lawyers. Perhaps none of these was "nearer," at least among those in the next generation, than John Adams. Gridley sponsored Adams for admission to the bar and took a personal interest in Adams's legal education. He included Adams in the Sodality. He invited Adams to stay at his house in Brookline and bequeathed Adams his legal practice. Clearly, on a personal as well as a professional level, John Adams was very important to Gridley, and had Gridley lived, that importance probably would have increased because Gridley's other favorite young lawyer, his son-in-law Joseph Dudley, died in 1767.

Given this relationship, it is reasonable to conclude that even if Gridley "was a Tory in heart," John Adams's influence on Gridley, like the Danas' influence on Trowbridge, would have "held him in check." It also seems likely that, had he lived, Jeremy Gridley would have chosen the same course that Trowbridge opted to take. When things began to heat up in Massachusetts, Trowbridge attempted to follow a middle course. When that proved impossible, he left the public scene, retiring with his books to the manse of Moses Parsons in Byfield, where "he devoted himself to legal research and the writing of essays on the law which survived in manuscript to impress another generation."[138]

Gridley left no manuscripts, but John Adams left many. And thankfully, Adams recorded in his diary that on October 25, 1758, he "went . . . to Mr. Gridley's, and asked the favour of his Advice what Steps to take for an Introduction to the Practice of Law in this County," thus saving this interesting and influential lawyer from an obscurity that would have been a loss to us all.[139]

NOTES

Introduction

1. *Diary and Autobiography of John Adams,* ed. L. H. Butterfield, vol. 1 (1961; New York: Atheneum, 1964), 54 (October 25, 1758).
2. Daniel R. Coquillette, ed., *The Law Reports, Part Two,* vol. 5 of *Portrait of a Patriot: The Major and Legal Papers of Josiah Quincy Junior,* ed. Daniel R. Coquillette and Neil Longley York (Boston: Colonial Society of Massachusetts, 2009), 875.
3. Clifford K. Shipton, *Sibley's Harvard Graduates: Biographical Sketches of Those Who Attended Harvard College,* vol. 7, 1722–1725 (Boston: Massachusetts Historical Society, 1945), 530.
4. Benjamin Lincoln Jr. to Dr. Joshua Parker (August 8, 1778), Benjamin Lincoln manuscripts, Massachusetts Historical Society, Boston.

Chapter One: Student, Teacher, Editor (1702–1733)

1. Clifford K. Shipton, *Sibley's Harvard Graduates: Biographical Sketches of Those Who Attended Harvard College* (hereafter Shipton, *Harvard Graduates*), vol. 7, 1722–1725 (Boston: Massachusetts Historical Society, 1945), 518.
2. *Second Report of the Record Commissioners of the City of Boston* (Boston, 1881), 160; Oliver Ayer Roberts, *History of the Military Company of Massachusetts now called the Ancient and Honorable Artillery Company of Massachusetts, 1637–1888* (Boston, 1897), 185; Zachariah Whitman, *The History of the Ancient and Honorable Artillery Company,* rev. ed., 2nd ed. (Boston, 1842), 168.
3. Roberts, *History of the Military Company,* 198; Whitman, *Ancient and Honorable Artillery Company,* 174.
4. Shipton, *Harvard Graduates,* 7:518; Roberts, *History of the Military Company,* 308; Whitman, *Ancient and Honorable Artillery Company,* 233.

5. Henry F. Jenks, *Catalogue of the Boston Public Latin School established in 1635 with a Historical Sketch* (Boston, 1886), 353. Jenks concludes that Gridley probably attended the school, but that the documents are not clear on the matter. Weighing in favor of his attendance is the fact that he was admitted to Harvard, which required a solid foundation in Greek and Latin, and that he subsequently taught at Boston Latin. Samuel Eliot Morison, *Three Centuries of Harvard, 1636–1936* (1936; Cambridge: Harvard University Press, 1963), 103.

6. Kenneth B. Murdock, "The Teaching of Latin and Greek at the Boston Latin School in 1712," *Transactions of the Colonial Society of Massachusetts* 27 (1932): 23–26.

7. Jenks, *Catalogue of the Boston Public Latin School*, 5; Morison, *Three Centuries of Harvard*, 103.

8. Jenks, *Catalogue of the Boston Public Latin School*, 5.

9. Richard Gridley, will dated February 2, 1713, 202, Suffolk County Probate Records, vol. 18 (1712–1715), the Church of Jesus Christ of Latter-day Saints Court Record Project, microfilm reel no. 0584133.

10. Shipton, *Harvard Graduates*, 7:518.

11. Thomas Jefferson Wertenbaker, *The Puritan Oligarchy* (New York: Grosset & Dunlop, 1947), 242.

12. Ibid., 328–29; James B. Bell, *A War of Religion: Dissenters, Anglicans, and the American Revolution* (New York: Palgrave Macmillan, 2008), 6.

13. Curtis P. Nettles, *The Roots of American Civilization: A History of American Life* (1938; New York: Appleton-Century Crofts, 1963), 298.

14. The Charter of the Province of the Massachusetts-Bay (1691), in *The Acts and Resolves, Public and Private, of the Province of Massachusetts Bay*, vol. 1 (Boston, 1869), 10–11; Bell, *War of Religion*, 14; Nettles, *The Roots of American Civilization*, 297–302.

15. Perry Miller, *The New England Mind: From Colony to Province* (1953; Boston: Beacon Press, 1961), 241; Shipton, *Harvard Graduates*, vol. 4, *1690–1700* (Boston: Massachusetts Historical Society, 1933), 124–25.

16. H. H. to Reverend Dr. Coleman, September 24, 1736, in William O. B. Allen and Edmund McClure, *Two Hundred Years: The History of the Society for Promoting Christian Knowledge, 1698–1898* (London, 1898), 257.

17. Shipton, *Harvard Graduates*, vols. 1–7 (Boston: Massachusetts Historical Society, 1873–1945).

18. Ibid., 7:514, 547, 615, 617, 601, 623.

19. John Langdon Sibley, *Biographical Sketches of Graduates of Harvard University*, vol. 3, *1678–1689* (Boston: Massachusetts Historical Society, 1885), 180–85.

20. Morison, *Three Centuries of Harvard*, 54.

21. Ibid., 57; Norman Fiering, "The First American Enlightenment: Tillotson, Leverett, and Philosophical Anglicanism," *New England Quarterly* 54, no. 3 (1981): 322.

22. Fiering, "The First American Enlightenment," 329–30.

23. The Reverend Benjamin Colman to Dr. White Kennett, November 1712, in Ebenezer Turell, *The Life and Character of the Reverend Benjamin Colman* (Boston, 1749), 123.

24. Fiering, "The First American Enlightenment," 309.

25. Ibid., 315.

26. Ibid., 313.
27. Ibid.
28. Morison, *Three Centuries of Harvard*, 68.
29. *New-England Courant*, May 7, 1722. Franklin referenced Tillotson's influence at Harvard, noting that "nothing worth mentioning" in *"The Temple of Theology"* except the fraudulent Contrivances of *Plagius* who . . . was diligently transcribing some eloquent Paragraphs out of *Tillotson's* Works, etc. to embellish his own." Ibid.
30. "Diary of Cotton Mather" (July 3, 1717), *Collections of the Massachusetts Historical Society*, 7th ser., 8 (1912): 463. See also Mather, "Diary" (July 11, 1718), ibid., 546; Mather, "Diary" (November 31 [sic], 1718), ibid., 565.
31. Josiah Quincy, *The History of Harvard University*, vol. 1 (Boston, 1860), 317.
32. "Cotton Mather's Suggestions on Points to be Inquired into Concerning Harvard College," in Quincy, *History of Harvard*, 1:558.
33. Ibid., 556–59. In referring to the "doctrines of grace," Mather probably was referring to the Calvinist tenet that those who obtain salvation do so not by their own free will (their works) but because of the sovereign grace of God.
34. Ibid., 559.
35. Ibid.
36. Ibid.
37. Quincy, *History of Harvard*, 1:319.
38. Ibid., 320.
39. Ibid., 319.
40. Ibid., 320; Kenneth Silverman, *The Life and Times of Cotton Mather* (New York: Harper & Row, 1984), 384.
41. Shipton, *Harvard Graduates*, 7:. Shipton cites no authority for this assertion.
42. Ibid.
43. *A Report of the Record Commissioners of the City of Boston*, vol. 13 (Boston, 1885), 170.
44. Charles Warren, *A History of the American Bar* (1911; New York: Howard Fertig, 1966), 164.
45. Morison, *Three Centuries of Harvard*, 29.
46. Ibid., 30.
47. Ibid., 62; *Transactions of the Colonial Society of Massachusetts* 13 (1908–9): 223, 225.
48. Jenks, *Catalogue of the Boston Public Latin School*, 330, 380, 861. Samuel Langdon, who entered Boston Latin in 1729, graduated from Harvard in 1740 and served as its president from 1774 to 1780. Shipton, *Harvard Graduates*, vol. 10, *1736–1740* (Boston: Massachusetts Historical Society, 1958), 508–28.
49. Ibid., 7:519; 4:242–43.
50. Ibid., 7:519.
51. Ibid., ; *A Report of the Record Commissioners of the City of Boston*, vol. 8 (Boston, 1883), 218; vol. 12 (Boston, 1885), 22.
52. Kenneth B. Murdock, "The Teaching of Latin and Greek at the Boston Latin School in 1712," *Transactions of the Colonial Society of Massachusetts* 12 (1908–9): 23–24.
53. "A Memorial offered to the Town at this Meeting by the Selectmen" (March 3, 1711), in *Report of the Record Commissioners of the City of Boston*, 8:78.
54. John Adams to Richard Cranch, September 2, 1755, in *The Works of John Adams*,

ed. Charles Francis Adams, vol. 9 (Boston, 1854), 27–28. Adams also had good things to say about his teaching experience. See *Diary and Autobiography of John Adams,* ed. L. H. Butterfield, vol. 1 (1961; New York: Atheneum, 1964), 13–14.

55. Library Inventory, Estate of Jeremy Gridley, Probate Records, Suffolk County, vol. 66, Massachusetts Archives and Commonwealth Museum, Boston (hereafter Gridley Library).Whenever reference is made to a historical figure's library, the question arises as to whether or not he or she actually read the books collected. The evidence indicates that Gridley was a voracious reader. Nevertheless, Gridley has been identified as "that persistent buyer but non-reader of legal works." Robert J. Taylor, "John Adams: Legalist as Revolutionist, *Proceedings of the Massachusetts Historical Society,* 3rd ser., 89 (1977): 62. The assertion cites a letter from John Adams to William Tudor in which Adams discusses his use of *Moore's Reports* in a political dispute in 1773. Adams states: "The owner of it [*Moore's Reports*], for alas master, it was borrowed was a buyer, but not a reader of books. It had been Mr. Gridley's." This was taken to mean that Gridley was "not a reader, of books," but the conclusion probably is incorrect. The book may once have belonged to Gridley, but in 1773 Gridley had been dead for six years. Whoever lent the book to Adams must have purchased it from Gridley's estate, and it was he, not Gridley, who "was a buyer, but not a reader of books."

56. Gridley Library.

57. *Diary and Letters of Thomas Hutchinson,* ed. Peter Orlando Hutchinson, vol. 1 (Boston, 1884), 13–14; Albert Matthews, "Teaching of French at Harvard College before 1750," *Transactions of the Colonial Society of Massachusetts* 27 (1913–14): 220. Thomas Hutchinson, a future governor of Massachusetts (1769–1773), also was a member of the club. Born in 1711, he was almost ten years younger than Gridley. Shipton, *Harvard Graduates,* vol. 8, *1726–1730* (Boston: Massachusetts Historical Society, 1951), 151.

58. Shipton, *Harvard Graduates,* 8:442, 42.

59. Ibid., 442. Both Gridley and Lovell had very limited financial resources. Green, whose father had a "comfortable fortune," probably paid more than his share. Ibid., 42.

60. The *News-Letter* was the first successful newspaper in the colonies. *Public Occurrences* debuted in Boston on September 25, 1698, but died the same day for want of a government license. Louis B. Wright, *The Cultural Life of the American Colonies, 1607–1767* (1957; New York: Harper & Row, 1962), 747n7.

61. Walter Isaacson, *Benjamin Franklin: An American Life* (New York: Simon & Schuster, 2003), 21.

62. Wright, *Cultural Life,* 243.

63. Charles Leslie Clark, "Boston and the Nurturing of Newspapers, 1690–1741," *New England Quarterly* 64, no. 2 (1991): 266, 269.

64. Although theologically conservative, Mather was in the forefront of the pre-Enlightenment movement in the colonies, which was marked by a rejection of Aristotelian scholasticism in favor of an understanding based on careful observation and experimentation. To Mather, science was "no enemy, but a very great incentive to religion." Those who thought otherwise were "fools and as little to be regarded as a monkey flourishing a broom stick." Cotton Mather, *The Christian Philosopher* (1757; Charlestown, MA, 1815), 8; Wertenbaker, *Puritan Oligarchy,* 253–58.

65. The most outspoken physician against inoculation was William Douglass, who

had been educated at the University of Edinburgh and held the only medical degree in Boston. Maxine Van de Wetering, "A Reconsideration of the Inoculation Controversy," *New England Quarterly* 58, no. 1 (1985): 46. Van de Wetering argues rather convincingly that Douglass's primary concern was not inoculation per se but "clerical meddling" in what he saw as the exclusive province of physicians. Ibid., 47.

66. *Boston News-Letter*, July 24, 1721. Inoculation was not without danger. Of the 242 people whom Boylston inoculated, six died from the procedure. John B. Blake, "The Inoculation Controversy in Boston: 1721–1722," *New England Quarterly* 25, no. 4 (1952): 497.

67. Increase Mather, *Several Reasons Proving that Inoculating or Transporting or Transplanting the Small Pox, is a Lawful Practice* (Boston, 1721), 1.

68. Isaacson, *Benjamin Franklin*, 21.

69. Ibid., 20; Isaiah Thomas, *The History of Printing in America, with a Biography of Printers*, 2 vols. (Albany, 1874), 1:106; Clark, "Boston and Newspapers," 250–60; Verner W. Crane, *Benjamin Franklin and a Rising People* (Boston: Little, Brown & Company, 1954), 10.

70. Clark, "Boston and Newspapers," 260; Carl Van Doren, *Benjamin Franklin* (New York: Viking Press, 1938), 20.

71. Clark, "Boston and Newspapers," 260.

72. Isaacson, *Benjamin Franklin*, 28.

73. Clark, "Boston and Newspapers," 261; Isaacson, *Benjamin Franklin*, 35; *New-England Courant* (Boston), September 30, 1723, advertisement, "James Franklin Printer in Queen-Street, wants a likely lad for an Apprentice."

74. G. B. Warden, *Boston, 1689–1776* (Boston: Little, Brown and Company, 1970), 90; Carl Bridenbaugh, *Cities in the Wilderness: The First Century of Urban Life in America, 1625–1725* (New York: Alfred A. Knopf, 1964), 303n1.

75. In June 1722, claiming a rather tame satirical piece critical of the government's anti-piracy efforts to be a "High Affront," the provincial council ordered Franklin jailed for several weeks. In January 1723, as a result of the *Courant's* "tendency" to "mock Religion," "injuriously" reflect upon "the Rever'd and faithful Ministers of the Gospel," and affront "His Majesty's government," the legislature forbade Franklin from publishing the *Courant* or any other newspaper in Massachusetts. Subsequently a grand jury dismissed the charges against him. *New-England Courant* (, June 11, 1722, February 11, 1723; Resolution of Council and House of Representatives, June 12, 1722, in Charles Augustus Duniway, *The Development of Freedom of the Press in Massachusetts* (New York: Longmans, Green, and Co., 1906), 163, 165–66; Joint Committee Report and Acceptance, January 15, 1723, in Duniway, *Development of Freedom of the Press*, 164.

76. Thomas, *History of Printing in America*, 1:112. In September 1732, in Newport, James Franklin founded the *Rhode Island Gazette*, that colony's first newspaper. Ibid.

77. *New-England Weekly Journal*, March 20, 1727.

78. Shipton, *Harvard Graduates*, 7:466. Both Byles and Gridley were in the Harvard class of 1725 and probably knew each other, but it seems unlikely that they were close. Though the son of a saddler, Byles was, after all, a Mather. Moreover, he was five years younger than Gridley and did not live on campus or eat in commons. Ibid., 465–66.

79. Thomas, *History of Printing in America*, 2:41–42.

80. *New-England Weekly Journal*, March 20, 1727.

81. Clark, "Boston and Newspapers," 262.

82. *New-England Weekly Journal*, August 21, 1727; July 29, 1728. Byles's tribute to Burnett earned him a poem in his honor which praised Byles as "a finish'd Poet in his blooming years" who "shines among the Stars." Ibid., August 5, 1728.

83. Shipton, *Harvard Graduates*, 7:472. Shipton considers Byles second only to Ann Bradstreet among Puritan poets "in fame and perhaps in ability." Ibid., 466.

84. Clark, "Boston and Newspapers," 263.

85. *Weekly Rehearsal*, September 27, 1731; Thomas, *History of Printing in America*, 1:125. The official name of the newspaper was the *Weekly Rehearsal*, but it was sometimes printed as the *Weekly Rehersal*.

86. *Weekly Rehearsal*, September 27, 1731.

87. Ibid.

88. Ibid.

89. *Weekly Rehearsal*, April 3, 1732.

90. *Weekly Rehearsal*, October 25, 1731; October 18, 1731; April 17, 1732.

91. *Weekly Rehearsal*, April 24, 1732.

92. *Weekly Rehearsal*, April 3, 1732; December 13, 1731.

93. *Weekly Rehearsal*, October 4, 1731; October 11, 1731; January 10, 1732; January 17, 1732.

94. One study concludes that all but six of the essays in the *Rehearsal* were drawn from other sources and that even those six are suspect. Joseph Buckingham, *Specimens of Newspaper Literature with Personal Memoirs, Anecdotes, and Reminiscences*, 2 vols. (Boston: Charles C. Little and James Brown, 1850), 1:273.

95. Sometimes the *Rehearsal* published slightly different fare such as extracts about the Spanish Inquisition taken from Joseph Morgan's translation of Muhammad Rabadan's *Mohometism Fully Explained*. *Weekly Rehearsal*, November 1, 1731. See Muhammad Rabadan, *Mohometism Fully Explained*, vol. 1, trans. Joseph Morgan (London: W. Mears, 1723–1725), 344–66.

96. *Weekly Rehearsal*, March 13, 1732.

97. *Weekly Rehearsal*, January 24, 1732.

98. Ibid.

99. Ibid.

100. *Weekly Rehearsal*, January 3, 1732.

101. Ibid.

102. Thomas, *History of Printing in America*, 1:125.

103. Ibid.

104. *Boston Evening-Post*, August 18, 1735.

Chapter Two: Gridley's Law Practice

1. *Legal Papers of John Adams*, ed. L. Kinvin Wroth and Hiller B. Zobel, vol. 1 (Cambridge: Harvard University Press, 1965), ci.

2. Clifford K. Shipton, *Sibley's Harvard Graduates: Biographical Sketches of Those Who Attended Harvard College* (hereafter Shipton, *Harvard Graduates*), vol. 4, 1690–1700 (Boston: Massachusetts Historical Society, 1933), 244.

3. Samuel L. Knapp, *Biographical Sketches of Lawyers, Statesmen, and Men of Letters*

(Boston, 1821), 199. The inventory of books in Gridley's estate includes at least thirty-four books dealing with religious subjects that were published prior to his admission to the bar, some of which he may have studied if he was preparing for the ministry. Inventory of Library, Estate of Jeremy Gridley, Probate Records, Suffolk County, vol. 66, Massachusetts Archives and Commonwealth Museum, Boston (hereafter Gridley Library).

4. Knapp, *Biographical Sketches of Lawyers*, 199.

5. See Charles R. McKirdy, "The Lawyer as Apprentice: Legal Education in Eighteenth Century Massachusetts," *Journal of Legal Education* 28, no. 2 (1976): 124–36, on which much of this discussion is based.

6. *Diary and Autobiography of John Adams*, ed. L. H. Butterfield, vol. 1 (1961; New York: Atheneum, 1964), 55.

7. It is possible that his father-in-law, Ezekiel Lewis, who had some legal knowledge, may have assisted Gridley, but with his mercantile business and governmental offices, Lewis was a busy man.

8. John Adams to Thomas Welsh, September 15, 1790, in *The Works of John Adams*, ed. Charles Francis Adams, vol. 9 (Boston, 1854), 572.

9. McKirdy, "Lawyer as Apprentice," 126.

10. Ibid., 13; Charles R. McKirdy, "Before the Storm: The Working Lawyer in Pre-Revolutionary Massachusetts," *Suffolk University Law Review* 11, no. 1 (1976): 54–56. Fees remained low in Massachusetts throughout the colonial period. John Adams noted a meeting of the bar in 1766 at which lawyer Robert Auchmuty Jr. "scolded and rail'd about the lowness of the Fees. This is Auchmuty's common Topick—In Jamaica Barbados, South Carolina, and N. York, a Lawyer will make an independent Fortune in Ten Years." *John Adams Diary and Autobiography*, 1:316 (July 28, 1766).

11. *John Adams Diary and Autobiography*, 1:63 (December 18, 1758).

12. Both Englishmen, Robert Auchmuty had studied law at the Middle Temple, and William Shirley had studied at the Inner Temple. John A. Schutz, *William Shirley: King's Governor of Massachusetts* (Chapel Hill: University of North Carolina Press, 1961), 4; John M. Murin, "The Legal Transformation of the Bench and Bar of Eighteenth Century Massachusetts," in *Colonial America: Essays in Politics and Social Development*, ed. Stanley N. Katz (Boston: Little, Brown and Company, 1971), 425–26.

13. *Diary and Autobiography of John Adams*, ed. L. H. Butterfield, vol. 3 (1961; New York: Atheneum, 1964), 273.

14. Ibid., 1:55 (October 25, 1758).

15. Ibid.

16. Coke wrote four *Institutes*. Published in 1628, Coke on Littleton was the *First Institute*. His *Second Institute* (1642) was a restatement of English law by means of a commentary on the principal statutes. The *Third Institute* (1644) was a treatise on criminal law which reviewed the pleas of the Crown, and the *Fourth Institute* (1644) described the history and jurisdiction of the courts. Theodore F. T. Plunknett, *A Concise History of the Common Law*, 5th ed. (1929; Boston: Little Brown and Company, 1956), 282.

17. John Adams to Jonathan Mason, August 21, 1776, in *Works of John Adams*, 9:432–33.

18. Lord Eldon to Mr. Farrier, October 14, 1807, in Horace Twiss, *The Public and Private Life of Lord Chancellor Eldon with Selections from his Correspondence*, vol. 2 (London, 1841), 51.

19. Diary of John Quincy Adams (March 8, 1788), Adams Papers, 102, Massachusetts Historical Society, Boston (hereafter MHS).

20. *The Private Correspondence of Daniel Webster*, ed. Fletcher Webster, vol. 1 (Boston, 1857), 14.

21. Joseph Story to William W. Story, January 23, 1831, in *Life and Letters of Joseph Story*, ed. William Story, vol. 1 (Boston: C. C. Little and J. Brown, 1851), 74. Story went on to say that when he finally completed the "formidable work," he "breathed a purer air, and . . . had acquired a new power." Ibid.

22. This discussion owes a large debt to William Holdsworth, *History of English Law*, 3rd ed., vol. 2 (1903; London: Methuen & Co., 1923), 573–89.

23. William Blackstone, *Commentaries on the Laws of England*, vol. 1 (Oxford: Clarendon Press, 1765), 73.

24. William Holdsworth, *History of English Law*, 3rd ed., vol. 5 (1903; London: Methuen & Co., 1923), 497.

25. Thomas Wood, *Institute of the Laws of England, or, the Laws of England in their Natural Order, according to Common Use* (London, 1720); *John Adams Diary and Autobiography*, 1:174 (November 26, 1760).

26. William Holdsworth, *History of English Law*, vol. 12 (London: Methuen & Co., 1938), 419. Along with Wood, it is likely that Gridley's legal education included works by other English civilian writers. Far less enchanted with custom and precedent than their common law counterparts, they believed in law founded on reason, systematic reform, and universal conceptions of justice. Daniel R. Coquillette, *The Civilian Writers of Doctors' Commons, London: Three Centuries of Juristic Innovation in Comparative, Commercial and International Law* (Berlin: Duncker & Humblot, 1988), 8–9, 18–21, 24.

27. *John Adams Diary and Autobiography*, 1:169 (November 14, 1750); Sir Mathew Hale, *The History and Analysis of the Common Law of England, written by a learned hand* (London, 1713); *Encyclopedia Britannica*, 11th ed., s.v. "Hale, Sir Matthew."

28. John Adams to Richard Rush, April 14, 1811, in "Some Unpublished Correspondence of John Adams," *Pennsylvania Magazine of History and Biography* 60, no. 4 (1936): 432–33; Holdsworth, *History of English Law*, 2:189–92, 236–43, 319–21, 569–70; Plunknett, *Concise History of English Law*, 18–19, 254–66, 278–79; Gridley Library.

29. John Adams to Richard Rush, April 14, 1811, in "Unpublished Correspondence of John Adams," 432–33; Plunknett, *Concise History of English Law*, 268–73.

30. John Adams to Richard Rush, April 14, 1811, in "Unpublished Correspondence of John Adams," 432–33; Plunknett, Concise *History of English Law*, 280; Gridley Library.

31. John Adams to Richard Rush, April 14, 1811, in "Unpublished Correspondence of John Adams," 432–33; Yale Law Library, Landmarks of Law, blogs.law.yale.edu/blogs/rarebooks/archive/2009/05/05 (accessed October 11, 2009); Gridley Library.

32. John Adams to H. Niles, January 14, 1818, in *The Works of John Adams*, ed. Charles Francis Adams, vol. 10 (Boston, 1856), 275. In the letter, Adams was quoting James Otis, who was quoting "his patron in the profession, Mr. Gridley." Ibid.

33. John Adams to Richard Rush, April 14, 1811, in "Unpublished Correspondence of John Adams," 432–33; *John Adams Diary and Autobiography*, 1:56 (October 26, 1753); 199 (January 27, 1761); 51 (January 24, 1765).

34. John Adams to Richard Rush, April 14, 1811, in "Unpublished Correspondence

of John Adams," 432–33; Yale Law School Library, www.vialibri.net (accessed October 13, 2009).

35. John Adams to Richard Rush, April 14, 1811, in "Unpublished Correspondence of John Adams," 432–33; *Encyclopedia Britannica*, 11th ed., s.v. "Cujas (or Cujacius), Jacques."

36. John Adams to Richard Rush, April 14, 1811, in "Unpublished Correspondence of John Adams," 432–33; *Encyclopedia Britannica*, 11th ed., s.v. "Domat, or Daumat, Jean."

37. *John Adams Diary and Autobiography*, 3:271–72. See also John Adams to Richard Rush, April 14, 1811, in "Unpublished Correspondence of John Adams," 432–33.

38. Gridley Library.

39. Ibid. Gridley's "Plan" also included the French jurist Jean Barbeyrac (1674–1744), whose main claim to fame were his notes and comments to his translations of Pufendorf and Grotius. John Adams to Richard Rush, April 14, 1811, in "Unpublished Correspondence of John Adams," 432–33; *Encyclopedia Britannica*, 11th ed., s.v. "Barbeyrac, Jean."

40. Gridley Library.

41. For an excellent discussion of the use of commonplace books as a pedagogical tool, see Daniel R. Coquillette, ed., *The Law Commonplace Book*, vol. 2 of *The Major Political and Legal Papers of Josiah Quincy Junior*, ed. Daniel R. Coquillette and Neil Longley York (Boston: Colonial Society of Massachusetts, 2007), 3–75.

42. For Rolle's "Advice," see "The Publishers Preface Directed to the Young Students of the Common-Law," in Henry Rolle, *Un abridgement des plusiers cases et resolutions del common ley alphabeticalment digest desouth severall titles/per henry Rolle* (London, 1668).

43. *John Adams Diary and Autobiography*, 1:55 (October 25, 1758). Apparently, not all of Gridley's law students followed this advice. One of them, Oxenbridge Thacher, told Adams that he was "sorry that he had neglected to keep a Common Place Book when he began to study Law, and he is half a mind to begin now." Ibid. One of Thacher's students, Josiah Quincy Jr. (1744–1775), kept an elaborate "Law Commonplace" consisting of a core of pre-indexed legal subjects, which, with his "Legis Miscellanea" of everything of interest that Quincy read in chronological order, and manuscript "Reports" of Massachusetts judicial proceedings that he had witnessed, all cross-referenced to one another, formed a "sophisticated" and effective "program to teach law." Coquillette, *Law Commonplace Book*, 11–25. In contrast, Adams's commonplace book was much less refined, with little cross-referencing or indexing. *Legal Papers of John Adams*, 1:4–25

44. Josiah Quincy, "Dedication of Dane Law College" (Cambridge, 1832), 17.

45. Charles R. McKirdy, "Massachusetts Lawyers on the Eve of the American Revolution: The State of the Profession," in *Law in Colonial Massachusetts, 1630–1800*, comp. Daniel R. Coquillette (Boston: Colonial Society of Massachusetts, 1984), 318–22. In 1768 the Essex County bar became the first county bar to set educational requirements for admission. G. Dexter, ed., "Record Book of the Suffolk County Bar," *Proceedings of the Massachusetts Historical Society* 19 (1881–82): 149. The Suffolk County bar accepted a modified version of the Essex bar requirements in 1771. Ibid., 150.

46. Peter E. Russell, *His Majesty's Judges: Provincial Society and the Supreme Court in Massachusetts, 1692–1774* (New York: Garland Publishing, 1990), 24. See also Claire Priest, "Currency Policies and Legal Development in Colonial New England," *Yale*

Law Journal 110, no. 8 (2001): 1301, and authorities cited therein; Peter Charles Hoffer, *Law and People in Colonial America*, rev. ed. (1992; Baltimore: Johns Hopkins Press, 1998), 79–80.

47. Charles R. McKirdy, "Lawyers in Crisis: The Massachusetts Legal Profession, 1760–1790" (Ph.D. diss., Northwestern University, 1969), appendix 1.

48. Ibid.

49. This discussion of the Massachusetts court system draws heavily from the excellent discussion in *Legal Papers of John Adams*, 1:xxxviii–xliv. See also McKirdy, "Before the Storm," 46, 49–50.

50. Act of June 18, 1697, ch. 8 (1697), *The Acts and Resolves, Public and Private, of the Province of Massachusetts Bay*, vol. 1 (Boston, 1869), 282.

51. Act of July 14, 1693, ch. 9 (1693), *Massachusetts Acts and Resolves*, 1:122; Act of November 1, 1692, ch. 18 (1692), ibid., 51–55; Act of October 22, 1692, ch. 22 (1692), ibid., 58–59.

52. Act of July 14, 1693, ch. 9 (1693), ibid., 122.

53. Act of June 18, 1697 (1697), ibid., 282; Act of June 16, 1699 (1699), ibid., 367–68.

54. Act of June 16, 1699, ch. 1 (1699), ibid., 367.

55. Ibid., 368–69. Certain counties were permitted to hold biannual sessions. Ibid.

56. Ibid., 367–68. Such appeals apparently entitled the appellant to a new trial by jury. *Legal Papers of John Adams*, 1:xxxix.

57. Act of June 15, 1699, ch. 2 (1699), *Massachusetts Acts and Resolves*, 1:369.

58. Ibid.; Act of June 15, 1699, ch. 2 (1699), ibid., 369; Act of June 18, 1697, ch. 9 (1697), ibid., 283–84.

59. Act of June 26, 1699, ch. 3 (1699), ibid., 370.

60. Act of June 3, 1701, ch. 2 (1701), ibid., 459–60.

61. Act of June 18, 1701, ch. 6 (1701), ibid., 466–67.

62. William E. Nelson, *Americanization of the Common Law: The Impact of Legal Change on Massachusetts Society, 1760–1830* (Cambridge: Harvard University Press, 1975), 16.

63. William Douglass, *Summary, Historical and Political, of the First Planting, Progressive Improvements, and Present State of the British Settlements in North America*, vol. 1 (Boston, 1749), 517.

64. This third bite was eliminated by legislation in 1754, which, noting that civil trials "upon appeals and reviews, have been grievously multiplied," provided that a loser in the Superior Court was not entitled to a second trial in that court if he or she already had lost in the inferior court. Act of June 18, 1701, *Massachusetts Acts and Resolves*, 1:466; Act of April 23, 1754, *Massachusetts Acts and Resolves*, vol. 3 (Boston, 1878), 378. The legal status of women in colonial Massachusetts was unclear. While unmarried women had the right to sue, a married woman's rights, in theory, were subsumed by those of her husband and she lost the right to bring suit. In practice, however, there were ways around this prohibition. Coquillette, *Law Commonplace Book*, 44–48.

65. Nelson, *Americanization of the Common Law*, 16. The Superior Court did not hear appeals from the province's probate courts. With one court in each county, these tribunals had cognizance over wills and intestacies. The governor and council, acting as a superior court of probate, heard appeals from the decisions of the county probate

judges. The governor and council also had jurisdiction over divorce cases. *Legal Papers of John Adams,* 1:xliv.

66. L. Kinvin Wroth, "The Massachusetts Vice Admiralty Court," in *Law and Authority in Colonial America: Selected Essays,* ed. George A. Billias (1965; New York: Dover Publications, 1970), 32–34.

67. Ibid., passim; *John Adams Legal Papers of John Adams,* 1:xliv; *Legal Papers of John Adams,* ed. L. Kinvin Wroth and Hiller B. Zobel, vol. 2 (Cambridge: Harvard University Press, 1965), 2:68, 98–100, 247–53, 352.

68. Massachusetts Superior Court, Suffolk County Minute Books (1734), Church of Jesus Christ of Latter-day Saints (hereafter LDS) Court Records Project, microfilm reel nos. 0946473, 0946472.

69. Massachusetts Superior Court, Suffolk County Minute Books (1736), LDS Court Records Project, reel no. 0946473.

70. *Boston Evening-Post t,* December 12, 1756; Massachusetts Superior Court, Suffolk County Minute Books (1738–1748), LDS Court Records Project, reel nos. 0946473, 0946475, 0946476, 0946477.

71. *Boston Gazette,* June 27, 1722.

72. *Boston Evening-Post,* January 10, 1737.

73. The minute books for each Superior Court session in Boston often identify at least one of the lawyers involved in a case, but the books are not consistent from session to session. While some provide the names of many attorneys, other do not name any for the entire term. Moreover, there are unreadable entries, and some use unclear or inconsistent abbreviations for attorneys' names.

74. Massachusetts Superior Court, Suffolk County Minute Books (1734), LDS Court Records Project, reel nos. 0946472, 0946473.

75. Massachusetts Superior Court, Suffolk County Minute Books (1736, 1738, 1739, 1740), LDS Court Records Project, reel nos. 0946473, 0946475, 0946476.

76. Massachusetts Superior Court, Suffolk County Minute Books (1739, 1749), LDS Court Records Project, reel nos. 0946475, 0946476.

77. Massachusetts Superior Court, Suffolk County Minute Books (1736–1739), LDS Court Records Project, reel no. 0946472).

78. Massachusetts Superior Court, Suffolk County Minute Books (February Term, 1738, no. 223), LDS Court Records Project, reel no. 0946473.

79. Massachusetts Superior Court, Suffolk County Minute Books (February Term, 1736, no. 297); August Term, 1739, no. 251), LDS Court Records Project, reel nos. 0946473, 0946475; *New-England Weekly Journal* (Boston), May 26, 1729 (Billings); Massachusetts Superior Court, Suffolk County Minute Books (February Term, 1736, no. 257), LDS Court Records Project, reel no. 0946473; *Boston News-Letter,* October 1, 1730 (Wood); Massachusetts Superior Court, Suffolk County Minute Books (February Term, 1738, no. 116), LDS Court Records Project, reel no. 0946474; *Boston News-Letter,* June 17, 1742 (Griggs).

80. Massachusetts Superior Court, Suffolk County Minute Books (August Term, 1740, no. 255), LDS Court Records Project, reel no. 0946476; *Weekly Rehearsal* (Boston), May 19, 1735 (Little); Massachusetts Superior Court, Suffolk County Minute Books (February Term, 1736, no. 256), LDS Court Records Project, reel no. 0946473; *New*

England Weekly Journal (Boston), June 17, 1728; Massachusetts Superior Court, Suffolk County Minute Books (August Term, 1739, no. 43), LDS Court Records Project, reel no. 0946475; *Boston Post-Boy*, December 26, 1763 (Brackett).

81. Massachusetts Superior Court, Suffolk County Minute Books (February Term, 1740, no. 211; August Term, 1736, no. 11; February Term, 1737, no. 244), LDS Court Records Project, reel nos. 0946475, 0946473, 0946474; *Boston Post-Boy*, April 27, 1767 (Isaac and Richard Gridley); Massachusetts Superior Court, Suffolk County Minute Books (August Term, 1740, no. 256), LDS Court Records Project, reel no. 0946476 (Henderson); Massachusetts Superior Court, Suffolk County Minute Books (August Term, 1736, no. 18), LDS Court Records Project, reel no. 0946473; *Boston News-Letter,* September 11, 1721 (Beal); Massachusetts Superior Court, Suffolk County Minute Books (August Term, 1738, no. 240), LDS Court Records Project, reel no. 0946473 (Gee).

82. Shipton, *Harvard Graduates*, vol. 6, *1713–1721* (Boston: Massachusetts Historical Society, 1942), 177–78; John Eliot, *A Biographical Dictionary containing a brief account of the first settlers and other eminent characters* (Boston, 1809), 215.

83. Massachusetts Superior Court, Suffolk County Minute Books (August Term, 1738, no. 239), LDS Court Records Project, reel no. 0946473 (Brattle); Massachusetts Superior Court, Suffolk County Minute Books (August Term, 1739, no. 259), LDS Court Records Project, reel no. 0946475 (Quincy).

84. Massachusetts Superior Court, Essex County Minute Books (Salem, October Term, 1736, no. 67), LDS Court Records Project, reel no. 0946472; Sibley, *Harvard Graduates,* vol. 3, *1678–1689* (Boston: Massachusetts Historical Society, 1885), 356–57; Shipton, *Harvard Graduates,* 6:250–57; D. Hamilton Hurd, *History of Essex County, Massachusetts, with Biographical Sketches of many of its Pioneers and Prominent Men,* vol. 1 (Philadelphia, 1888), xix.

85. Massachusetts Superior Court, Essex County Minute Books (Salem, October Term, 1736, nos. 44, 66), LDS Court Records Project, reel no. 0946472; Shipton, *Harvard Graduates,* vol. 5, *1701–1712* (Boston: Massachusetts Historical Society, 1937), 497; Hurd, *History of Essex County,* 1:xviii–xix.

86. Massachusetts Superior Court, Essex County Minute Books (Salem, November Term, 1738, no. 93), LDS Court Records Project, reel no. 0946472; Hurd, *History of Essex County,* 1:xviii–xix.

87. Summons (April 6, 1733), *Vassall v. Rogers,* Middlesex Inferior Court of Common Pleas, LDS Court Records Project, reel no. 900478, item no. 32515.

88. Shipton, *Harvard Graduates*, vol. 8, *1726–1730* (Boston: Massachusetts Historical Society, 1951), 521.

89. Shipton, *Harvard Graduates,* vol. 9, *1731–1735* (Boston: Massachusetts Historical Society, 1956), 350.

90. Meeting of Overseers of Harvard College (September 12, 1732), Superior Court of Massachusetts, Miscellaneous Papers, no. 35213, LDS Court Records Project, reel no. 900478.

91. Shipton, *Harvard Graduates*, vol. 7, *1722–1725* (Boston: Massachusetts Historical Society, 1945), 554.

92. Ibid.

93. Ibid.

94. Answer of Daniel Rogers (May 21, 1733), *Vassall v. Rogers*, Middlesex County Inferior Court of Common Pleas, Massachusetts County Court Files, vol. 249, no. 35,210, LDS Court Records Project, reel no. 900478.

95. Summons (April 6, 1733), *Vassall v. Rogers*, Middlesex County Inferior Court of Common Pleas, Massachusetts County Court Files, vol. 249, no. 35,215, LDS Court Records Project, reel no. 900478.

96. Indictment (May 21, 1733), *Case of Daniel Rogers*, Middlesex County Court of General Sessions, Massachusetts County Court Files, vol. 249, no. 35,218, LDS Court Records Project, reel no. 900478.

97. At a Meeting of ye President and Fellows of Harvard College at Cambridge, May 2, 1733, "Harvard College Records," *Publications of the Colonial Society of Massachusetts* 16 (1925): 610.

98. McKirdy, "Massachusetts Lawyers on the Eve of the Revolution," 325. For an example of one way that "hush money" worked, see John Adams to Col. Josiah Quincy, October 1761, in *John Adams Diary and Autobiography*, 1:223.

99. Answer (May 21, 1733), *Vassall v. Rogers*, Middlesex County Inferior Court of Common Pleas, Massachusetts County Court Files, vol. 249, no. 35,210, LDS Court Records Project, reel no. 900478.

100. At a Meeting of ye President & Fellows of Harvard College at Cambridge, July 30, 1733, "Harvard College Records," *Publications of the Colonial Society of Massachusetts* 16 (1925): 615.

101. Judgment (May 21, 1733), *Case of Daniel Rogers*, Middlesex County Court of General Sessions, Massachusetts County Court Files, vol. 249, no. 35,397, LDS Court Records Project, reel no. 900479.

102. Appeal (July 24, 1733), *Rogers v. Rex*, Superior Court of Massachusetts, Massachusetts County Court Files, vol. 249, no. 35,347, LDS Court Records Project, reel no. 900479.

103. Shipton, *Harvard Graduates*, 7:555. Rogers remained a tutor at Harvard until 1741, when he resigned to follow the revivalist George Whitefield as an itinerant preacher. In 1748 he was installed in the pulpit of a New Light church in Exeter, New Hampshire, a position he held until his death in 1785 at age seventy-eight. Ibid., 555–60.

104. White graduated from Harvard in Gridley's class (1725) and received his M.A. with Gridley in 1728. Gridley represented him in the August 1741 term of the Superior Court at Boston. Ibid., 619–20; Massachusetts Superior Court, Suffolk County Minute Books (August, 1741, no. 36), LDS Court Records Project, reel no. 0946475.

105. See text at notes 79–80; *Weekly Rehearsal* (Boston), June 26, 1732; September 18, 1732; October 2, 1732.

106. Shipton, *Harvard Graduates*, 7:520; Joseph S. Clark, *Historical Sketch of the Congregational Churches in Massachusetts from 1620 to 1858* (Boston, 1858), 151; *The West Church, Boston: Commemorative Service of the Fiftieth Anniversary of the Present Ministry and the One Hundred and Fiftieth of Its Foundation* (Boston, 1887), 13.

107. Shipton, *Harvard Graduates*, 7:520; R. G. F. Candage, "Jeremy Gridley," *Publications of the Brookline Historical Society* (Brookline, MA, 1903), 21; Charles M. Andrews, "The Boston Merchants and the Non-Importation Movement," *Publications of the Colonial Society of Massachusetts* 19 (1918): 161, 164. The "Fellowship Club," organized in 1742, was

chartered on February 2, 1754, as the Marine Society of Boston. See text at chapter 10, notes 53–58.

108. Shipton, *Harvard Graduates*, 7:520–21; Candage, "Jeremy Gridley," 27; *Proceedings in Masonry: St. John's Grand Lodge, 1733–1792; Massachusetts Grand Lodge, 1769–1792* (Boston, 1895), 40, 42.

109. John Adams to William Tudor, July 24, 1774, Tudor Papers, MHS.

110. *The Diaries of Benjamin Lynde and Benjamin Lynde, Jr. with an Appendix*, ed. Fitch E. Oliver (Boston, 1890), 51–52.

111. *Boston Post-Boy*, September 14, 1767; *Peter Oliver's Origins and Progress of the American Rebellion: A Tory View*, ed. Douglas Adair and John A. Schutz (Stanford: Stanford University Press, 1961), 36.

Chapter Three: The Land Bank Crisis (1740–1742)

1. *Journals of the Massachusetts House of Representatives* 20 (June 9, 1742): 34; *Boston News-Letter*, June 10, 1742.

2. Leonard Woods Labaree, ed., *Royal Instructions to British Governors, 1670–1776*, vol. 1 (New York: D. Appleton-Century Company, 1935), 388–89; A. C. Goodell Jr., "Attorneys-General of Massachusetts," *Proceedings of the Massachusetts Historical Society*, 3rd ser., 10 (1895–96): 285.

3. Attorney General Robert Raymond to Council of Trade, August 10, 1722, in *Calendar of State Papers: Colonial Series; America and the West Indies, 1722–1723* (London, 1934), 119.

4. Charter of the Province of the Massachusetts Bay (1691), in *The Acts and Resolves, Public and Private, of the Province of Massachusetts Bay*, vol. 1 (Boston, 1869), 12; Goodell, "Attorneys-General of Massachusetts," 286. See also *Journals of the Massachusetts House of Representatives* 9 (December 17, 1729): 182–85.

5. Charter of Massachusetts Bay (1691), 1:16; Goodell, "Attorneys-General of Massachusetts," 286. See also *Journals of the Massachusetts House of Representatives* 9 (December 9, 1729): 155–60; (December 19 1729): 200–202.

6. Goodell, "Attorneys-General of Massachusetts," 286; Labaree, *Royal Instructions*, 1:388–89; *Journals of the Massachusetts House of Representatives* 1 (June 8, 1716): 92 (Paul Dudley); (June 19, 1717): 213 (Dudley); *Journals of the Massachusetts House of Representatives* 2 (June 25, 1718): 45 (Dudley); (June 24, 1719): 161 (John Valentine); (July 19, 1720): 249 (Thomas Newton); *Journals of the Massachusetts House of Representatives* 5 (June 20, 1723): 45 (John Read); *Journals of the Massachusetts House of Representatives* 6 (June 12, 1724): 55 (Read); (June 15, 1725): 266 (Read); *Journals of the Massachusetts House of Representatives* 7 (June 21, 1726): 78 (Read); (June 28, 1727): 300 (Read). There were a few exceptions. In 1721 Governor Samuel Shute "negatived" John Read, who had been nominated by the legislature, and in 1728 Addington Davenport declined the nomination. *Journals of the Massachusetts House of Representatives* 3 (September 6, 1721): 120 (Read); *Journals of the Massachusetts House of Representatives* 8 (June 19, 1728): 232 (Davenport).

7. Labaree, *Royal Instructions*, 388–89 (change in italics); *Journals of the Massachusetts House of Representatives* 9 (May 28, 1729): 9. Apparently this change was based in part on

an opinion by the English attorney general to the Lords of Trade "that the nomination of an attorney general will be in the governor" as per the charter provision granting him the power to appoint "officers related to the courts." Attorney General Robert Raymond to Council of Trade, August 10, 1722, in *Calendar of State Papers*, 119–20.

8. *Journals of the Massachusetts House of Representatives* 9 (June 26, 1729): 11.

9. *Journals of the Massachusetts House of Representatives* 10 (June 4, 1731): 349 (Read); *Journals of the Massachusetts House of Representatives* 11 (July 4, 1732): 73 (Davenport): (June 22, 1733): 251 (Read); *Journals of the Massachusetts House of Representatives* 12 (June 12, 1734): 8 (Read); *Journals of the Massachusetts House of Representatives* 13 (July 2, 1735): 97 (Read); *Journals of the Massachusetts House of Representatives* 14 (June 23, 1736): 70 (William Brattle); *Journals of the Massachusetts House of Representatives* 15 (July 5, 1737): 118 (Brattle); *Journals of the Massachusetts House of Representatives* 16 (June 29, 1738): 97 (Overing); *Journals of the Massachusetts House of Representatives* 17 (July 11, 1739): 111 (Overing); *Journals of the Massachusetts House of Representatives* 18 (July 9, 1740): 86 (Overing); *Journals of the Massachusetts House of Representatives* 19 (July 31, 1741): 48 (Overing).

10. See note 9.

11. John A. Schutz, *William Shirley: King's Governor of Massachusetts* (Chapel Hill: University of North Carolina Press, 1961), 29; Claire Priest, "Currency Policy and Legal Development in Colonial New England," *Yale Law Journal* 110, no. 8 (2001): 1322.

12. Until the early 1740s, courts in Massachusetts applied the English doctrine of "nominalism." Under this rule, the payment of the nominal value of a debt satisfied a debtor's legal obligation even though the debt was paid in depreciated currency that, in reality, was not worth its face value. Priest, "Currency Policy," 1355–56.

13. Ibid., 1347–72.

14. Ibid., 1373–76.

15. Andrew McFarland Davis, "Provincial Banks Land and Silver," *Transactions of the Colonial Society of Massachusetts* 3 (1900): 10.

16. *Boston Weekly News-Letter*, July 16, 1741.

17. Davis, "Provincial Banks," 29. Davis maintains that the "pretense" that the "Bubble Act" originally applied to the colonies was "absurd" and "wicked." He points out that opinions of Great Britain's attorney general and the Board of Trade on November 16, 1735, and March 17, 1736, respectively, held that ventures like the Land Bank and the Silver Scheme were permissible in the colonies. Ibid., 29–30.

18. *Boston Weekly New-Letter*, July 16, 1741; Davis, "Provincial Banks," 28.

19. Davis, "Provincial Banks," 28.

20. "Novanglus," *Boston Gazette and Country Journal*, February 13, 1775.

21. *Boston Evening-Post*, October 5, 1741.

22. Some of these holdouts found it difficult to redeem the notes because they had sold them at a discount but could purchase them back only at face value. Andrew McFarland Davis, "Legislation and Litigation Connected with the Land Bank of 1740," *Proceedings of the American Antiquarian Society*, n.s., 2 (1896): 87.

23. William Shirley to Lords of Trade, April 30, 1742, in *Correspondence of William Shirley*, ed. Charles Henry Lincoln, vol. 1 (New York: Macmillan, 1912), 84.

24. *Journals of the Massachusetts House of Representatives* 19 (March 29, 1742): 214.

25. *An Account of the rise, progress and consequences of the two late schemes commonly call'd the land-bank or manufactory scheme and the silver scheme* (Boston, 1744), 52.

26. William Shirley to Lords of Trade, April 30, 1742, 1:85; *An Account of the land-bank*, 52.

27. Davis, "Legislation and Litigation Connected with the Land Bank of 1740," 91.

28. Schutz, *William Shirley*, 61.

29. *Journals of the Massachusetts House of Representatives* 20 (June 10, 1742): 34.

30. Schutz, *William Shirley*, 61–62.

31. See note 7. See also the Lords Justices to William Shirley, September 10, 1741, in *Correspondence of William Shirley*, 1:43.

32. *Journals of the Massachusetts House of Representatives* 20 (January 15, 1743): 156.

33. Ibid.

34. Andrew McFarlane Davis, "Partners in the Land Bank of 1740," *Publications of the Colonial Society of Massachusetts* 4 (1910): 194, 199.

35. Massachusetts Superior Court, Suffolk County Minute Books (February and August Terms, 1741), Church of Jesus Christ of Latter-day Saints Court Records Project, reel no. 0946475.

36. Read had first been elected to the council by the House of Representatives in 1741. Clifford K. Shipton, *Sibley's Harvard Graduates: Biographical Sketches of Those Who Attended Harvard College* (hereafter Shipton, *Harvard Graduates*), vol. 4, 1690–1700 (Boston: Massachusetts Historical Society, 1933), 375.

37. Shipton, *Harvard Graduates*, vol. 7, 1722–1725 (Boston: Massachusetts Historical Society, 1945), 224.

38. Schutz, *William Shirley*, 73.

39. Hiller B. Zobel, *The Boston Massacre* (1970; New York: W.W. Norton & Company, 1971), 105 (quoting Francis Bernard to Lord Hillsborough, December 12, 1768). For examples of attorneys general petitioning to be paid, see *Journals of the Massachusetts House of Representatives* 3 (June 30, 1721): 48; *Journals of the Massachusetts House of Representatives* 5 (August 27, 1723): 147; *Journals of the Massachusetts House of Representatives* 9 (July 10, 1729): 38; *Journals of the Massachusetts House of Representatives* 11 (April 13, 1733): 197.

40. Zobel, *Boston Massacre*, 105.

41. William H. Whitmore, *Massachusetts Civil List for the Colonial and Provincial Periods, 1630–1774* (Albany, 1870), 129; Shipton, *Harvard Graduates*, 7:521.

42. Charles R. McKirdy, "Before the Storm: The Working Lawyer in Pre-Revolutionary Massachusetts," *Suffolk University Law Review* 11, no. 1 (1976): 46, 58–59. The justices earned fees for performing their judicial and administrative functions. John Worthington, a Crown attorney and a justice of the peace, claimed full-term attendance as a justice even though he represented the Crown before the court on which he sat. Robert Taylor, *Western Massachusetts in the Revolution* (Providence: Brown University Press, 1954), 31–32.

43. John Adams to Abigail Adams (June 20, 1774), in *Adams Family Correspondence*, ed. L. H. Butterfield, vol. 1 (Cambridge: Belknap Press of Harvard University Press, 1963), 116–17. Loyalist Peter Oliver claimed that it was Adams's failure to gain a "Commission for the Peace" that drove him into rebellion. *Peter Oliver's Origin and*

Progress of the American Rebellion: A Tory View, ed. D. Adair and J. Schutz (Stanford: Stanford University Press, 1961), 83.

44. McKirdy, "Before the Storm," 49–50; *Legal Papers of John Adams,* ed. L. Kinvin Wroth and Hiller B. Zobel, vol.1 (Cambridge: Harvard University Press, 1965), xl; Taylor, *Western Massachusetts in the Revolution,* 28–29.

45. Shipton, *Harvard Graduates,* vol. 8, *1726–1730* (Boston: Massachusetts Historical Society, 1951), 727–28, 163–66.

46. Shipton, *Harvard Graduates,* vol. 9, *1731–1735* (Boston: Massachusetts Historical Society, 1956), 172–73; Shipton, *Harvard Graduates,* 7:251–52; Shipton, *Harvard Graduates,* vol. 6, *1713–1721* (Boston: Massachusetts Historical Society, 1942), 490–92.

47. *Legal Papers of John Adams,* 1:xxxix, n. 13.

48. Shipton, *Harvard Graduates,* 7:521.

Chapter Four: The *American Magazine* (1743–1746)

1. Frank Luther Mott, *A History of American Magazines,* vol. 1 (Cambridge: Harvard University Press, 1938), 78.

2. Joseph T. Buckingham, *Specimens of Newspaper Literature with Personal Memoirs, Anecdotes, and Reminiscences,* vol. 1 (Boston, 1850), 158; Isaiah Thomas, *The History of Printing in America with a Biography of Printers and an Account of Newspapers,* vol. 1 (Albany, 1874), 90, 106.

3. See, e.g., Charles Chauncy, *Seasonable Thoughts on the State of Religion in New England* (Boston: printed by Rogers and Fowle for Samuel Elliot, 1743); Giles Firmen, *The Real Christian, or A Treatise of Effectual Calling* (Boston: printed by Rogers and Fowle for J. Edwards and J. Blanchard, 1742).

4. Mott, *History of American Magazines,* 1:78.

5. See, e.g., *New-England Weekly Journal* (, December 9, 1735 ("Choice good Bohea Tea; also all sorts of Stationary and Cutlery Ware"); *Boston Evening-Post,* December 19, 1743 ("a collection of the most valuable Authors, viz. Shakespear, Sir Thomas Brown, . . . Mr. Dryden, . . . Mr. Pope").

6. Gridley probably was well acquainted with Green, Fowle, Eliot, and Blanchard. The Boston literary circle was small and the publishing business even smaller.

7. *Boston News-Letter,* January 27, 1743.

8. Ibid.

9. Ibid.

10. Ibid.

11. Walter Isaacson, *Benjamin Franklin: An American Life* (New York: Simon & Schuster, 2003), 116–18.

12. *The Christian History,* March 5, 1743. This publication lasted for two years, but in the words of one media historian, given its character, *The Christian History* "can scarcely be called a magazine." Mott, *History of American Magazines,* 1:78.

13. *Boston News-Letter,* March 10, 1743.

14. *Boston Weekly-Magazine,* March 2, 1743.

15. Ibid.; Isaiah Thomas, *The History of Printing in America with a Biography of Printers and an Account of Newspapers,* vol. 2 (Albany, 1874), 66.

16. *Boston Weekly-Magazine,* March 2, 1743.

17. *Boston News-Letter,* March 17, 1743.

18. Ibid.

19. Ibid.

20. John Blanchard, *A Sober Reply to a Mad Answer. In a Letter to M. A. Cresswell, occasioned by his letter to Mr. E. Turell, by a private brother* (Boston: Rogers and Fowle, 1742), 1, 16.

21. See *Boston Gazette,* February 1, 1743, February 8, 1743; *Boston News-Letter,* February 3, 1743, February 10, 1743.

22. See text at note 19.

23. In his *History of Printing in America,* 2:66, Isaiah Thomas maintains that there were four issues of the publication, but I could find only three.

24. The first issue was dated "September 1743," but the *American Magazine and Historical Chronicle* often was distributed a month after the date appearing on the masthead.

25. *American Magazine and Historical Chronicle,* September 1743, ii.

26. Ibid.

27. "Reflections on Inconsistency," *American Magazine and Historical Chronicle* (hereafter cited by article title, date, and page reference), March 1746, 120; "On Flattery and Morosity," April 1746, 169; "Of Cunning," August 1746, 369; "Haughtiness in Superiors towards Inferiors," November 1746, 493; "On Cursing and Swearing," December 1746, 11.

28. "Virtuous Love and Lust. A Vision," February 1744, 245; "Essay on the Passion of Love," April 1744, 329; "Education and the Power of Love," July 1745, 286.

29. "Reflections on Death," November 1744, 641; "An Essay on Happiness," November 1744, 645; "Of Style and Elocution," April 1745, 159; "Great TALKERS Exposed," April 1745, 160; "The Form of a Modern Love Letter," August 1744, 510; "A Caution against the ATTEMPTS OF LIBERTINE WITS," August 1744, 511.

30. "Description of China, From the French of Pere Du Halde," November 1744, 615; "Conclusion of the description of Greenland," May 1744, 399.

31. "Sir William Temple's Account of the Government of the United Provinces," September 1744, 558; "An Account of the College of Physicians in London," May 1745, 194; "A Succinct Account of Edinburgh Castle," January 1746, 24

32. "Comets from Rev. Mr. Rowning's 'Compendious System of Natural Philosophy,'" January 1744, 207; "The Weight and credit of popular Opinions, extracted from Dr. Boyle's Reflections on the Comet of 1680," January 1745, 30; "Literary Articles from the Hague . . . Planetary and Cometary Spheres . . . ," September 1745, 394.

33. "Philosophical Enquiries concerning the Virtues of Tar Water, etc. By Dr. George Berkeley," October 1744, 588; "Re Virtues of Tar Water," November 1744, 636; "Some Reflexions on Dr. Berkeley's Treatise on Tar Water," April 1745, 145; "On Tar Water," May 1745, 211.

34. "An Account of the Life of Sir Isaac Newton," January 1745, 8; "An ACCOUNT of the LIFE of John Locke, Esq.," September 1744, 540; "The Life of John Milton," June 1745, 239; "The LIFE of Dr. Sydenham," October 1745, 430; "The Life of Mr. John Jewell, an English Bishop," September 1745, 398. See *Encyclopedia Britannica,* 11th ed., s.v. "Sydenham, Thomas," and "Jewel, John."

35. "Mirth and Cheerfulness consistent with Religion," October 1744, 596; "The Church: A Religious Satire," July 1744, 477.

36. "On the Immortality of the Soul," May 1744, 377; "An Essay on Divine Judgments," July 1744, 458.

37. "An Apology for Religious Zeal," November 1744, 642; "Hypocrisy in Religion exposed and Sincerely recommended," February 1745, 71; "The Folly and Absurdity of Atheism," September 1745, 399.

38. *Boston News-Letter,* March 17, 1743.

39. *American Magazine and Historical Chronicle,* January 1746, 10, 12, 17, 19, 20, 22, 24, 27, 30, 32.

40. Respectively, January 1746, 27; March 1746, 124; July 1746, 323; October 1746, 457; November 1746, 501.

41. "Poetical Essays," June 1745, 264.

42. *American Magazine and Historical Chronicle,* March 1746, 144.

43. *American Magazine and Historical Chronicle,* October 1744, 608.

44. Edward W. R. Pitcher, *The American Magazine and Historical Chronicle (Boston 1743–1746)* (Lewiston, NY: Edwin Mellen Press, 2003), 2.

45. Mott, *History of American Magazines,* 1:79.

46. See, e.g., "A gentle hint to a few Gentlemen-Rakes," September 1743, 35 (from *Philadelphia Gazette*); "A Letter Concerning Two Scholars," March 1745, 122 (from *New York Post-Boy*).

47. *American Magazine and Historical Chronicle,* September 1743, ii.

48. See, e.g., "Extract from Vossius and his Treatise de Philogia," June 1745, 244, which Gridley took from the *Universal Spectator;* and "Means to recover persons thought to be drowned," June 1746, 265, which Gridley took from the *London Magazine,* which had taken it from *Philosophical Transactions.*

49. Louis B. Wright, *The Cultural Life of the American Colonies, 1607–1763* (1952; New York: Harper & Row, 1962), 246.

50. See text at note 11.

Chapter Five: Iron and Land

1. Clifford K. Shipton, *Sibley's Harvard Graduates: Biographical Sketches of Those who Attended Harvard College* (hereafter Shipton, *Harvard Graduates*), vol. 7, 1722–1725 (Boston: Massachusetts Historical Society, 1945), 524–25.

2. Ibid., 741. Although Oliver was more than ten years younger than Gridley, the two men shared a common interest in literature and poetry. Ibid.

3. Ibid., 737–38. The town's name is sometimes spelled "Middleboro."

4. Ibid.

5. Thomas Weston, *History of the Town of Middleboro, Massachusetts* (Boston: Houghton Mifflin and Company, 1906), 383–85.

6. Jeremy Gridley to James Otis Esq., June 18, 1743, Otis Family Papers, 1701–1800, Massachusetts Historical Society, Boston (hereafter MHS).

7. Arthur C. Bining, *British Regulation of the Colonial Iron Trade* (Philadelphia: University of Pennsylvania Press, 1933), 92.

8. Edward Pierce Hamilton, "Early Industry of the Neponset Valley and the Charles," *Proceedings of the Massachusetts Historical Society,* 3rd ser., 71 (1953–1957): 119.

9. 23 Geo. 2, c. 29, sec. 9.

10. The act carried high fines for violations. While in time it became studiously ignored by colonial iron manufacturers, until the end of the wars with France in America, when British regulars were much in evidence, American iron manufacturers showed little desire to erect the forbidden mills. Bining, *British Iron Regulation,* 86.

11. Weston, *History of Middleboro,* 360–61; Shipton, *Harvard Graduates,* 7:739.

12. Shipton, *Harvard Graduates,* 7:739.

13. Weston, *History of Middleboro,* 385.

14. Mary Elizabeth Ruwell, *Eighteenth-Century Capitalism: The Formation of American Marine Insurance Companies* (New York: Garland Publishers, 1995), 1.

15. Ibid., 10, 39–40; Christopher Kingston, "Marine Insurance in Britain and America, 1720–1844: A Corporate Institutional Analysis," *Journal of Economic History* 67, no. 2 (2005): 16–17.

16. Charles M. Andrews, *English Commercial and Colonial Policy,* vol. 4 of *The Colonial Period of American History* (New Haven: Yale University Press, 1938), 349–50. See also Curtis Nettels, "The Menace of Colonial Manufacturing," *New England Quarterly* 4, no. 2 (1931): 230–69.

17. Andrews, *English Commercial and Colonial Policy,* 350.

18. Ray Allen Billington, "The Origin of the Frontier Speculator as a Frontier Type," *Agricultural History,* 19, no. 4 (1945): 208; Roy Hidemichi Akagi, *The Town Proprietors of the New England Colonies* (1923; Gloucester, MA: Peter Smith, 1963), 175–76.

19. Petition of Samuel Heywood et al., in Albert Smith, *History of the Town of Peterborough, Hillsborough, New Hampshire* (Boston, 1876), 340; *Journals of the Massachusetts House of Representatives* 15 (December 6, 1737): 186.

20. Heywood Petition, in Smith, *History of Peterborough,* 340; *Journals of the Massachusetts House of Representatives* 15 (December 6, 1737): 186.

21. *Journals of the Massachusetts House of Representatives* 15 (December 6, 1737): 188.

22. Ibid.; Smith, *History of Peterborough,* 20.

23. Consent of the Governor (January 16, 1738), in Smith, *History of Peterborough,* 342.

24. List of Grantees or Settlers (March 17, 1738), ibid., 342–43.

25. Jonathan Smith, "The Proprietors of Peterborough," *Granite Monthly,* old ser., 39 (1907): 339–40.

26. Smith, "The Proprietors of Peterborough," 353; Jonathan Smith, "The Massachusetts and New Hampshire Boundary Line Controversy, 1693–1740," *Proceedings of the Massachusetts Historical Society,* 3rd ser., 43 (October 1909–June 1910): 77–88.

27. Meeting of Proprietors (November 29, 1738), in Smith, *History of Peterborough,* 344–45, 27.

28. *Boston Gazette,* June 16, 1740. This advertisement may have been placed by proprietor Peter Prescott, who sold off his land as quickly as possible. In early 1744 he enlisted in the Cape Breton expedition and probably had little to do with Peterborough after that. Smith, "The Proprietors of Peterborough," 346–49.

29. Smith, "The Proprietors of Peterborough," 351; Leonard A. Morrison, *The History of Windham, New Hampshire (Rockingham County), 1719–1883* (Boston, 1883), 124.

30. Petition of Hill and Fowle (January 26, 1748), in *Township Grants of Lands in New Hampshire in the Masonian Patent*, ed. Albert Stillman Batchelor, in *Provincial and State Papers of New Hampshire*, 40 vols. (Concord, NH, 1896), 28:185 (hereafter *Township Grants*).

31. Smith, "Massachusetts and New Hampshire Boundary Line Controversy," 79–84.

32. Ibid., 85; Otis Grant Hammond, "The Mason Title and Its Relation to New Hampshire and Massachusetts," *Proceedings of the American Antiquarian Society* (1916): 255.

33. David E. Van Devanter, *The Emergence of the Province of New Hampshire, 1623–1741* (Baltimore: Johns Hopkins University Press, 1976), 40–41.

34. Cornelius Moynihan, *Introduction to the Law of Real Property* (St. Paul: West Publishing Company, 1962), 38–39.

35. Ibid., 51, 60.

36. Van Devanter, *Emergence of New Hampshire*, 51–56.

37. Ibid., 60–61.

38. Hammond, "The Mason Title and Its Relations to New Hampshire and Massachusetts," 252–53.

39. Ibid., 255–56.

40. Ibid., 256–60.

41. Petition of Hill and Fowle (January 26, 1748), in *Township Grants*, 28:185.

42. Quitclaim to Peterborough (1748), ibid., 186.

43. Smith, *History of Peterborough*, 58.

44. Ibid., 29; John Hill to George Jaffrey, May 22, 1765, ibid., 49; Plan of Peterborough, 1765, in *Township Grants*, 27:192.

45. Charter of Dantzic, 1753, in *Township Grants*, 28:77–84.

46. Charter of Hereford (August 7, 1754), ibid., 28:80–85. Apparently, neither of these townships was developed as required by the grants and, in time, were granted to others. See, e.g., D. Hamilton Hurd, ed., *History of Merrimack and Belknap Counties, New Hampshire* (Philadelphia, 1885), 415. (In 1772, Masonian Proprietors granted Dantzic to John Fisher, who changed its name to Fisherfield.)

47. Portsmouth January 3, 1753, in *Documents and Records relating to the Province of New Hampshire*, ed. James M. Campbell, vol. 6 in *Provincial and State Papers of New Hampshire (Concord, NH, 1877)*, 55–56.

48. Gridley to Joseph Blanchard, February 24, 1753, in *Township Grants*, 28:186.

49. D. Donovon and Jacob A. Woodward, *The History of the Town of Lyndeborough, New Hampshire, 1735–1905*, vol. 1 (1906), 43–48.

50. See text at note 38.

51. Nicholas Fazakerley to Jeremiah Gridley, May 21, 1754, in Jeremy Belknap, *The History of Massachusetts*, vol. 1 (Boston, 1792), 365.

52. Andrew Cazneau to George Jeffries of the Masonian Proprietors, October 4, 1773, in *Provincial and State Papers of New Hampshire*, 27:229.

53. George Jeffries to Andrew Cazneau, October 23, 1773, in *Provincial and State*

Papers of New Hampshire, 27:230; Akagi, *Town Proprietors of the New England Colonies*, 241–43.

54. Alan Taylor, "A Kind of Warr': The Contest for Land on the Northeastern Frontier, 1750–1820, *William and Mary Quarterly* 46, no. 1 (1984): 13.

55. Ibid.

56. "The Proprietors holding under Lake & Clark, Plaintiffs against Proprietors from *Plymouth-Colony, Defendants[,] Plaintiffs State of the Case*" (1757), Early American Imprint Series, November 28, 2017, http://infoweb.newsbank.com/7.

57. George E. Kershaw, *The Kennebec Proprietors, 1744–1779* (Portland: Maine Historical Society, 1975), 154.

58. *Boston News-Letter*, May 23, 1754; *Boston Post-Boy*, May 27, 1754; *Boston Gazette*, May 28, 1754.

59. *Boston Evening-Post*, June 3, 1754.

60. Kershaw, *Kennebec Proprietors*, 156.

61. *Journals of the Rev. Thomas Smith and the Rev. Samuel Deane*, ed. William Willis (Portland: Joseph S. Bailey, 1849), 157. James Otis Jr. was Gridley's adversary in the earlier case, but now he represented the Kennebec Company. Robert Auchmuty represented Clark and Lake. Kershaw, *Kennebec Proprietors*, 156.

62. Although it had agreed to abide by the referees' decision, the Plymouth Company moved for and was granted a new hearing. The parties then settled with the Plymouth Company, grossly overpaying for land it overvalued. Kershaw, *Kennebec Proprietors*, 158.

63. Ibid., 157–58.

64. Docket of the Massachusetts Superior Court at Falmouth in Cumberland County (June 26, 1764, and June 25, 1765), microfilm, MHS; Akagi, *Town Proprietors of New England Colonies*, 248–50; Taylor, "A Kind of Warr," 11; Joseph Williamson, *History of the Town of Belfast in the State of Maine*, vol. 1 (Portland, 1877), 44–45.

65. Smith, "Proprietors of Peterborough," 355.

66. Ibid., 355–56.

Chapter Six: *Fletcher v. Vassall* (1752)

1. John Adams to Thomas Jefferson, May 3, 1816, in *The Works of John Adams*, ed. Charles Francis Adams, vol. 10 (Boston, 1856), 214.

2. See text at chapter 2, notes 87–103.

3. William Vassall to Simon Porter, April 10, 1784, *Proceedings of the Massachusetts Historical Society* 44 (1910–11): 211; Clifford K. Shipton, *Sibley's Harvard Graduates: Biographical Sketches of Those Who Attended Harvard College* (hereafter Shipton, *Harvard Graduates*), vol. 9, *1731–1735* (Boston: Massachusetts Historical Society, 1956), 349–51.

4. Benjamin Franklin to William Vassall, May 29, 1746, July 19, 1746, www.franklinpapers.org (accessed July 14, 2010). See also Margaret Barton Karty, "Franklin's World of Books," *Journal of Library History* 2, no. 4 (1967): 300.

5. Samuel Dexter to Dr. Belknap, February 23, 1795, *Collections of the Massachusetts Historical Society*, 5th ser., 3 (1877): 385.

6. Ibid.

7. John A. Schutz, *Legislators of the Massachusetts General Court, 1691–1780: A Biographical Dictionary* (Boston: Northeastern University Press, 1997), 220–21.

8. *The State of the Action Brought by William Fletcher against William Vassall, for Defamation: Tried in the Superiour Court at Boston, August Term, A.D. 1752* (Boston, 1753), 21 (testimony of Thomas Fletcher). This, the only account of the trial, was written by, or at the request of, William Fletcher, and although it appears to be generally trustworthy, its accuracy and balance obviously are open to question.

9. See, e.g., W. T. Baxter, *The House of Hancock: Business in Boston, 1724–1775* (Cambridge: Harvard University Press, 1745), for one merchant family's diverse commercial interests.

10. See, e.g., *State of the Action*, 19 (testimony of Thomas Hubbard), 25 (testimony of Stephen Greenleaf), 26 (testimony of John Gooch). This was not an uncommon practice. See Baxter, *House of Hancock*, 176.

11. *State of the Action*, 25 (testimony of John Dowse).

12. John J. McCuster and Russell R. Menard, *The Economy of British America: 1607–1789* (Chapel Hill: University of North Carolina Press, 1985), 335–36.

13. *State of the Action*, 35–36 (testimony of Thomas Cushing), 42–43 (testimony of Thomas Hubbard), 47–50 (testimony of Edmund Quincy).

14. Ibid., 21–22 (testimony of Edmund Quincy); William I. Roberts III, "Ralph Carr: A Newcastle Merchant and the American Colonial Trade," *Business History Review* 42, no. 3 (1968): 283.

15. See, e.g., *State of the Action*, 42–43 (testimony of Thomas Hubbard), 58–59 (testimony of John Gooch).

16. William Holdsworth, *A History of English Law*, vol. 9 (London: Methuen & Co., 1925), 261.

17. Ibid., 261, 263, 270.

18. "Respondent's Case," *Vassall v. Fletcher*, 1, King's Most Excellent Majesty in Council, British Library, *Vassall (William) Suit v. Fletcher*, 1754, Add. 36217 f. 44; Howard Miller Chapin, "New England Vessels in the Expedition against Louisbourg, 1745," *New England Historical and Genealogical Register* 77 (1923): 60.

19. Chapin, "New England Vessels in the Expedition against Louisbourg," 108.

20. One issue was whether British men-of-war that were part of the invasion fleet but at sea at the time of the capture were entitled to a share of the prize money. Paul Leicester Ford, "List of some Briefs in Appeal Cases tried before the Lords Commissioners of Appeals of Prize Cases of his Majesty's Privy Council which relate to America, 1736–1758," *Proceedings of the Massachusetts Historical Society*, 2nd ser., 5 (1889–90): 92.

21. Ibid. See also *Boston Gazette*, August 14, 1756; *Boston Post-Boy*, September 17, 1756.

22. *State of the Action*, 23 (testimony of Narries Vaughn).

23. Ibid., 34 (testimony of William Vassall).

24. Ibid.

25. Ibid., 37 (testimony of William Fletcher).

26. Ibid., 35 (testimony of William Vassall).

27. Ibid., 16–36.

28. Ibid., 9 (testimony of Jonathan Mayhew), 8 (testimony of Joseph Scott), 15 (testimony of Joseph Jackson).

29. Ibid., 15 (testimony of Isaac Freeman), 8 (testimony of Joseph Scott). A groat is an old English coin worth four pennies.

30. Ibid., 9–10 (testimony of Jonathan Mayhew). See also ibid., 11 (testimony of Joseph Royall), 11 (testimony of Joshua Richardson), 16 (testimony of John Billings), 7 (testimony of Joseph Scott); *Black's Law Dictionary*, 4th ed. (1951), 231.

31. Ibid., 10 (testimony of Jonathan Mayhew). See also ibid., 12 (testimony of Harrison Gray), 15 (testimony of Joseph Jackson), 7 (testimony of John Dennie).

32. Ibid., 9 (testimony of Jonathan Mayhew).

33. Ibid., 11 (testimony of Belcher Hancock and Joseph Royall), 10 (testimony of Ebenezer Miller), 11 (testimony of Joshua Richardson).

34. Ibid., 7–8 (testimony of Joseph Scott).

35. Ibid., 10 (testimony of Jonathan Mayhew).

36. Ibid., 13 (testimony of Hugh McDaniel).

37. Ibid., 15 (testimony of Joseph Jackson).

38. Ibid., 16 (testimony of Thomas Cushing).

39. Writ (October 25, 1751), *Fletcher v. Vassall*, Suffolk County Inferior Court of Common Pleas, microfilm no. 68677, Church of Jesus Christ of Latter-day Saints (hereafter LDS) Court Records Project, microfilm reel no. 915132.

40. This was a common tactic. See text at chapter 2, notes 63–65.

41. Writ (October 25, 1751), *Fletcher v. Vassall*, Suffolk County Inferior Court of Common Pleas, no. 68677, 5, LDS Court Records Project, reel no. 91532.

42. Shipton, *Harvard Graduates*, vol. 8, *1726–1730* (Boston: Massachusetts Historical Society, 1951), 508–11; *Legal Papers of John Adams*, ed. L. Kinvin Wroth and Hiller B. Zobel, vol. 1 (Cambridge: Harvard University Press, 1965), cxi.

43. Emory Washburn, *Sketches of the Judicial History of Massachusetts from 1630 to the Revolution in 1775* (Boston, 1840), 309. One of his law students recalled Trowbridge as studying "day and night, and to be so absorbed in contemplation, as, at the dining table, to not know what was on it, or who was at it." William Ellery to R. H. Dana (March 10, 1819), Dana Papers, 1809–1824 (1819 envelope), Massachusetts Historical Society, Boston (hereafter MHS).

44. *The Works of John Adams*, ed. Charles Francis Adams, vol. 4 (Boston, 1851), 6.

45. Ibid.

46. *Diary and Autobiography of John Adams*, ed. L. H. Butterfield, vol. 1 (1961; New York: Atheneum, 1964), 227.

47. John J. Waters Jr., *The Otis Family in Provincial and Revolutionary Massachusetts* (1968; New York: W. W. Norton & Company, 1975), 40, 50–52, 54–55.

48. Ibid., 65.

49. Washburn, *Sketches of the Judicial History of Massachusetts*, 213.

50. Waters, *Otis Family*, 68.

51. *John Adams Diary and Autobiography*, 1:316 (July 26, 1788).

52. Ibid., 71–72.

53. Ibid., 72.

54. *Diary and Autobiography of John Adams*, ed. L. H. Butterfield, vol. 2 (1961; New

York: Atheneum, 1964), 2:83 (May 25, 1773). Adams dismissed this criticism as the result of Tory "Prejudices." Ibid.

55. Waters, *Otis Family*, 72; Samuel White to James Otis Sr., May 29, 1741, Miscellaneous Bound, vol. 11, MHS.
56. *Legal Papers of John Adams*, 1:civ–cv.
57. Waters, *Otis Family*, 91–94.
58. *State of the Action*, 9–10 (testimony of Jonathan Mayhew).
59. John Adams to William Tudor, June 5, 1817, in *Works of John Adams*, 10:264.
60. John Adams to H. Niles, January 14, 1818, ibid., 10:275; Waters, *Otis Family*, 74.
61. John Adams to H. Niles, January 14, 1818, in *Works of John Adams*, 10:275.
62. Waters, *Otis Family*, 113.
63. John Adams to William Tudor, June 5, 1817, in *Works of John Adams*, 10:264.
64. Waters, *Otis Family*, 114.
65. Ibid., 114–15.
66. This was not the first time that the Otises had squared off in court. That occurred in September 1748 in the Plymouth County Inferior Court of Common Pleas, when James Jr. successfully defended the town of Duxbury against a claim by its pastor, the Reverend Samuel Veazie, who was represented by the elder Otis. Ibid., 114.
67. See text at chapter 2, note 48.
68. Shipton, *Harvard Graduates*, vol. 4, *1690–1700* (Boston: Massachusetts Historical Society, 1943), 561–63; *The History of the Colony and Province of Massachusetts-Bay by Thomas Hutchinson*, ed. Lawrence Shaw Mayo, vol. 3 (Cambridge: Harvard University Press, 1932), 63n.
69. Shipton, *Harvard Graduates*, 9:83; *Boston Post-Boy*, January 19, 1767.
70. Shipton, *Harvard Graduates*, vol. 6, *1713–1721* (Boston: Massachusetts Historical Society, 1942), 251–53.
71. Shipton, *Harvard Graduates*, vol. 7, *1722–1725* (Boston: Massachusetts Historical Society, 1945), 119.
72. Washburn, *Sketches of the Judicial History of Massachusetts*, 306.
73. Declaration, *Fletcher v. Vassall*, Suffolk County Inferior Court of Common Pleas (November 5, 1751), Massachusetts Superior Court, no. 68,677, LDS Court Records Project, reel no. 915132. See also *State of the Action*, 1–3. A copy of the writ filed in the Inferior Court was used in the Superior Court action "because it was not the practice to file a new writ for the Superior Court proceeding." *Legal Papers of John Adams*, 1:xiv.
74. *State of the Action*, 6.
75. Ibid., 5.
76. See text at notes 27–38.
77. *State of the Action*, 6. See also ibid., 7–9 (testimony of Joseph Scott), 13–14 (testimony of Thomas Gray), 9–10 (testimony of Jonathan Mayhew).
78. Ibid., 9–10 (testimony of Jonathan Mayhew), 10 (testimony of Ebenezer Miller), 11 (testimony of Belcher Hancock).
79. Ibid., 21. In defamation cases, "special damages" refers to a particular loss suffered by the plaintiff directly due to the defamation in question. John Bouvier, *Bouvier's Law Dictionary and Concise Encyclopedia*, 8th ed., vol. 1 (1839; St. Paul: West Publishing Company, 1914), 759.

80. *State of the Action*, 21–23 (testimony of Edmund Quincy), 25–26 (testimony of Stephen Greenleaf), 29 (testimony of Thomas Bell).

81. Ibid., 34 (testimony of Daniel Manwarring and Gibbins Sharp, shipwrights). See also ibid., 33 (testimony of Jacob Emmons).

82. Ibid., 21.

83. Ibid.

84. Ibid. By this time, the trial had been relocated from the old Town Hall House to Faneuil Hall. The court had ordered the move because of the "Numerous Audience" that had been drawn by the "examination of such a Number of Gentlemen and the Importance of the Case." Ibid.

85. Ibid., 34.

86. Ibid., 34–35.

87. Ibid. Vassall claimed that Fletcher bet Gray that he had a better barrel of pork than Gray did, and then "order'd his Cooper in packing the Pork, to put the best Pieces on the top of the Barrel." Ibid.

88. Ibid., 35–36. See ibid., 36, for copies of the agreement and the decision.

89. Ibid., 36.

90. Ibid.

91. Ibid., 37.

92. Ibid.

93. Ibid. At the time of the trial, Trowbridge was the Massachusetts attorney general. It was accepted practice for Crown attorneys to represent clients in civil cases.

94. *State of the Action*, 34.

95. Eighteenth-century English law distinguished between written defamation (libel) and oral defamation (slander).

96. William Holdsworth, *History of English Law*, vol. 8 (London: Methuen & Co., 1925), 333.

97. W. Blake Odgers, *The Law of Libel and Slander*, vol. 1 (1876; Philadelphia, 1887), 40; Thomas Starkie, *A Treatise on the Law of Slander, Libel, Scandalum Magnatum and False Rumors* (London, 1813), 16–17.

98. Starkie, *Treatise on the Law of Slander*, 20, 123–129, 310–11.

99. See text at notes 31–34.

100. See text at notes 36–37.

101. Massachusetts Superior Court Minute Book (November 14, 1752), New Action no. 26, LDS Court Records Project, reel no. 946479.

102. "Appellant's Case," *Vassall v. Fletcher*, 2, King's Most Excellent Majesty in Council, 2, British Library, *Vassall (William) Suit v. Fletcher*, 1754, Add. 36217 f. 44.

103. James Otis to George Johnston, January 25, 1765, *Proceedings of the Massachusetts Historical Society*, 3rd ser., 43 (1909): 206.

104. Massachusetts Superior Court Minute Books, LDS Court Records Project, reel nos. 946478, 946479, 946480.

105. *Joselyn v. Engs*, Continued Action no. 54, Minute Book, Massachusetts Superior Court (Boston, August 1755), LDS Court Records Project, reel no. 946479.

106. Petition of William Vassall to Governor and Council, February 18, 1755, Massachusetts Archives, vol. 44, 153, LDS Court Records Project, reel no. 2322758.

107. Sharon Hamby O'Connor and Mary Sarah Bilder, "Appeals to the Privy Council before American Independence: An Annotated Digital Catalogue," *Law Library Journal* 104, no. 1 (2012): 85–86. The subcommittee usually included the chief justice of the King's Bench or Common Pleas. Ibid., 85.

108. See text at notes 39–41.

109. "Appellant's CASE," 3, *Vassall v. Fletcher,* King's Most Excellent Majesty in Council, British Library, *Vassall (William) Suit v. Fletcher,* 1754, Add. 36217 f. 44.

110. Ibid.

111. Ibid.

112. "Respondent's CASE," *Vassall v. Fletcher,* 3, King's Most Excellent Majesty in Council, British Library, *Vassall (William) Suit v. Fletcher,* 1754, Add. 36217 f. 44.

113. Ibid.

114. George Adrian Washburne, *Imperial Control of the Administration of Justice in the Thirteen American Colonies* (New York: Columbia University Press, 1923), 136; *Acts of the Privy Council of England,* Colonial Series, vol. 4, AD 1745–1766 (1911; Nendeln [Liechtenstein]: Kraus Reprint, 1966), 226.

115. *State of the Action,* 35.

116. "Appellant's CASE," 1–2, *Vassall v. Fletcher,* King's Most Excellent Majesty in Council, British Library, *Vassall (William) Suit v. Fletcher,* 1754, Add. 36217 f. 44.

117. *Journals of the Massachusetts House of Representatives,* 29, 4; ibid., 30, 4; ibid., 31, 4.

118. Petition of William Vassall (September 17, 1754), Massachusetts Archives, vol. 44, 9, LDS Court Records Project, reel no. 2322758.

119. Shipton, *Harvard Graduates,* 9:353.

120. "Mr. William Vassall. Petition to the Governor and ye Council" (February 18, 1755), Massachusetts Archives, vol. 44, 154, LDS Court Records Project, reel no. 2322758.

121. Shipton, *Harvard Graduates,* 9:353.

122. Ibid., 354; *State of the Action,* 28 (testimony of John Tudor).

123. Shipton, *Harvard Graduates,* 8:465, 467. The prize was valued at £300,000. Eliza Susan Quincy, "Josiah Quincy, Sr.," *Pennsylvania Magazine of History and Biography* 3, no. 2 (1879): 183.

124. Shipton, *Harvard Graduates,* 7:107.

125. Fletcher, *State of the Action,* 11 (testimony of Joseph Royall). See also testimony of Joseph Richardson ("an old Ship or Vessel that was so bad that Mr. *Quincy* would not send her to Sea"), ibid.

126. *Willliam Vassall v. Edmund Quincy,* New Action no. 40, *William Vassall v. John Tudor,* New Action no. 41, Massachusetts Superior Court (Boston, February 18, 1755), LDS Court Records Project, reel no. 946479.

127. *John Tudor v. William Vassall,* Massachusetts Superior Court (Boston, February 17, 1756), LDS Court Records Project, reel no. 947005.

128. Shipton, *Harvard Graduates,* 9:354.

129. Ibid.

130. Elizabeth Murray to James Murray, 1755, in *Letters of James Murray, Loyalist,* ed. Nina Moore Tiffany (Boston, 1901), 104–5; Edmund Quincy to William Vassall, September 4, 1755 (complains of "very Singular Losses & Disappointments in Business"), Houghton Library, Harvard University, Cambridge.

131. *Boston Evening-Post*, January 9, 1758. Shipton maintains that Gridley, along with Foster Hutchinson and Thomas Flucker, were named bankruptcy commissioners in the case. Shipton, *Harvard Graduates*, 7:110. According to the contemporary reports, however, Joseph Green, not Gridley, was the third commissioner. See, e.g., *Boston Evening-Post*, January 9, 1758; *Boston Post-Boy*, January 16, 1758; *Boston Gazette*, January 16, 1758.

132. Elizabeth Murray to James Murray, 1755, in *Letters of James Murray*, 105; Shipton, *Harvard Graduates*, 9:354.

133. Shipton, *Harvard Graduates*, 9:354.

134. James Otis Jr. to William Vassall (in London), October 22, 1753, Houghton Library, Harvard University.

135. James Otis Jr. to William Vassall (in London), September 29, 1753, Houghton Library, Harvard University.

Chapter Seven: The House of Representatives

1. H. G. F Candage, "Jeremy Gridley," *Publications of the Brookline Historical Society* (1903): 3; Clifford K. Shipton, *Sibley's Harvard Graduates: Biographical Sketches of Those Who Attended Harvard College* (hereafter Shipton, *Harvard Graduates*), vol. 7, 1722–1725 (Boston: Massachusetts Historical Society, 1945), 525.

2. *Massachusetts Centinel* (Boston), June 15, 1785; *Letters of a Loyalist Lady: Being the Letters of Ann Hulton, Sister of Henry Hulton, Commissioner of Customs at Boston, 1767–1776* (Cambridge: Harvard University Press, 1927), x–xi.

3. Michael C. Batinski, *Jonathan Belcher: Colonial Governor* (Lexington: University Press of Kentucky, 1996) 55.

4. *Massachusetts Centinel* (Boston), June 15, 1785; *Boston Evening-Post*, February 22, 1768; Candage, "Jeremy Gridley," 3–4.

5. Shipton, *Harvard Graduates*, 7:521.

6. Ibid.

7. *Muddy River and Brookline Records*, vol. 1, 1634–1838 (1875), 180–217. Of the thirty-seven times that Brookline chose a moderator between May 1755 and June 1767, Gridley was elected twenty-two times. Ibid.

8. Ibid., 157–217; Shipton, *Harvard Graduates*, 7:525.

9. John J. Waters Jr., *The Otis Family in Provincial and Revolutionary Massachusetts* (1968; New York: W. W. Norton, 1975), 84.

10. *Boston Gazette*, June 2, 1755.

11. Ibid.

12. Francis G. Walett, "The Massachusetts Council, 1766–1774: The Transformation of a Conservative Institution," *William and Mary Quarterly*, 3rd ser., 6, no. 4 (1949): 605.

13. William E. Nelson, *Americanization of the Common Law: The Impact of Change on Massachusetts Society, 1760–1830* (Cambridge: Harvard University Press, 1975), 13.

14. Ibid., 14. The governor also had the power, with the consent of the council, to use the militia to enforce the law. Ibid.

15. Waters, *Otis Family*, 87.

16. John A. Schutz, *William Shirley: King's Governor of Massachusetts* (Chapel Hill: University of North Carolina Press, 1961), 122.

17. Ibid.

18. The problem of having too few patronage positions to dole out in order to secure support was one that plagued most colonial governors most of the time. See Bernard Bailyn, *The Origins of American Politics* (New York: Alfred A. Knopf, 1968), 73–80.

19. John A. Schutz, "Succession Politics in Massachusetts, 1730–1741," *William and Mary Quarterly*, 3rd ser., 15, no. 4 (1956): 511–14.

20. Batinski, *Jonathan Belcher*, xiv.

21. Schutz, "Succession Politics in Massachusetts," 508; Schutz, *William Shirley*, 11.

22. Waters, *Otis Family*, 78, 87.

23. Schutz, *William Shirley*, 38.

24. Ibid., 71.

25. Ibid., 69–73.

26. Bailyn, *Origins of American Politics*, 116–17.

27. Ibid., 84–92.

28. *Journals of the Massachusetts House of Representatives* 32 (May 30, 1755): 10; 32 (June 4, 1755): 23.

29. Thomas Thumb, *The Monster of Monsters: A true and faithful Narrative of a most remarkable Phenomenon lately seen in this Metropolis* . . . (July 1754). While the author of the pamphlet remains a mystery, its likely printer was Zechariah Fowle, Daniel's younger brother, whom Daniel probably assisted in some manner. Isaiah Thomas, *History of Printing in America with a Biography of Printers, and an Account of Newspapers*, vol. 1 (Albany, 1874), 133. Royal Tyler, who had been brought before the House after Daniel Fowle had vaguely implicated him in the pamphlet's publication, brought a separate action solely against the House messenger. Daniel Fowle, *A Total Eclipse of Liberty* (Boston, 1755), 12–13; Thomas, *History of Printing in America*, 1:134; *Journals of the Massachusetts House of Representatives* 32 (June 4, 1755): 23.

30. Summons (May 24, 1755), Suffolk County Inferior Court of Common Pleas, Massachusetts Court File (1755), vol. 436, no. 74517, Church of Jesus Christ of Latter-Day Saints (hereafter LDS) Court Records Project, microfilm reel no. 915447.

31. *Journals of the Massachusetts House of Representatives* 32 (June 11, 1755): 59.

32. Ibid.

33. Ibid.

34. Leonard W. Levy, *Freedom of Speech and Press in Early American History: A Legacy of Suppression* (1960; New York: Harper & Row, 1973), 15; Mary Patterson Clarke, *Parliamentary Privilege in the American Colonies* (1943; New York: Da Capo, 1971), 2.

35. Levy, *Freedom of Speech*, 15–16.

36. Clarke, *Parliamentary Privilege*, 69–70.

37. Ibid., 117.

38. Levy, *Freedom of Speech*, 16.

39. Harold L. Nelson, "Seditious Libel in Colonial America," *American Journal of Legal History* 3, no. 2 (1959): 168.

40. See text at chapter 1, note 75.

41. *Journals of the Massachusetts House of Representatives* 32 (June 4, 1755): 59.

42. Ibid.

43. Suffolk County Inferior Court of Common Pleas, Massachusetts Superior Court File (1755), vol. 256, no. 74879 (first Tuesday of October 1755), LDS Court Records Project, reel no. 915447.

44. Ibid.

45. Ibid.

46. *Fowle v. Hubbard* (March 1755), Records of the Superior Court of Judicature, vol. 1757–1759, 24, LDS Court Records Project, reel no. 947005.

47. Order, *Fowle v. Hubbard* (Boston, February 13, 1757), Records of the Superior Court of Judicature, vol. 1757–1759, 24, LDS Court Records Project, reel no. 947005.

48. *Journals of the Massachusetts House of Representatives* 32 (June 4, 1755): 109.

49. Ibid. (February 14, 1756): 332.

50. Ibid. (February 13, 1756): 327.

51. Ibid. (April 12, 1756): 453.

52. *Journals of the Massachusetts House of Representatives* 33 (May 28, 1756): 11–12, 17.

53. *Journals of the Massachusetts House of Representatives* 32 (February 18, 1756): 341.

54. *Journals of the Massachusetts House of Representatives* 33 (August 13, 1756): 104.

55. Francis Parkman, *Montcalm and Wolfe: France and England in the New World*, vol. 1 (1884; Boston: Little, Brown and Company, 1927), 198–201; Fred Anderson, *Crucible of War: The Seven Years' War and the Fate of Empire in British North America, 1754–1788* (2000; New York: Vintage Books, 2001), 87–88.

56. Anderson, *Crucible of War*, 88.

57. Ibid., 94–105.

58. Parkman, *Montcalm and Wolfe*, 1:242–43, 256–62, 307–26; Anderson, *Crucible of War*, 110–23.

59. Schutz, *William Shirley*, 227–29; Anderson, *Crucible of War*, 137–39.

60. *Journals of the Massachusetts House of Representatives* 32 (February 23, 1756): 360.

61. *Journals of the Massachusetts House of Representatives* 32 (April 17, 1756): 480.

62. *Journals of the Massachusetts House of Representatives* 33 (July 1, 1756): 76, (August 15, 1756): 108.

63. Anderson, *Crucible of War*, 141.

64. Ibid., 157

65. William S. Fields and David T. Hardy, "The Third Amendment and the Issue of the Maintenance of Standing Armies: A Legal History," *American Journal of Legal History* 35, no. 4 (1991): 395–402.

66. The Petition of Right (June 7, 1628), Charles I, c. 1, in *Select Documents of English Constitutional History*, ed. George Burton Adams and H. Morse Stephens (London: Macmillan, 1939), 340–41.

67. Fields and Hardy, "Third Amendment," 403–4.

68. Ibid., 404–5.

69. "The Declaration of Rights," in *Readings in European History*, ed. James Harvey Robinson, vol. 2 (New York: Ginn & Company, 1906), 367.

70. Adams and Stephens, *Select Documents of English Constitutional History*, 457–58.

71. "An Act for Punishing Officers and Soldiers who shall mutiny or desert their Majestyes Service and for punishing false Musters," 2 Will. & Mar. sess. 2, c. 6 (Chapter

6, Rot. Parl., pt. 3 no. 5), British History Online, www.law-library.rutgers.edu (accessed December 23, 2010) (hereafter Mutiny Act).

72. "An Act for punishing mutiny and desertion; and for the better payment of the army and their quarters" (London, 1757), Eighteenth Century Collections Online (accessed January 6, 2011).

73. Ibid.

74. *Oxford Dictionary of National Biography*, www.oxforddnb.com (accessed August 11, 2017); Stanley McCrory Pargellis, *Lord Loudoun in North America* (1933; Hamden, CT: Archon Books, 1968), 42–43.

75. *Diary and Autobiography of John Adams*, ed. L. H. Buttrfield, vol. 3 (1961; New York: Atheneum, 1964), 266.

76. Samuel Davies to——McCullock, August 11, 1758, *Transactions of the Colonial Society of Massachusetts* 19 (1916–17): 24.

77. Parkman, *Montcalm and Wolfe*, 1:412.

78. *Oxford Dictionary of National Biography*, www.oxforddnb.com (accessed August 11, 2017).

79. Pargellis, *Loudoun in North America*, 43.

80. Ibid., 44.

81. The Mutiny Act was amended to extend it to the colonies in three of its particulars: discipline of British soldiers serving abroad (1723); application to provincial troops serving with regulars (1754); and a provision for a legal basis for recruiting (1756). None of these dealt with quartering. Pargellis, *Lord Loudoun in North America*, 189.

82. Fred Anderson, *A People's Army: Massachusetts Soldiers and Society in the Seven Years' War* (Chapel Hill: University of North Carolina Press, 1984), 13.

83. Pargellis, *Lord Loudoun in North America*, 190.

84. Lord Loudoun to William Pitt, March 10, 1757, in *Correspondence of William Pitt When Secretary of State with Colonial Governors and Naval Commissioners in America*, ed. Gertrude Selwyn Kimball, vol. 1 (New York: Macmillan, 1906), 19–20.

85. Lord Loudoun to the Duke of Cumberland, August 29, 1756, in *Military Affairs in North America, 1748–1756: Selected Documents from the Cumberland Papers in Windsor Castle*, ed. Stanley M. Pargellis (New York: D. Appleton-Century Company, 1936), 231; Pargellis, *Loudoun in North America*, 195–96; Alan Rogers, *Empire and Liberty: American Resistance to British Authority, 1755–1763* (Berkeley: University of California Press, 1974), 82–83.

86. Pargellis, *Lord Loudoun in North America*, 198–99; *Messages from the Governors Comprising Executive Communications to the Legislature and Other Papers Relating to Legislation from the Organization of the First Colonial Assembly in 1683 to and Including the Year 1906 with Notes* (Albany: J. B. Lyon Company, 1909), 1604n3; *Documents Relative to the Colonial History of New York*, vol. 7 (Albany, 1856), 204.

87. Lord Loudoun to William Denny, December 22, 1756, in *Minutes of the Provincial Council of Pennsylvania*, vol. 7 (Harrisburg, 1851), 374.

88. Ibid., 258–59.

89. Lord Loudoun to William Denny, December 22, 1756, ibid., 379.

90. Pargellis, *Lord Loudoun in North America*, 201–2.

91. Ibid., 191; *The Acts and Resolves, Public and Private, of the Province of Massachusetts Bay*, vol. 15 (Boston: Wright & Potter, 1908), 293 (February 27, 1755).

92. Pargellis, *Lord Loudoun in North America*, 191.

93. *Massachusetts Acts and Resolves*, 15:626; Rogers, *Empire and Liberty*, 84.

94. Loudoun, Diary, vol. 2 (January 26, 1757), Loudoun Collection, Huntington Library, no. HM1717, 11, San Marino, CA (hereafter Huntington Library).

95. Lord Loudoun to the Duke of Cumberland, November 1756, in Pargellis, *Military Affairs in North America*, 269.

96. See text at notes 85–86.

97. See text at notes 88–90.

98. Lord Loudoun to the Duke of Cumberland, November 1756 ("I shall take care to keep up my Claim, to every thing included in the *Mutiny Act*"), in Pargellis, *Military Affairs in North America*, 269; Loudoun to Pitt, March 10, 1757, in *Pitt Correspondence*, 1:20.

99. Rogers, *Empire and Liberty*, 84.

100. Jeremiah Gridley to Gilbert McAdam, February 26, 1757, Loudoun Collection, LO 2929, Huntington Library.

101. See Rogers, *Empire and Liberty*, 84.

102. Jeremiah Gridley to Gilbert McAdam, February 26, 1757, Loudoun Collection, LO 2929, Huntington Library.

103. See text at chapter 6, notes 68–69.

104. Shipton, *Harvard Graduates*, vol. 8, *1726–1730* (Boston: Massachusetts Historical Society, 1951}, 149–50; Bernard Bailyn, *The Ordeal of Thomas Hutchinson* (Cambridge: Harvard University Press, 1974), 40.

105. Bailyn, *Ordeal of Thomas Hutchinson*, 40.

106. Ibid., 40–41; Malcolm Freiberg, "Thomas Hutchinson: The First Fifty Years (1711–1761)," *William and Mary Quarterly*, 3rd ser., 15, no. 1 (1958): 52–53; Pargellis, *Lord Loudoun in North America*, 214.

107. Bailyn, *Ordeal of Thomas Hutchinson*, 40; Freiberg, "Thomas Hutchinson: The First Fifty Years," 53; Pargellis, *Lord Loudoun in North America*, 216

108. *Proceedings in Masonry: St. John's Grand Lodge, 1733–1792; Massachusetts Grand Lodge, 1769–1792* (Boston, 1895), 5–6.

109. Ibid., 48–49.

110. Ibid., 49. The three were Captain Harry Charteris, Captain Gilbert McAdam, and Loudoun's secretary, John Appy.

111. McAdam was the son-in-law of Christopher Kilby, a Boston merchant and Loudoun confidant, who had served as the agent for Massachusetts in London and subsequently became a partner in the London firm of Baker-Kilby, one of the major suppliers of British forces in North America. Pagellis, *Loudoun in North America*, 167, 390; Shutz, *William Shirley*, 32, 42, 226, 234; William T. Baxter, *The House of Hancock: Business in Boston, 1724–1775* (Cambridge: Harvard University Press, 1945), 58, 95–96, 136.

112. Jeremiah Gridley to Gilbert McAdam, February 26, 1757, Loudoun Collection, LO 2929, Huntington Library.

113. Ibid.

114. Ibid.
115. Ibid.
116. Ibid.
117. Ibid.
118. *Massachusetts Acts and Resolves*, 15:666, 671.
119. Lord Loudoun to William Shirley, August 2, 1756, in *Correspondence of William Shirley, Governor of Massachusetts and Military Commander in America, 1731–1760*, ed. Charles Henry Lincoln, vol. 2 (New York: Macmillan, 1912), 495.
120. Lord Loudoun to the Duke of Cumberland, November 22, 1756, December 26, 1756, in Pargellis, *Military Affairs in North America*, 275; Loudoun to Cumberland, October 3, 1756, ibid., 241.
121. In Rogers, *Empire and Liberty*, 47.
122. Anderson, *A People's Army*, 111. According to Governor Charles Lawrence of Nova Scotia, recruiting officers in North America were "met with every Obstacle the People could throw in their way." Lawrence to Lord Halifax, December 9, 1755, in Pargellis, *Military Affairs in North America*, 155.
123. Pargellis, *Lord Loudoun in North America*, 86.
124. Franklin Thayer Nichols, "The Organization of Braddock's Army," *William and Mary Quarterly*, 3rd ser., 4, no. 2 (1947): 136; John Shy. *Toward Lexington: The Role of the British Army in the Coming of the American Revolution* (Princeton: Princeton University Press, 1965), 39.
125. George Farquhar, *The Recruiting Officer* (The Hague, 1710), 35.
126. Nichols, *Braddock's Army*, 136.
127. Ibid., 146–47.
128. Lord Loudoun to the Duke of Cumberland, October 3, 1756, in Pargellis, *Military Affairs in North America*, 241.
129. Ibid.
130. Rogers, *Empire and Liberty*, 45.
131. Captain Harry Charteris to Lord Loudoun, June 11, 1757, Loudoun Collection, LO 3816, Huntington Library.
132. Jeremiah Gridley to Lord Loudoun, June 6, 1757, Loudoun Collection, LO 3797, Huntington Library.
133. Captain Harry Charteris to Lord Loudoun, June 11, 1757, Loudoun Collection, LO 3816, Huntington Library.
134. Ibid.
135. Ibid.
136. Jeremiah Gridley to Lord Loudoun, June 6, 1757, Loudoun Collection, LO 3797, Huntington Library.
137. 28 George II, c. 35, sec. 8.
138. Jeremiah Gridley to Lord Loudoun, June 6, 1757, Loudoun Collection, LO 3797, Huntington Library.
139. Ibid. Under the English rules of evidence at the time, interested persons, which included parties, were barred from testifying. *Legal Papers of John Adams*, ed. L. Kinvin Roth and Hiller Zobel. vol. 1 (Cambridge: Harvard University Press, 1963), 117n21.

140. Jeremiah Gridley to Lord Loudoun, June 6, 1757, Loudoun Collection, LO 3797, Huntington Library.

141. Parkman, *Montcalm and Wolfe*, 1:484–86; Anderson, *Crucible of War*, 207–8.

142. Parkman, *Montcalm and* Wolfe, 1:485–87; Anderson, *Crucible of War*, 179, 196–99.

143. Thomas Pownall to William Pitt, December 1,1757, September 4, 1757, in *Pitt Correspondence*, 1:128, 101.

144. *Massachusetts Acts and Resolves*, vol. 16 (Boston, 1909), 67. See also Thomas Pownall to William Pitt, September 24, 1757, in *Pitt Correspondence*, 1:113.

145. *The History of the Colony and Province of Massachusetts-Bay by Thomas Hutchinson* (hereafter Hutchinson, *History of Massachusetts*), ed. Lawrence Shaw Mayo, vol. 3 (Cambridge: Harvard University Press, 1936), 46.

146. Ibid.

147. Ibid.

148. Ibid.

149. Thomas Pownall to William Pitt, December 1, 1757, in *Pitt Correspondence*, 1:128; Hutchinson, *History of Massachusetts*, 3:46.

150. *Massachusetts Acts and Resolves*, vol. 4 (Boston, 1890), 47–48; Thomas Pownall to William Pitt, December 1, 1757, in *Pitt Correspondence*, 1:128.

151. J. Alan Rogers, "Colonial Opposition to the Quartering of Troops during the French and Indian War," *Military Affairs* 34 (1970): 9–10. See also John A. Schutz, *Thomas Pownall: British Defender of American Liberty* (Glendale, CA: A. H. Clark Co., 1951), 115.

152. Thomas Pownall to Lord Loudoun, December 15, 1757, Loudoun Collection, LO 5014, Huntington Library.

153. Hutchinson, *History of Massachusetts*, 3:47.

154. Lord Loudoun to William Pitt, February 14, 1758, in *Pitt Correspondence*, 1:186–87.

155. Quoted in Hutchinson, *History of Massachusetts*, 3:47n.

156. Jeremiah Gridley to Christopher Kilby, January 10, 1758, Loudoun Collection, LO 5421, Huntington Library. For Pownall's early optimism that the ranger company would be raised, see Thomas Pownall to William Pitt, September 24, 1757, in *Pitt Correspondence*, 1:113.

157. Ibid.

158. Ibid.

159. Jeremiah Gridley to Christopher Kilby, January 28, 1758, Loudoun Collection, LO5485, Huntington Library.

160. Ibid.

161. Schutz, *Pownall*, 125.

162. Thomas Pownall to William Pitt, March 14, 1758, in *Pitt Correspondence*, 1:203.

163. Ibid.

164. William Pitt to Governors, December 30, 1757, in *Pitt Correspondence*, 1:135–36.

165. Ibid., 136.

166. Ibid., 138.

167. Ibid.

168. *Massachusetts Acts and Resolves*, 4:135.

169. Ibid.

170. Jeremiah Gridley to Lord Loudoun, March 12, 1758, Loudoun Collection, LO 5758, Huntington Library.
171. Ibid.
172. Ibid.
173. See text at notes 114–18.
174. Jeremiah Gridley to Lord Loudoun, June 6, 1757, Loudoun Collection, LO 3797, Huntington Library.
175. *John Adams Legal Papers*, 1:cxi–cxii, civ–cv, cxiii; Charles R. McKirdy, "Massachusetts Lawyers on the Eve of the American Revolution: The State of the Profession," in *Law in Colonial Massachusetts, 1630–1800*, comp. Daniel R. Coquillette (Boston: Colonial Society of Massachusetts, 1984), 348, 351, 355.
176. Jeremiah Gridley to Lord Loudoun, June 6, 1757, Loudoun Collection, LO 3797, Huntington Library.
177. Ibid. Although Gridley downplayed the financial rewards a regimental command in the militia could bring, they were not insignificant. Colonels made money on the purchase of uniforms, on handling their soldiers' pay, and on selling certain luxuries to enlisted men. They also could profit on spoils seized from enemy territory. Schutz, *William Shirley*, 97.
178. Jeremiah Gridley to Lord Loudoun, June 6, 1757, Loudoun Collection, LO 3797, Huntington Library.
179. Jeremy Gridley to Lord Loudoun, March 12, 1758, Loudoun Collection, LO5758, Huntington Library.
180. Ibid. See note 111 for "Mr. Kilby."
181. *Muddy River and Brookline Records*, 1:186.

Chapter Eight: Gridley's Law Practice in the 1750s and 1760s

1. Massachusetts Superior Court, Suffolk County Minute Books (February 9, 1754), Church of Jesus Christ of Latter-day Saints (hereafter LDS), Court Records Project, microfilm reel no. 0946479.
2. John A. Schutz, *William Shirley: King's Governor of Massachusetts* (Chapel Hill: University of North Carolina Press, 1961), 84, 118, 124, 139–69; Clifford K. Shipton, *Sibley's Harvard Graduates: Biographical Sketches of Those Who Attended Harvard College* (hereafter Shipton, *Harvard Graduates*), vol. 9, *1731–1735* (Boston: Massachusetts Historical Society, 1956), 365–67.
3. John Winsor, *The Memorial History of Boston including Suffolk County, Massachusetts, 1630–1880*, vol. 2 (Boston, 1861), 374–75.
4. Ellen Susan Bulfinch, *The Life and letters of Charles Bulfinch, Architect, with other Family Papers* (Boston, 1896), 32.
5. *Samuel Waldo v. Susanna Waldo*, Massachusetts Superior Court, Suffolk County Minute Books (August 14, 1742), LDS Court Records Project, reel no. 0946476; *Samuel Waldo v. Ebenezer Thornton*, Massachusetts Superior Court, Suffolk County Minute Books (August 18, 1747), LDS Court Records Project, reel no. 09466477; *Samuel Waldo v. John Ernest Knotchel*, Massachusetts Superior Court, Suffolk County Minute Books (August 1755), LDS Court Records project, reel no. 0947479.

6. Schutz, *William Shirley*, 10, 42, 92. At his death in 1759, Waldo's estate was valued at over £52,000. Gary B. Nash, "Urban Wealth and Poverty in Pre-Revolutionary America," *Journal of Interdisciplinary History* 6, no. 4 (1978): 570n49.

7. *Samuel Turner v. Stephen Sewall*, Massachusetts Superior Court, Suffolk County Minute Books (August 1758), LDS Court Records Project, reel no. 0946480; *Robert Mason v. Eliakim Hutchinson*, Massachusetts Superior Court, Suffolk County Minute Books (February 17, 1756), LDS Court Records Project, reel no. 0946479; *Thomas Hutchinson v. Nathaniel Barber*, Massachusetts Superior Court, Suffolk County Minute Books (February 17, 1756), LDS Court Records Project, reel no. 0946479.

8. *Diary and Autobiography of John Adams*, ed. L. H. Butterfield, vol. 1 (1961; New York: Atheneum, 1964), 294n1. See *Benjamin Hallowell v. William Hambleton*, Massachusetts Superior Court, Suffolk County Minute Books (August 20, 1754), LDS Court Records Project, reel no. 0946479; *William Hallowell v. Benjamin Hallowell*, Massachusetts Superior Court, Suffolk County Minute Books (August 17, 1756), LDS Court Records Project, reel no. 0946479.

9. Edmund S. Morgan and Helen M. Morgan, *The Stamp Act Crisis: Prologue to Revolution* (1953; New York: Collier Books, 1963), 16; *Peter Oliver's Origin and Progress of the American Rebellion: A Tory View*, ed. Douglass Adair and John Schutz (Stanford: Stanford University Press, 1961), 52n9 (a "beautiful home").

10. Massachusetts Superior Court Minute Books, Suffolk County (1757, 1763), microfilm, Massachusetts Historical Society, Boston (hereafter MHS).

11. Ibid. Suffolk County had 124 new filings in 1757 and 209 in 1763; Bristol County went from 34 to 98; and Hampshire and Berkshire counties from 34 to 96. Ibid.; Massachusetts Superior Court Minute Books, Bristol County (1757, 1763), Hampshire and Berkshire counties (1757, 1763), MHS.

12. *Diary and Autobiography of John Adams*, ed. L. H. Butterfield, vol. 3 (1961; New York: Atheneum, 1964), 276.

13. John Adams to William Tudor, December 18, 1816, in *The Works of John Adams*, ed. Charles Francis Adams, vol. 10 (Boston: Little, Brown and Company, 1856), 233.

14. Ibid.

15. *John Adams Diary and Autobiography*, 3:176.

16. John Adams to William Tudor, December 18, 1816, in *Works of John Adams*, 10:233.

17. Daniel R. Coquillette, ed., *The Law Reports, Part One (1761–1765)*, vol. 4 of *Portrait of a Patriot: The Major Legal and Political Papers of Josiah Quincy, Junior*, ed. Daniel R. Coquillete and Neil Longley York (Boston: Colonial Society of Massachusetts, 2009), 156.

18. Arthur M. Alger, "Barristers at Law in Massachusetts," *New England Historical and Genealogical Register* 31 (1877): 207; *Legal Papers of John Adams*, ed. L. Kinvin Wroth & Hiller B. Zobel, vol. 1 (Cambridge: Harvard University Press, 1965), lxxixn177.

19. Daniel R. Coquillette, *The Law Reports, Part Two (1765–1772)*, vol. 5 of *Portrait of a Patriot: The Major Legal and Political Papers of Josiah Quincy Junior*, ed. Daniel R. Coquillette and Neil Longley York (Boston: Colonial Society of Massachusetts, 2009), 690. The editors of the *Legal Papers of John Adams* theorize that the lack of statutory

authority for the distinction between barristers and attorneys "may have prevented both bench and bar from objecting or seeking to apply sanctions" to lawyers like Quincy who ignored the rules. *Legal Papers of John Adams*, 1:lxxixn77.

20. *John Adams Diary and Autobiography*, 1:70. The problem was an old one. In 1720, the Massachusetts General Court had attempted to provide an incentive to competence. It ordered that "if the plaintiff in any action suffer a nonsuit, through the default, negligence or omission of his attorney that drew the writ, . . . by mislaying the action or otherwise, such attorney shall draw a new writ without fee." *The Acts and Resolves, Public and Private, of the Province of Massachusetts Bay*, vol. 1 (Boston, 1869), 622–23. As of 1760, the only formal requirements for practice in the county courts were contained in very general court orders or bar agreements. An order of the Middlesex County Court of Common Pleas was typical: "Ordered that no Person who has not been sworn as Attorney in this Court or in the Superior Court of Juda. Etc. (altho sworn in any other infer. Court in any other county) shall be entitled to the Fee of an attorney in this Court." Minute Book of the Middlesex Court of Common Pleas (December Term, 1748), MHS. The Worcester County Court of Common Pleas passed a similar rule in 1757. Joseph Willard, "Address before the Members of the Bar of Worcester, Massachusetts, October 2, 1829," in *Addresses Before Members of the Bar of Worcester, Massachusetts* (1879), 41.

21. *John Adams Diary and Autobiography*, 1:235–36 (February 2, 1763).

22. Ibid., 236.

23. Benjamin Kent "damned" Otis, and some lawyers suggested "removing all Commerce or Connection" with him. Gridley preached moderation. He said that Otis should be treated "dryly and decently." Ibid.

24. James Hovey to Robert Treat Paine, October 22, 1764, Robert Treat Paine Papers, MHS.

25. G. W. Gawalt, *The Promise of Power: The Emergence of the Legal Profession in Massachusetts, 1760–1840* (Westport, CT: Greenwood Press, 1979), 17.

26. *John Adams Diary and Autobiography*, 1:316. A "sennight" is seven days and nights, i.e., a week.

27. *Legal Papers of John Adams*, 1:lxxix.

28. *John Adams Diary and Autobiography*, 1:316.

29. See note 17.

30. For some cases, no lawyer is indicated.

31. For some cases, no lawyer is indicated.

32. Shipton, *Harvard Graduates*, vol. 7, *1722–1725* (Boston: Massachusetts Historical Society, 1945), 524–25.

33. Shipton, *Harvard Graduates*, vol. 8, *1726–1730* (Boston: Massachusetts Historical Society, 1951), 39–40.

34. *John Adams Diary and Autobiography*, 1:251, 3:285–86. See text at chapter 10, notes 92–95.

35. Augustine Jones, *The Life and Work of Thomas Dudley, The Second Governor of Massachusetts* (Boston, 1899), 58–65, 160–61. Dudley was elected governor in 1634, 1640, 1645, and 1650. Ibid., 161.

36. John Langdon Sibley, *Harvard Graduates*, vol. 2, *1659–1677* (Cambridge, MA, 1881), 168.

37. Shipton, *Harvard Graduates*, vol. 5, *1701–1712* (Boston: Massachusetts Historical Society, 1937), 244–52. William's older brother Paul (1675–1751) had attended the Inns of Court and, at the time of his death in 1751, had served on the Massachusetts Superior Court for thirty-three years, the last six as chief justice. All six of his children died in infancy. Shipton, *Harvard Graduates*, vol. 4, *1690–1700* (Boston: Massachusetts Historical Society), 42–53.

38. Shipton, *Harvard Graduates*, 5:244–52. For the following discussion, this chart may be helpful:

Thomas Dudley (1576–1653)
|
Governor Thomas Dudley (1647–1720)
|
Paul Dudley (1675–1751)   William Dudley (1686–1743)
                                                |
Thomas Dudley (1731–1769)   Joseph Dudley (1732–1767)   Daughters

39. William Dudley had six children—two sons, Thomas and Joseph, and four daughters—living at the time of the dispute. Dean Dudley, *The Dudley Genealogies and Family Records* (Boston, 1848), 84–85.

40. Cornelius J. Moynihan, *Introduction to the Law of Real Property* (St. Paul: West Publishing Co., 1962), 29–30.

41. Ibid., 37–40.

42. *Black's Law Dictionary*, 4th ed. (St. Paul, MN, 1951), 1355.

43. *Massachusetts Acts and Resolves*, 1:44 (emphasis added).

44. Coquillette, *The Law Reports, Part One*, 110–12. Manchaug (or Manchage) was an Indian town in Worcester County, Massachusetts. It was located near the present town of Oxford, which is about fifty miles southwest of Boston. Daniel Gookin, "Historical Collections of the Indians of New England," *Collections of the Massachusetts Historical Society* 1 (1792): 189.

45. Coquillette, *The Law Reports, Part One*, 112.

46. Ibid., 110.

47. Ibid.

48. Edmund Trowbridge to William Bollan, October 5, 1762, Dana Papers, 1674–1769 (1761–1764 envelope), MHS.

49. Edmund Trowbridge to William Bolan, November 18, 1763, Dana Papers, 1674–1769 (1761–1764 envelope), MHS; Shipton, *Harvard Graduates*, vol. 6, *1713–1721* (Boston: Massachusetts Historical Society, 1742), 80–86.

50. Apparently at some point Auchmuty replaced Kent. William Sullivan, *Address to the Suffolk Bar* (Boston, 1825), 34. Auchmuty was the son of lawyer Robert Auchmuty (d. 1751). Quincy's account of the initial hearing mentions Kent but not Auchmuty. Conversely, Auchmuty is quoted in the second hearing and Kent is not.

51. Coquillette, *The Law Reports, Part One*, 114, 118, 119, 121, 126.

52. Ibid., 114.

53. Ibid., 114–16.

54. Ibid., 114, 117.

55. Ibid., 122–23; see also 118.

56. Ibid., 127.

57. Ibid., 120.

58. Edmund Trowbridge to William Bollan, October 5, 1762, Dana Papers, 1674–1769 (1761–1764 envelope), MHS. See, e.g., *Cases with Opinions of Eminent Council, in Matters of Law, Equity, and Conveyances* (Dublin, 1791). See also Charles Sweet, "Contingent Remainders and Other Possibilities," *Yale Law Journal* 27, no. 8 (1918): 986.

59. Edmund Trowbridge to William Bollan, October 5, 1782, Dana Papers, 1674–1769 (1761–1764 envelope), MHS.

60. Ibid.

61. Samuel M. Quincy, ed., *Reports of Cases Argued and Adjudged in the Superior Court of Judicature of the Province of Massachusetts Bay Between 1761 and 1222. By Josiah Quincy, Junior* (Boston, 1865), 25n9; Coquillette, *The Law Reports, Part One*, 115.

62. Coquillette, *The Law Reports, Part One*, 117.

63. Coquillette suggests that the court chose not to explain its decision to avoid any chance that its reasoning might "tempt the Privy Council to interfere." Ibid., 115.

64. Ibid.

65. For example, Justices Cushing, Lynde, and Danforth had served on the provincial council with William Dudley and his brother Paul. Lynde's diary is peppered with notes of social engagements with one brother or the other, and the two were pallbearers at the funeral of Lynde's father-in-law. Shipton, *Harvard Graduates*, 6:250–57; Schutz, *William Shirley*, 281; William Henry Whitmore, *The Massachusetts Civil List for the Colonial and Provincial Periods, 1630–1774* (Albany, 1870); *The Diaries of Benjamin Lynde and Benjamin Lynde, Jr.* (Boston, 1880), 146.

66. Coquillette, *The Law Reports, Part One*, 118.

67. Ibid. (emphasis added to final nine words).

68. Edmund Trowbridge to William Bollan, November 18, 1763, Dana Papers, 1764–1769 (1761–1764 envelope), MHS.

69. Ibid.

70. Coquillette, *The Law Reports, Part One*, 111, 115.

71. Ibid., 120.

72. Ibid., 119.

73. Ibid., 126.

74. Ibid., 179–87.

75. Ibid., 398.

76. Ibid., 234–44.

77. Ibid., 72–74.

78. Ibid., 237.

79. Ibid., 140.

80. *Boston Post-Boy*, September 28, 1767.

81. In his *Biographical Dictionary* (1809), John Eliot put it this way: "[Thomas and Joseph Dudley] were very unlike their ancestors. Instead of preserving the honour and dignity of a family which had been illustrious for more than a hundred years, they seemed to prefer the manners of ordinary life, and very soon were mingled with the people who make up the common mass of human society." John Eliot, *Biographical*

Dictionary containing a Brief Account of the First Settlers and other Eminent Characters among the Magistrates, Ministers, Literary and Worthy Men in New England (Boston, 1809), 162–63.

82. Shipton, *Harvard Graduates*, 7:40.

83. Depositions of William Sitwell, Samuel Brooks, and John Mann (March 3, 1766), Court Files (86586–86857) (1725–1766), Suffolk County, Massachusetts, no. 86728, LDS Court Records Project, reel no. 0925065; Coquillette, *The Law Reports, Part One*, 248n1; Coquillette, *The Law Reports, Part Two*, 478n1.

84. Certification of William Sheaf (October 10, 1765), Massachusetts Court Files, Suffolk County, Miscellaneous Papers, no. 86617, LDS Court Records Project, reel no. 0925065; Coquillette, *The Law Reports, Part One*, 248n1; Coquillette, *The Law Reports, Part Two*, 246, 478n1. Freeman had been a witness in William Fletcher's case against William Vassall. Thomas Fletcher probably was William's brother. See chapter 6.

85. Order (February 12, 1763), *Scollay v. Dunn*, Massachusetts Archives, vol. 1763–64, folio 107, 107–9; examination of John Dunn (June 23, 1759), Suffolk County Court Files, no. 79773, LDS Court Records Project, reel no. 0914995.

86. Order (February 12, 1763), *Scollay v. Dunn*, Massachusetts Archives, vol. 1763–64, folio 107, 107–9; examination of John Dunn (June 23, 1759), Suffolk County Court Files, no. 79773, LDS Court Records Project, reel no. 0914995.

87. Order (February 12, 1763), *Scollay v. Dunn*, Massachusetts Archives, vol. 1763–64, folio 107, 107–9; examination of John Dunn (June 23, 1759), Suffolk County Court Files, no. 79773, LDS Court Records Project, reel no. 0914995.

88. Coquillette, *The Law Reports, Part 2*, 478n1.

89. *Legal Papers of John Adams*, 1:xcvi.

90. Order (February 12, 1763), *Scollay v. Dunn*, Massachusetts Archives, vol. 1763–64, 108, Massachusetts Archives and Commonwealth Museum, Boston (hereafter MACM); *Quincy's Reports*, 75n1. A "libel" is the plaintiff's initiatory pleading in an admiralty proceeding, corresponding to a declaration, bill, or complaint. *Black's Law Dictionary*, 1060.

91. Richard B. Morris, "Legalism versus Revolutionary Doctrine in New England," *New England Quarterly* 4, no. 2 (1931): 212–13; *Legal Papers of John Adams*, 1:57.

92. Coquillette, *The Law Reports, Part One*, 257.

93. L. Kinvin Roth, "The Massachusetts Vice Admiralty Court and Federal Admiralty Jurisdiction," *American Journal of Legal History* 6, no. 4 (1962): 265, 359; Coquillette, *The Law Reports, Part One*, 261.

94. Order (February 12, 1763), *Scollay v. Dunn*, Record Book, Massachusetts Superior Court, vol. 1763–1764, 188, MACM; *Quincy's Reports*, 75n1. A writ of prohibition is an order issued by a superior court to an inferior court commanding it to cease all proceedings with regard to a matter. *Black's Law Dictionary*, 1377. In England, the writ of prohibition was a product of parliamentary statute. Although that statute did not extend to the colonies, the courts there assumed that they had the right to issue such writs. Carl Ubbelohde, The *Vice Admiralty Courts and the American Revolution* (Chapel Hill: University of North Carolina Press, 1960), 95.

95. *Scollay v. Dunn*, Massachusetts Superior Court Record Book, vol. 1763–1764, 108, Massachusetts Archives, Record 1763, folio 107, MACM; Coquillette, *The Law Reports, Part One*, 248.

96. Ibid.

97. Morris, "Legalism versus Revolutionary Doctrine," 212–13.

98. Earlier, Scollay had attempted to settle with Dunn for £150. Affidavit of Joseph Cordis (October 21, 1765), *Dunn v. Scollay*, Massachusetts Court Files, no. 86627, LDS Court Records Project, reel no. 0925065.

99. Justice Chambers Russell, who was also the admiralty judge, probably had recused himself. Coquillette, *The Law Reports, Part One*, 266–67.

100. Wroth, "Massachusetts Vice Admiralty Court," 264. The discussion of admiralty jurisdiction in the text draws on Wroth's first-rate analysis.

101. Ibid., 264, 347.

102. Ibid., 264, 351.

103. Ibid., 266, 347–48, 351. The colonial vice admiralty courts operated at three different levels. First, on a local level, the courts heard and determined the disputes and problems of merchants and mariners. Second, from the late seventeenth century on, they were concerned with the enforcement of the trade acts. And third, in time of war, they acted as prize courts with authority to condemn captured enemy vessels and cargos. Ubbelohde, *Vice-Admiralty Courts*, 15.

104. Coquillette, *The Law Reports, Part One*, 250–51.

105. Ibid., 254.

106. Ibid.

107. Ibid., 252.

108. Ibid., 250.

109. Ibid., 252.

110. Ibid., 252–54, 259; Wroth, "Massachusetts Vice Admiralty Court," 347.

111. Coquillette, *The Law Reports, Part One*, 254.

112. Ibid.

113. Ibid., 254–56.

114. Ibid.

115. Ibid., 256.

116. Ibid.

117. Ibid.

118. Ibid., 258.

119. *Massachusetts Acts and Resolves*, 1:15. I have updated the spelling of a few words.

120. Coquillette, *The Law Reports, Part One*, 26.

121. Ibid.

122. Ibid., 260.

123. Ibid., 258.

124. Ibid., 260–62.

125. Ibid., 262.

126. Ibid.

127. Ibid., 264. See ibid. for an insightful and comprehensive treatment of Hutchinson's decision.

128. Ibid., 264.

129. Order, *Scollay v. Dunn*, Massachusetts Archives, Supreme Court Record Books, vol. 1766–1767, 10, MACM; Coquillette, *The Law Reports, Part Two*, 478.

130. James Otis to George Johnston, January 25, 1765, *Proceedings of the Massachusetts Historical Society*, 3rd ser., 43 (1909): 206. See also, e.g., *Boston Gazette*, May 18, 1761; *Boston Evening-Post*, July 19, 1762; *Boston Evening-Post*, May 23, 1763.

131. *Boston Gazette*, March 15, 1756. See, e.g., *Boston Post-Boy*, December 12, 1757 (paving and repairing Boston Neck); *Boston Evening-Post*, December 13, 1762 (repairing Faneuil Hall).

132. *New York Mercury*, May 26, 1760.

133. *Letters and Diary of John Rowe, Boston Merchant, 1759–1762, 1764–1779*, ed. Anne Rowe Cunningham (Boston: W. B. Clarke Company, 1903), 74.

134. James Otis to George Johnston, January 25, 1765, *Proceedings of the Massachusetts Historical Society*, 3rd ser., 43 (1909): 206.

135. *Boston Gazette*, September 16, 1765; *Boston Post-Boy*, November 11, 1765.

136. Coquillette, *The Law Cases, Part Two*, 478–80.

137. Order, Massachusetts Archives, Superior Court Record Book, vol. 1766–1767, 12, MACM.

138. Rowe, *Diary*, 105.

139. *John Adams Diary and Autobiography*, 1:321.

140. Record of *Jenny Slew v. John Whipple, Jr.*, "Records of the Inferior Court of Common Pleas," in George H. Moore, *Notes on the History of Slavery in Massachusetts* (New York, 1866), 113.

141. Thomas Franklin Waters, *Ipswich in the Massachusetts Bay Colony*, vol. 2 (Ipswich: Ipswich Historical Society, 1917), 217.

142. *Diary and Autobiography of John Adams*, ed. L. H. Butterfield, vol. 2 (1961; New York: Atheneum, 1964), 50.

143. Ibid., 1:110.

144. *Works of John Adams*, ed. Charles Francis Adams, vol. 2 (Boston, 1850), 290n1.

145. Ibid.

146. See text at chapter 3, note 37.

147. Emory Washburn, *Sketches of the Judicial History of Massachusetts from 1630 to the Revolution in 1775* (Boston, 1840), 232. See also Sullivan, *Address to Suffolk Bar*, 34 (Kent was a "very inferior man").

148. Washburn, *Judicial History of Massachusetts*, 232.

149. Massachusetts Superior Court Record Books, Suffolk County (February 13 and August 8, 1738), LDS Court Records Project, reel no. 0946373; ibid. (February 21 and August 15, 1758), MHS; ibid. (April 15 and August 26, 1766), MHS.

150. *Fanueil v. Pompey*, Superior Court of Judicature, vol. 1752–53, 238, Massachusetts Archives; Suffolk Files Collection, vol. 432, 42, MACM. The Superior Court remanded "the said Pompey . . . to the said Fanueil." Apparently the decision was reversed not on the merits but rather on a pleading defect of some other nonsubstantive reason. Ibid.

151. Record of *Jenny Slew v. Jonathan Whipple, Jr.*, "Records of the Inferior Court of Common Pleas," in Moore, *Notes on Slavery in Massachusetts*, 113–14.

152. Record of *Jenny Slew v. Jonathan Whipple, Jr.*, "Records of the Superior Court of Judicature," in Moore, *Notes on Slavery in Massachusetts*, 114.

153. Record of *Jenny Slew v. Jonathan Whipple, Jr.*, "Records of the Inferior Court of

Common Pleas," in Moore, *Notes on Slavery in Massachusetts*, 113. Much of this discussion draws on the insights found in *Legal Papers of John Adams*, 2:52–55.

154. *Legal Papers of John Adams*, 2:54.
155. Ibid.
156. *Massachusetts Acts and Resolves*, 1:578.
157. See, e.g., An Act for the Registration of Free Negroes, etc., ibid., 1:606.
158. By implication, Massachusetts statute law restricted slavery to people of color, specifically Negroes, mulattos, and Native Americans. See, e.g., An Act Relating to Mulato and Negro Slaves, ibid., 1:519; An Act to Encourage the Importation of White Servants (distinguishes between "Indian Slaves" and "white servants"), ibid., 1:634.
159. *Legal Papers of John Adams*, 2:53.
160. *The Institutes of Justinian with English Introduction, Translation, and Notes*, ed. Thomas Collett Sandars (1853; London: Longmans, Green and Co., 1922), 7.
161. The fifth justice, Chambers Russell, was on a ship bound for London. Shipton, *Harvard Graduates*, 9:56–87.
162. *Legal Papers of John Adams*, 2:53.
163. Ibid., 54.
164. Ibid.
165. Ibid.
166. Ibid.
167. Ibid.
168. Ibid.
169. Ibid., 54–55.
170. Record of *Jenny Slew v. Jonathan Whipple, Jr.*, "Records of the Superior Court of Judicature," in Moore, *Notes on Slavery in Massachusetts*, 114.
171. Ibid.

Chapter Nine: The Writs of Assistance (1760–1761)

1. Peter Orlando Hutchinson, *The Diary and Letters of His Excellency Thomas Hutchinson*, vol. 1 (London, 1884), 64–65.
2. *Boston News-Letter*, April 7, 1763.
3. Charles R. McKirdy, "Lawyers in Crisis: The Massachusetts Legal Profession, 1760–1790" (Ph.D. diss., Northwestern University, 1969), 37–40; John M. Murrin, "The Legal Transformation: The Bench and Bar of Eighteenth-Century Massachusetts," in *Colonial America: Essays in Politics and Social Development*, ed. Stanley M. Katz (Boston: Little, Brown and Company, 1971), 434.
4. Clifford K. Shipton, *Sibley's Harvard Graduates: Biographical Sketches of Those Who Attended Harvard College* (hereafter Shipton, *Harvard Graduates*), vol. 8, *1726–1730* (Boston: Massachusetts Historical Society, 1951) 163–64. Hutchinson was aware of this weakness; Thomas Hutchinson to John Sullivan, March 29, 1771 ("I never presumed to call myself a Lawyer"), Thomas Hutchinson Letter Books, vol. 27, 239, Massachusetts Historical Society, Boston (hereafter MHS).
5. *Diary and Autobiography of John Adams*, ed. L. H. Butterfield, vol. 1 (New York: Atheneum, 1964), 168.

6. [Oxenbridge Thacher], *Considerations on the Election of Counsellors Humbly Offered to the Electors* (Boston, 1761).

7. *John Adams Diary and Autobiography*, 1:225

8. *The Papers of Francis Bernard, Governor of Massachusetts, 1760–1769*, ed. Colin Nicolson, vol. 1 (Boston: Colonial Society of Massachusetts, 2007), 3–7.

9. Ibid., 3–6; Bernard Bailyn, *The Ordeal of Thomas Hutchinson* (Cambridge: Harvard University Press, 1974), 45–47.

10. Benjamin Lynde Sr. served as chief justice from 1728 to 1745, Paul Dudley from 1745 to 1751, and Stephen Sewall from 1752 to 1760. McKirdy, "Lawyers in Crisis," appendix 1.

11. Murrin, "The Legal Transformation," 435.

12. Shipton, *Harvard Graduates*, vol. 6, *1713–1722* (Boston: Massachusetts Historical Society, 1942), 250–54.

13. See text at chapter 6, note 72.

14. Neither Russell nor Oliver had any formal legal training. Russell (1713–1766) had a mercantile background. He was appointed judge of the Massachusetts Vice Admiralty Court in 1746. The next year he was appointed a judge on the Middlesex Inferior Court, and in 1752 he was named to the Superior Court. In 1747 Oliver was appointed to the Plymouth Inferior Court. In 1756 he was elevated to the Superior Court. *Legal Papers of John Adams*, ed. L. Kinvin Wroth and Hiller B. Zobel, vol. 1 (Cambridge: Harvard University Press, 1965), cviii–cix, civ; Shipton, *Harvard Graduates*, vol. 9, *1731–1735* (Boston: Massachusetts Historical Society, 1956), 81–87; Shipton, *Harvard Graduates*, 8:737–63.

15. Stephen Sewall (1702–1760) was an aberration. Appointed chief justice in 1752 at age fifty, he was the youngest man ever selected for the position. His immediate predecessor, Paul Dudley (1675–1751), was seventy when he was appointed in 1745, and the average age at appointment of Dudley's predecessors was sixty-two.

16. Murrin, "The Legal Transformation," 436.

17. Shipton, *Harvard Graduates*, 6:220, 236–39.

18. *Legal Papers of John Adams*, 1:cvi.

19. Edmund Trowbridge to William Bollan, July 15, 1762, in "Jasper Mauduit: Agent in London for the Province of Massachusetts-Bay, 1762–1765," *Collections of the Massachusetts Historical Society* 74 (1918): 60; Colin Nicolson, *The "Infamas Govener": Francis Bernard and the Origins of the American Revolution* (Boston: Northeastern University Press, 2001), 63.

20. Shipton, *Harvard Graduates*, vol. 7, *1722–1725* (Boston: Massachusetts Historical Society, 1945), 11–13, 15. Early in his legal career, Brattle apparently enjoyed some recognition. He was appointed a justice of the peace. The House of Representatives elected him attorney general several times only to have the governor negate their choice. He also sat as a special justice on the Superior Court in 1749. At least some of these appointments probably stemmed more from Brattle's social standing than from his legal ability. He was never made a barrister of the Superior Court. Ibid., 10–11.

21. *Sundry Rules and Directions for drawing up a regiment, posting the officers, etc.* (Boston, 1733).

22. Shipton, *Harvard Graduates*, 7:16–17. When he was twenty-three, Brattle had

been elected to the House of Representatives and served several more terms, after which he took a hiatus for about twenty years until his election in 1754. Ibid., 12, 16.

23. Jonathan Belcher to Richard Waldron, May 25, 1741, quoted ibid., 14.

24. In Emory Washburn, *Sketches of the Judicial History of Massachusetts from 1630 to the Revolution in 1775* (Boston, 1840), 209–10.

25. John J. Waters Jr. and John A. Schutz, "Patterns of Massachusetts Colonial Politics: The Writs of Assistance and the Rivalry between the Otis and Hutchinson Families," *William and Mary Quarterly*, 3rd ser., 24, no. 4 (1967): 551–52.

26. To soothe the colonel's disappointment, the Otis family received several military contracts. Waters and Schutz, "Patterns of Massachusetts Colonial Politics," 554n23.

27. John J. Waters Jr., *The Otis Family in Provincial and Revolutionary Massachusetts* (1968; New York: W. W. Norton & Company, 1975), 104–5.

28. James Otis Sr., Memorandum, ca. August 15, 1757, in Waters, *Otis Family*, 105.

29. Waters and Schutz, "Patterns of Massachusetts Colonial Politics," 555–56.

30. Ibid., 555–57.

31. James Otis, *Boston Gazette*, April 4, 1763. When Otis went public with these allegations two years after the fact, Hutchinson claimed that when he had met with Otis, Hutchinson gave him "no reason to suppose that I was determined to refuse the place" or would support Otis's father for it. *Boston News-Letter*, April 7, 1763.

32. *John Adams Diary and Autobiography*, 1:226 (June 6, 1762). See also William Gordon, *The History of the Progress and Establishment of the Independence of the United States of America*, vol. 1 (London, 1788), 141.

33. *Boston News-Letter*, April 7, 1763.

34. Edmund Trowbridge to William Bollan, July 15, 1762, Dana Papers, 1674–1769, Massachusetts Historical Society, Boston (hereafter MHS); Francis Bernard to the Earl of Shelburne, December 22, 1766, in *Bernard Papers*, 1:403.

35. *John Adams Diary and Autobiography*, 1:25.

36. James Otis, *Boston Gazette*, April 4, 1763.

37. *John Adams Diary and Autobiography*, 1:226.

38. Ibid., 236.

39. Quoted in Bailyn, *Ordeal of Thomas Hutchinson*, 49.

40. Nicolson, *The "Infamas Govener,"* 63.

41. Ibid.

42. Ibid.

43. Bailyn, *Ordeal of Thomas Hutchinson*, 47.

44. Lawrence Henry Gipson, *The Coming of the Revolution, 1763–1775* (1954; New York: Harper & Row, 1962), 34. Three years after appointing Hutchinson, Bernard credited "the steadiness of the Judges of the supreme court" with bringing the smuggling in Boston under control. Francis Bernard to the Earl of Egremont, October 25, 1763, in *Bernard Papers*, 1:426.

45. John Adams to Dr. J. Morse, November 29, 1815, in *Works of John Adams*, ed. Charles Francis Adams, vol. 10 (Boston: Little, Brown and Company, 1856), 183. See also John Adams to William Tudor, August 6, 1818 (Hutchinson "had been appointed on purpose to sanction the writ"), ibid., 343. Some find no basis for Adams's conclusion.

See, e.g., James Truslow Adams, *Revolutionary New England, 1691–1776* (Boston: Atlantic Monthly Press/Little Brown, 1923), 272n.; Nicolson, The *"Infamas Govener,"* 63.

46. Daniel R. Coquillette, ed., *The Law Reports, Part One,* vol. 4 of *Portrait of a Patriot: The Major Political and Legal Papers of Josiah Quincy Junior,* ed. Daniel R. Coquillette and Neil Longley York (Boston: Colonial Society of Massachusetts, 2009), 201; Stephen B. Presser and Jamil S. Zainaldin, *Law and American History: Cases and Materials* (St. Paul: West Publishing Co., 1980), 61.

47. Colliquette, *The Law Reports, Part One,* 199.

48. John Adams to William Tudor, March 29, 1817, in *Works of John Adams,* 10:247; John Adams to Dr. Morse, November 29, 1815, ibid., 183.

49. John Adams to William Tudor, March 29, 1817, ibid., 248. See, e.g., O. M. Dickerson, "Writs of Assistance as a Cause of the Revolution," in *The Era of the American Revolution,* ed. Richard B. Morris (New York: Columbia University Press, 1939), 42; James M. Farrell, "The Writs of Assistance and Public Memory: John Adams and the Legacy of James Otis," *New England Quarterly* 79, no. 4 (2006): 534, for arguments that the importance of Otis's speech has been exaggerated.

50. *Legal Papers of John Adams,* ed. L. Kinvin Wroth and Hiller B. Zobel, vol. 2 (Cambridge: Harvard University Press, 1965), 98.

51. Ibid.; Larry Sawers, "The Navigation Acts Revisited," *Economic History Review,* new ser., 45, no. 2 (1992): 262–63. The Acts of Trade also forbade colonial manufacture of certain products. Ibid., 263.

52. *Legal Papers of John Adams,* 2:99.

53. Thomas C. Barrow, *Trade and Empire: The British Customs Service in Colonial America, 1660–1775* (Cambridge: Harvard University Press, 1967), 72–77.

54. 12 Car., c. 19; M. H. Smith, *The Writs of Assistance Case* (Berkeley: University of California Press, 1978), 42.

55. Smith, *Writs of Assistance Case,* 42.

56. Ibid., 42–45.

57. 13 & 14 Car. 2, c. 11 sec. 5(2); Smith, W*rits of Assistance Case,* 43. When enacted in 1662, the Act of Frauds did not apply to the colonies. The "Act for preventing Frauds and regulating abuses in the Plantation Trade" (7 & 8 Wm. III, c. 22) of 1696 gave colonial customs officers the powers of their English counterparts. *Legal Papers of John Adams,* 2:111; Farrell, "The Writs of Assistance and Public Memory," 535.

58. Coquillette, *The Law Reports, Part One,* 204–6.

59. *Legal Papers of John Adams,* 2:131n93. Accord: Coquillette, *The Law Reports, Part One.* 203.

60. William J. Cuddihy, "'A Man's House is his Castle': New Light on an Old Case," *Reviews in American History* 5, no. 1 (1979): 65; Smith, *Writs of Assistance Case,* 37.

61. Smith, *Writs of Assistance Case,* 31, 37.

62. Farrell, "Writs of Assistance in the Public Mind," 535.

63. *Legal Papers of John Adams,* 2:108–9.

64. Gipson, *The Coming of the Revolution,* 36; Presser and Zainaldin, *Law and American History,* 61. Prior to 1755, when Hutchinson advised him that the practice was unlawful, Governor Shirley, acting on his own authority, had issued search warrants "to the officers of the customs to enter." *The History of the Colony and Province of*

Massachusetts Bay by Thomas Hutchinson, ed. Lawrence Shaw Mayo, vol. 3 (Cambridge: Harvard University Press, 1936), 92.

65. Gipson, *The Coming of the Revolution*, 28, 30.

66. Barrow, *Trade and Empire*, 169; Presser and Zainalden, *Law and American History*, 62.

67. Gipson, *The Coming of the Revolution*, 28; Barrow, *Trade and Empire*, 160–62; *Legal Papers of John Adams*, 2:100.

68. Barrow, *Trade and Empire*, 163–68.

69. See text at chapter 8, note 94, for a discussion of writs of prohibition.

70. Maurice H. Smith, "Charles Paxton, Founding Stepfather," *Proceedings of the Massachusetts Historical Society*, 3rd ser., 94 (1982):15–17.

71. *Boston Gazette*, September 19, 1752.

72. Francis Bernard to the Earl of Halifax, May 17, 1765, in *The Papers of Francis Bernard, Governor of Massachusetts, 1760–1769*, ed. Colin Nicolson, vol. 2 (Boston: Colonial Society of Massachusetts, 2012), 272–73; Emily Hickman, "Colonial Writs of Assistance," *New England Quarterly* 5 (1932): 88.

73. Smith, "Charles Paxton," 19.

74. Coquillette, *The Law Reports, Part One*, 203.

75. *Reports of Cases Argued and Adjudged in the Superior Court of Judicature of Massachusetts Bay Between 1761 and 1772. By Josiah Quincy, Junior*, ed. Samuel M. Quincy (Boston, 1865), 402.

76. Ibid., 404–5.

77. John C. Miller, *Origins of the American Revolution* (Boston: Little Brown & Company, 1943), 46.

78. *Quincy's Reports*, 553.

79. Miller, *Origins of the American Revolution*, 46; Smith, "Charles Paxton," 19–20; Presser and Zainaldin, *Law and American History*, 62. Governor Bernard was well aware of the problem that Rhode Island presented: "The greatest difficulty which attends the execution of the Laws of trade here arises from the great liberty which is allowed in some other colonies. The Merchants here complain, with some show of reason, of the hardship they suffer by being Subject to restraints, which their Neighbors in Ports almost under their Eye are quite Strangers to." Answer of Governor Bernard to Queries of the Board of Trade, September 5, 1763, in *Bernard Papers*, 1:403.

80. *Boston Post-Boy*, July 2, 1759; Barrow, *Trade and Empire*, 123, 169. From 1755 to 1757, Barons had been secretary to his wife's brother, the governor of New York. Apparently he obtained the collector position through the support of the Earl of Halifax, president of the Board of Trade. Smith, *Writs of Assistance*, 185. Governor Bernard maintained that Barons's actions were in "direct opposition to Common sense & reason" and to "his Obligations his Duty & his interest." Francis Bernard to Thomas Pownall, July 12, 1761, in *Bernard Papers*, 1:126.

81. *Legal Papers of John Adams*, 2:160n44; Barrow, *Trade and Empire*, 170.

82. Deposition of Ebenezer Richardson, February 27, 1761, transcript, Great Britain, Public Record Office, London, Treasury, bundle 408, Library of Congress. This deposition, like the others cited in this discussion, was taken in the action against Barons brought by surveyor Charles Paxton which ultimately led to Barons's removal as

collector in June 1761. *Boston Evening-Post*, June 29, 1761; *John Adams Legal Papers of John Adams*, 2:160n44.

83. Deposition of Charles Paxton, February 18, 1761, transcript, Great Britain, Public Record Office, London, Treasury, bundle 408, Library of Congress.

84. Smith, "Charles Paxton," 21.

85. Deposition of Charles Paxton, February 18, 1761, transcript, Great Britain, Public Record Office, London, Treasury 1, bundle 408, Library of Congress; Smith, *Writs of Assistance*, 193–94.

86. Ibid.

87. *Quincy's Reports*, 412–13, 541n1.

88. Otis had been acting as a deputy to William Bollan, who had held the position of advocate general since October 1742. When Bollan was in England, Otis carried out his duties. *Bernard Papers*, 1:160n1. It is not clear exactly when Otis resigned his admiralty position. According to Paxton, Otis resigned immediately prior to the merchants' meeting. Deposition of Charles Paxton, February 18, 1761, transcript, Great Britain, Public Records Office, London, Treasury 1, bundle 408, Library of Congress. Adams maintains that Otis resigned when he was pressed to be more rigorous in enforcing the trade and navigation acts. James Adams to William Tudor, February 25, 1818, in *Works of John Adams*, 10:29. Accord: Waters, *Otis Family*, 120.

89. Francis Bernard to the Lords of Trade, August 6, 1761, in *Bernard Papers*, 1:133, 136n5. Paxton won a verdict and judgment at the February 1762 term of the Superior Court. *Legal Papers of John Adams*, 2:113n21.

90. *Diary and Autobiography of John Adams*, ed. L. H. Butterfield, vol. 3 (New York: Atheneum, 1964), 275. Adams began his autobiography in the fall of 1802. Ibid., 1:lxviii.

91. See, e.g., John Adams to Dr. J. Morse, November 29, 1815, in *Works of John Adams*, 10:182–83; John Adams to William Tudor, March 29, 1817, ibid., 246; John Adams to Hezekiah Niles, January 14, 1818, ibid., 274–75; John Adams to Benjamin Waterhouse, March 25, 1817, in *Statesman and Friend: Correspondence of John Adams with Benjamin Waterhouse, 1784–1822*, ed. Worthington Chauncey Ford (Boston: Little, Brown and Company, 1927), 129–31, for Adams's repetition of this account. See Smith, *Writs of Assistance Case*, 134–36, for a detailed, if unpersuasive, argument in support of the accuracy of Adams's account. Among others, Gipson, *Coming of the Revolution*, 34; Presser and Zainoldin, *Law and American History*, 61, also rely on Adams's version.

92. *Quincy's Reports*, 409; Ellen E. Brennan, *Plural Office Holding in Massachusetts* (Chapel Hill: University of North Carolina Press, 1945), 39; Smith, *Writs of Assistance Case*, 134.

93. *Quincy's Reports*, 422–24; *Legal Papers of John Adams*, 2:134n105.

94. *Legal Papers of John Adams*, 2:113n22. Quincy's account of the writs case is titled "Paxton's Case," and Paxton's was the first writ granted. Colliquette, *The Law Reports, Part One*, 194; *Quincy's Reports*, 51, 418–22.

95. *Quincy's Reports*, 412–13; *Legal Papers of John Adams*, 2:113n21.

96. *Quincy's Reports*, 413–14.

97. *Legal Papers of John Adams*, 2:113.

98. See text at note 91.

99. Hutchinson, *History of Massachusetts*, 3:68. Sewall's "doubts" may have arisen from an article in the March 1760 issue of the *London Magazine* which reached Boston prior to Sewall's death. The article maintained that writs of assistance had "never been granted without an information under oath, that the person applying for it [had] reason to suspect that prohibited or uncustomed goods [were] concealed in the house or place which he desired a power to search." "The History of the Last Session of Parliament," *London Magazine*, March 1760, 126. This, of course, was entirely different from the manner in which writs routinely had been issued in Massachusetts. Smith, *Writs of Assistance*, 133–42; Presser and Zainaldin, *Law and American History*, 61.

100. According to John Adams, the "Merchants of Salem and Boston applied to Mr. Pratt, who refused and to Mr. Otis and Mr. Thacher, who accepted." John Adams to William Tudor, March 29, 1817, in *Works of John Adams*, 10:247. In a later letter to Benjamin Waterhouse, however, written at about the same time (March 25, 1817), Adams states that Otis asked Prat to assist him. *Statesman and Friend*, 130.

101. John Adams to William Tudor, March 29, 1817, in *Works of John Adams*, 10:245.

102. Shipton, *Harvard Graduates*, vol. 10, *1736–1740* (Boston: Massachusetts Historical Society, 1958), 233. In March 1761, Prat was appointed New York's chief justice. Ibid. In May 1760, Prat had acted as advocate general of admiralty in the action against Erving's brigantine *Sarah*. He may have thought it inappropriate and politically unwise to change sides in so short a time frame. *Quincy's Reports*, 554.

103. John Adams to Hezekiah Niles, January 14, 1818, in *Works of John Adams*, 10:276.

104. Ibid., 275.

105. *Legal Papers of John Adams*, 2:135.

106. Ibid., 138.

107. Smith, *Writs of Assistance Case*, 292.

108. Ibid.

109. McKirdy, "Lawyers in Crisis," 199–200.

110. Hutchinson, *History of Massachusetts*, 3:75.

111. Ibid.; Shipton, *Harvard Graduates*, 10:323.

112. John Adams to Hezekiah Niles, February 13, 1818, in *Works of John Adams*, 10:285.

113. Hiller B. Zobel, *The Boston Massacre* (New York: W. W. Norton, 1970), 9.

114. *John Adams Diary and Autobiography*, 3:276.

115. *Legal Papers of John Adams*, 2:134n.103. No copy of Adams's "Abstract" in his own hand has been found. This discussion relies on the version found in the *Legal Papers of John Adams*, 2:134–44, which is a distillation of all known versions of the "Abstract." Ibid., 122.

116. Ibid., 210.

117. Smith, *Writs of Assistance Case*, 286–87, 317–18.

118. Ibid., 87.

119. *Legal Papers of John Adams*, 2:127.

120. *John Adams Diary and Autobiography*, 3:114. Four years later, Governor Bernard stated that "the Arguments in Court from the Bar & upon the Bench lasted 3 days." It is not clear whether he is referring only to the argument in February, or to those in both February and November. Francis Bernard to the Board of Trade, November 30, 1765, in *Bernard Papers*, 2:427.

121. Ibid., 114.
122. *Legal Papers of John Adams*, 2:123.
123. Ibid., 136.
124. Ibid., 136–37.
125. Ibid.
126. Ibid., 137.
127. Ibid., 137–38.
128. Ibid., 138.
129. Ibid.
130. Ibid.
131. John Adams to Benjamin Waterhouse, March 25, 1815, in *Statesman and Friend*, 131.
132. *Legal Papers of John Adams*, 2:139.
133. Ibid.
134. Ibid., 140.
135. Ibid., 141.
136. Ibid., 125.
137. Ibid., 141, 126. Gridley had cited William Hawkins's *Treatise of Pleas of the Crown; or a system of the principal matters relating to the subject digested under proper heads*, first published in 1716, which was an influential treatise on English criminal law.
138. *Legal Papers of John Adams*, 2:141.
139. Ibid., 144.
140. Ibid.
141. Smith, *Writs of Assistance*, 333.
142. Hutchinson, *History of Massachusetts*, 3:68.
143. Ibid.
144. Ibid.
145. Ibid.; Thomas Hutchinson to Secretary Conway, October 1, 1765, in *Quincy's Reports*, 414n2.
146. Memorandum by William Bollan "relating to the proceedings at Boston with respect to illicit Trade, ec.," in Smith, *Writs of Assistance*, 540–41.
147. Ibid., 541.
148. Ibid.
149. Ibid., 392–93.
150. Superior Court of Massachusetts, August 1761 Term, Suffolk County (1750–1762), 239, Church of Jesus Christ of Latter-day Saints, Court Records Project, reel no. 947006; *John Adams Diary and Autobiography*, 1:224; *Boston Gazette*, November 13, 1761.
151. Colliquette, *The Law Reports, Part One*, 202–4.
152. Ibid., 200–202.
153. Ibid., 194–96.
154. Smith, *Writs of Assistance Case*, 403.
155. Coquillette, *The Law Reports, Part One*, 204.
156. Ibid., 206.
157. Ibid.; Paul de Rapin's *Histoire d'Angleterre* (1724–1727), a multivolume history of England, was one of the first comprehensive English histories.
158. Coquillett, *The Law Reports, Part One*, 206.

159. Ibid.
160. John Adams to William Tudor, March 24, 1817, in *Works of John Adams*, 10:247. See also John Adams to Benjamin Waterhouse, March 25, 1817, in *Statesman and Friend*, 247.
161. Smith, *Writs of Assistance Case*, 283.
162. *Quincy's Reports*, 539–40.
163. Smith, *Writs of Assistance Case*, 280. Accord: *Quincy's Reports*, 536 ("Gridley's argument hard to meet").
164. Smith, *Writs of Assistance Case*, 280.
165. Ibid., 334.
166. Ibid., 335.
167. Ibid.
168. *Quincy's Reports*, 532.
169. Smith, *Writs of Assistance Case*, 398 (With Bollan's "blockbuster," Otis's argument "was destroyed beyond all possibility of salvage").
170. *Legal Papers of John Adams*, 2:117.
171. Smith, *Writs of Assistance Case*, 285.
172. Ibid.
173. Ibid., 291.
174. Ibid., 270. Smith never explains what he means by the term "whig," which is unfortunate because in different eras and in different situations it has had different meanings. In fact, the persistence of the term in English politics between the mid-sixteenth and mid-nineteenth centuries has been attributed to its "essential unmeaningness." *Encyclopedia Britannica*, 11th ed., s.v. "Whig and Tory." From the context in which it is used in his book, it would seem that to Smith, a "whig" was one opposed to the exercise of British authority in British America.
175. Smith, *Writs of Assistance Case*, 270.
176. See text at chapter 3, notes 3–5, 29–31.
177. *Writs of Assistance Case*, 270.
178. Shipton, *Harvard Graduates*, 7:526.
179. Jeremiah Gridley to Gilbert McAdam, February 2, 1757, Loudoun Collection, LO 2929, Huntington Library. See text at chapter 7, notes 112–18.
180. Smith, *Writs of Assistance Case*, 283.
181. Ibid.
182. Ibid., 284.
183. Ibid., 284–85.
184. See text at chapter 7, notes 132–40.
185. Deposition of Robert Temple, February 25, 1761, transcript, Great Britain, Public Records Office, London, Treasury, bundle 408, Library of Congress.
186. Ibid.
187. Francis Bernard to Thomas Pownall, July 12, 1761, in *Bernard Papers*, 1:126.
188. Smith, *Writs of Assistance Case*, 292.
189. Ibid.
190. John K. Reeves, "Jeremy Gridley, Editor," *New England Quarterly*, 17, no. 2 (1944): 265. Smith also attempted to make something out of Adams's comment in an 1818 letter that after Otis's argument, "Mr. Gridley himself seemed to me to exult inwardly

at the glory and triumph of his pupil." John Adams to William Tudor, August 6, 1818, in *Works of John Adams*, 10:342. Putting aside the obvious difficulty in determining whether or not someone is exulting "inwardly," Adams's statement must be read in context with another he made in a letter a year earlier that Gridley "said everything that could be said in favor of [the writ]." John Adams to William Tudor, March 27, 1817, in *Works of John Adams*, 10:247.

191. Shipton, *Harvard Graduates*, 7:527.

192. John Adams to William Tudor, July 9, 1818, in *Works of John Adams*, 10:327.

Chapter Ten: Sugar and Stamps (1762–1766)

1. John Adams to B. Niles, January 14, 1818, in *The Works of John Adams*, ed. Charles Francis Adams, vol. 10 (Boston, 1856), 276.

2. John J. Waters Jr., *The Otis Family in Provincial and Revolutionary Massachusetts* (Chapel Hill: University of North Carolina Press, 1968), 142.

3. Ibid., 138–39; Elizabeth Brennan, *Plural Office-Holding in Massachusetts, 1760–1780* (Chapel Hill: University of North Carolina Press, 1945), 41.

4. Thomas Hutchinson to William Bollan, April 24, 1762, in "Jasper Mauduit: Agent in London for the Province of Massachusetts-Bay, 1762–1765," *Collections of the Massachusetts Historical Society* 74 (1918): 29.

5. Waters, *The Otis Family*, 140. The salaries were reduced from £750 to £700 per year. Ibid.

6. Francis Bernard to John Pownall, April 25, 1762, in *The Papers of Francis Bernard, Governor of Colonial Massachusetts, 1760–1769*, ed. Colin Nicolson, vol. 1 (Boston: Colonial Society of Massachusetts, 2007), 200–202. Many in the House of Representatives mistrusted Bollan because he was a friend of Hutchinson's and an Episcopalian. Waters, *The Otis Family*, 140; Bernard Bailyn, *The Ordeal of Thomas Hutchinson* (Cambridge: Harvard University Press, 1974), 58.

7. Francis Bernard to Lord Barrington, May 1, 1762, in *The Barrington-Bernard Correspondence and Illustrative Matter, 1760–1770*, ed. Edward Channing and Archibald Cary Coolidge (Cambridge: Harvard University Press, 1912), 51–52; Waters, *The Otis Family*, 141–42.

8. *The History of the Colony and Province of Massachusetts-Bay by Thomas Hutchinson*, ed. Lawrence Shaw Mayo, vol. 3 (Cambridge: Harvard University Press, 1936), 69.

9. Waters, *The Otis Family*, 143.

10. Francis Bernard to John Pownall, April 25, 1762, in *Bernard Papers*, 1:200.

11. Francis Bernard to Lord Barrington, February 27, 1762, in *Barrington-Bernard Correspondence*, 50. See also *Journals of the House of Representatives of Massachusetts* 28, pt. 2 (February 27, 1762): 282.

12. Francis Bernard to Lord Barrington, February 20, 1762, in *Bernard-Barrington Correspondence*, 50.

13. About the same time, Joseph Otis, another of the colonel's sons, was named sheriff of Barnstable County. Waters, *The Otis Family*, 142.

14. Ibid., 138.

15. Francis Bernard to Lord Barrington, May 1, 1762, in *Barrington-Bernard*

Correspondence, 51–52; Francis Bernard to Board of Trade, April 13, 1762, in *Bernard Papers*, 1:193–94. See also *Journals of the Massachusetts House of Representatives* 38, pt. 2 (March 6, 1762): 299.

16. Waters, *The Otis Family*, 144; Hutchinson, *History of Massachusetts*, 3:71.

17. Waters, *The Otis Family*, 145–46; Francis Bernard to John Powell, April 25, 1762, in *Bernard Papers*, 1:201–2; Bailyn, *The Ordeal of Thomas Hutchinson*, 58–59.

18. Oxenbridge Thacher to Benjamin Prat, 1762, in *Proceedings of the Massachusetts Historical Society*, 1st ser., 20 (1882–83): 47.

19. Israel Williams (1763), in Henry Lefavour, "The Proposed College in Hampshire County in 1762," *Proceedings of the Massachusetts Historical Society*, 3rd ser., 66 (1936–1941): 53.

20. Josiah Quincy, *The History of Harvard University*, vol. 2 (Cambridge, MA, 1840), 105. Oxenbridge Thacher believed that Williams was partially motivated by "his son's being placed . . . something lower in a class at our college than befitted ye. son of a king." Oxenbridge Thacher to Benjamin Prat, 1762, in *Proceedings of the Massachusetts Historical Society*, 1st ser., 20 (1882–83): 47.

21. Israel Williams to William Smith (1762), in *Proceedings of the Massachusetts Historical Society*, 1st ser., 20 (1882–83): 47n. The quote refers to the legal opinion of Smith, whom Williams also consulted. Williams says of Smith's opinion that "Mr. Gridley was of the same." Ibid.

22. Oxenbridge Thacher to Benjamin Prat, 1762, in *Proceedings of the Massachusetts Historical Society*, 1st ser., 20 (1882–83): 48.

23. Waters, *The Otis Family*, 141.

24. Lafavour, "The Proposed College in Hampshire County," 61.

25. Francis Bernard to Board of Trade, April 12, 1762, in *Bernard Papers*, 1:191.

26. Israel Williams, 1762, in Lafavour, "The Proposed College in Hampshire County," 60. See also Francis Bernard to Board of Trade, April 12, 1762, in *Bernard Papers*, 1:191.

27. Israel Williams, 1762, in Lafavour, "The Proposed College in Hampshire County," 62.

28. Oxenbridge Thacher to Benjamin Prat, 1761, in *Proceedings of the Massachusetts Historical Society*, 1st ser., 20 (1882–83): 48. The remonstrance was drafted by the Reverend Jonathan Mayhew, who claimed that the proposed college met with "an almost universal uneasiness and alarm; not only as we think the scheme itself of bad tendency, but also because we generally suppose that the Governor has no such authority as he asserts, and has thus assumed to himself, of granting Charters." Jonathan Mayhew to Thomas Hollis, April 6, 1762, in "Jasper Mauduit," 70n1.

29. Quincy, *History of Harvard University*, 2:110. Bernard's version is different. He explained that he "put a stop to the Charter, still insisting on the King's right of granting Charters, tho' I did not think proper to perfecting this particular one." Francis Bernard to Board of Trade, April 12, 1762, in *Bernard Papers*, 1:191.

30. Bailyn, *The Ordeal of Thomas Hutchinson*, 57.

31. *Boston Gazette*, April 11, 1763. See also *Boston Gazette*, April 4, 1763.

32. Waters, *The Otis Family*, 147–48.

33. *Boston Evening-Post*, May 23, 1763.

34. Gilman M. Ostrander, "The Colonial Molasses Trade," *Agricultural History* 30, no. 2 (1956): 77.

35. Ibid., 78–79.

36. Ibid.

37. Albert B. Southwick, "The Molasses Act—Source of Precedents," *William and Mary Quarterly*, 3rd ser., 8, no. 3 (1951): 393–98.

38. 6 Geo. 2, c. 13.

39. Historians differ as to how injurious the duty would have been had it been effectively enforced. In "The Colonial Molasses Trade," 80, Ostrander argues that an enforced act would have seriously disrupted colonial commercial life. *Accord*: John W. Tyler, *Smugglers and Patriots: Boston Merchants and the Advent of the American Revolution* (Boston: Northeastern University Press, 1986), 79. *Contra*: Lawrence Henry Gipson, *The Coming of the American Revolution, 1763–1775* (New York: Harper & Row, 1954), 63–64.

40. John C. Miller, *Origins of the American Revolution* (Boston: Little, Brown and Company, 1943), 99.

41. Edmund S. Morgan and Helen M. Morgan, *The Stamp Act Crisis: Prologue to Revolution*, rev. ed. (1953; New York: Collier Books, 1963), 43n20.

42. Great Britain's national debt had increased from £73 million in January 1755 to £137 million in January 1763. Allen S. Johnson, "The Passage of the Sugar Act," *William and Mary Quarterly*, 3rd ser., 16, no. 4 (1959), 507–8.

43. Ibid., 508.

44. Tyler, *Smugglers and Patriots*, 67–68.

45. *Massachusetts Gazette*, September 22, 1763.

46. Ibid.

47. Ibid.; Gipson, *The Coming of the Revolution*, 60.

48. John J. McCusker, introduction to "Trade in the Atlantic World," *Business History Review* 79, no. 4 (2005): 707.

49. Johnson, "The Passage of the Sugar Act," 510; Gipson, *The Coming of the Revolution*, 60n15.

50. Charles Jenkinson to the Commissioners of the Customs, July 22, 1763, in Johnson, "The Passage of the Sugar Act," 510.

51. See, e.g., *Boston Post-Boy*, January 2, 1764 (Boston); *Boston Evening-Post*, January 2, 1764 (Salem); *Boston Gazette*, January 16, 1764 (Falmouth).

52. Francis Bernard to Richard Jackson, January 7, 1764, in *The Papers of Francis Bernard, Governor of Colonial Massachusetts, 1760–1769*, ed. Colin Nicolson, vol. 2 (Boston: Colonial Society of Massachusetts, 2012), 29. Concerned about the adverse economic effects of the new act on Massachusetts, Bernard claimed that he "could write a Volume against this measure." Francis Bernard to John Pownall, October 20, 1763, ibid., 1:428. See also Francis Bernard to Richard Jackson, August 3, 1763, ibid., 229; Answers to the Queries of the Board of Trade, September 5, 1763, ibid., 401.

53. Charles M. Andrews, "The Boston Merchants and the Non-Importation Movement," *Transactions of the Colonial Society of Massachusetts* 20 (1916–17): 161, 163.

54. Ibid., 164.

55. Nathaniel Spooner, *Gleanings from the Records of the Boston Marine Society, Through its First Century, 1742 to 1842* (Boston, 1879), 10.

56. *Manual of the Constitution and By-Laws of the Boston Marine Society, Begun June 1, 1742, Incorporated February 2, 1754* (Boston, 1896), 9.

57. R. G. F. Candage, "Jeremy Gridley," *Publications of the Brookline Historical Society* (1903): 21.

58. Mary Elizabeth Ruwell, *Eighteenth Century Capitalism: The Formation of American Marine Insurance Companies* (New York: Garland Publishing, 1993), 32, 39.

59. Andrews, "Boston Merchants and the Non-Importation Movement," 166.

60. "State of the Trade," *Transactions of the Colonial Society of Massachusetts* 19 (1916–17): 382–90.

61. Thomas Gray, Edward Payne, Joshua Winslow, and Joseph Green to Gurdon Salstonstal and Nathaniel Shaw, January 9, 1764, *Transactions of the Colonial Society of Massachusetts* 19 (1916–17): 381. Plymouth, Marblehead, Newbury, and Salem submitted similar memorials. *Journals of the Massachusetts House of Representatives* 40 (December 27, 1763): 132.

62. Andrews, "Boston Merchants and the Non-Importation Movement," 166.

63. According to John W. Tyler, the composition of the committee was "five merchants (including two distillers) with heavy interest in the West Indies, two traders with southern Europe, and at least three known smugglers: Solomon Davis, Edward Payne, John Rowe." Tyler, *Smugglers and Patriots*, 74.

64. Ibid.

65. Edmund S. Morgan, ed., *Prologue to Revolution: Sources and Documents on the Stamp Act Crisis, 1764–1766* (Chapel Hill: University of North Carolina Press, 1959), 4–23.

66. Ibid., 42.

67. Morgan and Morgan, *The Stamp Act Crisis*, 42.

68. Jasper Mauduit to the Speaker of the House of Representatives, March 13, 1764, "Jasper Mauduit," 146n1.

69. Jasper Mauduit to the House of Representatives, May 26, 1764, in Morgan, *Prologue to Revolution*, 27.

70. John L. Bullion, *A Great and Necessary Measure: George Grenville and the Genesis of the Stamp Act, 1763–1765* (Columbia: University of Missouri Press, 1982), 115. A stamp tax was not unprecedented in Massachusetts. In 1755 the General Court had passed an act imposing duties on specified documents. *The Acts and Resolves, Public and Private of the Province of Massachusetts Bay*, vol. 3 (Boston, 1873), 793–94.

71. Thomas Cushing to Jasper Mauduit, June 22, 1764, "Jasper Mauduit," 160.

72. Morgan and Morgan, *The Stamp Act Crisis*, 86–88.

73. Thomas Cushing to Jasper Mauduit, November 11, 1764, "Jasper Mauduit," 167.

74. Thomas Cushing to Jasper Mauduit, November 17. 1764, ibid., 170–71; Hutchinson, *History of Massachusetts*, 3:82–83.

75. Hutchinson, *History of Massachusetts*, 3:83.

76. Bullion, *A Great and Necessary Measure*, 159–60; Morgan and Morgan, *The Stamp Act Crisis*, 120.

77. Stamp Act, Preamble, 5 Geo. 3, c. 2; Hiller B. Zobel, *The Boston Massacre* (New York: W. W. Norton, 1970), 24.

78. Morgan and Morgan, *The Stamp Act Crisis*, 80. In England the fee was £6. Ibid.

79. Ibid., 81.

80. Bullion, *A Great and Necessary Measure*, 104–6.
81. Ibid., 166.
82. Thomas Whately to John Temple, May 10, 1755, "The Bowdoin and Temple Papers," *Collections of the Massachusetts Historical Society*, 6th ser., 9 (1897): 55.
83. *Boston Evening-Post*, April 8, 1765; *Boston Post-Boy*, April 8, 1765; *Boston News-Letter*, April 11, 1765.
84. Hutchinson, *History of Massachusetts*, 3:58; Samuel G. Drake, *The History and Antiquities of Boston* (Boston, 1856), 650.
85. Hutchinson, *History of Massachusetts*, 3:58; Drake, *History and Antiquities of Boston*, 650. More than one thousand homeless was a large percentage of Boston's population, which in 1765 numbered about fifteen thousand. Zobel, *The Boston Massacre*, 5.
86. *Boston Gazette*, January 30, 1764, February 13, 1764.
87. *Boston Evening-Post*, January 30, 1764.
88. Morgan and Morgan, *The Stamp Act Crisis*, 48–49.
89. Governor Bernard put Wheelright's debt at £170,000. Francis Bernard to Board of Trade, April 8, 1765, in *Bernard Papers*, 2:236–37.
90. James Otis to George Johnstone, January 25, 1765, *Proceedings of the Massachusetts Historical Society*, 3d ser., 43 (1909): 205.
91. Francis Bernard to Board of Trade, April 8, 1765, in *Bernard Papers*, 2:237.
92. James Otis to George Johnstone, January 25, 1765, *Proceedings of the Massachusetts Historical Society*, 3d ser., 43 (1909): 205. Governor Bernard also likened Wheelright's failure to "an earthquake." Francis Bernard to Lords of Trade, April 8, 1765, in *Bernard Papers*, 2:237.
93. *Boston Gazette*, May 6, 1765, May 20, 1765; *Boston Evening-Post*, May 6, 1765; *Boston News-Letter*, May 9, 1765. The only significant exception was the June 3, 1765, number of the *Boston Gazette*. Addressing Section 57 of the act, which allowed the trial of violations of its provisions to be heard in admiralty, the paper editorialized "that the Americans are not only to have their Monies taken from them without Consent, but to be deprived of another darling Privilege, viz. Trials by Jury."
94. *Journals of the Massachusetts House of Representatives* 42 (June 6, 1765, June 8, 1765): 108–11.
95. *Boston Gazette*, July 1, 1765. The *Gazette*'s article was taken verbatim from a report in the *Newport (Rhode Island) Mercury*, June 24, 1765, which did not accurately describe what had taken place in Virginia. It omitted one of the resolves that had been adopted by the Virginia legislators and included three that had been proposed but rejected as too extreme. These three had asserted that the Virginia legislature had the right to tax Virginians, and that Virginians had no obligation to pay taxes imposed by any other authority, and branded any person who said that anyone other than the Virginia assembly had the right or power to tax Virginians as "an enemy of his Majesty's Colony." Ibid.; *Bernard Papers*, 2:296n3; Morgan and Morgan, *Stamp Act Crisis*, 120–30.
96. Hutchinson, *History of Massachusetts*, 3:86n.
97. *Works of John Adams*, 10:287.
98. *Boston Gazette*, July 8, 1765. At the time of his conversation with Adams, Thacher was dying of smallpox contracted from an unsuccessful attempt at inoculation. He

died on July 9, 1765. Clifford K. Shipton, *Sibley's Harvard Graduates: Biographical Sketches of Those Who Attended Harvard College* (hereafter Shipton, *Harvard Graduates*), vol. 10, *1736–1740* (Boston: Massachusetts Historical Society, 1958), 327.

99. See, e.g., *Boston Gazette*, July 22, 1765, July 29, 1765, August 5, 1765.

100. *Boston Gazette*, August 12, 1765.

101. The psalm praises God for all he has done for the Israelites, including: "When they went from one nation to another, from one kingdom to another people; He suffered no man to do them wrong: . . . Saying Touch not mine anointed, and do my prophets no harm."

102. *Boston Gazette*, August 12, 1765.

103. Ibid.

104. Apparently what followed came as no surprise to Governor Bernard. In describing the situation prior to the Stamp Act riots, Bernard blamed the *Boston Gazette*, which "has swarmed with Libells of the most atrocious kind. These have been urged with so much Vehemence, & so industriously repeated, that I consider them as Preludes to Action." Francis Bernard to Board of Trade, August 15, 1765, in *Bernard Papers*, 2:301.

105. Ibid., 302; *Boston Gazette*, August 19, 1765.

106. *Boston Gazette*, August 19, 1765.

107. Francis Bernard to Lord Halifax, August 14, 1765, in Morgan, *Prologue to Revolution*, 108.

108. Ibid.

109. Colin Nicolson, *The "Infamas Govener": Francis Bernard and the Origins of the American Revolution* (Boston: Northeastern University Press, 2001), 118. There is a school of thought which holds that while the demonstration against the Stamp Act had been planned by others, the actions against Oliver were spontaneous. See, e.g., Dirk Horder, *Crowd Action in Revolutionary Massachusetts, 1765–1780* (New York: Academic Press, 1977), 102.

110. Andrew Eliot to Thomas Hollis, August 27, 1765, *Collections of the Massachusetts Historical Society*, 4th ser., 4 (1858): 407. See also Francis Bernard to Board of Trade, August 15, 1765, in *Bernard Papers*, 2:30

111. Morgan and Morgan, *The Stamp Act Crisis*, 160–61.

112. Hutchinson, *History of Massachusetts*, 3:87.

113. Francis Bernard to Board of Trade, August 15, 1765, in *Bernard Papers*, 2:303.

114. *Boston Gazette—Supplement*, August 19, 1765; John Avery to John Collins, August 19, 1765, in *Extracts from the Itineraries and Other Miscellaneous of Ezra Stiles, D.D., L.L.D., 1755–1794, with a Selection from His Correspondence*, ed. Franklin Bowditch Dexter (New Haven: Yale University Press, 1916), 437.

115. *Boston Gazette—Supplement*, August 19, 1765.

116. *Boston Evening-Post*, August 19, 1765; Andrew S. Walmsley, *Thomas Hutchinson and the Origins of the American Revolution* (New York: New York University Press, 1999), 67.

117. Hutchinson, *History of Massachusetts*, 3:88.

118. Ibid.

119. Ibid.

120. *Boston Gazette*, August 19, 1765.

121. *Boston Gazette,* September 2, 1765.

122. Ibid.; "Quincy Diary," *Proceedings of the Massachusetts Historical Society,* 1st ser., 4 (1860): 47; *Deacon Tudor's Diary,* ed. William Tudor (Boston, 1896), 18–19.

123. *Boston Gazette,* September 2, 1765.

124. Ibid.; "Quincy Diary," 47.

125. Thomas Hutchinson to Richard Jackson, August 20, 1765, in Richard K. Hosmer, *The Life of Thomas Hutchinson* (Boston, 1896), 91–92.

126. Ibid., 92.

127. Ibid.

128. Thomas Hutchinson to Richard Jackson (August 30, 1765), ibid., 92–93. Among the items lost were a collection of papers that Hutchinson had collected over the years to form a basis for a public archive. Bailyn, *The Ordeal of Thomas Hutchinson,* 35. See also *Boston Gazette,* September 2, 1765; Hosmer, *Life of Thomas Hutchinson,* appendix A (catalogue of Hutchinson's losses).

129. Hutchinson, *History of Massachusetts,* 3:90. See also *Deacon Tudor's Diary,* 20 ("some hundreds of people looking on . . . , I was one . . . who did nothing").

130. Thomas Hutchinson to Richard Jackson, August 30, 1765, in Hosmer, *Life of Thomas Hutchinson,* 93. The "Castle" was a fort in Boston Harbor.

131. Daniel R. Coquillette, ed., *The Law Reports, Part Two,* vol. 5 of *Portrait of a Patriot: The Major Political and Legal Papers of Josiah Quincy Junior,* ed. Daniel R. Coquillette and Neil Longley York (Boston: Colonial Society of Massachusetts, 2009), 450, 452–55.

132. "Quincy's Diary" (August 27, 1765), 48–49

133. See, e.g., *Boston Gazette,* September 2, 1765 ("every face was gloomy, and we believe every heart affected"); Thomas Hutchinson to Edward Jackson, August 30, 1765, in Hosmer, *Life of Thomas Hutchinson,* 93 ("the people in general expressed the utmost detestation of this unparalleled outrage'); *Deacon Tudor's Diary,* 20 ("there was Universal Lamentation for the Destruction done"); Jonathan Mayhew to Thomas Hutchinson, n.d., in Shipton, *Harvard Graduates,* vol. 11, *1741–1750* (Boston: Massachusetts Historical Society, 1960), 465 (I "have a deep sympathy with you and your distressed family").

134. *Diary and Autobiography of John Adams,* ed. L. H. Butterfield, vol. 1 (1961; New York: Atheneum, 1964), 264–65 (December 18, 1765).

135. Thomas Hutchinson to Richard Jackson, June 6, 1765, Thomas Hutchinson Letter Books, Massachusetts Archives, vol. 26, 276, Massachusetts Archives and Commonwealth Museum (hereafter MACM); James Murray to William Hooper, July 6, 1765, in *Letters of James Murray Loyalist,* ed. Nina Moore Tiffany and Susan I. Lesley (Boston, 1901), 115; *Boston Evening-Post,* December 30, 1765.

136. *John Adams Diary and Autobiography,* 1:264 (December 8, 1765).

137. Hutchinson, *History of Massachusetts,* 3:93.

138. Ibid. In taxing legal documents, the ministry had made a conscious decision to profit from the proverbial litigiousness of the colonials. Thomas Whately to Jared Ingersoll, n.d., "A Selection from the Correspondence and Miscellaneous Papers of Jared Ingersoll," ed. Franklin B. Dexter, *Papers of the New Haven Historical Society* 9 (1918): 28n4.

139. Morgan and Morgan, *The Stamp Act Crisis*, 175–81.

140. *Boston Post-Boy*, December 16, 1765; *Boston Gazette*, December 16, 1765.

141. *Boston News-Letter*, December 19, 1765; Henry Bass to Samuel Savage, December 19, 1765, *Proceedings of the Massachusetts Historical Society*, 3d ser., 44 (1910–11): 688–89.

142. *Boston News-Letter*, December 19, 1765; Document, December 17, 1765, Dana Papers, 1674–1769 (1765–1769 envelope), Massachusetts Historical Society, Boston (hereafter MHS). Hutchinson claimed that Oliver resigned after "finding his family in terror and great distress," with no hope of protection. Hutchinson, *History of Massachusetts*, 3:88.

143. *Boston Evening-Post*, December 23, 1765 ("The Custom-House in this Town is now opened for the Clearing out of Vessels, a Certificate being given. That no Stamp-Papers are to be had").

144. Richard Dana to Edmund Dana, November 4, 1765, Dana Papers, 1674–1769 (1765–1769 envelope), MHS.

145. See, e.g., *Boston News-Letter*, November 28, 1765; *Boston Evening-Post*, December 2, 1765.

146. *Boston News-Letter*, November 28, 1765; *Boston Evening-Post*, December 2, 1765.

147. *Boston Gazette*, December 2, 1765.

148. James Otis, *The Rights of the British Colonists Asserted and Proved* (Boston, 1764), 37; *John Adams Diary and Autobiography*, 1:295 (January 1, 1766). See also [James Otis,] *A Vindication of the British Colonies, Against the Aspersions of the Halifax Gentleman* (Boston, 1765) (Parliament had the right); [James Otis,] *Remarks on the Defense of the Halifax Libel, on the British American Colonies* (Boston, 1765) (same); *Peter Oliver's Origin and Progress of the American Revolution: A Tory View*, ed. Douglass Adair and John Schutz (Stanford: Stanford University Press, 1961), 51 (Daniel Dulany's claim that only Americans could tax themselves was "high Treason'); James Otis, *Considerations on Behalf of the Colonists* (London, 1765), 40 (Parliament had no right to tax); *Boston Gazette*, January 13, 1766 (same).

149. See, e.g., Richard B. Morris, "Legalism versus Revolutionary Doctrine in New England," *New England Quarterly* 4, no. 2 (1931): 206; Morgan and Morgan, *The Stamp Act Crisis*, 232; Edwin C. Surrency, "The Lawyer and the Revolution," *American Journal of Legal History*, 8, no. 2 (1964): 206, for a contrary view.

150. In Alfred E. Jones, *The Loyalists of Massachusetts; Their Memorials, Petitions, and Claims* (London: Saint Catherine Press, 1930), 155.

151. *John Adams Diary and Autobiography*, 1:299–300 (January 20, 1766). Lawyer John Lowell (1743–1802) remained loyal to the administration until 1774, when he reluctantly changed sides and, eventually, became chief judge of the United States District Court of Massachusetts. Charles R. McKirdy, "Massachusetts Lawyers on the Eve of the Revolution: The State of the Profession," in *Law in Colonial Massachusetts, 1630–1800*, comp. Daniel R. Coquillette (Boston: Colonial Society of Massachusetts, 1984), 347. Daniel Farnham (1719–1799), an early opponent of the radicals, later moderated his views. Ibid., 343. John Chipman (1722–1768) probably leaned against the Stamp Act. He was chosen for the committee to instruct Marblehead's representative with regard to it. Shipton, *Harvard Graduates*, 10:276.

152. Robert J. Taylor, *Western Massachusetts in the Revolution* (Boston: Brown University Press, 1954), 55.

153. Israel Williams to Thomas Hutchinson, December 28, 1767, Massachusetts Archives, vol. 25, 2, MACM.

154. *Boston Evening-Post*, March 28, 1766.

155. *John Adams Diary and Autobiography*, 1:264 (December 8, 1765).

156. Ibid.

157. Registry Department of the City of Boston, *Records Relating to the Early History of Boston*, 39 vols. *(Boston: Rockwell and Churchill, 1889)*, 20:189.

158. Ibid., 26:158–59.

159. Ibid., 159. See also Coquillette, *The Law Reports, Part Two*, 504–6.

160. City of Boston, *Records Relating to the Early History of Boston*, 16:159.

161. *John Adams Diary and Autobiography*, 1:265–66 (December 19, 1765).

162. Ibid., 266.

163. Ibid., 266–67. Apparently this requirement was not strictly enforced. Josiah Quincy Jr.'s notes on the proceedings indicate "that he transcribed the arguments himself, and did not rely on circulated copies." Coquillette, *The Law Reports, Part Two*, 505.

164. *John Adams Diary and Autobiography*, 1:267.

165. Ibid.

166. Ibid., 512.

167. Ibid., 514.

168. Ibid., 515.

169. Ibid., 517–20.

170. Ibid., 520.

171. Ibid., 521.

172. Ibid., 521–22.

173. Ibid., 521–23. Gridley's "impossibility" argument was founded on a civilian maxim from Justinian's *nemo tenetur ad impossibitia* (and Coke on Littleton's *lex cognit ad impossibilia*)—no one is obligated to perform the impossible. Ibid., 509. Like Gridley, Adams and Otis also drew on civilian maxims as well as classical English sources. Coquillette finds the "sophistication" of their research "impressive" and "historically significant" in view of the fact that not one of the three had attended a law school. Otis and Adams were products of the legal apprenticeship system. Ibid., 505–13. Gridley was self-taught.

174. Francis Bernard to Henry Seymour Conway, December 21, 1765, in *Bernard Papers*, 2:444.

175. Coquillette, *The Law Reports, Part Two*, 523n3.

176. *John Adams Diary and Autobiography*, 1:270–71 (December 23, 1765).

177. Ibid., 292 (January 13, 1766) (Suffolk County); ibid., 308 (April 10, 1766) (Plymouth County); Thomas Hutchinson to ———, January 2, 1766, Massachusetts Archives, vol. 26, 377 (Admiralty), MACM.

178. *John Adams Diary and Autobiography*, 1:305 (March 11, 1766); ibid., 308 (April 15, 1766); ibid., 310–11 (April 29, 1765); Thomas Hutchinson to Thomas Hutchinson Jr., April 15, 1766, Massachusetts Archives, vol. 26; Thomas Hutchinson to William Bollan,

December 1768, Thomas Hutchinson Letter Books, Massachusetts Archives, vol. 26, 362, MACM.

179. Thomas Hutchinson to———, January 2, 1766, Thomas Hutchinson Letter Books, Massachusetts Archives, vol. 26, 37–78, MACM.

180. *Journals of the Massachusetts House of Representatives* 42 (January 23, 1766): 214–15; Massachusetts Archives, vol. 44, 584–86 (February 4, 1766), Church of Jesus Christ of Latter-day Saints (hereafter LDS) Court Records Project, reel no. 2322758.

181. Massachusetts Archives, vol. 44, 578 (February 14, 1766), LDS Court Records Project, reel no. 2322758.

182. *John Adams Diary and Autobiography*, 1:310–11 (April 29, 1766). Adams claimed that, during the proceedings, he "kept an obstinate silence." Ibid.

183. Thomas Hutchinson to———, April 27, 1766, Massachusetts Archives, vol. 26, 441–42, MACM.

184. *John Adams Diary and Autobiography*, 1:312n1 The act had been repealed on March 19, 1766. Official notice of the repeal reached Governor Bernard on May 31, 1766. *Bernard Papers*, 3:13.

Chapter Eleven: Death and Legacy

1. *Boston Gazette*, March 31, 1766; *Boston Evening-Post*, April 28, 1766.
2. *Boston Evening-Post*, June 2, 1766.
3. Colin Nicolson, *The "Infamas Govener": Francis Bernard and the Origins of the American Revolution* (Boston: Northeastern University Press, 2001), 144. Nicolson estimates that radical strength in the House went from about one-third to two-thirds of its membership. Ibid.
4. *The History of the Colony and Province of Massachusetts Bay by Thomas Hutchinson*, ed. Lawrence Shaw Mayo, vol. 3 (Cambridge: Harvard University Press, 1936), 107. According to Thomas Hutchinson, some "of the governor's friends thought Mr. Otis would be of less importance in the chair than out of it, and advised in the negative. But the governor did not think with them." Ibid.
5. *Diary and Autobiography of John Adams*, ed. L. H. Butterfield, vol. 1 (1961; New York: Atheneum, 1964), 313 (May 28, 1766).
6. Hutchinson, *History of Massachusetts*, 3:107; *The Diaries of Benjamin Lynde and Benjamin Lynde, Jr.* (Boston: 1880), 191; Francis G. Walett, "The Massachusetts Council, 1766–1774: The Transformation of a Conservative Institution, *William and Mary Quarterly*, 3rd ser., 6, no. 4 (1949): 607.
7. *Journals of the House of Representatives of Massachusetts* 43, pt. 1 (May 28, 1765): 5–10; Nicolson, *The "Infamas Govener*," 144–45.
8. *John Adams Diary and Autobiography*, 1:313 (May 29, 1766).
9. Speech of Governor Bernard to the Council and House of Representatives, May 29, 1766, in *Speeches of the Governors of Massachusetts from 1765 to 1775; and the Answers of the House of Representatives to the Same*, ed. Alden Bradford (Boston, 1818), 75.
10. Ibid.
11. Answer of the House of Representatives, June 3, 1766, ibid., 79.

12. Ibid.

13. Speech of the Governor to the Council and House of Representatives, June 3, 1766, ibid., 82.

14. Answer of the House of Representatives, June 24, 1766, ibid., 94.

15. Hutchinson, *History of Massachusetts*, 3:113–14; Nicolson, *The "Infamas Govener,"* 146.

16. Gertrude E. Meridith, *The Descendants of Hugh Amory, 1605–1805* (London: Cheswick Press, 1901), 140. See also Francis Bernard to the Earl of Shelburne, November 14, 1766, in *The Papers of Francis Bernard, Governor of Colonial Massachusetts, 1760–1709*, ed. Colin Nicolson, vol. 3 (Boston: Colonial Society of Massachusetts, 2013), 242.

17. An Act For Granting General Compensation To The Sufferers And For Free And General Pardon, Indemnity And Oblivion To The Offenders In The Late Times (1766), in *The Acts and Resolves, Public and Private, of the Province of Massachusetts Bay*, vol. 4 (Boston, 1890), 903–4.

18. Nicolson, *The "Infamas Govener,"* 147. On May 13, 1767, the Privy Council disallowed the act, but by then the victims had received the money. Hutchinson, *History of Massachusetts*, 3:115; Nicolson, *The "Infamas Govener,"* 150; Francis Bernard to the Earl of Shelburne, October 15, 1767, in *Bernard Papers*, 3:415.

19. *Letters and Diary of John Rowe*, ed. Anne Rowe Cunningham (Boston: W. B. Clarke Company, 1903), 115. See also *Boston Evening-Post*, December 1, 1766.

20. "An act to amend and render more effectual in his Majesty's dominions in America, an act passed in the present session of parliament intitled, An act for punishing mutiny and desertion, and for the better payment of the army and their quarters," 5 Geo. 3, c. 33.

21. Speech of Governor Bernard to the House of Representatives, February 17, 1767, in *Speeches of the Governors of Massachusetts*, 107–8.

22. Message from the House of Representatives to the Governor, February 4, 1767, ibid.,107.

23. Hutchinson, *History of Massachusetts*, 3:123.

24. Answer of the House of Representatives, January 31, 1767, in *Speeches of the Governors of Massachusetts*, 109.

25. A Message from his Excellency the Governor by his Secretary, February 7, 1767, *Journals of the Massachusetts House of Representatives* 43 (February 7, 1767): 260.

26. Ibid., 294–95 (February 17, 1767).

27. Ibid., 296.

28. A Message from the Honorable Board, ibid., 368 (March 7, 1765).

29. Ellen E. Brennen, *Plural Office-Holding in Massachusetts, 1760–1780* (Chapel Hill: University of North Carolina Press, 1945), 89.

30. John Cushing to Thomas Hutchinson, December 15, 1766, in John J. Waters Jr., *The Otis Family in Provincial and Revolutionary Massachusetts* (1968; New York: W. W. Norton & Company, 1975), 165–66.

31. Clifford K. Shipton, *Sibley's Harvard Graduates: Biographical Sketches of Those Who Attended Harvard College* (hereafter Shipton, *Harvard Graduates*), vol. 9, *1731–1735* (Boston: Massachusetts Historical Society, 1956), 86–87.

32. *Diary of John Rowe*, 127 (March 25, 1767). See also *Boston Post-Boy*, March 30, 1767; *Boston Gazette*, March 30, 1767.

33. Shipton, *Harvard Graduates*, vol. 7, *1722–1725* (Boston: Massachusetts Historical Society, 1945), 526; *Mein and Fleeming's Massachusetts Register with an Almanac for the Year MDCCLXVII* (Boston, 1767), 20, 42.

34. *Boston Post-Boy*, June 1, 1767.

35. Francis Bernard to the Earl of Shelburne, June 6, 1767, in *Bernard Papers*, 3:367.

36. *Diary of John Rowe*, 127 (March 25, 1767); *Boston Gazette*, March 30, 1767. Because Gridley was unhappy about Sewall's appointment as "Special Attorney General," the title was changed to "Solicitor General," the "first Officer of the Kind ever known in the Province." Daniel R. Coquillette, ed., *The Law Reports, Part Two*, vol. 5 of *Portrait of a Patriot: The Major Political and Legal Papers of Josiah Quincy Junior*, ed. Daniel R. Coquillette and Neil Longley York (Boston: Colonial Society of Massachusetts, 2009), 578n.

37. John Pierce Memoirs, 218 (September 1820), Massachusetts Historical Society, Boston (hereafter MHS).

38. *John Adams Diary and Autobiography*, 1:316 (July 28, 1766).

39. *Muddy River and Brookline Records, 1634–1838* (1875), 216.

40. *Diary of John Rowe*, 136 (June 24, 1767).

41. Ibid., 141 (September 11, 1767); ibid., 141–42 (September 12, 1767); John Pierce Memoirs, 218 (September 1829), MHS. According to church records, Gridley died of a "rising of the lights," that is, lung problems. "First Parish Church Records of Baptisms, Marriages and Deaths, for 100 Years," *Publications of the Brookline Historical Publications Society* (1897): 119.

42. H. G. F. Candage, "Jeremy Gridley," *Publications of the Brookline Historical Society* (1903): 31.

43. *Diary of John Rowe*, 141 (September 12, 1767).

44. *Boston Post-Boy*, September 14, 1767.

45. Ibid.

46. Alden Bradford, *Biographical Notices of Distinguished Men in New England: Statesmen, Patriots, Physicians, Lawyers, Clergymen and Mechanics* (Boston, 1852), 213.

47. Ezra Stiles to Charles Chauncy (1767), in Shipton, *Harvard Graduates*, 7:528. See also text at chapter 2, notes 3–4, 106.

48. Charles Chauncy to Ezra Stiles, September 26, 1767, in *Extracts from the Itineraries and Other Miscellaneous of Ezra Stiles, D.D., L.L.D., 1755–1794, with a Selection from His Correspondence*, ed. Franklin Bowditch Dexter (New Haven: Yale University Press, 1916), 444.

49. Ibid.

50. *Diary and Autobiography of John Adams*, ed. L. H. Butterfield, vol. 2 (1961; New York: Atheneum, 1964), 38 (July 22, 1771).

51. *Boston Evening-Post*, March 27, 1769.

52. See, e.g., *Boston Evening-Post*, January 25, 1768, February 22, 1768, April 25, 1768.

53. *Diary and Autobiography of John Adams*, ed. L. H. Butterfield, vol. 3 (1961; New York: Atheneum, 1964), 285.

54. Ibid., 1:55 (October 25, 1758).

55. John Eliot, *A Biographical Dictionary* (Boston, 1809), 257. See also Samuel Knapp, *Biographical Sketches of Eminent Lawyers, Statesmen and Men of Letters* (Boston, 1821), 207 (Gridley "was too chivalrous for his own interest and that of his friends"); Emory

Washburn, *Sketches of the Judicial History of Massachusetts* (Boston, 1840), 212 (Gridley "was indifferent to the acquisition of wealth").

56. See text at chapter 7, note 4.

57. See text at chapter 2, note 10.

58. Minute Books of the Superior Court of Massachusetts, 1757–1759, microfilm copies, MHS.

59. *Diary of John Rowe*, 61 (September 11, 1764), 100 (June 24, 1766).

60. Ezra Stiles to Charles Chauncy, 1767, in Shipton, *Harvard Graduates*, 7:528.

61. *John Adams Diary and Autobiography*, 1:83 (April 1759).

62. Charles Chauncy to Ezra Stiles, September 26, 1767, in *Itineraries of Ezra Stiles*, 444.

63. Coquillette, *The Law Reports, Part Two*, 875.

64. John Adams to William Tudor, June 5, 1817, in *The Works of John Adams*, ed. Charles Francis Adams, vol. 10 (Boston, 1856), 264.

65. *John Adams Diary and Autobiography*, 1:54–56 (October 25, 1758).

66. Ibid., 236 (February 5, 1763).

67. *The Diary and Letters of His Excellency Thomas Hutchinson*, ed. Peter Orlando Hutchinson, vol. 1 (London, 1886), 64; *Peter Oliver's Origin and Progress of the American Revolution: A Tory View*, ed. Douglass Adair and John Schutz (Stanford: Stanford University Press, 1961), 36.

68. *John Adams Diary and Autobiography*, 1:83 (April 8, 1759).

69. Knapp, *Biographical Sketches of Eminent Lawyers*, 199; Washburn, *Sketches of the Judicial History of Massachusetts*, 211.

70. Eliot, *Biographical Dictionary*, 237.

71. Knapp, *Biographical Sketches of Eminent Lawyers*, 200.

72. Washburn, *Sketches of the Judicial History of Massachusetts*, 211.

73. Candage, "Jeremy Gridley," 15.

74. See, e.g., Knapp, *Biographical Sketches of Eminent Lawyers*, 200; Candage, "Jeremy Gridley," 15.

75. John K. Reeves, "Jeremy Gridley, Editor," *New England Quarterly* 17, no. 2 (1944): 273.

76. Ibid., 281.

77. John Adams to Catherine McCauley (August 9, 1770), in *The Works of John Adams*, ed. Charles Francis Adams, vol. 9 (Boston, 1854), 332; *John Adams Diary and Autobiography*, 1:255n1.

78. *The True Sentiments of America* (London, 1768), iii.

79. *John Adams Diary and Autobiography*, 1:258n1.

80. Charles Chauncey to Ezra Stiles, December 12, 1768, in *Itineraries of Ezra Stiles*, 446–47.

81. Edward Everett, *Orations and Speeches on Various Occasions*, vol. 1 (Boston, 1870), 140n.

82. Shipton, *Harvard Graduates*, 7:254.

83. Ever critical of Gridley, Charles Chauncy, who considered the piece "one of the best yt. has been wrote," claimed that anyone who knew Gridley "must at once know

he was not the writer of that piece." Charles Chauncy to Ezra Stiles, December 16, 1768, in *Itineraries of Ezra Stiles,* 446.

84. *Boston Post-Boy,* September 14, 1767.

85. *John Adams Diary and Autobiography,* 1:83 (April 8, 1759).

86. Charles Chauncy to Ezra Stiles, September 26, 1767, in *Itineraries of Ezra Stiles,* 443–44.

87. Charles Warren, *A History of the American Bar* (1911; New York: Howard Fertig, 1966), 81.

88. The price of this first-class education seems to have been relatively modest. For example, Gridley contracted with Andrew Oliver "to educate his Son Daniel Oliver liberally in Law during three Years . . . for ye Sum of Ten pounds per annum." Agreement to educate Daniel Oliver in the Law (April 2, 1763), Hutchinson-Oliver Papers, 1658–1774, MHS. Of course, Gridley also received young Oliver's services as a law clerk as part of the arrangement.

89. *John Adams Diary and Autobiography,* 3:270–71.

90. Ibid., 1:56 (October 26, 1758).

91. Ibid., 1:157–58. Charles Viner, *A General Abridgement of the Law and Equity,* 23 vols. (1741–1753); John Lilly, *The Practical Register; or a General Abridgment of the Law* (1719); John Mallory, *Modern Entries in English* (1734–35); Sir Edward Coke, *A Book of Entries* (1674); William Rastal, *Collection of Entries* (1566).

92. Invited by Gridley for weekends at his "Country Seat," Adams "went but once, though [Gridley] urged so much and so often that I was afraid he would take offence at my Negligence." *John Adams Diary and Autobiography,* 3:286.

93. Ibid., 1:251 (January 24, 1765). Samuel Fitch, a graduate of Yale (1742), was admitted as a barrister by the Massachusetts Superior Court in 1762. Charles R. McKirdy, "Massachusetts Lawyers on the Eve of the Revolution: The State of the Profession," in *Law in Colonial Massachusetts, 1630–1800,* comp. Daniel R. Coquillette (Boston: Colonial Society of Massachusetts, 1984), 343–44.

94. *John Adams Diary and Autobiography,* 1:251 (January 24, 1765). The meetings were not stuffy affairs. According to Adams, Gridley's "conversation was too amusing and instructive to leave Us very earnest Wishes for Books." Ibid., 3:285–86.

95. Ibid., 255 (February 21, 1765).

96. Ibid., 1:255–58. Gridley's legacy of outstanding law students reached years beyond John Adams's generation. Gridley's student Oxenbridge Thacher (1719–1765) had two students—Josiah Quincy Jr. (1744–1775) and John Lowell (1743–1802). Quincy was a radical leader in the years leading up to the American Revolution. John Lowell became a United States district judge and a Circuit Court judge. Lowell's law students included Christopher Gore (1758–1827), who became governor of Massachusetts and a United States senator, and Harrison Gray Otis (1765–1848), who also served in the U.S. Senate. One of Gore's law students was Daniel Webster (1782–1852), a U.S. senator and secretary of state. Among those who studied in Webster's office were Charles Francis Adams (1807–1886) and Robert Charles Winthrop (1809–1894). Adams was a U.S. senator and ambassador to England. Winthrop served as speaker of the U.S. House of Representatives and as a U.S. senator. See Daniel R. Coquillette, ed., *The Law Commonplace Book,* vol. 2 of *Portrait of a Patriot,* ed. Daniel R.

Coquillette and Neil Longley York (Boston: Colonial Society of Massachusetts, 2007), 76–77, for a very helpful chart showing five generations of Gridley's law students and their legal progeny.

97. See Charles R. McKirdy, "A Bar Divided: The Lawyers of Massachusetts and the American Revolution," *American Journal of Legal History* 16, no. 3 (1975): 205.

98. Shipton, *Harvard Graduates,* 9:581.

99. Shipton, *Harvard Graduates,* vol. 8, *1726–1730* (Boston: Massachusetts Historical Society, 1951), 29–30.

100. Inventory of Library, Estate of Jeremy Gridley, Probate Records, Suffolk County, Massachusetts, vol. 66, MACM (hereafter Gridley Library).

101. *John Adams Diary and Autobiography,* 1:251 (January 24, 1765).

102. Bernard Bailyn, *The Ideological Origins of the American Revolution* (Cambridge: Harvard University Press, 1967), 25–26.

103. Ibid., 25.

104. Ibid., 27.

105. Ibid.; *John Adams Diary and Autobiography,* 3:271–72.

106. Gridley Library.

107. Caroline Robbins, "Algernon Sidney's *Discourses Concerning Government*: Textbook of Revolution," *William and Mary Quarterly,* 3rd ser., 4, no. 3 (1947): 267–96; Bailyn, *Ideological Origins,* 34–35; Gridley Library.

108. John Pierce Memoirs (September 13, 1820), 217–18, MHS.

109. John Adams to Josiah Quincy, February 9, 1811, in *Works of John Adams,* 9:630.

110. Ezra Stiles to Charles Chauncy, 1767, in *Itineraries of Ezra Stiles,* 443n1.

111. Lorenzo Sabine, *The American Loyalists: Or, Biographical Sketches of Adherents to the British Crown in the War of the Revolution* (Boston, 1847), 338–39.

112. See text at chapter 7, note 112.

113. Jeremy Gridley to Gilbert McAdam, February 26, 1757, Loudoun Collection, LO 2929, Huntington Library, San Marino, CA (hereafter Huntington Library).

114. John Adams to William Tudor, March 24, 1817, in *Works of John Adams,* 10:247.

115. M. H. Smith, *The Writs of Assistance Case* (Berkeley: University of California Press, 1978), 283.

116. See text at note 35.

117. See text at chapter 10, note 173.

118. Speaking of Gridley's funeral procession, John Rowe confided to his diary, "I do not much approve of such parade & show but . . . it was his Relatives desire." *Diary of John Rowe,* 142 (September 12, 1767).

119. Shipton, *Harvard Graduates,* 7:10–23.

120. Ibid., 9:199–223.

121. Franklin Bowditch Dexter, *Biographical Sketches of the Graduates of Yale College with Annals of the College History,* vol. 1 (New York, 1885), 658–60.

122. Shipton, *Harvard Graduates,* vol. 16, *1764–1767* (Boston: Massachusetts Historical Society, 1972), 20–23.

123. "Col. Richard Gridley," "Portraits and Profiles of Chief Engineers," mlloyd. org/gen/Macomb/text/coe/htm (accessed April 25, 2012); Daniel Thomas Vose Huntoon, *History of the Town of Canton* (Cambridge, 1893), 368–79.

124. *Weekly Rehearsal*, January 3, 1732.

125. *Boston News-Letter*, March 17, 1743.

126. Jeremy Gridley to Gilbert McAdam, February 26, 1757, Loudoun Collection, LO 2929, Huntington Library.

127. *Legal Papers of John Adams*, ed. L. Kinvin Wroth and Hiller B. Zobel, vol. 2 (Cambridge: Harvard University Press, 1965), 114.

128. See text at chapter 10, note 173.

129. Francis Bernard to Lord Halifax, August 14, 1765, in *Prologue to Revolution: Sources and Documents on the Stamp Act Crisis, 1764–1766*, ed. Edmund S. Morgan (New York: W. W. Norton & Company, 1959), 107–8.

130. Ibid., 108.

131. Thomas Hutchinson to Richard Jackson, August 30, 1765, in James K. Hosmer, *The Life of Thomas Hutchinson* (Boston, 1896), 92.

132. James Gordon to William Martin, September 10, 1765, *Proceedings of the Massachusetts Historical Society*, 2nd ser. (1899–1900): 13.

133. The North End and South End mobs, two well-organized collections of bullyboys, annually fought each other on Guy Fawkes Day and bore a deep-seated animosity toward authority in general. Hiller B. Zobel, *The Boston Massacre* (New York: W. W. Norton, 1970), 26–27. In the 1740s, the town experienced three significant riots, the last in 1747, over an impressment sweep in Boston. Ibid., 26.

134. *History of St. John's Lodge of Boston* (Boston, 1917), 221.

135. Ibid., 213.

136. Theophilus Parsons, *Memoir of Theophilus Parsons, Chief Justice of the Supreme Judicial Court of Massachusetts* (Boston, 1859), 28–29.

137. Ibid., 28.

138. Shipton, *Harvard Graduates*, 8:519.

139. *Adams Diary and Autobiography*, 1:54.

INDEX

Note: "JG" refers to Jeremiah Gridley.

Abercrombie, James, 101
Act for preventing Frauds and regulating abuses in the Plantation Trade, 1696 (Eng.), 144
Act for the further enforcement of His Majesty's Revenue of Customs, 1763 (Eng.), 160, 165
Act of Frauds, 1662 (Eng.), 135–36, 143–44, 149–50
Act to Prevent Frauds and Concealment of his Majesty's Customs, 1660 (Eng.), 134–35, 144, 145–46, 149–50
Adams, John: on barristers, 106; on closed courts, 171, 174, 191; "Dissertation on Canon and Feudal Law," 189, 191; on JG's erudition, 189; on JG's health, 185; JG's law practice, inheritance of, 186; on JG's oratorical ability, 188; on JG's personality, 187; JG's relations with, 1, 21–24, 190–91, 199; on Thomas Hutchinson, 127; on judges' attire, 106; on judges' qualifications, 127; on justices of the peace, 41; on Benjamin Kent, 122; on Land Bank problems, 38; on legal education, 20; *Legal Papers of John Adams* (Wroth and Zobel), 108, 140, 150, 189; on Lord Loudon, 90; on networking, 33; on Col. James Otis, 70; on James Otis, 143, 155; on *Slew v. Whipple*, 121–22; on Stamp Act supporters, 173–74; Superior Court bar, admission to, 147; on teaching, 11; on unsworn legal practitioners, 107–8; on William Vassall, 65; on writs of assistance case, 133, 139–40
Adams, John Quincy, 21
Adams, Samuel, 11, 175, 178
Addison, Joseph, 11. See also *Freeholder, The*; *Spectator, The*
admiralty law, 116–17. See also *Dunn v. Scollay*
Allen, Samuel, 58–59. See also Masonian Proprietors
Allen, Thomas, 58–59. See also Masonian Proprietors
Almon, John, *The True Sentiments of America*, 189
American Magazine (Philadelphia), 45
American Magazine and Historical Chronicle, 43–52, 84; competition of, 44–46; demise of, 52; essays in, 48–50; founders of, 43–44; marketing of, 44; news content of, 47–48; plagiarism and imitation, 47, 51–52; poetry in, 50; tone of, 49
American Revenue Act, 1764 (Eng.). See Sugar Act
Andros, Edmund, 5–6
Apthorp, Charles, 105
Ashley, Jonathan, 46
attorney general: dispute over right to appoint, 34–36; JG appointed, 184; JG nominated, 39–41
Auchmuty, Robert (father): legal opinion on land, 58, 61; legal practice, 20, 27, 28; Vice Admiralty Court judge, 40

Auchmuty, Robert (son): cases as attorney (see *Dudley v. Dudley; Dunn v. Scollay; Elwell v. Pierson;* writs of assistance case); Vice Admiralty Court, advocate general of, 149

Baker, William, 86
Baker v. Mattocks, 115
Banister v. Henderson, 114
Barons, Benjamin, 138–39; Francis Bernard on, 153; on JG's politics, 153. *See also* smuggling
Beal, Othiel, 29
Belcher, Jonathan, 183; attorney general dispute, 36; on William Brattle, 129; Land Bank crisis, 37–39; politics, 56, 82, 183, 188–89
Bernard, Francis: background of, 127–28; Benjamin Barons, 153; charter for new college, 157–58; Chief Justice dispute, 128, 130–32; governor, appointment as, 127–28; JG, appointment of, 154, 184; on James Otis, 131; Otis family, relations with, 155–58; Charles Paxton, support of, 138; politics, 155–58, 180–85; smuggling, efforts against, 132–33; Stamp Act, 168, 172, 175, 177–78
Bill of Rights, 1689 (Eng.), 89
Biographical Dictionary, A (Eliot), 188–89
Blackstone, William, 22, 150
Blanchard, Joshua: *American Magazine and Historical Chronicle,* 43–44, 52; background of, 43–44; *Boston Weekly-Magazine,* 45; Great Awakening, 46
Bollan, William: colonial agent, replaced as, 156; legal practice of, 20, 27–28; William Shirley, ally of, 40; Sugar Act, 162; writs of assistance case, 147
Boston, fires in, 165
Boston Evening-Post, 18, 158–59, 172, 189
Boston Gazette, 46, 130, 166–67, 172–73
Boston News-Letter, 12, 44, 45, 47, 172
Boston Post-Boy, 185, 188, 189
Boston Weekly-Magazine, 45–46, 50
Bouquet, Henry, 92
Bourne, Shearjeshub, 195
Brackett, Anthony, 29
Bracton, Henry de, *De Legibus & Consuetudinibus Angliae,* 23
Braddock, Edward, 87
Bradford, Andrew, *American Magazine* (Philadelphia), 45

Brattle, William: background and reputation of, 129; Francis Bernard, opponent of, 156; Chief Justice dispute, 129; JG, client of, 29; loyalist, 195; opinions about, 129
British regulars: desertion of, 96–98; recruitment of, 96. *See also* quartering of troops
Britton, 23
Byles, Mather, 14–15

Campbell, John. *See* Loudoun, Lord
Cato's Letters (Gordon and Trenchard), 192
Censor, The (London), 12
Charter of Massachusetts, 5, 34, 36
Chauncey, Charles: on JG's erudition, 189–90; on JG's personality, 187; on JG's religion, 186
Checkley, Anthony, 34
Cheever, Ezekiel, *A Short Introduction to the Latin Tongue,* 5
Chief Justice dispute, 128–33; Francis Bernard, 128, 132–33; William Brattle, claim to seat, 129; Thomas Hutchinson, claim to seat, 30–31, 126–27, 131; Col. James Otis, claim to seat, 129–31; James Otis, attacks on Thomas Hutchinson's claim, 127, 130–31
Chipman, John, 173–74
Christian History, The, 45
Chubb, Thomas, 66
Cicero, 192
Clark and Lake Company, 62–63
Cockle, James, 139–40
Coke, Edward: *Commentaries on Littleton,* 21–22; poem on, 51; reputation of, 21
Colman, Benjamin, 7
Commentaries on Littleton (Coke). *See* Coke, Edward
Compendiosa Institutionum Justiani Tractato: In Usum Collegiorum (van Muyden), 23
Coquillette, Daniel, 108, 112, 113, 117. *See* also *Quincy's Reports*
Corpus Juris Canonici, 23
Corpus Juris Civilis, 23
Cottman, George, 96
council, 81; membership dispute, 183–84
courts: county courts of general sessions, 26, 41–42; county inferior courts of common pleas, 26; Court of Vice Admiralty, 27, 116–19, 134, 136–38; justices

of the peace, 26, 41–42; probate courts, 210–11n65; Superior Court, 25–27
Craftsman, The (London), 12
Croswell, Andrew, 46
Cujacius, Jacques, *Paratitla*, 23–24
Cushing, John: background and reputation of, 128; cases as judge (see *Dudley v. Dudley; Dunn v. Scollay; Fletcher v. Vassall; Slew v. Whipple*)
Cushing, Thomas, 66, 69, 163, 180
Cushing, William, student of JG, 190, 192
Cushing family, 113
customs enforcement, 133–38

Dana, Caleb, 97–98
Dana, Francis, influence on Edmund Trowbridge, 199
Dana, Richard, 199; on closed courts, 172; desertion case, 98, 103; family, 198–99; reputation of, 128–29
Danforth, Samuel: *Dudley v. Dudley*, judge of, 111; *New-England Weekly Journal*, 14
Dantzic (Newbury), New Hampshire, 60
Davenport, Addison, 25
Davies, Samuel, on Lord Loudoun, 90
Declaration of Rights, 1689 (Eng.), 88
defamation, 75–76. See also *Fletcher v. Vassall*
De Hominis et Civis (Pufendorf), 24
De Jure Maritimo et Navali (Molloy), 119
De Juris Naturali, Gentium et Civill (Justinian I), 124
De Legibus & Consuetudinibus Angliae (Bracton), 23
Discourses Concerning Government (Sidney), 193
Domat, Jean, *Lois civiles dans leur ordre naturel*, 24
Dominion of New England, 4
Douglass, William, 204–5n65
Dudley, Abigail (née Gridley): first marriage to Joseph Dudley, 108; second marriage to John Gray, 115. See also *Dudley v. Dudley*
Dudley, Governor Joseph: attorney general appointment, 34; background of, 109; will of, 109–11, 112, 113. See also *Dudley v. Dudley*
Dudley, Governor Thomas, 109. See also *Dudley v. Dudley*
Dudley, Joseph (JG's son-in-law): claim to inheritance, 109, 111; death of, 115, 199; JG, law student of, 108–9; marriage, 108; Sodalitas member, 109. See also *Dudley v. Dudley*
Dudley, Paul 34–35, 48, 49
Dudley, Thomas, 109, 110–11, 112–13. See also *Dudley v. Dudley*
Dudley, William, 109–13. See also *Dudley v. Dudley*
Dudley family, 113. See also *Dudley v. Dudley*
Dudley v. Dudley, 108–15; arguments, 111–12; background facts of, 109; case attorney, Robert Auchmuty as, 111; case attorney, JG as, 111–12, 114; case attorney, Benjamin Kent as, 111; case attorney, James Otis as, 111; case attorney, Edmund Trowbridge as, 111–12, 113–14; case judge, John Cushing as, 111, 114; case judge, Samuel Danforth as, 111, 113; case judge, Benjamin Lynde as, 111, 114; case judge, Thomas Hutchinson as, 111, 113; case judge, Peter Oliver as, 111, 114; case judge, Chambers Russell as, 111; case judge, Stephen Sewall as, 111; decision, 113–14; issues, 109–10; law involved, 109–10; will terms, 110
Dunn, John, 116, 121. See also *Dunn v. Scollay*
Dunn v. Scollay, 115–21; admiralty jurisdiction, 118–19; admiralty proceedings, 116; appeal, 119–21; arguments, 118–20; background of, 115–16; case attorney, Robert Auchmuty, 116, 119; case attorney, JG as, 116, 118–20; case attorney, James Otis as, 117, 120; case attorney, Oxenbridge Thacher as, 117, 119, 120; case judge, John Cushing as, 118, 119, 120; case judge, Thomas Hutchinson as, 118, 119–21; case judge, Benjamin Lynde, 118, 119; case judge, Peter Oliver, 118, 119, 120; common pleas proceedings, 121; Superior Court proceedings, 117–20

economic panic, 2, 121, 165–66
Edmund Quincy and Sons, 79
Eliot, Andrew, 168
Eliot, John, *A Biographical Dictionary*, 188–89
Eliot, Samuel, 43, 46–47, 52. See also *American Magazine and Historical Chronicle*
Ellery, William, 199
Elwell v. Pierson, 114–15
Englishman, The (London), 11

Erving, John, 138
Examiner, The (London), 12

Fanueil v. Pompey, 123
Farnham, Daniel, 173–74
Farquhar, George, 96
Fazakerley, Nicholas, 61
Fleta, 23
Fletcher, Thomas, 66, 73–74, 115. See also *Dunn v. Scollay; Fletcher v. Vassall*
Fletcher, William: business, 66; Louisbough, Quebec, 66–67; William Vassall, dealings with, 67. See also *Fletcher v. Vassall*
Fletcher v. Vassall, 65–67; appeal to Privy Council, 76–77; arguments, 72–73, 75; background of, 67–69; case attorney, JG as, 71, 73–74, 79; case attorney, Col. James Otis as, 69–71; case attorney, James Otis as, 71–72, 73–74, 78–79; case attorney, Edmund Trowbridge as, 69; case judge, John Cushing as, 72, 74; case judge, Benjamin Lynde as, 72, 74; case judge, Chambers Russell as, 72, 74; case judge, Richard Saltonstall as, 72, 74; case judge, Stephen Sewall as, 72, 74; evidence, 73–75; initial proceedings, 69, 72–73; judgment, 76; law of defamation, 75; post-appeal proceedings, 77–79
Flynt, Henry, 7
Fortesque, John, *In Praise of the Laws of England*, 23
Fowle, Daniel: *American Magazine and Historical Chronicle*, 43, 45, 46; *The Monster of Monsters*, 84–85. See also *Fowle v. Hubbard*
Fowle, John, Jr., 56, 60
Fowle v. Hubbard, 84–86. See also Fowle, Daniel
Franklin, Benjamin: *General Magazine* (Philadelphia), 45; on Harvard College, 8; on Benjamin Kent, 122; William Vassall, correspondence with, 65
Franklin, James: arrested, 85, 205n75; *New-England Courant*, 13–14, 15, 17. See also *New-England Courant*
Freeholder, The (London), 11
Freeman, Isaac, 115–16
Freethinker, The (London), 12
French and Indian War, 54, 59–60, 83–84, 87–88, 98; John Abercrombie, commander in chief, 101; Braddock defeat, 87; British policy, 136; British regulars, desertion of, 96–97; British regulars, friction with colonials, 95–96; British regulars, recruitment of, 96; Canada, invasion of, 98; Crown Point fort, 83, 87–88; Fort William Henry, fall of, 98; French incursions, 83–84; JG, iron works of, 54; Lord Loudoun, 88, 101; Louisbourg, Quebec, 98; Peterborough, New Hampshire, effect on, 59–60; William Pitt, 101–2. See also British regulars; Loudoun, Lord; quartering of soldiers
French Wars, 2. See also French and Indian War; King George's War

Gardner, Silvester, 63
Gee, Joshua, 29
General Court (Massachusetts legislature). See council; House of Representatives
General Magazine (Philadelphia), 45
Gentleman's Magazine, The (London), 47
Glanville, Ranulf de, *Tractatus de Legibus*, 23
Gordon, Thomas, *Cato's Letters*, 192
governor of Massachusetts, responsibilities of, 81
Gray, Harrison, 74–75
Gray, Thomas, 74
Great Awakening, 2, 46
Green, Joseph, 12
Greenleaf, Stephen, 73
Gridley, Abigail (née Lewis), 11, 80
Gridley, Abigail. See Dudley, Abigail (née Gridley)
Gridley, Benjamin, 173
Gridley, Isaac, 29, 40, 56
Gridley, Jeremiah (JG)
—background and personal life: birth, 4; children, 11, 53; death and funeral, 185–86; house in Boston, 53; house in Brookline, 80; lineage of, 4; marriage of, 11; personality of, 187; religion of, 19, 32, 185–86
—education: Boston Latin, student at, 5; erudition, 42, 189; Harvard College, student at, 5–9; library of, 2, 11–12, 23–24, 186, 192–93
—law practice: John Adams, left practice to, 186; admission to bar, 19; income from, 186–87; land speculators, representation of, 60–63; litigation, amounts at issue,

76; litigation, volume of, 28, 106, 186–87; nature of, 29, 76, 105–6. See also *Baker v. Mattocks*; *Banister v. Henderson*; *Dudley v. Dudley*; *Dunn v. Scollay*; *Elwell v. Pierson*; *Fletcher v. Vassall*; *Fowle v. Hubbard*; *Slew v. Whipple*; *Vassall v. Rogers*; writs of assistance case
—mentorship: John Adams as law student of, 1, 21–24, 190–91, 199; Boston Latin, teacher at, 9–11; William Cushing as law student of, 190, 192; Joseph Dudley as law student of, 108; law students of, 190; legal studies of, 19–25; James Otis as law student of, 71, 190; Benjamin Prat as law student of, 190; Samuel Swift as law student of, 192; Oxenbridge Thacher as law student of, 190, 209n43
—opinions: British regulars, defense of, 97; on the House of Representatives' privileges, 84–86; on Thomas Hutchinson, 126; on marine insurance, 161; on marriage, 20; on Masonian Proprietors' rights, 60–61; on Massachusetts legal studies, 21; on a militia colonelcy, 103; on a new college, 157–58; on quartering troops, 95; rebellion, position on, 193–99; on Stephen Sewall, 95; on various law books, 21–24; on wealth, 186
—public work: attorney general, appointed, 184; attorney general, elected, 39–50; House of Representatives, attorney for, 84–86; House of Representatives, elections to, 80–81, 184–85; House of Representatives, Lord Loudoun's agent in, 94–95, 100–102, 193–94; House of Representatives committees, member of, 84–88; justice of the peace, appointed, 41–42; militia colonelcy, seeks and receives appointment to, 103–4, 184; municipal offices held, 80; search for favor and place, 103–4, 184; Superior Court Chief Justice, passed over, 128. See also *Fowle v. Hubbard*
—social reputation and engagement: Fellowship Club member, 32; Marine Society member, 161, 187; Masons member, 32, 94, 197–98; as a networker, 32; oratory proficiency, 143, 188; reputation of, 1, 37, 187–88; sociability of, 187; Society for Encouraging Trade and Commerce member, 32, 161–62; Sodalitas founding, 108–9, 191–92; writer, reputation as a, 188–89. See also Adams, John; Chauncey, Charles
—ventures outside law practice: business opportunities, 54–55; as an editor (see *American Magazine and Historical Chronicle*; *Weekly Rehearsal*); iron mill, investment in, 53–54; land speculation, 55–60, 63–64; wealth of, 63–64, 186–87. See also Peterborough, New Hampshire
Gridley, John, 5
Gridley, Joseph, 4
Gridley, Richard (brother of JG), 29, 40, 56, 195–96
Gridley, Richard (father of JG), 4–5
Griggs, Jacob, 29
Grotius, Hugo: *Jure Belli ac Pacis Libres Tres*, 24; *Mare Liberum*, 24

Hale, Matthew, *The History and Analysis of the Common Law of England*, 22–23
Hall, Andrew, 75, 78
Hallowell, Benjamin, 106, 169, 198
Hancock, Belcher, 73
Harvard College, 5–9; closed, 165; curriculum, 10, 30–32; proposed new college, 157–58. See also *Vassall v. Rogers*
Hawley, Joseph, 63, 174
Henderson, John, 29
Hereford, New Hampshire, 60
Hill, John, 56, 60
Hiller, Joseph, 27–28, 31
History and Analysis of the Common Law of England, The (Hale), 22–23
History of Harvard University, The (Quincy), 158
History of the American Bar, A (Warren), 190
Hollis, Thomas, *The True Sentiments of America*, 189
Hope, Thomas, 66
House of Representatives, 81; privileges of, 84–86
Hubbard, Thomas, 42, 66, 84–86. See also *Fowle v. Hubbard*
Hutchinson, Eliakim, 42, 106
Hutchinson, Francis, 193
Hutchinson, Thomas, 42; barristers, designates, 106–7; cases as judge (see *Dudley v. Dudley*; *Dunn v. Scollay*; writs of assistance case); Chief Justice, 106–7, 126; council member, 180, 183–84; French club member, 204n57; on JG, 126; JG, client

Hutchinson, Thomas (*continued*)
of, 106; JG on Hutchinson, 126; Lord
Loudoun, relationship with, 94, 95, 100;
Otis family feud, 129–32, 226–29; on
politics, 156; quartering of troops, 94, 95,
100, 193–94; on Stamp Act, 170–71; Stamp
Act riots, victim of, 169–70. *See also* Chief
Justice dispute
Hutchinson family, 113

In Praise of the Laws of England (Fortesque),
23
Institute of the Laws of England (Wood), 22
Institutiones Juris Canonici (Lancelloti), 23
Intelligencer, The (London), 11–12
Iron Act of 1750 (Eng.), 54

Jefferson, Thomas, 65
Jeffries, John, 42
Johnson, William, 87
Johnston, William, 57
Jure Belli ac Pacis Libres Tres (Grotius), 24
Justinian I, *De Jure Naturali, Gentium et
Civill*, 124

Kennebec Proprietors. *See* Plymouth
Company
Kent, Benjamin: John Adams on, 122;
background and reputation of, 40,
122–23, 129; cases as attorney (see *Dudley
v. Dudley; Fanueil v. Pompey; Slew v.
Whipple*); Benjamin Franklin on, 122;
Emory Washburn, on, 122–23
Kilby, Christopher, 104, 232n111
King George's War, 83; Louisbourg,
Quebec, 48, 66–67; Peterborough, New
Hampshire, 57; politics, effect on, 83–84
Knapp, Samuel, 188–89

Lancelloti, Giovanni Paolo, *Institutiones
Juris Canonici*, 23
Land Bank: background of, 36–37;
establishment of, 37; opposition to, 37–38;
termination of, 38. *See also* attorney
general; Belcher, Jonathan; Gridley,
Jeremiah; Shirley, William
land speculation, 55–64. *See also* Clark and
Lake Company; Masonian Proprietors;
Peterborough, New Hampshire;
Plymouth Company
Lane, Andrew, 27–28, 40
Lauchlen, Samuel, 61

Lechmere, Thomas, 140
Legal Papers of John Adams (Wroth and
Zobel), 108, 189
legal profession: John Adams, on, 106;
barristers, designation of, 106–7; fees,
20, 186–87; rules relating to, 1, 25, 107–8;
status of, 27; unlicensed practitioners,
27–28, 107–8; volume of litigation, 25, 106
Leonard, Daniel, 173–74
Leonard, George, 180
Leverett, John, 6–7
Lewis, Ezekiel, 11, 19, 29, 31
Lewis, Ezekiel, Jr., 56
Lincoln, Benjamin, Jr., 3
Little, John, 29
Littleton, Thomas, 22
Locke, John, 193
Lois civiles dans leur ordre naturel (Domat), 24
London Magazine (London), 47, 48, 51
Loudoun, Lord (John Campbell, Earl of):
John Adams on, 90; background and
reputation of, 90; colonial troops, on,
95–96; as commander in chief, 88, 101;
Samuel Davies on, 90; JG, dealings with,
94–97, 100–104; Thomas Hutchinson,
dealings with, 94; Louisbourg, Quebec,
98; on Francis Parkman, 90. *See also*
French and Indian War; quartering of
troops
Lovell, John, 10–11, 12
Lowell, John, 173–74
Loyal Nine, 168, 172. *See also* Stamp Act;
Stamp Act riots
Lynde, Benjamin, JG client, 29, 33
Lynde, Benjamin, Jr.: Chief Justice
candidate, 128; council member, 180; JG,
client of, 29, 33; land speculation, 60–61.
See also *Dudley v. Dudley; Dunn v. Scollay;
Fletcher v. Vassall*
Lynde family, 113

Mare Liberum (Grotius), 24
Marine Society, 161, 187
Marion, Joseph, 27–28
Mason, John, 58
Mason, John Tufton, 58–59
Masonian Proprietors: Samuel Allen, 58–59;
Thomas Allen, 58–59; JG, employed by,
60–61; land holdings of, 58; organization,
59; Peterborough, New Hampshire,
59–60; squatters, 59
Masons, 32, 90

Mather, Cotton, 14–15; Harvard College, 8–9; scientist, 204n64; smallpox inoculation controversy, 13
Mather, Increase, 6, 8, 14, 15
Mauduit, Jasper, 156, 157, 163
Mayhew, Jonathan, 68–69, 73
McAdam, Gilbert, 94–95, 102
Miller, Ebenezer, 73
Molasses Act, 1733 (Eng.), 159–60
Molloy, Charles, *De Juri Maritimo et Navali*, 119
Monster of Monsters, The (Fowle), 84–86. See also *Fowle v. Hubbard*
Montcalm, Marquis de, 98. See also French and Indian War
Montesquieu, 193
Morison, Samuel Eliot, 7, 10
Mutiny Acts (Eng.), 89, 182

Navigation Acts. See trade acts
Newbury, New Hampshire, 60
New-England Courant, 13–14
New-England Magazine, 52
New-England Weekly Journal, 14–15
newspapers, 12–14. See also names of individual newspapers
Northey, Edward, 35

Oliver, Andrew: Francis Bernard, advisor to, 183; on James Otis, 131–32; Thomas Pownall, advisor to, 130; Stamp Act riots, victim of, 167–68; stamp distributor, 164–65, 172. See also Stamp Act riots
Oliver, Peter: background and reputation of, 53, 128; business opportunities, 54–55; cases as judge (see *Dudley v. Dudley; Dunn v. Scollay; Slew v. Whipple*); council member, 180; family, 53, 164–65; on JG, 53, 188, 197–98; iron mill partner with JG, 53–54; on James Otis, 131; Superior Court appointment, 130
Otis, Colonel James: John Adams on, 70; attorney general, service as, 70–71, 103; background and reputation of, 70–71, 85, 156; cases as attorney (see *Fletcher v. Vassall; Fowle v. Hubbard*); council member, 155–56; JG, friendship with, 71; JG, retained by, 54; House of Representatives, member of, 70–71, 85, 103; Thomas Hutchinson, feud with, 129–30; justice of the peace, sat as a, 70–71; William Shirley, ally of, 71, 129–30;

Superior Court, aspirations to, 130–31. See also Chief Justice dispute
Otis, James: John Adams on, 71; as admiralty advocate general, 139, 141; background of, 71–72; Francis Bernard, feud with, 155–58; cases as attorney (see *Baker v. Mattocks; Dudley v. Dudley; Dunn v. Scollay; Fletcher v. Vassall*; writs of assistance case); Chief Justice dispute, 130–32; Richard Dana on, 71; on economic panic, 166; JG, law student of, 71; House of Representatives, elected speaker of, 180; House of Representatives, elected to, 155; Thomas Hutchinson, feud with, 129–32, 155–58; instability of, 131–32, 156, 167, 173; Andrew Oliver on, 131–32; Peter Oliver on, 131; Stamp Act, 167, 173, 176–77; writings, 192–93. See also Chief Justice dispute; Otis, Colonel James; smuggling; Stamp Act
Overing, John, 36, 39, 40

Paratitla (Cujacius), 23
Parkman, Francis, on Lord Loudoun, 90
Parsons, Joseph, 29
Parsons, Moses, 199
Parsons, Theophilus, 198
Paxton, Charles, 137–39, 140. See also smuggling
Peterborough, New Hampshire: development of, 56–57, 59–60; dispute with Masonian Proprietors, 57–60; grant of, 55–56; JG as proprietor of, 56–57, 63–64
Petition of Right, 1628 (Eng.), 88
Phipps, William, 34, 39
Phips, Spencer, 130
Pickman, Benjamin, 29
Pitt, William, 101–2. See also French and Indian War
Plowden's Commentaries, 23, 170
Plymouth Company (Kennebec Proprietors), 62–63
politics, 81–82; 1762–1766, 155–58, 165; 1766–1767, 180–85
Pownall, Thomas: as governor, 94, 127, 130; Benjamin Prat, relationship with, 129; quartering troops, 98–100; raising troops, 100–102
Prat, Benjamin, 61, 63, 129, 141, 187; law student of JG, 190, 194. See also writs of assistance case

Prescott, Peter, 56, 220n28
Prince, Thomas, 17, 45
Prince, Thomas, Jr., 45
Privy Council (Eng.), 26–27, 58, 76–77. See also *Dunn v. Scollay*; *Fletcher v. Vassall*
Pufendorf, Samuel: JG's view on, 192–93; *Law of Nature and Nations*, 24
Putnam, James, 20, 190

Quartering Act of 1765 (Eng.), 182–83
quartering of troops: Albany, New York, 91; England, 88–89; legal authority for, 90–91; New York, New York, 91; Massachusetts, 92–94, 95, 98–100, 182–83; Philadelphia, Pennsylvania, 91–92. See also French and Indian War; Loudoun, Lord; Mutiny Acts
Quincy, Colonel Josiah, 143
Quincy, Edmund: bankruptcy of, 79; on William Fletcher, 73; William Fletcher, bondsman for, 79; JG, client of, 29
Quincy, Josiah: *The History of Harvard University*, 158; on legal studies, 24
Quincy, Josiah, Jr.: on barristers, 107; on Thomas Hutchinson's appearance, 170–71; notes on writs of assistance case, 147–48. See also *Quincy's Reports*
Quincy, Samuel, *Quincy's Reports*, 112
Quincy's Reports (Quincy Jr.), 108, 112. See also Quincy, Samuel

Read, John: attorney general, 36; cases as attorney (see *Vassall v. Rogers*); council member, 40; law practice of, 27–28; legal education of, 20; legal opinion on land ownership, 58, 61
"Resolves of the Virginia Assembly, on debating the Stamp Act" (*Boston Gazette*): James Otis on, 167; reaction to, 166–67; Oxenbridge Thacher on, 167
Robie, Thomas, 7
Rogers, Daniel, 30, 65. See also *Vassall v. Rogers*
Rogers, Gamaliel, 43, 45
Rogers, George, 42
Rowe, John, 121, 182, 185, 187
Ruggles, Timothy, 103, 195
Russell, Chambers: background and reputation of, 72, 128; cases as judge (see *Dudley v. Dudley*; *Fletcher v. Vassall*); death of, 185; Superior Court appointment, 137; as Vice Admiralty Court judge, 72, 137

Sabine, Lorenzo, 193
Salem-Canada, New Hampshire, 60–61
Saltonstall, Mary, 30
Saltonstall, Richard, 72, 74, 130. See also *Fletcher v. Vassall*
Sanders, Edmund, Reports, 23
Scollay, John: background and reputation of, 121; bankruptcy of, 121; John Dunn sues, 116. See also *Dunn v. Scollay*
Scott, Joseph, 73
Sewall, Jonathan, 185
Sewall, Stephen: background and reputation of, 72, 106; cases as judge (see *Dudley v. Dudley*; *Fletcher v. Vassall*); death of, 126–27; quartering of troops, 94–95, 193–94; on writs of assistance, 139–41
Shaw, Lieutenant, 97
Sheridan, Thomas, *The Intelligencer*, 11–12
Shipton, Clifford, on JG, 9
Shirley, William: French and Indian War, 87–88; as governor, 38, 82–83, 99; JG, relation to, 105; King George's War, 83–84; Land Bank, 38–39, 82–83; law practice of, 20, 27, 28; Col. James Otis, political ally of, 71, 130; quartering of troops, 92; smuggling, attempts to reduce, 136–37
Short Introduction to the Latin Tongue, A (Cheever), 5
Shute, Samuel, 35
Sidney, Algernon, *Discourses Concerning Government*, 193
Sitwell, John, 115–16
Silver Scheme, 37
Sketches of the Judicial History of Massachusetts (Washburn), 123
Slew, Jenny, 122, 123, 125. See also *Slew v. Whipple*
Slew v. Whipple, 121–25; John Adams on, 121–22; arguments, 123–25; background of, 122; case attorney, JG as, 121, 123–25; case attorney, Benjamin Kent as, 122–23; case judge, John Cushing as, 125; case judge, Peter Oliver as, 125; decision, 124–25; law involved, 23–24; Jenny Slew, 122; John Whipple Jr., 122
small pox epidemics, 2; 1721, 13; 1764, 165

Smith, W. H., *The Writs of Assistance Case*, 141, 143, 149–50: on JG's arguments in case, 149–50; on JG's motives in case, 150–54; on James Otis's arguments in case, 149–50; rebuttal to, 141–42, 150–54; on Oxenbridge Thacher's role in case, 141. *See also* writs of assistance case
Smith, William, 157–58
smuggling: Benjamin Barons, complicity in; 138–39; customs enforcement, 132–35, 160–61; Charles Paxton's attempts to reduce, 137–38; William Shirley's attempts to reduce, 136–37; as treason, 136
Society for Encouraging the Trade and Commerce, 32, 161–62. *See also* Sugar Act
Spectator, The (London), 10, 11
Stamp Act, 1765 (Eng.): background of, 162–63; colonial opposition to, 163–64, 165, 166–67; Congress, 166; George Grenville promotes, 162–63, 164; provisions of, 164–65; public sentiment on, 172–73; repeal of, 179, stamp distributors, 164–65. *See also* Stamp Act: court and customs office closures; Stamp Act riots
Stamp Act: John Adams on, 2, 172, 175–76, 178; court and customs office closures, 171–72, 178–79; Richard Dana on, 172; JG on, 175, 177–78, 195–95; Thomas Hutchinson on, 171, 178–79; legal profession response to, 173–74; James Otis on, 2, 176–78; petition to reopen courts, 175–76
Stamp Act riots, 167–71; August 14, 1765, 167–68; August 15, 1765, 168–69; August 26, 1765, 169–70; JG on, 197–98; Loyal Nine, 168; response to, 168; victim compensation, 181–82
Steele, Richard. *See Englishman, The*; *Spectator, The*
Stiles, Ezra, 193
St. Lawrence, Joseph, 40
Story, Joseph, 21
Story, William, 169
Sugar Act, 1764 (Eng.): background of, 158–60; enactment of, 162; George Grenville as architect of, 160, 163; opposition to, 161–62; provisions of, 160, 162–63; Society for Encouraging Trade and Commerce, opposed to, 161–62

Swift, Jonathan: *The Examiner*, 11–12; *The Intelligencer*, 11–12
Swift, Samuel, 192

Telltale, The, 10
Temple, John, 172
Temple, Robert, 153
Thacher, Oxenbridge: John Adams on, 142; cases as attorney (see *Dunn v. Scollay*; writs of assistance case); death of, 173; JG, law student of, 11–12, 190; law practice of, 187; on new college proposal, 158; opposition to Thomas Hutchinson, 127; on James Otis, 132; on Stamp Act, 173; on "Virginia Resolves," 167
Tillotson, John, 7
Tractatus de Legibus (Glanville), 23
trade acts (Eng.): enforcement of, 133–39, 160–61; provisions of, 133–34. *See also* Molasses Act; smuggling; Sugar Act; writs of assistance; writs of assistance case
Trenchard, John, *Cato's Letters*, 192
Trowbridge, Edmund: John Adams on, 69; as attorney general, 69; background and reputation of, 69, 103; cases as attorney (see *Dudley v. Dudley*; *Fletcher v. Vassall*; *Fowle v. Hubbard*); House of Representatives, member of, 85–86; on James Otis, 131; retirement of, 198–99; Superior Court, appointed to, 184
True Sentiments of America, The (Almon and Hollis), 189
Tudor, John, 78–79

van Muyden, Johannes, *Compendiosa Institutionum Justiani Tractato: In usum Collegiorum*, 23
Vassall, Leonard, 30–31. *See also Vassall v. Rogers*
Vassall, William: John Adams on, 65; background of, 30, 65–66; William Fletcher, relationship with, 67; Benjamin Franklin, correspondence with, 65; JG, relationship with, 71. *See also Fletcher v. Vassall*; *Vassall v. Rogers*
Vassall v. Rogers, 30–32; arguments, 32; case attorney, JG as, 31–32; case attorney, John Read as, 31; factual background of, 30–31; issues in, 31–32

Vinnius, Arnold, 23
Voltaire, 193

Wainright, John, 29
Waldo, Samuel, 2, 42, 105–6
Waldo, Samuel, Jr., 63
Warren, Charles, *A History of the American Bar*, 190
Washburn, Emory, *Sketches of the Judicial History of Massachusetts*, 72, 122, 188
Webster, Daniel, 21
Weekly Rehearsal, 15–18, 51, 196
Wendell, Jacob, 105
West Church, 32
Whately, Thomas, 164–65
Wheelright, Nathan, 166
Whipple, Benjamin, Jr., 122. See also *Slew v. Whipple*
White, Nathaniel, 32
White, Samuel, 103
Wigglesworth, Edward, 7–8
Wilbraham, Randle, 112
Williams, Israel, 157
Williams, Nathaniel, 5, 10
Winslow, John, 81
Wolcott, Oliver, 63
Wood, Amos, 29, 32

Wood, Thomas, *Institute of the Laws of England*, 22
Worthington, John, 63, 174
writs of assistance: description and purpose, 133–34; legal basis of, 135–36; in Massachusetts, 136
writs of assistance case, 126–54; John Adams, report on, 142–43; arguments, 143–46, 148–49; background of, 133–41; case attorney, Robert Auchmuty as, 148; case attorney, JG as, 142–44, 148–49; case attorney, James Otis as, 1, 141, 145–48; case attorney, Oxenbridge Thacher as, 141–42, 145, 148; case judge, Thomas Hutchinson as, 141–42, 146–47; criticism of, 149–54; decision, 146–47, 149; JG, legacy after, 133; James Otis, legacy after, 133; Josiah Quincy Jr., report on, 147–48
Writs of Assistance Case, The (Smith), 141, 143, 149–50. See also Smith, W. H.
Wroth, L. Kinvin, *Legal Papers of John Adams*, 108, 140, 150

Young, Alexander, 86

Zobel, Hiller B., *Legal Papers of John Adams*, 108, 140, 150

www.ingramcontent.com/pod-product-compliance
Lightning Source LLC
Chambersburg PA
CBHW031707230426
43668CB00006B/145